What People Are Sa[ying about]
The Angel and the D[ragon]

"Interesting, sad, informative and moving, this is a book which ougnt to be read by every parent in difficulty."

Michael Korda
author, *Country Matters* and *Charmed Lives*

"*The Angel and the Dragon* is not only an anguished, gripping memoir about the descent of the author's son into madness. It is the best examination of the complexities of mental illness—and of modern psychiatry's inadequacies to understand and treat it—that I have ever read."

John Horgan
author, *The Undiscovered Mind*

"*The Angel and the Dragon* is a remarkable book and a gripping read—a vivid, sophisticated account of a parent's bewildered struggle to respond to his beloved son's psychotic despair. Anyone trying to understand a loved one's illness and today's psychiatric treatments should read this book."

T. M. Luhrmann
author, *Of Two Minds: The Growing Disorder in American Psychiatry*

"*The Angel and the Dragon* seems often like a detective story as we are taken forward and backward in time looking for reasons behind seemingly senseless, unrelated actions. But this father's relentless search to understand his son's suicide is in fact a love story whose tenderness is often found in the spaces between the lines. The meaning of Charley's life did not end that day when he parked his bike on an overpass and jumped to his death on the Santa Monica Freeway. It waits to be created by each reader who sifts through the facts and pieces that his father has strung together in a prose that never panders for tears. Those of us who have tried to come to the rescue of a loved one afflicted by a profound mental illness can attest to the honesty and truthfulness of this work. And through it Charley lives on."

Dan E. Weisburd
founder and former editor of
The Journal of the California Alliance for the Mentally Ill

The Angel
and
the Dragon

A Father's Search for Answers to
His Son's Mental Illness and Suicide

JONATHAN AURTHUR

Health Communications, Inc.
Deerfield Beach, Florida

www.hci-online.com

Library of Congress Cataloging-in-Publication Data

Aurthur, Jonathan, 1948-
    The angel and the dragon : a father's search for answers to his son's mental illness and
suicide / Jonathan Aurthur.
        p.   cm.
    Includes bibliographical references and index.
    ISBN 0-7573-0052-9 (tp)
    1. Aurthur, Charley, d. 1996 2. Mentally ill—United States—Biography. 3. Suicide
victims—United States—Biography. 4. Aurthur, Jonathan, 1948- 5. Parent and child. I. Title.

RC464.A93 A933 2002
616.89'0092—dc21
[B]
                                                                                        2002068664

Publisher: Health Communications, Inc.
            3201 S.W. 15th Street
            Deerfield Beach, FL 33442-8190

Cover design by Larissa Hise Henoch
Inside book design by Dawn Von Strolley Grove
Dragon sculpture on back cover by Francisco Hernández Cruz, Oaxaca, Mexico

To Jenny, Lin, Shizuko . . .
and Charley, in Memoriam

Contents

Introduction

In the fall of 1996 my twenty-three-year-old son, Charley, committed suicide after five years of intermittent but severe mental illness, numerous hospitalizations and several other suicide attempts, two of which failed only miraculously. Charley was variously diagnosed as manic-depressive, schizophrenic and schizoaffective, and put on a number of medications (sometimes five or six at once), but nothing in the end saved him from his own encroaching sense of exhaustion and isolation.

The Angel and the Dragon is an account of my experience with Charley and his and my attempts—and his mother's and sister's—to deal with a crisis that seemed to erupt out of nowhere and that none of us would ever fully understand, a crisis that had both physical and spiritual aspects but in the end remained both more and less than it seemed. In the course of trying to help Charley, who lived with me for much of the five years he was ill, I read and learned a great deal about the current state of psychiatry and particularly psychopharmacology (treatment of mental illness with medications), hoping that the Decade of the Brain, as the 1990s were called, would provide answers. At first, convinced that Charley had a chemical imbalance that could be cured or at the worst successfully treated with psychiatric medications, I embraced the "brain-disorder" theory of mental illness, convinced that it provided a practical and humane understanding of Charley's illness that he could embrace as well because it was both simple and "destigmatizing"—a brain disorder, after all, is nobody's fault. And at times he did seem to embrace it, but never completely and never for long, because the theory and the treatment it led to didn't correspond to his actual experience or needs. Either the medications didn't help enough, or else their side effects—physical discomfort, a deadening of perception, a spiritual flattening—seemed worse than the disease. Even more fundamentally, medication-based treatment (a lot of drugs and a little therapy and human interaction) did not speak to Charley's illness the way Charley himself perceived it, and thus ultimately failed to enlist his capacities for recovery. As part of showing this, I include in my narrative numerous passages from Charley's own journals and poems and letters, which present his own perceptions and analysis of what was happening to him.

As Charley's periodic crises continued to erupt and grow worse despite medication and psychotherapy, I became skeptical of the brain-disease model. As a result, part of *The Angel and the Dragon* is an attempt to understand the question of what mental illness is and isn't, and how (and why) so many of the current medical treatments fail to live up to their claims. My aim is, through one concrete story, to give an idea of the nuance and complexity of what many have come to see (I believe self-defeatingly) as a straightforward issue of physical ailment and physical treatment. I also offer an alternative theory and practice of mental illness treatment known as the "psychosocial rehab" model, which, unlike the psychopharmacological model, seeks to "treat the person, not the disease." (Appendix E has contact information for two alternative recovery facilities whose theories and practices I discuss in the book.)

NOTE: For privacy reasons, some names of people and places have been changed.

Prologue

On Saturday, November 2, 1996, a photograph appeared in the *Santa Monica Outlook* accompanied by a brief text. The photo shows a police officer standing on an otherwise deserted freeway, holding a clipboard and bending over, examining the pavement. A few feet behind him is a tarpaulin covering something close to the ground. The text reads:

Bicyclist Jumps Off Bridge

A CHP officer conducts an investigation on the westbound Santa Monica Freeway where a Santa Monica man apparently jumped to his death off the Lincoln Boulevard overpass on Friday morning.

The driver of a Porsche was taken to an area hospital for head and neck injuries, after the man fell on his car, Santa Monica police Sgt. Garry Gallinot said.

The incident occurred at 8:43 A.M. The westbound side of the freeway was closed until 11 A.M.

"Witnesses indicated he rode his bicycle to the overcrossing, climbed over the railing, looked down for a few minutes and jumped," Gallinot said.

The 23-year-old man was pronounced dead at the scene.

His name was not released because relatives had not been notified.[1]

The twenty-three-year-old man's name was Charley Aurthur, my son. The text was wrong in one detail. I *had* been notified of his death a couple of hours after it happened, although not by the police. Charley had jumped from the overpass while I was at work on Friday morning. A little before eleven, a representative of the Los Angeles County coroner's office, finding my address on Charley's driver's license recovered from his body, came to my apartment looking for me. When he found no one there he knocked on the door of a neighbor, who was home and had my number at work. The neighbor called me.

This call was the last in a series of phone calls about Charley I had been getting for more than five years. Five years and three months and six days, actually, since July 26, 1991, also a Friday. Calls from highway patrolmen, calls from school physicians and school counselors, calls from heart surgeons, calls from detectives, calls from psychiatrists and psychotherapists of various persuasions, calls from relatives, calls from Charley's friends, calls from Charley himself. Calls ranging from confusing to disquieting to horrifying to miraculous to horrifying. Calls that echo now in my memory like the clang of nails closing a coffin.

Some of the calls had that sound at the time—the jangling phone the clanging gong of impending doom. Others didn't. All were part of a drama whose meaning I am still trying to understand, a drama that began in confusion and misunderstanding, evolved (at least for me) into some kind of certainty, and then dissolved again into confusion with no hope of any final understanding. But perhaps through the telling of the story, letting Charley speak for himself as much as possible, some more of him and the meaning of his life and death will be revealed.

2

Wrong Turn at Yosemite

The First Day of the Rest of His Life

Tuesday morning, July 30, 1991

"You've got a very sick boy there," said Dr. Thomas Gray, M.D., Ph.D., psychiatrist/psychoanalyst, looking at me and Lin, my ex-wife, from across his desk through glasses that drooped slightly on his nose. We were sitting in his office, having met him for the first time fifteen minutes before. He had just spoken privately—also for the first time—with Charley, who had stomped out of his office after ten minutes, eyes averted, muttering, "He asks too many questions" as he passed us in the waiting room. He was now somewhere in the hallway or perhaps downstairs in front of the building, smoking. At least I hoped he was. I hoped he hadn't wandered off somewhere. Or run away. Or God knows what. Four days earlier he had come back from a brief trip to Yosemite, changed somehow, and I couldn't figure out what was happening.

"I think he's probably psychotic, reacting to internal stimuli—hearing

3

voices," Dr. Gray continued. "That's why he's having a hard time answering questions. There's a lot we don't know going on in his mind that he doesn't seem to want to tell us. It's creating, um, a lot of confusion for him, and it's taking a long time to process our questions."

Tom Gray said this all in a calm, slightly halting voice. He looked to be in his forties, our generation. Soft features, light brown hair graying at the temples; Scotch-Irish, I thought, maybe Welsh. Quiet, a little shy sounding, not full of himself or his degrees or decades of practice. Humble, even.

Which is what made his matter-of-fact use of the word "psychotic" so chilling. Everybody used it as a joke, of course—Lin had a phony college sweatshirt that said "Psychotic State" across the front—but till now I had never heard it in connection with anybody I actually knew.

"I think he needs to be hospitalized," Dr. Gray was saying. "Given the auto accident, I'm, um, a little concerned for his safety. We don't know what caused it, and he won't tell us. I think he needs to be under supervision." Dr. Gray was on staff at the mental health center at St. John's Hospital half a block away. The psychiatric unit had an excellent nursing staff. He could vouch for the care Charley would receive.

Hospitalized? That word, at least in a psychiatric context (I was used to Charley going to emergency rooms for broken bones and lacerations), was as bad as "psychotic." The only experience I had ever had with mental hospitals had been twenty-five years earlier in New York when my mother, in the throes of a midlife crisis, had swallowed sleeping pills and been put in a psych ward for observation after having her stomach pumped. But she had gotten out in a few days and never been back, and my memory of the place was dim. My only other strong associations with psychiatric hospitals were *One Flew over the Cuckoo's Nest* and *The Bell Jar*, Nazi nurses and electroshock and lobotomies.

What was going on? Dr. Gray had known Charley for a total of ten minutes, and Charley apparently hadn't even said much. Psychiatric unit? What did Dr. Gray know that we, Charley's parents for eighteen and a half years, didn't? Or more likely, what had he inferred from the little Charley had said before stomping out? I glanced at Lin to see if she was as confused as I was.

For me it was a continuation of a confusion I had been feeling, more and more acutely, since the previous Friday, when the first call came, the first nail.

It had been from the California Highway Patrol (CHP) in Mammoth Lakes near Yosemite. Yosemite was two hundred miles northeast of Santa Monica, where I lived and where Charley was staying with me for the summer. He had driven my car up three days earlier to meet Lin and go camping with her and two cousins.

He had been in an accident, the CHP officer was saying on the phone. Driving out of the campgrounds that morning to come back to L.A. Charley had gotten lost on a mountain road and run the car into a ditch. It was unclear why; weather conditions were good and no other car was involved. Charley, who seemed fine physically, had been taken to the local hospital, examined and CAT-scanned for head injury. Nothing appeared wrong or irregular. There were no signs of drugs or alcohol.

Then the officer asked me, after the briefest pause, whether Charley had a history of mental illness.

No, I said. Why?

He had been acting odd, the cop said, gunning the engine when the CHP arrived, trying to drive out of the ditch. I asked why that was odd. Well, the cop answered after another slight pause, the car didn't seem drivable. In addition, Charley had been on the wrong road, going in the opposite direction from L.A., and didn't seem to understand that when they questioned him. Later, at the hospital, he had walked out of the ER half-dressed, gone into a convenience store and picked up a sweatshirt in plain view of everybody, just taken the sweatshirt and headed out of the store, so he hadn't been arrested, just led back to the hospital.

The cop asked again if I was sure Charley didn't have a history of mental illness. I said of course I was sure. What about the family? Any history of schizophrenia? Delusions? No, I answered. (What was the guy talking about?) I said it sounded like Charley was in shock. Yes, possibly, the officer said. We talked a minute longer, he giving me names and phone numbers, and that was that.

I left work immediately and rode home on my bicycle—the crashed car in Yosemite was the only one I owned—trying to figure out how to get Charley back to L.A. That was my only real concern now. Of course it was too bad about the accident. But Charley had been in many accidents, many hospitals, in his day. He had been accident-prone since he was old enough to run into doors and dive off porches, a sort of lifelong "terrible two" Lin and I had nicknamed "Emergency Room Charley" when he was still little. In fact, he hadn't been to the ER for a couple of years now, so he was about due for a trip. This one didn't even sound that bad; no broken bones this time, no lacerations. Too bad about the car, of course, but really, who cared? Charley was okay, that was the main thing. Even the CHP officer hadn't denied that the strange behavior could be explained as shock.

Neither had he mentioned, nor was I aware of at the time, the skepticism with which people familiar with such matters have come to view single-car accidents that seem to happen for no reason.

As a result of this unawareness I was hopeful when I met Charley at the airport later that night, even though I could see right away that something was wrong, or at least different. His face was flushed and his expression was a little dreamy as he sauntered into the waiting area, smiling when he saw me, giving me an affectionate hug but holding off my return hug so that the pack of cigarettes he was fumbling for in his breast pocket wouldn't get crushed. Yes, flushed, dreamy, glad to see me but also a little—what? preoccupied? above it all? By now I'd learned a little more than what the CHP officer had told me and was anxious to find out from Charley exactly what had happened, since the new information didn't quite add up either. A mental health worker in Mammoth Lakes, a woman named Sydney Quinn who had helped care for Charley at the hospital and arranged his flight home, had told me during one of several phone conversations a few hours earlier that Charley had talked about suffering from insomnia; it was the reason, he had told her, for the accident. She asked me whether Charley had been depressed, since insomnia often is a symptom of depression. No, I said, Charley didn't have a history of depression and had seemed fine up to the time he left Santa Monica to go to Yosemite. Ms. Quinn also mentioned some "bizarre writing" the CHP had found in the ditched car, a notebook of Charley's where he talked about "everybody being down on him." She didn't have the notebook, though (and I never found it later), so she didn't know anything more about it. Neither did I, I told her.

Later in the evening I'd spoken with Lin, reaching her in Santa Cruz (south of San Francisco) where she had gone for the weekend after driving out of Yosemite separately from Charley that morning. (Lin lived a few miles from me—in Culver City, like Santa Monica a part of greater Los Angeles—but was planning to move to Santa Cruz the following week.) She hadn't been as surprised as I'd thought she would be when I told her what had happened. She said she'd been a little worried about Charley herself and had even considered not letting him drive that morning. He hadn't been himself since he'd arrived at the campgrounds three days earlier complaining of insomnia. He'd been acting a little wild from the beginning, which she had attributed to the stress of the long drive through the unfamiliar desert and mountains. The first afternoon he had gotten a bicycle from somewhere, and when she followed him in her car to a recreation area, he'd ridden recklessly, darting into the road without looking for cars. That night there was a full moon and he hadn't been able to sleep. He'd seemed moonstruck, running around in the woods, jumping off picnic tables. The next night there had been an incident. Charley had stood too near a girl about his own age, fixated on her. When he wouldn't let her alone, the girl told her father and the father complained to the campground director, and Lin had to talk to the father to calm him down. Charley had continued acting strange, running around the woods. Then, at four in the morning, he had come into her tent and crawled into her sleeping bag as he did when he was a little boy, saying he was scared. Lin had wondered whether he was on drugs. When she asked him he said yes, he'd been smoking a little pot.

Which seemed to explain things. That and Yosemite itself, Lin said. A park employee she had talked to about Charley told her that the wild beauty of the place had a reputation for making people a little crazy when they were there, which made her feel better; Charley had always been impressionable. But he had seemed sober and alert in the morning, saying he had slept and was fine driving, so she'd let him go. Now, of course, she was second-guessing herself. But like me she had no reason to think Charley wasn't basically all right. For all his accident-proneness he had always been mentally stable, rational and reliable. If he said he could drive, he could drive.

I had thought about all this as I waited for Charley's plane to get in, hoping that the shock from the accident had worn off during the two-hour flight, that he'd gotten a little sleep or at least rest and would be able to tell me what had happened. Of course, I was vaguely aware that the "moonstruck" stuff, like the "bizarre writing" stuff, contradicted my shock-from-the-accident theory. It meant that he had been acting strange before the car crash, not just after. But how strange, and for how long? Now, here at the airport in the presence of Charley himself, I quickly saw that I wouldn't be getting any simple, sensible answers from him, at least not right away. He didn't volunteer any information about the crash, which was a little odd but then again *not* odd given the traumatic nature of the experience and the shock that he still seemed to be experiencing. But at the same time he was *here,* with me, alive and safe, a little flushed and spacey (but who wouldn't be after the kind of day he'd had?), and his physical presence made everything else secondary. Despite his history of emergency rooms and other minor idiosyncrasies I had always felt a certain basic confidence in Charley and his older sister Jenny. Jenny was twenty, about five-eight, a honey-blonde. After a few slightly white-knuckle years of early adolescence (white-knuckle for *me*), she had settled down and was now taking advanced placement classes at Santa Monica College, getting ready to transfer to UCLA. Charley was tall as well, slim and handsome in the androgynous way of a David Bowie or River Phoenix, also honey blond with soft brown eyes and eyelashes like palm fronds, his sister and mother's beauty translated into male terms. He had survived his freshman year at a tough school, Reed College in Portland, Oregon, Lin's alma mater. At the end of school in May he had come to L.A. to stay with me and work for the summer to help pay for school. He had found a job busing tables at a Greek restaurant three blocks from my apartment, working evenings and sometimes lunches. During the day when I was at work he played Bach, Beethoven, Chopin and Scott Joplin on a little upright piano I'd rented for him.

All that had been up to Tuesday. This was Friday. Whatever was going on now, less than four days later, how bad could it be?

Charley couldn't have agreed more. As we drove home from the airport in a borrowed car, he waved off what I hoped were my not excessive, and not excessively parental, questions. He'd had insomnia at Yosemite, the effects of the full moon. He'd been tired when he drove out of the campsite, was listening to Beethoven's "Emperor" piano concerto on the tape player, became distracted by the music's intensity, made a wrong turn. None of it important. I tried not to push it, and we reached home without any further real discussion. It was only later that evening, when I mentioned how philosophical he seemed to be about the accident, that he said he had "become a philosopher" and began showing some interest in the conversation, talking about how he had achieved "god" or "cosmic" consciousness. He said it had come from TM—transcendental meditation—which he had been practicing for the past few weeks to help him sleep. "I've got good karma," he told me, and he asked me whether I was familiar with the nine stages of consciousness that led to god consciousness.

No, I wasn't. I was vaguely aware that he had been meditating and going to some kind of self-realization center in Pacific Palisades near where we lived, so the stuff about TM was not a total surprise. Lin had practiced it sometimes as a relaxation technique, so I thought he might have gotten the idea from her. But what he was talking about now—cosmic consciousness—was new. Did it relate to the accident? Charley said no, he hadn't been meditating at Yosemite.

We had quickly reached an impasse. I wanted to talk about the accident; he, to the extent he wanted to talk at all, wanted to talk about enlightenment. But what do you say to someone—particularly your eighteen-year-old kid—who has god consciousness? And anyway, we didn't talk that much. Conversation tended to be difficult. When I said something or asked a question, Charley would tend to look at me blankly for a few seconds before answering. Another time that evening when I communicated concern he said, "Don't worry, Dad. I'm fine. Reeeally. I know you're worried about me. Don't be," in a kind of sweet, stroking voice.

Later as I lay in bed, trying to sleep—it was after midnight—I suddenly heard the piano through my bedroom wall. I opened the door into the living room, which doubled as Charley's bedroom in my tiny apartment. Charley was playing Chopin as if in a trance, his eyes closed, his body hunched over. But the playing was odd, too fast for his fingers. Every few seconds the music seemed to veer off into a jumble of notes. "Charley," I whispered, "it's kind of late."

Again the delay before he seemed to hear me; then, again, the sweet smile. "Ohhhh, Okaaaay, Dad. Sorry." He stopped playing. I told him to try and sleep, he'd had a very long day.

The next morning he claimed to have slept. He also announced that instead of going back to Reed he wanted to study piano at the San Francisco Conservatory of Music or Juilliard in New York.

Huh? I thought. Where had *that* idea come from? The fact that there were major problems with it—such as that Charley hadn't applied to either school—didn't seem to bother him. My reaction was dismissed as typical Dad negativity and old-fogeyism. "Come on, Dad, you're always like that. It's always 'no' with you. You're always trying to rain on my parade. You won't have to pay for any of it."

"Oh? Then who will?"

"Mom."

"Mom ran out of money with the first year of Reed."

"Then I'll pay. I'll get the money. Don't worry about it. That's why I want to study music. I'm gonna make a lot of money and pay you back everything you ever spent on me just to get you off my back. I'll support you in your old age. . . ."

"Which is starting in about twenty minutes." A family joke.

Charley's characterization of me was not entirely unfair. I had been opposed to his going to Reed, a private college that cost twenty-plus-thousand dollars a year. He could go to UCLA or another University of California school, like Jenny. But Lin, a Reed alumna, had wanted Reed and had paid almost the entire first-year tuition herself, going into serious debt. Charley's grades had been good enough to entitle him to some financial aid for his second year, so continuing Reed was possible (barely) if he applied for grants and loans and saved money from his summer job. But so far he hadn't done much, and as of now his return to Reed at the end of August—only four weeks away—was by no means a done deal.

Going to the San Francisco Conservatory or Juilliard, on the other hand, was pure fantasy. Even if Charley were somehow able to audition and be admitted so late, a new school would mean starting over and paying full tuition for at least the first year. Apart from the time and the money there was the question of—well, not talent, exactly, but level of commitment and prepared-ness. Charley was a gifted pianist, but an amateur, and had never before shown interest in being more. So why was he suddenly talking about world-class music conservatories?

I could see that he was serious, however, so I tried to deal with the whole thing rationally. I happened to have a coworker whose husband had gone to Juilliard, so I called them on Saturday and arranged for the four of us to have lunch and chat. We met at a little restaurant in Venice. Charley was polite but rather aloof. The husband talked about how hard it was to get into Juilliard, how all the students had been studying since they were two, what competitive and joyless drones they were. Charley nodded. There was always San Francisco Conservatory, he said, if Juilliard didn't work out.

Later Saturday afternoon he borrowed my bicycle to go to the local mall. He arrived home a couple of hours later saying he had bought a watch but then given it away to a homeless guy on the street.

I asked why. "He looked like he needed a watch," Charley said, smiling slightly and saying no more, enjoying my puzzlement. And I *was* puzzled. Giving away watches was not like Charley. More cosmic consciousness? I wasn't sure; he seemed less lofty now, less dreamy, more excitable, although his mood varied. With me he was relatively low-key. On the phone with friends he seemed to get more animated. He was talking a lot to one in particular, his new best friend, Kit Henderson. I had never met Kit, who was several years older than Charley and lived a couple of hundred miles up the coast. They had been planning a trip to New Orleans for the following week. They talked several times over the weekend. Charley would take the phone into my bedroom and close the door. I didn't eavesdrop but I could hear his voice through the wall. It was fast and chattery, a lot of laughing.

As I watched his growing jitteriness and the continued denial about the accident I was starting to have doubts about New Orleans. Should he go anywhere now, much less to a town famous for serious partying? Kit was older and theoretically more mature, but then again, I didn't know him. Weeks later, when I finally met him, I asked whether during the phone calls he had been having second thoughts about making the trip in light of the car crash. No, Kit said. He hadn't known about the crash. Charley hadn't mentioned it.

By Sunday Charley was becoming more jittery and anxious. I was becoming worried, too. I had thought I would welcome the fading of his dreamy complacency as evidence that the shock was wearing off and he was finally becoming aware of his narrow escape. But what was happening now was no better, and my growing anxiety caused me periodically to violate my strategy of nonintrusive calm. I would sit across from him at the kitchen table and say, "Charley, look at me, I'm trying to talk to you. I'm very concerned about what happened, the fact that you could have been seriously hurt. And I'm very concerned that you don't seem to get it. Don't you understand what happened?" I repeated this hectoring several times over the weekend, hoping he'd suddenly snap out of his daze, look at me with a smile, say in his old humorous voice, "Thanks, Pop, I needed that," give me a hug and then pick me up by the waist.

But he didn't, and his refusal to acknowledge any problem was starting to bother me. The second or third day after his return I cooked a huge breakfast—his favorite, fried eggs and ham and cheese on a croissant (known as "Oeuf McMoeuf") and home-fries and onion, which he and Jenny called *papas,* Spanish for "potatoes" (as in "Papa's *papas*"). He barely touched his food, which both concerned and annoyed me (why wasn't he responding to my great parenting?). I had asked him to do the dishes before we went out for a walk. He went to the sink and I went into my room to get ready. When I came out a few minutes later he was standing at the sink, motionless, the dishes untouched.

"Charley!" I barked, and his shoulders jumped and he turned around with a startled look. "Do the dishes so we can get out of here! Come *on!*"

He nodded and turned back to the sink and began doing the dishes, slowly.

I immediately regretted what I'd said and how I'd said it. I was not consciously trying to be cruel—it was more frustration—but even then I could see clearly how out of place my impatience was. He was not himself, and I should have been acting accordingly. I will always remember that startled look.

Sunday night brought more sleeplessness for both of us. A waspish buzz of anxiety permeated the apartment, the feel of a shorting power line. As it grew late Charley came into my room and lay down next to me. I tried to comfort him as I had when he was little and couldn't sleep. I rubbed his shoulders and chanted in an undulating, singsong voice: "Pretend you're a jellyfish, swimming in the ocean, being carried this way and that, not a bone in your body. . . ."

He closed his eyes at the old routine. Then: "What am I afraid of?"

I said I didn't know, but that it was okay to be anxious after what he'd been through with the accident. He talked some more about how he had become a philosopher, achieved cosmic consciousness. I said that being a philosopher didn't seem to be helping with his current distress. "I'm a distress philosopher," he said.

After a while we both relaxed, lying in bed side by side, the buzz of anxiety dissipating for a time.

But not his god consciousness. He asked me what I wanted; he could get it for me.

The next morning, Monday, after another restless night, Charley began having anxiety attacks and bouts of weeping. I took him to my regular doctor, giving him an account of the recent accident and the X ray and CAT scan at the hospital in Mammoth that seemed to rule out injury. The doctor gave him a quick physical exam and prescribed Xanax, an antianxiety drug. He suggested that Charley see a psychiatrist and recommended one he knew a few blocks away. The diagnosis he wrote on the referral slip was "morbid depression." When we got home I called the psychiatrist, Dr. Gray, and made an appointment for the next morning.

The Second Crash

Alprazolam. Brand name: *Xanax*
Pharmacology: Anxiolytic—Antipanic
Indications: For the management of anxiety disorders or the short-term symptomatic relief of symptoms of excessive anxiety . . .
   Warnings: *Alprazolam is not recommended for use in patients whose primary diagnosis is psychosis or depression.*[1] (emphasis added)

By Monday afternoon Charley's condition was worse, and for the first time in either of my kids' lives, I started to feel helpless.

By now, Lin had gotten back from Santa Cruz, and she came to my apartment for dinner. Charley ate almost nothing and was alternately distracted and accusatory when we tried to talk to him. Everything would be okay, he said, if we just let him alone. Lin, like me, could see that something was seriously wrong. She could also see that I was suffering from lack of sleep, so she decided to take Charley back to her condo for the night; he could help her pack for her move to Santa Cruz. Before they left I asked her to come to the session with Dr. Gray the next morning to talk and (I hoped) come to some kind of agreement about what to do next. Lin was reluctant; she didn't like psychiatrists and didn't see why Charley should have to go to one.

This resistance was typical of what was going on between Lin and me. It was only a few days after the car crash, but we were already having basic disagreements over what the problem was and how to deal with it. Having seen Charley's new behavior only after the accident, I was still sure it was some kind of physical or psychological shock and that he needed some kind of professional care. Lin, who disliked Western medicine and doctors anyway, had observed Charley's moon madness at Yosemite before the accident and thought his condition was more spiritual than physical, possibly even something positive if handled right. Perhaps he needed an acupuncturist, or a healer. But despite our differences and Lin's distrust of psychiatry, she agreed to meet with Dr. Gray. I gave her the bottle of Xanax, and she and Charley headed back to Culver City to pack.

Late that night—it was after one and I was still awake—the phone rang. It was a Reed classmate of Charley's named Brian Marsh calling from New York. He had just gotten off the phone with Charley, who had called him from Lin's (at about 3 A.M. Brian's time). They had talked at some length, and now Brian wanted to discuss the conversation with me. "I'm very worried about Charley," he said, and described how disoriented Charley had sounded. "The first thing he asked me was, 'Does anybody really know anything?' He's worried that he's lost everything he ever knew. Charley kept asking if I was in his reality. He kept talking about transcendental meditation and referring to 'his reality' as if it were one of many realities."

We talked for quite a while and I learned a lot. Brian told me how hard freshman year had been for Charley, how isolated and depressed he had been much of the time, how he tended to take philosophical questions too seriously, a tendency aggravated by the unending Portland rain. Charley didn't have a lot of friends at school, which was hard for him because he wanted people to love him, Brian said. "Charley is real scared that people don't love him. He just wants to love people and to read Tolstoy. He wants to *meet* Tolstoy." He particularly needs to know that his parents love him, Brian added.

I mentally shrugged this off. Of course. How could Charley possibly have any doubts that his parents loved him?

Brian also talked about an episode the previous Halloween, when Charley had taken some kind of hallucinogenic seeds from a plant I had never heard of (it sounded like "iawaska") and acted crazy in the student union, breaking lightbulbs. He lost his watch and shoes and felt intense fear of not knowing what was going on around him.

I had not known about this, I told Brian. I had been in touch with Charley a few days after Halloween and he seemed normal, and I was not aware of any particular problems and stresses then or later, other than that he sometimes talked about having trouble sleeping and once toward the beginning of the year called me with some concern, wanting help with a paper on *Antigone*. But none of it had sounded like anything other than normal college anxiety, and he had appeared to get through the year all right.

Brian mentioned several times that he thought Charley might want to take a break from Reed, maybe a semester. "Reed is very easy about leaves of absence."

This conversation with Brian Marsh had taken place late Monday night. Now, Tuesday morning, eight sleep-deprived hours later, Lin and I were sitting across the desk from Dr. Gray, who had just proposed putting Charley in the St. John's psychiatric ward.

Lin was shaking her head. She liked the idea even less than I did. She told Dr. Gray that she thought Charley was going through some kind of spiritual crisis. He obviously needed help, but a psychiatric ward? Locked up? Wouldn't that just upset him more and make things worse? "No, I really don't want to do that," she said.

Dr. Gray listened, nodding. Of course the decision was up to Charley and us. He wrote out a prescription for an antipsychotic drug called Navane to replace the Xanax, and said Charley should start taking it immediately. Based on his reaction, we would determine what to do next. Maybe the medication would be enough, Dr. Gray said, although his voice lacked conviction. When we left the office Lin took Charley with her so I could go to work.

I went to my apartment to get cleaned up and dressed. As I was putting on my clothes the two of them suddenly appeared at my door. "Here, take your son," Lin said as Charley walked silently past me into my bedroom and closed the door. She made a face as she watched him disappear.

"What happened?" I asked.

"He's acting like a total jerk. We went to Izzy's"—a nearby deli—"to have breakfast and he just started acting up. He wouldn't talk to me, engage with me, anything. He wouldn't eat, just messed around with his food like a two-year-old. Then when I went to pay the bill he started picking up money from other tables, other people's tips, and putting them on ours—pissing off the waitresses. I can't deal with him. I'll talk to you later." She left.

"I'm Being Devoured by Tigers"

Thiothixene: Brand name: ***Navane.*** Thiothixene is an antipsychotic agent of the thioxanthene series [useful in the management of schizophrenia and other psychotic disorders.] . . . ***Thiothixene's mode of action has not been clearly established.***

Adverse Effects: *Behavioral:* The most common side effects are initial and transient drowsiness, restlessness and agitation and insomnia. Other adverse reactions reported less frequently are weakness or fatigue, excitement, depression and headache. . . . ***Toxic confusional states may occur on rare occasions.*** *Neurological:* The incidence and nature of extrapyramidal symptoms, including akathisia, pseudo-parkinsonism and dystonic reactions, are similar to those encountered with the piperazine phenothiazines, but thiothixene is more likely to produce akathisia. They are usually controlled by reduction of dosage and/or administration of antiparkinson drugs depending on the type and severity of symptoms.

Dosage: The usual optimal dosage of thiothixene is in the range of 15 to 30 mg daily. In most conditions, the initial dosage should be 5 to 10 mg daily. The dosage should be gradually increased to the optimally effective level based on patient response. . . . ***The dosage should be reduced to the lowest possible maintenance level as soon as possible.***[2] (emphasis added)

Charley spent most of the rest of the day either on my bed or on his futon, increasingly withdrawn. He tried the piano a couple of times, but his playing was becoming completely incoherent and he soon gave up entirely. He listened to the stereo once or twice, particularly David Bowie, his favorite singer, standing right next to the turntable, almost in a trance. But as he became more withdrawn, the music tapered off.

Neither of us slept much that night. Charley was by now openly delusional, at one point thinking I was Brian Marsh and that he was in New York. He picked up the phone and listened intently, apparently thinking he was hearing a voice. "What are you thinking about?" I asked in the early hours of Wednesday morning. It was a question I hated being asked myself and would soon learn to avoid.

"The beauty of reality," Charley answered. Then, some time later: "I'm being devoured by tigers."

By early morning he was lying rigid on his futon, almost catatonic. I was exhausted. I hadn't gone to work Monday or Tuesday, and knew I couldn't leave Charley like this; it wouldn't work for either of us. I was a proofreader and copy editor for an accountancy firm. The work I did demanded concentration and attention to detail, and even if I could go to my job and concentrate knowing he was here, lying curled up on the futon all day, who would take care of him? What if he got up and wandered outside into traffic? He had almost killed himself a few days before. On the other hand, I couldn't lock him in the apartment.

I tried to think rationally. In the long run I had no doubt he would get over whatever was wrong with him, but I had no idea when. In his current state he was in no position to take care of himself. Lin was going to Santa Cruz in the next couple of days. I couldn't simply not work indefinitely. I was an hourly employee; if I didn't work, I didn't get paid. Lack of sleep and an increasing sense of helplessness were starting to break me down, and what good would I be to Charley or anybody else if I cracked up or lost my job? He was obviously sick. St. John's Hospital was only eight blocks from my apartment. Lobotomies were no longer legal. Weren't hospitals there to take care of sick people and help them get better?

Lin agreed to come to my apartment Wednesday morning to relieve me; even with my night off Monday, when Charley had stayed at her condo, I had gotten almost no real rest since Friday. She and I talked on the phone early Wednesday morning, and I told her I wanted to put Charley in the hospital. She continued to resist, wanting to take him to a healer and try acupuncture and some other things like herbal remedies first.

I called Dr. Gray at about 6 A.M., got his answering machine and had him paged. When he called me back I explained the situation, including Lin's hesitations. He said he understood them. I asked what he thought about the acupuncture idea, my strategy being to negotiate with Lin and do both: first we would take Charley to acupuncture, then, barring a miracle, to St. John's. Dr. Gray said that acupuncture wouldn't help. It wouldn't hurt, but it was a question of time. The sooner Charley got full-time care the better. We talked about the basic mechanics of getting him admitted.

When Lin arrived a little later, Charley was curled up rigid and motionless on the futon facing the wall. I thought the deterioration was a result of his deepening psychosis; Lin thought it was just as likely the side effects of the medication I was now giving him, which Dr. Gray had warned might cause stiffness (he had prescribed a second medication to counteract it).

By this point I didn't care what was causing what; one way or the other Charley was going to the hospital. Lin still resisted, but she was starting to crack too. "Oh God, I think we're losing him forever," she said as she looked down at the back of her darling boy.

"No we're not," I said with a confidence I tried not to analyze too carefully. "He'll be fine. We just need to get him to people who can help him."

"By giving him medicine like this, that makes him stiff and immobile? Look at him. Do you see him getting better? I don't."

"He will. I know he will. The medication takes time to work. We can't leave him like this. Look at him. I've had it, Lin."

She still wanted to take him for acupuncture, but when he showed no more willingness to do that than to go to the hospital she finally gave in.

It took both of us to rouse him and get him dressed. By now he was so disoriented that he didn't understand when we told him where he was going; he thought he was getting ready for work. Heart-rending as this was—even with all that had happened we were only gradually realizing how clouded his mind was—the delusion about going to work also got him out of his stupor long enough to get dressed in his white busboy shirt and black slacks. He even examined himself in the mirror and carefully brushed his hair—this was someone who ten minutes before had not seemed able to move—so that when we led him out to Lin's car he actually looked good enough to go to work.

But we weren't going to work. I drove. Lin sat with Charley in the back, hugging him. In a moment we passed the street that led to his job. "Turn there, Dad," Charley said, pointing in the direction of the restaurant.

"You're not going to work, Charley," I said. "We're taking you to the hospital."

"You missed the turn, Dad."

The Gospel According to St. John's

There are two ways of getting into a psychiatric hospital: voluntary and involuntary. Although Charley was not exactly brought to St. John's by force, and thus his initial admission was at least technically voluntary, once he was admitted and saw what was happening he demanded to leave, so Dr. Gray put him on a seventy-two-hour involuntary hold known as a 5150, a legal procedure by which people can be psychiatrically hospitalized against their will for one or more of three reasons: They are a danger to others, they are a danger to themselves, or they are gravely disabled (unable to care for themselves). Charley's hold was based on criteria two and three. He was put in the hospital's locked ward, the third floor of the mental-health center. (There was also an unlocked ward on the second floor for voluntary patients.)

How did I feel about putting my "favorite son" under lock and key among strangers who were giving him heavy medications whose nature I barely understood? I felt awful. I also felt vastly relieved, and at least for the time being, the immediate relief overwhelmed the more general awfulness. I felt that we—I—had made the best of a bad situation. Despite knowing Dr. Gray for a total of one day, I trusted him and his hospital; if he said Charley would get good care, Charley would get good care. Lin remained far less confident, tending to think that I'd caved in to Western patriarchy in general and the medical establishment in particular, more out of self-interest than concern for Charley. At this point I was prepared to live with that even though part of me agreed with her. I knew that some of my motives were selfish. The previous five days—such a short time!—had seemed like forever. It wasn't only the increasing tension in the air, the electricity of torment generated partly by Charley's inner conflicts and partly by my response to them. It was also my sense that I had no idea what was going on and no effective way to deal with it; what was happening was totally beyond my experience as a parent or as a human being. Is there anything more exhausting and demoralizing than the feeling of being adrift, alone? The term "grasping at straws" refers to the phenomenon of drowning sailors mistaking slivers of wood floating near them for logs. I felt I was drowning in ignorance and confusion, and Dr. Gray and his method of care were the only things I could see that might save me and Charley from going down.

I visited him for the first time the next morning, buzzed into a locked elevator and up to the third floor, which had another lock on the door into the actual ward. The ward was small, twenty beds or so. Patients ranged from people like Charley, middle class with families and insurance, to the mentally ill homeless brought in by the police. The windows were large and allowed a lot of light in, and the patient rooms and hallway and common area were spacious enough not to seem suffocating. Except for the endless drone of the TV in the common room the place didn't seem too bad.

For the first two days Charley didn't have his own room; he stayed in a special observation area—the third locked door between him and the outside world. It was next to the nurses' station, separated by a wall fitted with a nonbreakable glass window. The room was a drab, depressing place with scuffed, dirty walls, a lot of stainless steel and no privacy. That was on purpose; he was there so the staff could keep an eye on him. When I arrived to see him the day after he was admitted he was still not himself, although no longer catatonic. He spoke to me mainly in French and I tried to respond in French, and none of it made much sense in any language. But at least he was talking, not lying in the fetal position. I was feeling renewed myself after sleeping well for the first time in almost a week, and had no doubt he would soon get better. But Charley really hated being locked up, and as we spoke he demanded to know how long it was going to last. He claimed the female nurses had sexual designs on him, although he admitted they hadn't actually done anything yet except look at him lustfully. I made it clear that in principle I didn't want him there either, and that his mother and I loved him and wouldn't desert him. Later I called Dr. Gray, who was having at least one inpatient therapy session with him every day. I mentioned the remark about the nurses. Dr. Gray said that hypersexuality was a common symptom of people experiencing psychosis. I thought about the incident with the female camper at Yosemite.

Over the next few days I had a hard time knowing how Charley was doing because I still couldn't distinguish between the effects of the psychosis and the effects of the antipsychotic medication. So-called antipsychotics like Thorazine, Haldol or Navane (which Charley was on) are also known as neuroleptics—a term that means "seizing the brain." Webster's defines *neuroleptic* as "tranquilizer." Neuroleptics are in fact major tranquilizers that attack the central nervous system, and people taking them tend to develop side effects known as *extrapyramidal symptoms,* which can include a stiff, shuffling walk, shaking, sometimes drooling, and a dazed, narcotized expression—all of which psychiatrists attempt to mitigate with additional medications like Artane or

Cogentin, which were originally developed for parkinsonism.

When the anti–side effects medication started to work after a couple of days, some of the stiffness and near-catatonia Charley had developed in my apartment the day before he was hospitalized began to disappear, and he seemed to me visibly improved. He became more conversant and coherent, and even began to get some of his personality—Dr. Gray called it his "sparkle"—back. But whenever I stopped by the nurses' station at the end of visiting hours and expressed my cheery view that he was getting better, the staff, trained to distinguish the symptoms of psychosis from the side effects of the medication, told me that he was still hearing voices and "responding to internal stimuli." Despite the physical improvement, in other words, he was still psychotic. The antipsychotics took time to work.

Charley went into the hospital on Wednesday morning, July 31. The following Monday I had a long phone conversation with Dr. Gray. I mentioned something Charley had said the first or second time I visited him, when he was still in the holding area next to the nurses' station and speaking mostly French. "Dad, I don't have to be Franz Liszt, do I?" he had suddenly asked in English— Franz Liszt being reputedly the greatest pianist of all time.

"Of course you don't have to be Franz Liszt. Is that what you think?"

"Kind of."

The discussion moved on before I could find out what he meant, but although confused by the question I also felt relieved because it seemed to indicate that the mental fever was breaking. Days later, as Charley became more lucid, I asked him whether he remembered the question about Liszt. He said yes.

"What did you mean by it?"

"I meant I'd been Franz Liszt in a former life. Beethoven, too."

He said this a little too easily. "Former lives" was fairly mainstream Southern California New Age speak, used, I suspected, to hide what he had really meant, which was that he had actually thought he *was* Franz Liszt in *this* life, or at least a new incarnation. Or both.

"That's a pretty big burden," I said. We talked some more and I tried to answer what I thought was the underlying question, whether he had to achieve some supernatural greatness to justify his existence.

When I mentioned this to Dr. Gray on the phone, he said the Liszt remark was in keeping with what Charley had told him. By then they had had five or six talk therapy sessions. Charley had opened up a little, and Dr. Gray tried to let me know some of what had been said without completely violating doctor-patient confidentiality. Charley felt he was a terrible burden on Lin and me. "He feels he didn't do well enough at school. He feels he has to accomplish something remarkable to justify the expense. He has to grow up very rapidly, to transform himself into something remarkable. He's very lucid in his ability to talk about it."

Further, Dr. Gray said, drugs hadn't been involved in the breakdown at Yosemite. The story Charley had told Lin about smoking pot was untrue, a red herring. So what had caused the psychosis? Acute insomnia, for one thing. Charley told Dr. Gray that he had almost completely stopped sleeping for several weeks. He had taken up transcendental meditation as a relaxation technique, but then became attracted to its more spiritual and mystical aspects. (Months later he would write about TM, "I enjoy it immensely—physically and cerebrally. I can achieve all cosmic, god and unity consciousness. I have the ability to see all the beauty in the world as if I were the Creator. And I have the ability to perceive the unified field. I know this is true because I achieved this before"—at Yosemite.) Charley had been working to change his mental state, to leap onto a higher plane where he would have the power to overcome the practical obstacles in his life. He would accomplish great things—become a great pianist, bring world peace—and by doing so justify his existence to the world, his parents and himself.

When the three-day hold expired, Charley again demanded to be released. Dr. Gray then put him on a fourteen-day hold—the next thing up from a three-day hold. Charley then went to a patients' rights advocate to get the new hold overturned. He had a hearing on the Wednesday after he was admitted. It was basically a show trial. Even the patients' rights advocate didn't seem very enthusiastic about his getting out—Charley was clearly not well—and the municipal court judge presiding found in Dr. Gray's favor, although Dr. Gray dropped criterion two, danger to himself, from the hold. He didn't think Charley was a danger to himself anymore, just gravely disabled.

Once his appeal to lift the hold failed, Charley saw that how long he stayed locked up depended on Lin and me and Dr. Gray, who could lift the hold whenever he wanted or else start a new one when the old one ran out (this could continue for a while, although not indefinitely). Hospitalization then became a matter of day-to-day negotiation, of begging and guilt tripping, of haggling and persuasion and bribery. A slightly exaggerated form, in other words, of ordinary parent-child relations. "Dad, get me out of here!" Charley would plead every time I visited or talked to him on the phone, and my reply would always be, "Hang in there a little longer, Charley, you seem to be getting better. Chill for a couple of more days."

"You don't know what it's like in here!"

"It doesn't seem so bad. You'll get out soon. I promise. How 'bout if I bring you Pancho's"—food from our favorite Mexican restaurant—"tomorrow?"

"Yeah, and Benson & Hedges Export Blues. Two packs. And more quarters."

The quarters were for the two pay phones in the hall near the ward's common room. The patients' rights movement of the 1960s and 1970s had brought a certain dignity to the psych ward. Patients had phone access to the outside world as long as they had calling card numbers or change. They could call out for pizza or other take-out. A list of their rights was posted in the ward (these included freedom from coercion and involuntary shock therapy, and the right to talk to a patients' rights advocate). Among the daily group classes was one on self-assertiveness. The staff seemed to be humane. Not even Charley ever complained of being abused. But he hated the Navane, and even a benevolent asylum is still an asylum. "Elopement risk," said a handmade sign on the locked door into the ward the first time Lin and I visited (and subsequently), and we wondered what it meant. Were a couple of the patients trying to sneak out and get married? No, we were told. "Elopement" was hospitalese for "escape," and the posting meant that staff were supposed to be extra careful when they opened and closed the locked doors. We soon found out who the elopement risk was.

Over time he seemed to relax a little, though, and became less demanding about being released. I even had the impression that he wanted to stay for a while, although he desperately wanted to move from the third floor to the unlocked ward one flight below, where the less-acute patients stayed. In fact, moving to "the second floor" was the carrot Dr. Gray held out if Charley cooperated, and he actually did move downstairs for the last four days of his stay.

It was no doubt self-serving of me to think that Charley really did want to be hospitalized. But only partly. Time would show that he had his own fears about being "a danger to himself." I also think that he was benefiting from his daily therapy with Dr. Gray, and he knew it. If he could use me as the bad guy, the one who was forcing him to remain locked up, then he could stay put temporarily and still maintain his pride.

Once it became known—with Charley's permission—where he was, visitors started arriving. His sister Jenny came, and various friends. Kit Henderson of the now-postponed New Orleans trip flew into town the first weekend and stayed with Charley every minute of every visiting hour. I had never met him before, although we had talked on the phone. On Saturday we introduced ourselves and had dinner together after visiting hours. Kit seemed utterly devoted to Charley, overinvolved if anything. Lin had met and talked to Kit a little herself, and eventually we began to suspect that he was in love with Charley. We weren't homophobic and we didn't care about Kit's sexual preferences—or Charley's, for that matter. But we were beginning to wonder whether sexual pressures and uncertainties centered on the planned trip to New Orleans had had something to do with the breakdown.

His pattern in the hospital was uneven but generally positive. Sometimes he sounded like "him," as my girlfriend Janet said, sometimes he just sounded crazy. I found out later that he thought he could hypnotize people just by staring at them. The same day I talked to Dr. Gray on the phone about Liszt— Charley had been in the ward five days—Jenny and I visited him and she asked what he was afraid of. "Oh, the world in general," Charley answered. He seemed afraid of world conflict, although he'd never shown much interest in current events before; I'd never seen him read a newspaper. His fears alternated with grandiosity, the two sometimes seeming to exist almost simultaneously.

Jenny asked if they had art therapy at the hospital.

"That's my whole life," Charley replied. The whole world was art, he said, and he was a performance artist. The next day I visited him alone and he said, "I have special talents. I can make the wind blow. I can make the sun shine"—then added, as he saw me shift uncomfortably in my chair, "Maybe I'm exaggerating."

But I had no idea whether he really meant it. Sometimes the delusions seemed to exist side by side with rationality, elbowing each other, fighting for position like two big centers under the basket in a basketball game. Or were the expressions of sanity just a con? Dr. Gray talked about how he thought Charley was learning to mask his delusions. But when I mentioned the claims of supernatural powers, Dr. Gray seemed unconcerned. They were common to people in Charley's condition and would clear up automatically as the medication kicked in, he said, although they did indicate the need for ongoing talk therapy. I mentioned that during the "I can make the wind blow" conversation Charley had also hinted to me for the first time that the accident at Yosemite was not an accident, that it had resulted from his attempt to prove his immortality. Dr. Gray agreed. He had already heard it from Charley himself, but had said nothing to me (I assumed for confidentiality reasons). But now that Charley had mentioned it himself, Dr. Gray filled in the details in a kind of roundabout way. "In that kind of 'higher' state," he said, "where they think they're communicating directly with God or through some higher consciousness, *people have been known to do things like close their eyes when they're driving and take their hands off the wheel.*"

Oh my God, I thought, no wonder Charley hadn't wanted to talk about the crash. No wonder he had started having panic attacks.

Oh, Yes, the Car

With Charley temporarily taken care of, I turned to other matters I had neglected since his return from Yosemite. One of these was the car, which had been towed from the crash site to a Union 76 station near Mammoth in a town called Lee Vining. So the Friday evening after Charley went into St. John's, a week after the crash, I borrowed my girlfriend Janet's old Toyota station wagon, found a California map, drank some coffee and started up toward Yosemite, still not sure about what I would do about the car if it looked reparable, but glad to have an excuse to get away for a day or so. I headed northeast out of L.A. and onto Highway 395, threaded through the desert toward the eastern Sierra Nevada and Death Valley, passed through Lone Pine and Bishop, and arrived near Lee Vining around five Saturday morning. After sleeping for a few hours in the back of Janet's car I made my way into town, a tiny collection of houses, gas stations, restaurants and tourist shops pressed up against the mountains overlooking Mono Lake. My plan had been to get the car taken care of first thing and head back to L.A. before it got really hot, and the day before I had called the owner of the gas station to tell him I was coming. But when I got to the station shortly after it opened, he wasn't there. His wife told me that there was a forest fire some way away, and he was lugging water to the fire-fighters and would be gone for a few hours. He had the only key to the shed that held the car.

The best-laid plans . . . But by now I was getting used to having no control over anything, so I waited in the growing August desert heat, proud of my newfound serenity, occasionally strolling around the tiny town, wondering what I would do with the car when the station owner got back. Would he rent me a tow bar? Did he even have one that would fit Janet's car, or would I have to go back to L.A. and drive up again in a pickup truck with a tow attachment? Was Janet's little Toyota even big enough to tow my heavier '84 Ford through the desert?

The day was becoming stuporously hot. Still no gas station owner. I periodically gazed down at Mono Lake to the east, denuded, its water level reduced by sixty feet after seventy years of being pumped into the bottomless development maw of L.A., a city Charley basically hated, hundreds of miles to the south. The lake really did look like the surface of the moon. I felt like I had landed in a parallel world. The only people in town seemed to be young Swedish and German backpackers, rangy big-jointed Wotans and Brunnhildes wearing shorts and kneesocks who could have stepped out of a Leni Riefenstahl movie, tall and straight as the surrounding pines and with about the same percent body fat. Mono Lake could be a postapocalypse setting, and these were the survivors. What had not killed them had made them stronger.

I wandered around some more. Even after a couple of hours I wasn't getting impatient. The guy with the key would get back when he got back. Why was I in such a hurry to get back to L.A. anyway?

Another hour or two and he arrived, apologizing for making me wait. We walked to the shed and he opened the door into the corrugated darkness. It took my desert-light-assaulted eyes a few seconds to adjust. At first I couldn't make out the car. Then I did, and all worries about tow bars and pickups vanished. "Oh my God," I said.

In front of me in the darkness was a flattened and deformed monstrosity that looked like some odd, squatty fungus, a deformed metal mushroom, not a car. I could see a caved-in roof with a number of huge dents, a front that was a dirty, mangled bouquet of jagged metal edges. The car looked like it had gone though a compactor.

"It looks like it flipped over at least—what, two or three times, doesn't it?" I asked, just to have something to say.

"Yeah, he took quite a spill," the garage owner said. He left me alone to go to his office and do the paperwork; he had agreed to take the car as payment for the tow.

I continued to stare. Talk about postapocalypse. For the first time I understood why the CHP officer had thought Charley must be crazy to think he could drive this thing out of the ditch; for the first time, the true magnitude of what had happened hit me. How, how, had Charley walked away from this? I thought of stories I'd heard about drunks walking away from accidents where other sober people lay dead, surviving through some sort of loose-limbed obliviousness. Maybe Charley had been feeling that kind of obliviousness, both life threatening and life saving at the same time.

In the end he was in the hospital for sixteen days, the length of stay determined less by his mental condition than my financial one. My company's mental-health insurance, which was fairly good as medical insurance goes in the United States, had a lifetime limit of twenty thousand dollars for each covered person (Charley was covered as my dependent). St. John's, which had a preferred provider arrangement with my insurance company, charged about eight hundred dollars a day, of which I paid about eighty out of pocket. At the rate we were going, the whole twenty thousand would be gone in less than a month. I talked about this to Dr. Gray. Should I blow Charley's whole lifetime allowance on this one hospitalization? Probably not, he replied, you may want to keep some in reserve. So although I knew that for Charley every day in the hospital was an eternity, I also knew—and told him—that he would be out soon, hold or no hold.

Dr. Gray's remark about keeping some of the twenty thousand in reserve registered on me only dimly at the time. I didn't believe Charley would ever have another episode like this; it was (as my brother, Charley's Uncle Tim, called it) a nervous breakdown, a one-time event caused by a unique set of

circumstances that would never recur. Charley would recover fully and permanently, I was sure of it. Dr. Gray didn't agree or disagree. The first week, in
accordance with standard psychiatric practice outlined in the American
Psychiatric Association's *Diagnostic and Statistical Manual of Mental Disorders
(DSM)*, he described Charley's condition as "brief reactive psychosis," a term
that basically means "he's acting crazy and we don't know why." Within a few
days he was revising this first opinion. "It's not brief reactive psychosis," he told
me on day nine, because brief reactive psychosis "goes away within three to
five days."[3] He suggested tentatively that Charley might be suffering from
manic-depressive illness and considered putting him on lithium along with the
Navane. Lithium had a "more benign" profile than the neuroleptics, Dr. Gray
said, and Charley could take both it and Navane and then start tapering off on
the Navane. If he didn't show signs of relapse he could stop the Navane
entirely, then possibly even taper down on the lithium. Trial and error over
time would determine which medication he needed, if any.

All such questions were rendered moot, however, when Charley actually left
the hospital. At an exit meeting held in a hospital lounge on August 13, the
evening before his release, he announced to me, Dr. Gray and Lin, who had
come down from Santa Cruz, that once he left St. John's he would not take
any medication—Navane, lithium, or anything else. "Hospitals are bad for the
psyche," he said—especially "meds," a psychiatric jargon word he hated. Dr.
Gray advised him to keep taking the medication, or at least taper off gradually
under a psychiatrist's care. Charley didn't want to hear it and stomped out of
the lounge.

The three of us who remained were once again left staring at each other. I
said it looked like the hospital's assertiveness training classes were paying off.

What should we do now? I couldn't force Charley to take his medication,
and I knew Lin was still basically opposed to the whole idea of medication
anyway. Tonight in the hospital lounge was only the second time she and Dr.
Gray had met. Although she had gone along with Charley's hospitalization, she
acted as if it and everything and everyone related to it were my department.
"Does he really need to keep taking the medication?" she asked now. "It just
seems so bad—what it does to him."

"I've been doing this a long time," Dr. Gray said. "I saw too much of the *I
Never Promised You a Rose Garden* kind of stuff twenty-five years ago—people

being hospitalized for months without medication, smearing the walls with their feces. The medication helps to avoid a lot of that."

I glanced at Lin. Dr. Gray didn't sound like a dope-pusher to me, a shill for the drug companies. He was a psychoanalyst as well as a psychiatrist; he knew it wasn't all just brain chemistry. Plus he genuinely liked Charley, and I think Charley was beginning to like him. He didn't want to turn Charley into a zombie. But of course Lin would shrug all this off. Sure, Dr. Gray was an okay guy, she would say. But his mindset was set.

Now, in the lounge, I asked him what he thought would happen when Charley went off the medication.

"The Navane might last, um, four to six weeks in his bloodstream and continue to have an effect. After that I'm not sure. A couple of trips to the county psych ward are often required before a person gets tired of going through this."

I shuddered inwardly, but it was an abstract shudder. I didn't think such dire warnings applied to us. "So what do you think the outlook for him is?" I asked.

"I really don't know at this point. With situations like Charley's there are, um, generally three possible outcomes. In about a third of the cases, the person gets over the first episode and it never happens again. In another third of the cases, the person gets on a medication that works, and they can deal with it successfully from then on. In the final third of cases, the medication doesn't work and you then have ongoing problems." He told us to watch for insomnia, a danger sign of oncoming mania. He suggested sleeping pills. He also said to discourage Charley from experimenting with transcendental meditation, at least the god consciousness part. As a relaxation technique, fine. But be careful. One of the hallmarks of Charley's condition was megalomania, and the spiritual aspects of TM—the striving for god consciousness and so on—could feed into that.

We talked a little about the megalomania, Charley's belief that he could bring everyone together and achieve world peace. The messiah complex was very common in these situations, Dr. Gray said—"I've seen it a million times." It indicated the need for ongoing psychotherapy. Charley, however, had also refused to consider that once he was out of St. John's. So now we were faced with the prospect of his getting out the next day, drug and therapy free.

I walked over to the hospital the next morning to get him. He greeted me with quiet triumph at being released. He seemed fairly rational, although it was hard for me to tell. But certainly a million percent better than when he'd been at my apartment the couple of days before I hospitalized him. We went to Izzy's, scene of the tip-grabbing episode two and a half weeks earlier, to have lunch. His hands were shaking. "See what the Navane does to me, Dad?" he said as he raised his glass. "How can I function like that?" He asked me to help him put mustard on his sandwich.

How could I not sympathize? During the past two weeks I had talked about antipsychotics to everybody I could find, including a woman therapist even Lin respected, looking for something other than the official "patriarchal Western medicine" party line. Everybody said that in some cases such medications, nasty as they were, were necessary because they beat the alternatives: florid psychosis, possible suicide, total disaster. But nobody liked them (even Dr. Gray had wanted to move Charley from neuroleptics to lithium). Now, with him refusing to take anything, I was fervently hoping he had been right all along, that he really didn't need medication. It was a reversal of our roles of a week before when he'd hidden behind my decision to keep him in the hospital, protesting volubly but going along. Now I protested about his going off the medication, but also went along.

The hospitalization had forced the cancellation of the New Orleans trip, but a few days after Charley's release Kit Henderson came back to L.A. and he and Charley drove up to San Francisco, a city Charley loved, to visit his twenty-one-year-old Aunt Ella and her husband Chris, both artists. "They're my people, Dad," he'd told me when I wondered whether he should leave town. They'd take care of his ills. They wouldn't lean on him to take medication. He would be free of doctors and parents. I shrugged. I couldn't force him to stay, and San Francisco was a kind of consolation prize after the failed New Orleans trip and the two weeks in the psych ward.

On August 23, nine days after Charley left St. John's, my phone rang, another coffin nail. It was an old man's voice, paper-thin, dry as an Illinois drought. "Jonathan, this is Bob Tideman." Lin's father, calling from his home in San Francisco. "It's about Charley. He's back in the hospital." Bob sounded tired. He had been operated on for prostate cancer a few months before and still hadn't really recovered. He may also have been starting to feel the effects of the liver cancer, as yet unknown, that would kill him two years later.

I asked what had happened. Bob told me what the police had told him. Charley had become fixated on a young woman he'd seen on the street, then followed her to a store where she worked, claiming she was somebody he knew who was destined to be with him. He refused to go away and she had called the police. They had taken him to San Francisco General Hospital—the county psych ward. He was on a seventy-two-hour hold.

Years later he wrote an account of these days from his internal perspective. He talked about staying with Kit Henderson at Ella and Chris's in a kind of surreal fog, which included mental telepathy.

> The thoughts that ensued for the next forty-eight hours don't belong on paper. The notions behind madness are like dreams, only more personal and more unfathomable. But to state the facts: I thought I was in love and destined to betroth a young woman I knew from SF Conservatory when I was taking lessons there [in high school]. I weirded up at some little greeting card/craft shop (God knows how I chose it) insisting I see Allison. Where's Allison? Eventually the girl behind the counter got fed up, locked me out and called the cops. And that was my second psych ward.

San Francisco General

Bob's call was actually not a total surprise. The previous day Charley had called me, sounding very spacey, like after Yosemite only more so. I don't remember the conversation, but he ended by saying "I love you" in an ethereal, almost beatific way, which worried me. Normally he only said he loved me a little grudgingly, and only after I said I loved *him*.

I didn't go to San Francisco. I was still exhausted from the last month, and there were already plenty of people up there to minister to him, including grandparents and numerous aunts and uncles and his mother only eighty miles away in Santa Cruz. They had all criticized me for the way I had handled Charley's first hospitalization and then had supported his decision to stay off medication when he arrived in San Francisco. Good. Let *them* deal with him.

He had visitors every day, family and others. "My [former] piano teacher, Richard, even paid me a visit at one point during my sojourn," Charley wrote in his later account.

It was great to see him. I envied immediately how well dressed he was. He was headed to work, some nice hotel where he played. I tried to talk seriously to him about my profound revelations a few months back. When I mentioned "immortal consciousness" he looked away, vexed. "Well, you know," he said. "We all have to shit, we have to eat, we all have to . . . buy food." After my mystical experience is that what it all comes to?

He stayed at San Francisco General for about two weeks "of humiliation" (he wrote), hating what he described as the power-tripping staff, the lousy food and his fellow patients, many of them the mentally ill homeless, the most insulted and injured of the insulted and injured.

So why had he gotten himself locked up again if he hated psych wards so much? It was pretty much as Dr. Gray had predicted. The new San Francisco breakdown was actually a continuation of the first breakdown that had begun at Yosemite and been suppressed by the two weeks of antipsychotic medication at St. John's. The psychosis flared up again when he went off the medication, just as Dr. Gray had worried it would. When Charley was put back on Navane at San Francisco General the psychosis began to subside again.

This time the recovery was real despite the uncongenial environment. Charley was released after about ten days into the care of his grandparents Bob and Meighen and lived with them for a couple of months, finally beginning to act a little chastened. "Dear Dad," he wrote me at the beginning of September while still in the hospital,

> How grand it is! Grand to be in the constant state of receiving therapy. As I lie on the couch watching a tennis match, it's therapy. When I walk around on the patio with a cigarette, it's therapy. When I read about Tolstoy's life on his estate Yasnaya Polyana, it's therapy. Knowing this counterbalances the restlessness which is integral to being in the hospital. Everybody, Dad, is just a little bit crazy. Now that I know this I can live my own life and quit worrying about being a prophet who brings world peace. As long as I am at peace with myself peace will surround me. The main objective though is not to let it envelop me.

A few days after his release he decided to stop taking the Navane again— he really hated the extrapyramidal side effects of stiffness and slowness and the mental effect of being "knocked out"—but this time he promised to do it gradually after I argued with him. During the second week of September, now at his grandparents', he wrote me,

> Dearest Dad, I very much appreciate the sympathy you've shown during my time of crisis. I don't know what I would do if I didn't have your intellect to help me. It is true my illness has been depressing and so poorly defined also. It is as if I have no direction to guide me. I'll continue the Navane as long as I must. I plan to see a psychiatrist on the 20th. I have a piano lesson tomorrow. If only I didn't feel so stiff I could practice more.

A few days later he sent me a postcard saying he had cut the Navane dosage in half on his own because "I shan't wait for someone else to monitor me." But then the very next day:

> Please excuse . . . the insolent remark about not letting someone else monitor my medication. I am still taking the medication. Tonight I bought some artane (prescribed by Dr. Gray) since I've run out of cogentin (prescribed at SFGH) which are for the side effects of the Navane. If it is not I who choose to reduce the Navane dosage, who is? I should know since it is my body. I also know you're afraid I might have a relapse. I can just about promise you I shall not.

The conflictedness of his thinking is apparent not only from one day to the next but from one sentence to the next. Still, this time the recovery was real. While at his grandparents' Charley stopped taking all medication, but there was no relapse. My girlfriend Janet and I flew to San Francisco the first weekend in October to visit him and some friends of hers, a gay couple. Charley seemed almost well, although when the five of us went to the Castro Street gay pride fair on Sunday and stood at a corner waiting for the light to change he started to step off the curb into traffic and I had to grab him and pull him back. But a photo Janet took of the two of us an hour later shows him present and accounted for. A few weeks later he moved to Santa Cruz to live with his mother, taking the year off from Reed. Lin took him to a doctor specializing in body chemistry and amino acid therapy and he was put on a number of amino acids and other mineral supplements to try to improve his neurotransmitter (mood) functioning. Toward Christmas I got a card from him with a painting on the front that reminded me of a 1960s-era psychedelic poster. It pictured a pope standing in the middle of a Rorschach-like forest of blue water drops and ice crystals. Superimposed on the pope was a faint crucifix of light. "I liked the cover painting, *Enlightenment,*" Charley wrote inside. "This is how I felt while I was in Yosemite." He also told me he was signing up for classes at a community college:

> I'm taking the maximum units so maybe I can reactivate what's left of my brain cells. One of the few goals I have presently is to be able to get married one day, in five to fifteen years, and have kids whom I can engage with and educate as thoroughly as you and Mom were able to.

So now, four or five months after the moon madness and crash in Yosemite, Charley was recovered, off antipsychotics and on amino acids. This seemed to confirm my opinion that he had suffered a one-time nervous breakdown, an essentially physical short-circuiting brought on by stress—or possibly, Lin and I speculated, a flashback to the bad "iawaska" trip of the previous Halloween that Brian Marsh had told me about (Charley had said the two episodes had a lot in common). At any rate, it was over.

Charley himself, according to Dr. Gray and the San Francisco General medical records (which I read years later), attributed the episode to insomnia, which may have been true to a degree. Prolonged sleeplessness can cause psychosis, and Charley had been experiencing insomnia in the weeks before he went camping. But that was clearly an inadequate explanation; if it had been true, sleep would have solved the problem. It also begged the questions: What had caused the insomnia, and why had it become so severe now? Dr. Gray had mentioned one possibility: the pressure Charley felt to do well in school and justify his mother's sacrifices and what he saw as her and my expectations, and the related uncertainties about what he was going to do at the end of the summer. The fantasies of going to music school and becoming a great concert pianist were ways of leaping over the actual roadblocks in his life: difficulties getting financial aid, ambivalence about Reed with its academic pressures, guilt over the burden he felt himself to be on his parents.

Another area of stress was worry and uncertainty regarding the now-aborted New Orleans trip. It took a while for Lin and me to learn the details, but we had been right about Kit Henderson. He *was* in love with Charley, and even though he didn't reveal his feelings explicitly until after Yosemite (he wrote a passionate, and very inappropriately timed, declaration of love letter

while Charley was locked up at San Francisco General), Charley had been feeling doubts and pressures about the trip. But these doubts were not merely the
discomfort of a straight man being pursued by a gay one; they were doubts
about his own sexuality. One form his psychosis had taken was, as Charley put
it himself, "a battle of the sexes" in his head. Two conflicting voices, one male
and one female, importuned him, demanding that he make a decision about
whether to be a man or a woman. In the San Francisco General medical
records one psychologist wrote about how in therapy Charley expressed "conflicting feelings about sexuality and pressure from friend Kit Henderson (five
years older) to engage in sexual relationship with him. Patient also had a male
friend in college[4] who expressed desire for sexual relationship with patient.
Patient seems ambivalent re: sexuality and feels he needs to make a decision."

Periodically from then on he would think that he had made the decision—
to be a man—but the conflict would never really be resolved, although in normal times it seemed resolved enough to give him some level of comfort. In late
September, for example, after he moved in with Bob and Meighen, Charley
wrote me that Meighen was fixing up a bedroom for him that had previously
belonged to one of her daughters, Aunt Justine. "She has even decided to present it in a more masculine motif than it was before. How happy I am to be a
man, without losing traits of androgyny." As I learned much later, both parts of
that last sentence—the desire for masculinity and the androgyny—were important for understanding Charley and his doubts and instabilities.

But for the present things remained peaceful, and all of us were hugely
relieved, not least of all Charley. For there was an irony in his breakdown. As
dangerous and awful as that breakdown was and as much suffering as it caused
him, Yosemite and the psych wards that came after solved, at least temporarily,
his immediate problems. The New Orleans trip was canceled, and decisions
about Reed were indefinitely postponed. Whatever else they are or are not,
psychotic breakdowns—what Charley called "trips to the underworld"—are
effective ways of getting out of the obligations of *this* world.

Now Charley was back in a charmed approximation of this world—the
low-stress semiparadise of Santa Cruz, living with his mother and pondering
his future at leisure. Lin, who had been living with her sister since moving up
in August, rented a house for herself and Charley to give him more room and
stability. That and the amino acids seemed to do the trick. His recovery lasted
almost a year.

3

"The Brightest Little Boy in the Whole Park"

Derelict Keys

Culver City, California, is an odd-shaped city within greater Los Angeles that on a map looks like a long-necked goose, airborne, about to head out over the Pacific Ocean. Few outside Los Angeles have ever heard of this odd goose of a city, which seems unfair, since it has at least as much claim as another part of L.A., Hollywood, to be the "home of the movies." It was Culver City, not Hollywood, that was the home of the quintessential "Hollywood" studio, Metro-Goldwyn-Mayer, which meant that in the late '30s, the American film industry's golden age, Oz's yellow-brick road twisted and Dorothy's ruby shoes shimmered in Culver City, not in Hollywood proper, a few miles to the northeast. And there was much more to Culver City than just MGM. *Gone with the Wind*'s Atlanta was built and then burned at Selznick Studios in Culver City. A year or so later, Orson Welles built *Citizen Kane*'s Xanadu at RKO Pictures, a couple of blocks from Selznick. So one could justly claim that the two most

37

beloved Hollywood movies, and the single greatest one, were not made in Hollywood at all, but in Culver City.

And it was to Culver City that Lin, Jenny, Charley and I moved in the summer of 1982, coming from Chicago and renting an apartment about five blocks from MGM.

Among its other oddities, Culver City is known for having the world's shortest Main Street. It starts at Washington Boulevard on the south and extends northward a couple of hundred feet to an alley, which, for some long-lost reason of municipal history, is the boundary between Culver City and the city of Los Angeles proper. On the other side of the alley, what was Main Street is no longer a Culver City street but an L.A. street called Bagley Avenue. Main Street, in other words, is less than a block long.

In the early 1980s, if you had turned west off Main Street/Bagley Avenue into that nameless alley and headed toward the interior of the block, you would have soon come to a dilapidated little one-story commercial building on the left, fronted by a little junk-strewn yard. A sign hung on the door of the building announcing a piano repair shop. Sometime around 1984 or 1985— we'd been living in L.A. for about two years, now—Lin noticed the shop and walked in to browse, eventually making friends with one of the owners, a woman named Sandra Aichee who with her husband was running the business on a shoestring. The Aichees, who lived on the premises, also bought and sold used pianos, and one day Lin saw one that she took a fancy to, an ugly old upright dating to the early part of the century—dark, dirty brown in color, its surface rough and cracked. She paid six hundred dollars for it—fifty dollars a month (we were living as hand-to-mouth as the Aichees at that point)—and along with the piano bought a series of twelve lessons and a couple of thin teaching books of music. She had studied piano briefly as a child and thought she might like to start playing again, and Sandra began coming to her apartment to teach her. After a couple of sessions, however, Lin began realizing that she really wasn't very interested.

Charley, it turned out, was. As Lin sat one day with Sandra during the second or third lesson, plunking dutifully at the little Bach minuet in front of her, she noticed Charley, then twelve, just home from school, standing in the living room doorway watching. Later, after Sandra left and Lin had gone into her room, she suddenly heard the piano being played, just a few odd notes, then a scale. She walked back into the living room. Charley was sitting on the piano bench fingering the keys. He had never taken any notice of classical music; his tastes ran to the standard teen fare of the mid-'80s: David Bowie, Duran Duran, Depeche Mode and Run DMC. He had never expressed any interest in playing an instrument. But now he seemed suddenly taken with the ugly old bear of a piano, and at first he didn't notice his mother watching him. Then he sensed she was there and turned. She walked over.

"Hi, Sweet Potato."

"Hi, Mom."

"Would you like to take piano lessons?"

"Not really," he replied, and got up from the piano and left the room. Lin said no more about it for a few days. But then early one evening she came home from work and saw Charley, long since arrived home from school, sitting at the keyboard teaching himself basic fingering from one of the thin teaching books. Now it was Mom's turn to watch as, unaware of her presence, he spread his two still small hands across the middle of the keyboard, playing the C scale. Not wanting to repeat her error, Lin kept going into her room. But she listened as he played the scale several times, a little more assured each time. She doubled back and stood in her bedroom doorway, watching him in profile a few feet away, concentrating intently as he played the simple notes, then moved his hands up the keyboard to play a higher scale. He seemed to be at home. Lin continued to watch. She had only used three or four of the twelve lessons she had bought from Sandra Aichee. She was very busy these days, didn't have much time to practice, and was thinking that Charley might need the piano more than she did. Soon afterward she asked him again whether he wanted to take lessons, and this time he said yes without hesitation. He used up the rest of the lessons and then continued studying, soon becoming Sandra's prize pupil.

Not too long after he began taking lessons Charley played for me for the first time, one of the pieces from the book with the Bach minuet. I was no longer living with Lin and the kids and hadn't known he played, so when I came over to visit one evening and he sat me down and told me he was going to perform for me I was amazed at his quick proficiency. I had been a fanatical music devotee in my teens and studied piano for two years, desperately wanting to be good but lacking talent, and I had never gotten as far as he'd gotten in a couple of months. He was still a beginner, however, without a background in listening to piano music—I don't think he had ever even heard a Bach recording—so he didn't have a sense of how the music should sound. When he played, concentrating on getting the notes right, he pounded.

"That's incredible, Charley," I said. "But you're pounding. Don't pound. Think of the music as a stream and not a bunch of notes. Let it flow."

He only had to be told once. It was as if he had been waiting for this simple instruction, and when he began playing again he didn't pound. Despite occasional mistakes, the piece "flowed like oil," as Mozart liked to say, and I never heard him pound again.

The Journals

Besides being intensely musical Charley was intensely verbal. By the time he was twelve or thirteen he wrote as well as most adults, and he began keeping a journal when he was fifteen. It eventually comprised about a dozen notebooks, which, although I knew they existed, I never read during his lifetime, and then not for a year after his death. One of the first entries goes as follows:

> I have a memory, nothing really special. I had just come out of a movie with my father, and we started walking home. We had just seen a film at the Meralta in old Culver City. The day was bright and fresh and there's always a pleasant sensation when coming out of a dark theatre into a sunny day that warms the spirit. I said to my father out of the blue "Dad I'm happy." I think I was happy just because I was spending time with Dad and it was a Saturday so I could play all day and wouldn't have to go to bed early. Not a care in the world. I wonder now what my father thought of this beatific mood that came from apparently nowhere.

When I read this fifteen or so years later, I actually did remember the "Dad I'm happy" incident. It happened in 1983 or 1984, when Charley was ten or eleven. I remember it not so much because the feeling it expressed was atypical—it wasn't—but because Charley's sudden spontaneous and unforced expression of happiness was so charming. It was a kind of Stendhalian moment, the sudden little sunburst of words that Fabrizio del Dongo or Lucien Leuwen might have uttered while riding alone on horseback (and in dashing uniform) in some leafy French or Italian glade in summertime after being smiled at by a beautiful young women passing in a carriage. What greater gift could a parent receive from a child?

The joy itself, however, did not appear unusual to me at the time. Lin and I had always thought of Charley as being basically a happy little boy. From infancy he possessed a special charm and (if the term can apply to someone preverbal) wit, a kind of charismatic gaiety that was noticeable even to strangers, who seemed instinctively to hook into his particular quickness and animation. One time when he was barely a toddler I took him to the park and bought him a balloon on a string. He examined it for a moment—I'm not even sure he had ever seen a balloon before—and suddenly began in a very single-minded and serious manner to punch it back and forth while holding the string in his fist, a look of intense concentration on his face. An old lady was walking by and stopped to watch. After a couple of seconds she turned to me and said matter-of-factly, "The brightest little boy in the whole park."

He learned to talk early. And clearly. I would give him his bath—he was about a year and a half old—and wrap him in a towel and hold him up to the mirror over the sink and put his face to mine. I would point to his reflection. "There's the other Charley," I would say. "Two Charleys." "Two Charleys," he'd repeat, and I'd say, pointing to my reflection and mispronouncing my name, "And who's that? Is that Jona*fin*?"

"No, Jona*thin*."

Soon he was doing numbers. I would say, "Charley, what's two plus five?" He would think quietly for a minute and then say, "Seven." I'd look at him in amazement. "How did you know that?" He'd give me a serious look. "I *thinked* about it." That "thinked about it" became part of our family lore.

He had excellent hand-eye coordination. He never showed any interest in team sports; I think he was just too individualistic. But he could beat me at computer football by the time he was seven and later excelled at hacky-sack (the little soft leather ball kept in the air by being bounced on the side of the foot or toe), juggling, ice-skating, skateboarding, walking on his hands and tennis. It was this athleticism and (it seemed) total faith in his own body that seemed to drive him to overextend himself and periodically land in the hospital and earn the nickname Emergency Room Charley. From the time he was old enough to walk he was falling off porches headfirst, running into glass doors, slicing himself on the edges of tin cans, falling out of trees, and breaking various bones from skateboard and dune buggy accidents. Once I offered him a big reward if he went a year without landing in the ER. I never had to pay.

Aside from his accident-proneness, Charley suffered from migraine headaches starting from the time he was five (his mother and Grandpa Bob had them too). He also had a proclivity for alcohol—wanting sips of people's drinks, for example, when he was little—and by eleven or twelve was sneaking beers. Naturally this concerned me, because there was alcoholism in my family and I had done the same thing at his age and later developed a drinking problem. I talked to him a few times about alcohol as he got into his teens, trying to describe in a nonalarmist way our family patterns and how he needed to be aware of potential problems and think about what he was doing. He nodded and said he understood.

His distinct personality expressed itself early. From infancy he showed certain characteristics different from those of Jenny, who was born two years earlier, lived in the same environment, and for Lin and me formed an obvious basis for comparison. Both were breast-fed, Charley till he was over two, when Lin weaned him. Jenny weaned herself much earlier. She tended to go to sleep easily. Charley, aside from his difficulties sleeping, was a finicky eater throughout childhood and early adolescence to the point where it became part of the family culture that Jenny "was always a good eater" who ate all of whatever you shoveled down her throat whereas Charley fussed. This fussiness eventually disappeared for the most part, however, and his eating habits became fairly normal.

In school he sometimes seemed to have a hard time concentrating on his work, but his teachers loved him and were almost apologetic when, as happened almost every year, they called Lin and me in for a conference to discuss his problems finishing assignments and handing in work on time. None of it particularly worried me; it was all within the bounds of normal problems. I thought I knew Charley pretty well. He and I spent a lot of time together, playing catch or reading or going to the movies, and he was always conversant and engaged, more so, I thought, than I had often been at his age. I never remember him visibly depressed or brooding, whereas I had begun having bad bouts of depression, very noticeable to others, when I was ten. Other people who knew him had the same impression. One of his favorite teachers, Lucille Van

Ornam from Culver City Middle School, recently wrote me the following description of Charley at twelve:

> In 7th grade Charles was in one of my top favorite classes of all time, language arts core. It was a fine group of kids, and I have more happy memories of them than of any other class I ever taught. . . . His desk most of the year was front & center. I often taught from the middle or back of the room, and my memory of Charles is that so often when I'd glance his way I'd see him in profile, smiling at something the class was doing. It was never a grin of mischief or monkey business, just a smile of enjoyment. I can see him as clearly as if it were still 1985. Such a beautiful boy! Some people object to the use of the world *beautiful* to describe a male. But "handsome" isn't adequate for Charles: He was beautiful. . . .
>
> In high school he wrote to me during teacher appreciation week. His words were so sweet, I was bowled over. He said he wanted me to know that the letter wasn't a class requirement but that he was doing it simply because he wanted to. He paid me specific compliments such as "You corrected our papers perfectly."

This is a typical description. From birth Charley was doted on and spoiled by everybody. It was easy to love Charley because he was so lovable, so capable of eliciting affection with his sweetness and wit. And yet, also from birth, he manifested a certain jitteriness or restlessness, a lack of grounding that was not merely geographical, but rather a more fundamental tendency to feel psychologically rootless, out of his element. Several years before he started keeping a regular journal he began a diary that lasted only a few entries. This is from late January 1985, the year he was in Mrs. Van Ornam's class. He was having problems with a girl. He had just turned twelve:

> Hi, it's getting late. I hate life. The world is very unhappy. I don't know why. I really hate the world. Don't think I'm saying this because Anna is mean. I hate the world, it's mad. I don't understand how a person can be in this hell for up to eighty years.
>
> I'm a toy to Anna. She plays with you then leaves you alone. She plays and plays some more until you're broken. Loving her is like loving a wall, it's useless. I'm getting some grass tomorrow and am gonna blaze. Not to forget my problems but to get out of this nasty world for a couple maybe a few hours and be happy. Think how expensive being happy forever would be.
>
> Def. *Unhappiness*—life on earth. Love, a sad person, Charley.
>
> P.S. Don't think I say this because of Anna. No no no no no.

But most of this sense of oppression, almost theatrical in its intensity, remained unknown to those who knew him. Almost always it was obscured by his charm and energy and humor, and it would be years before I began to see the skittishness, accident-proneness and very occasional anomie as anything more than growing pains.

Parenthood: No Statute of Limitations

Children are our punishment for the sin of lust.

(My journal)

I became a parent relatively young for my generation. I was twenty-two and twenty-four when Jenny and Charley were born, so by the time I entered my forties, when many of my contemporaries were just starting families, my kids were close to college age and I was feeling cocky. When a friend or coworker would gripe about something their two- or six-year-old had done, I would give them a slightly sadistic smile and say, "Don't worry. The first eighteen years are the hardest." But in late 1991, as we all recovered from Yosemite and its aftermath, I was beginning to wonder. Charley had turned eighteen the January before his breakdown. The main problems were supposed to be over by now. Sure, Lin and I were responsible for him until he was twenty-one, and we accepted our obligation to get both him and Jenny through college, despite differences over which college or colleges. But we had assumed that once all of us had squeezed through the most treacherous straits of early adolescence— avoiding the Scylla of hormonal imbalance and the Charybdis of high school substance abuse and drunk driving—the worst would be over.

We read the papers, of course. We had abstract knowledge of kids who suffered breakdowns or crises at around the age Charley was now. During my senior year in high school a student in the class ahead of me, Alan J. Glickman, committed suicide during his freshman year at college, and some time later his parents came back to the high school and set up an annual award in his name for intellectual promise or leadership or some such, which I happened to win the first year it was given out. (The inevitable joke was that the award was to go to someone in the hopes they would "follow in the footsteps of Alan J. Glickman.") But that was about as close as Lin or I had gotten to the extreme adolescent angst and drama that led to breakdowns and suicides.

This is not to say that what Charley had experienced during his break-down—the grandiosity, the talk of being Liszt, of achieving immortality—was completely out of family character. The extreme forms his fantasies took were unprecedented, but not the fantasies themselves. When I was fourteen a family friend asked me what I wanted to be when I grew up. "A genius," I answered, only half-joking. "You already *are* that," she said, trying to hide a smile. "Can you be more specific?" "Sure. I want to be Leonardo DaVinci." When I was fifteen I decided one sleepless night to make a movie out of *Crime and Punishment*. Jean-Paul Belmondo would play Raskolnikov. I was sure he'd agree—my screenplay would make it the role of a lifetime. Maybe they'd let me direct. I actually got to the point of blocking out scenes before I abandoned the idea as a little more than I could handle, given the amount of homework I had that year.

By sixteen I was even more bumptious (my father's term for me). One of my favorite pieces of music was the bass aria "The Trumpet Shall Sound" from Handel's *Messiah,* especially the trumpet that accompanied the voice. I wrote a letter to my paternal grandfather, Willie, who was a mentor to me, saying I wanted to become like "a Handelian trumpet," shafting high and clear into the night like a pillar of light, illuminating the universe. I wrote my freshman essay at college that year on Aeschylus's *Prometheus Bound* because I identified with Prometheus, the fire bringer. The next year I turned my sophomore essay into a summation and further expansion of all human knowledge based on my reading of Norman O. Brown's *Life Against Death* mixed with Chaucer and my own special brand of Zen Buddhism. The paper was only supposed to be fifteen to twenty typed pages. Ha! I *spit* on your fifteen to twenty pages! It used to take me fifteen to twenty pages to clear my throat. I was one of those kids who when the teacher says write a thousand-word composition and everybody else is groaning, waves his little hand and asks, ignoring the glares of hatred from his classmates, "Miss So and So, are we allowed to write *more* than a thousand words?" So, after ruthless cutting, my sophomore essay, entitled "Guilt and the Dream of Romance," came in at a lean and mean forty-three pages. It began with the sentence, "All human beings are basically unhappy," and went on from there.

I was, in other words, no stranger to grandiosity and angst. Neither was Lin.

She wrote her senior paper at Reed on William Faulkner's *Light in August* and the tragic vision. Her thesis was that we humans are doomed by the universe to spend our lives painfully striving to be good, but even when we do achieve goodness the universe swats us down like flies. And it's our fault.

Where had the self-inflation come from? Partly from our genes, perhaps, definitely from our family backgrounds and the *zeitgeist*. My parents were both writers and members of the New York left-wing cultural intelligentsia, people for whom quirkiness and originality and a certain amount of neurosis were tools of the trade. They were the Freudian generation. There was something wrong with you if you *weren't* in psychoanalysis.

Lin's background was different from mine but also out of the mainstream. When she was five her mother died. The immediate cause of death was untreated diabetes, but underlying that was poverty and neglect. Lin's father, Bob, a lifelong follower of the nineteenth-century economic reformer Henry George, had given up an engineering career and planted his wife and three small children (Lin was the eldest) at a farm in rural Illinois to go about Chicago as an unpaid lecturer spreading George's gospel of the "single tax." Lin inherited Bob's idealism, although it took a different form. In spring 1964, as she was completing the Faulkner paper and graduating from Reed, she volunteered to go to Mississippi as part of the Freedom Summer black voter registration project. When news came during her week of training in Ohio that three civil rights workers already in Mississippi had been kidnapped and probably killed by the Klan, Lin and her fellow trainees were encouraged to drop out if they had any doubts. She didn't. ("I couldn't *wait* to get to Mississippi," she said later.) Three years after that she joined the Peace Corps and went to Nigeria in the middle of the Biafran civil war. About two years after that, she and I met while doing work with a radical documentary film group in Venice, California; it was the heyday of the antiwar and black liberation movements and we were involved in both, studying Marx and other radical thinkers as well. In many ways we were an ill-matched pair. I was twenty-one, Lin was six years older. Although not quite a virgin I had never had an extended relationship. She had been married twice. I had dropped out of college and only worked a few months in my life. She had not only graduated college but had been in world-class hotspots and held a variety of jobs. I was still a kid, in other words; she was a grown-up. But I started following her around anyway. I kept moving in with her, and she kept moving out. She finally agreed to stop moving out if I agreed to have a baby. Her mother had died at twenty-seven, the same age she was now, and she could feel the clock ticking.

A few months later, around the time she got pregnant, we got out of film work and began doing direct grassroots organizing, mainly in working-class communities, and continued doing it for thirteen years, first in Los Angeles, then in New York City, finally in Chicago. Jenny was born in California in 1971, Charley in New York in 1973. Both spent their early childhoods in Chicago, where we lived for seven years before completing the cycle and returning to L.A. in 1982. For reasons of age and temperament, our marriage never really worked, and we separated for good in 1983. A year earlier we had quit organized political activity owing to disagreements with the people we had been working with, although we hadn't given up our political views. We never regretted our years of study and organizing, we never felt duped, we never decided that Big Brother had needs, too. We still thought capitalism was a self-inflated sham that would eventually be seen as such. How can a system last forever whose very being depends on manipulating people into buying larger and larger quantities of things they don't need, all the while prattling on about how spiritually uplifting it is? While still in Chicago Lin had gone back to school and gotten her M.A. in urban planning. I made money by proofreading and copyediting, working on a screenplay at night and on weekends—one reason for our move back to L.A.—about early New Orleans jazz, how America's music grew out of the cesspool of segregation and postslavery oppression of blacks in the South. We tried to remain as active as we could in the different protest movements (disarmament, prochoice, antinuke, anti-Contras, anti–Gulf War) of the day.

As they grew up, the kids looked on our activism, and later on our ex-activism, with skepticism or respect, or both, depending on their stage of development. Although we were fairly broke some of the time, especially in the early years, Jenny and Charley were never deprived, although a couple of times during adolescent-parent arguments they accused Lin and me of not having taken advantage of our backgrounds and education to become more successful—we were underachievers, in other words. But I never had the sense that they felt isolated or marginalized by our nonmainstream views or lifestyle—the fact, for example, that we lived for years in minority neighborhoods where

Jenny and Charley were sometimes the only white kids on the block. They always made friends, and the diversity of their environment was more a gift than an affliction, I was assured later as they developed into broad-minded, good-hearted, progressive young adults. Lin and I were never cultists, and while we always explained to them why we thought capitalism didn't work we never tried to indoctrinate or quarantine them. (Which would have been impossible anyway, given the necessities of life. In Chicago, for example, they attended a Southern Baptist day-care center because Lin and I were both working and it was the only day care available.) As a result, as they grew older they seemed to adopt a fairly tolerant and easy-going, even humorous, view of their somewhat odd parents' somewhat odd views and curricula vitae. "Dad, were you and Mom yuppies?" Charley asked in 1984 or 1985, soon after the word was invented. "No, we were *yuckies*," I replied. "Young urban communists." Charley thought that was very funny.

But family values are family values, histories histories, subtexts subtexts. Charley didn't follow in our political footsteps, but wasn't it possible, I wondered after Yosemite, that Lin's and my temperaments and histories were in a way relevant to his breakdown? Did each of us, perhaps, as Lin later said half-seriously, have some kind of "recessive gene" for mania that when combined in Charley became dominant? We had become activists because we wanted to save the world; was it such a stretch that he would want single-handedly to achieve world peace? He came by his hifalutinness naturally, in other words. And what's wrong with a little hifalutinness, especially when you're young? I mean, why *start* life cowering and defeated? There's plenty of time for that later on. What's wrong with a little ambition, even when it's a little full of itself, especially when it doesn't involve bombing small agrarian countries and killing the spotted owl?

My point is that in the aftermath of Charley's breakdown at Yosemite I tended to view it and him through the lens of my own experience. I'd had some tough times as a teenager too—hell, as an adult. I had been a problem drinker until I was almost thirty-two, only quitting when I realized I had to choose between alcohol and everything else. I chose everything else and, my character flaws notwithstanding, stayed engaged in the world. As a result I hadn't paid much attention to Charley's references to god consciousness and the nine stages of whatever. To me it was all static, cross talk, slightly annoying interference with the real program—the real Charley—but of no real consequence once we corrected his chemical imbalance and helped him through his breakdown. I thought (to carry on the radio metaphor) that once we got his antennae properly placed and jiggled his tuning knob and got it exactly on the right frequency, not a little off as it was now, the cross talk would disappear naturally. He was like me, I kept telling myself, just a younger and slightly more confused version. Which of course was a comforting thought. After all, I was the devil I knew. It never occurred to me that what I thought was cross talk was for him the real program, and that he was jiggling the knob too, only in a different direction.

Some lives are poetry, others are prose. Shakespeare's plays are neatly divided between the two, the nobility like Hamlet and the Henrys speaking mostly in flush left, ragged right iambic pentameter, the base, plebian slobs like Brutus and Falstaff and Rosencrantz and Guildenstern speaking in rhythmless justified text. I had always preferred the base, plebian slobs, and even as a very ambitious and pretentious young person with dreams of being a great artist—"a bumptious youth," as my father called me one time—I always had the sense that my Book of Life would be written in the vulgate, not high Latin. And when my kids came along and grew up I thought of them as prose artists as well. I wasn't the only parental influence, of course. They had their mother's qualities as well as mine, but when all was said and done, all the papers on Faulkner and tragedy written and filed away, Lin was an earthling too. Jenny certainly was. And so was Charley, I thought. He was too much like me, like us, to get too far out into space. And if he did, it would be temporary. And in the final analysis, what was the point of worrying anyway? I had no control.

Well, I was right about the no control part. But I was wrong to think that Charley's life was prose like mine. That basic misreading of his nature, my insistence on casting him in my own mold (and shadow), led me, post-Yosemite, in his nineteenth year when the hard part was supposed to be over, to misunderstand what was happening.

Insomnia—or, "Do I Have Genius?"

Tiredness, thoughts, lying down, darkness, thoughts, a desire to sleep, thoughts, more thoughts, changing position, thoughts, seriousness, fear of sleeplessness, thoughts, a conscious effort to sleep, more seriousness, fatigue, a

conscious effort to not make a conscious effort to sleep, more fear, anxiety, a fear
of looking at the time, frustration, another thought, passive resistance, despair,
another position, more thoughts, a cigarette perhaps, more frustration, work
tomorrow, more fatigue, warm milk perhaps, meditation perhaps, feigned sleep,
changing position, another thought, feigned indifference, more frustration, etc.,
the chirping of birds, dawn, tiredness.

("Insomnia," Charley's journal, June 1991,
about six weeks before Yosemite)

The insomnia, for example. I always had trouble going to sleep as a kid and
never saw Charley's childhood and adolescent sleep problems as something to
worry about unduly. It was his active mind, I told him, which was a good thing.
So even after he had started college I would heat him up some milk or rub his
back, telling him to pretend he was a jellyfish swimming in the ocean. It had
worked when he was little.

Years later when I read his journals, I realized that as he had grown up his
problems with sleep had grown too. He talks about this specifically a few
months before Yosemite:

During the summer [of 1988] after tenth grade when I was fifteen I stayed
a week in San Francisco with my grandparents and [nineteen- and twenty-year-
old] aunts, Ella and Justine. While I was there, a feeling overcame me which I'd
never known before. It was like I had seen a light which was awaiting me. I discovered the energy of my intellect. I was so overcome by my thoughts I experienced insomnia for the first time.

This episode, Charley goes on to say, made him decide to move from Los
Angeles, a place "inimical to life and destructive to the mind altogether," to San
Francisco to live with his grandparents and their assorted children, some not
much older than he. For two years he attended, apparently happily, a small and
remarkably inexpensive private high school that seemed to cater to oddball
kids. He was mentored by Grandpa Bob the Henry Georgeite, hollow-cheeked
and parchment-voiced, a courtly, old-fashioned intellectual with white hair
and a moustache and a perfectionist speaking style.

Leaving L.A. and his parents was a big step. But I think the "insomnia for
the first time" experience had an importance beyond impelling Charley to
leave home. His description of being overcome with a hitherto-unknown

feeling, of seeing a "light" awaiting him, of experiencing great intellectual energy, indicates that he was experiencing mania for the first time, or more precisely a mild form of mania called hypomania, which is characterized by an elevated and expansive mood, heightened energy, restlessness, and decreased need for sleep. I believe this episode, and similar ones that followed over the next three years, including the Halloween bad "iawaska" trip, were precursors to the full-fledged psychotic breakdown at Yosemite. They marked a growing instability of mood that grew out of Charley's temperament but was new in its increasing intensity and the forms it took. My evidence for this comes from his journal. About a year after the insomnia episode in San Francisco, for example, he wrote the following:

> At this moment I lust. I feel an insatiable appetite for life. I want to embrace people. I want to feel. I want each of my five senses to be satisfied. I want more than happiness. I want my body to become one with the world and I want my soul to penetrate those of others. I want too much. I've finally realized that I must act. I must and will do because my spirit must be fulfilled. I will no longer contemplate why I don't do. I will contemplate and act simultaneously. I must have. I must experience. I will write because I want to be a writer. . . . I will be a genius. An extraordinary one. I will be courteous to mankind. I will appreciate nature and all its aesthetic qualities. I will love. I will love some more than others. I might cry but I will enjoy that. I might enjoy misery because I will write about it later. I will learn but I have no choice in that matter. I will act and think and do and contemplate and execute and circumspect and proceed and introspect. And if my principles fall and I have only remaining shattered ideals? Then I shall find some new ones because I cannot limit myself to a specific code of ethics.

The entry immediately following, dated May 10, 1989, at 3 A.M., reads in part:

> A moment ago I lay awake in bed in darkness while the whispering wind filled my head and the draft from the window cooled my neck and face. I could not stop thinking those clear, well formed thoughts that never leave me alone. I have such a vivid existence, I know now, for my mind is so powerful. . . . I am so young. Why must I learn myself so quickly? so soon? It is somewhat frightening. Maybe it is all an illusion. But would I have so much motivation if it were? Who would say? I will discipline my talent. My talent, hah! How can I

flatter myself so? Where is the proof? Isn't a talent, a special one something we have no control over? But do I have control or am I misleading myself or shall I go mad? I want so much to be exceptional, even extraordinary. I will write. Could a talent be a talent if one is aware of it and wants that talent? Who could answer me? I want to be articulate. I am so much afraid of deceiving myself. Where would I be then? Perish the thought.

There is more here than ordinary adolescent histrionics, evidenced especially by the sentence-to-sentence shifts in tone. Charley was quite capable of writing clearly and rationally in his journals and elsewhere. But these entries are neither clear nor rational. The writer is experiencing some kind of heightened mood and sense of self, some kind of elation although there is no way to know what caused it—lack of sleep, drugs, alcohol or something else. The elation is not entirely joyous. It is too powerful to be purely positive; it is also confusing, even disquieting. There is a sense of fear, of being overwhelmed. Going hand in hand with the "inflated self-esteem" of hypomania—for example, Charley's conviction that he "can see beyond what others cannot"—there is the fear that it is all illusion; there is desperation underlying the elation.

". . . Or Shall I Go Mad?"

The fear of going mad crops up a number of times in Charley's pre-Yosemite journal. The language is theatrical, but given his later history, the fear is no doubt real. The next reference to going mad comes a few months after the one above, during a tempestuous love affair he was having with a high-school classmate named Stephanie, who apparently came from a troubled family. Charley was in a hurry to grow up, to escape adolescent confusion, to take on the mantle of adulthood like that worn by Grandpa Bob (in whose house he was living), a snowy-haired paterfamilias with ten children by three wives. Saving Stephanie would make him a man, Charley believed. Early in their relationship he writes,

She asks sincerely, "Why are you so nice to me?" I say "I like being nice to you." "Thank you" she says. She grew silent. Absorbed in reverie. It then dawned upon me. It slowly illuminated in my mind. It was a memory of something my grandfather once said. "Women need to be taken care of." He then quoted someone. It goes something like this: "'He who husbands the crops shall reap from them the benefits.'" I then told Stephanie "I'm going to take care of you." And she said "Promise?" And I said "I will." At that moment, I could swear, a new sort of peace existed. . . . *I felt, for a moment, at least that I had a certain place to be.* I kind of had a worthwhile position. I would take care of her, emotionally and "spiritually" if you care to say so. I finally had something to do. Everything else that followed would come naturally. I know I felt complete for a few moments and I really cared. As I write these words I feel, it seems strange saying it, but like a man. I discovered what it is a little bit to play a male role in a relationship. Despite anything that happens, I will remain responsible for Stephanie in this sense. I will be obligated until she can take care alone. (emphasis added)

But within days this "new sort of peace" was shattered when Charley sabotaged the relationship in the most childish way imaginable, by picking up and reading a pornographic comic book in Stephanie's presence, causing her to "walk out in anger, disgust and worst of all, silence." He hopes "we shall forgive and forget. If she looks away in silence, refusing to talk to me I shall go mad. This is what happens when I give a girl my soul, my heart and my faith. She will find ways to alter it, manipulate me and torment me to hell" (shades of his diary regarding Anna when he was twelve).

They patched things up, but not for long. The very neediness that had made Stephanie so attractive quickly became overwhelming as Charley realized that he had taken on an impossible task, saving another person. Still, the tempest-tossed love affair lurched on until he returned to Los Angeles for the summer to work. Writing while traveling south in his Aunt Justine's van:

The first day of my journey to Los Angeles has proved to be a sad one. It is unusual. A strong sensation of gloom has overwhelmed me, physically and emotionally. . . . All my energy is being absorbed into the dark moroseness. It dawned upon me a short while ago why I feel this way. I hadn't realized it before but it is the loss of Stephanie that is affecting me, hurting my spirit. This is an unprecedented state of agony, quite new to me. . . . I am almost incapable of writing about it.

Despite Charley's penchant for self-dramatization, the pain is not merely rhetorical, or routine. It would soon become familiar. Part of his encroaching depression came from having to go back to L.A., which he didn't like most of the time. But when he returned to San Francisco a couple of months later for his senior year of high school his mood wasn't much better. He writes in September 1989:

> Honestly, I cannot see how I will be able to endure this f---ing senior year. . . . I hate myself for having no hope but I am helpless. I am lonely as it is. Will I feel less lonely when I am among my peers? Those kids whom I just can't relate to. Many of whom dislike me for having self-confidence. They think I am totally secure.

And this was at a school he liked! But to the depressive, heaven itself is worse than hell, because in heaven he can blame no one but himself for his hellish torment.

Another experience a few months later again raised the fear of going mad. After working only three days and making (in his own words) an "exorbitant effort to impress" his employers, Charley was fired from a job he had coveted—busing tables in a fancy Italian restaurant in San Francisco. He had invested great hopes in the job, counting on the income to help him be more self-sufficient and less of a perceived burden on his grandparents. A letter to me after his second night on the job expresses his delight:

> Dear Dad, Tonight was the second night working at "La Traviata," the Italian restaurant in the Mission District. I'm very happy with my job. It's the finest restaurant I've seen in SF and the coolest job I've ever had. The manager and the owners are exceedingly kind. It's almost overwhelming. I couldn't even begin to compare the ambiance to Flakey Jake's [a West Los Angeles hamburger joint where he had worked briefly the previous summer]. The money's good too. I can tell you more about it later. I just finished up my 1st semester, the last significant portion of my high school career. I'm going to have an interview at a piano school next week and maybe take lessons.
>
> Well that's all the good news I can think of right now. I hope you're doing well. I'll probably be down before March. Take care. Love . . .

The ax fell the next night, wielded by the same owners he had praised to me so warmly. The firing was a major blow, particularly troubling in its seeming lack of a reason. When he asked repeatedly why he had been let go after so little time and no prior warnings, all the management would say was that they needed somebody who could do more. The seeming arbitrariness of the firing may have added to Charley's growing sense of being at the mercy of capricious, random forces; he talked about it for years afterward and I don't think he ever recovered from the humiliation. This sounds overdramatic. Everybody gets fired or laid off some time or other, often unfairly. But Charley's ego was very fragile, and the overwhelming sense of rejection was real. In a way this may be the whole point. The drama of his life was the playing out of that fragility, that instability, of ego.

After complaining bitterly of the injustice of being fired he writes in his journal:

> I now plan to devote a great deal of time to writing. I have no choice. I have to develop my writing skills, or I will go mad. Who knows what I'll write. I may throw some stories together. Whatever I do, my little note pad, please be patient and tolerant with me, for I am an arrogant, lonely, crazed adolescent who has too much on his mind. I will try, though, because I am driven.

The next entry, undated but from around the beginning of February 1990, shortly after he turned seventeen, is a poem entitled "The Rain":

> *Melancholy is each drop*
> *Of rain that falls atop*
> *My roof. On this January evening*
> *I think I hear the weeping*
> *Of the angels who shed*
> *Countless tears above my bed.*

By May he had successfully weathered high school and done well academically—and the depression seemed worse than ever. This entry is called "Idle Thoughts of Distress":

> What have I to say in my state? I can think of nothing but confusion. Every thought has a negative conclusion and I don't know what to write. I have virtually no one to talk to. I can't sleep. I would if I could 'cause the day that follows a good night's sleep has an advantage over one that doesn't. School is an

utter bore. I am alone, alone, alone; tired of myself, of my intellect, my worries, my fears, and nebulous ambitions. So alone, so hungry for fulfillment. Jobless, idle, bored, and yet I have my whole life ahead of me. . . . The f---ed-up thing is, I am the source of my problems, I create them. . . . Dissatisfaction is my ailment.

"I feel anger at the moment," he had written the previous spring (when things were going *well* with Stephanie):

It is not a good feeling. I am upset because I . . . I don't really know. It seems like I have no home anymore because I have two. I sometimes don't know who I am. I am so young and yet I care like an old person. I do not have the flippant carefree attitude a boy should have. It feels like I'm taking so much of the world's heart into my own.

The Wanderer

But why? Why the wanderlust, the feeling of rootlessness and having no home? Was it only some genetic proclivity, an inborn skittishness, or were there elements of nurture along with nature at work? As one of the two people most responsible for making Charley feel at home in the world, I tended to dwell on the nature part, not wanting to blame myself for his feelings of insecurity and (I first learned from Brian Marsh) doubts about his parents' love. I adored Charley and often told him so (well, I used the word "love," not "adore"). I never had any doubts about where he belonged and who loved him, so why should he? If anything, Lin was even closer to him. There was never a more affectionate and generous mother—generous to a fault, I sometimes thought, as in our differences over where he should go to college. Our love for him being a given, then, as deeply rooted as anything can be, how could anybody, most of all Charley, doubt it?

But doubt it he did, it seemed, although the evidence is mostly indirect and not always objective. In his San Francisco General medical records, for example, the discharge summary reports that his San Francisco family (grandparents and aunts) "view the patient's difficulties as a result of the patient's perception that his parents do not love him." A couple of years after that, Charley met a Native American shaman, who wrote in response to something (now lost) that Charley had told him, "In your childhood you feel you experienced a lack of love and in reality there may have been a lack. That lack drove you to do bizarre things and have bizarre dreams." The San Francisco General records also indicate, in the words of one therapist, "feelings that surround his nuclear family & about parents' divorce."

The last comment may shed some light. Lin's and my marriage had always been unstable. We had separated several times in the 1970s, once for a year and a half, and even when we were together things were seldom harmonious for long. After moving with the kids from Chicago to California in 1982 we separated for good in the spring of 1983, when Charley was ten, and his writings indicate that he took the divorce harder than we knew at the time. Lin and I never had any extensive discussions with the kids or family therapy to deal with the separation, which wasn't even as formal as a divorce because we had never been legally married. One day I simply moved out—at first temporarily, and only to a tiny bachelor apartment a half-mile away; but by tacit consent the temporary soon became permanent. Despite the divorce (I call it that), Lin and I stayed close friends. I saw her and the kids all the time, and Jenny and Charley stayed with me weekends in a kind of informal joint custody arrangement. For the first two years after the divorce I actually became the custodial parent during the summers, moving into Lin's larger apartment to live with the kids while she moved into my little bachelor pad and paid me child support. Even during the school year, when Lin lived with the kids, I had access to her apartment and went over on weekday afternoons while she was at work (I worked nights) to spend time with Charley (Jenny was always with friends), help with his homework and walk with him to the park to throw the football. The four of us continued doing things (dinners, holidays, even occasional trips) as a family. Part of the togetherness stemmed from Lin's and my genuine affection for each other, part of it from a desire to provide the kids with continuity and security. We thought we'd succeeded. The very informality and relative comity of the whole arrangement, and the fact that we remained close, made us think they were adjusting without major trauma. Jenny did; Charley seemed to.

Another factor in Charley's life that may have contributed to a feeling of not-at-homeness was the birth order dynamic. He had an older sister who cast a wide shadow, especially as they entered adolescence. Although they had been very close when they were little and would always love each other, their lives in L.A. had gone in separate directions, the more gregarious Jenny developing a broad network of friends and an active social life from which the more solitary Charley felt excluded. That social life soon turned disruptive. The year after the divorce (and the minute she hit puberty), Jenny began acting up in ways (smoking, drinking, breaking curfew) that were normal in the context of urban America but which severely tested Lin and me—separated, both working—at the time. For a while Jenny became the squeaky wheel, which may have caused us to take the quieter Charley for granted and not give him the emotional attention he needed despite the considerable time and energy we both spent on him.

Going back even further into his life history was the question of his and my personal relationship. A couple of years after his breakdown at Yosemite he wrote a poem called "Knock on Wood," which begins:

> "Knock on wood," said his father with a grin and a chuckle,
> And jestingly tapped his son's head with his knuckle.
> To Woody's father it was no small revelation
> That such fun could be got from the boy's appellation.
> He was five at the time and not long thereafter
> Would he become the source of indefatigable laughter.

Others follow the father's example, treating Woody as an object of fun, and eventually the boy turns into a piece of wood.[1] Charley read the poem out loud to me at least once, and I remember not liking it very much. I don't remember what, if any, discussion followed. I might have asked him whether he thought I teased him too much. I had sometimes done what the father does in the poem, tap Charley's head with my knuckle and make a "tock" sound with my tongue for good luck. Could he have actually taken such silliness seriously? I did have a tendency to tease him and Jenny, just as I teased everybody else; it was a male family trait and part of my New York Jewish cultural background. (Upper Manhattan Jewish background in particular, it seems. Groucho Marx, Steven Sondheim and Tom Lehrer are three other upper-Manhattanites known for their astringency and "poisoning pigeons in the park" style of humor. I never set out to emulate them; it came more naturally than that.) For example, when Charley was less than two, Lin and I took him to the zoo. He seemed fascinated by the tiger, and as they peered at each other through the cage bars I said something like, "You know, I think the tiger's hungry, Charley. He's looking at you and thinking to himself, 'Yum! I wish I had a *biiiiig* French roll, with some mustard, and mayonnaise and lettuce, and then I could put that little boy on it. Yum!'"

"Daddy, you *teasin'* me!" he said indignantly. I gave him a hug and said I was sorry for teasing him, as I always did when he objected to what I meant to be oblique expressions of love, the modus operandi of a person who tended to be emotionally shy or blocked and had difficulty expressing affection directly.

Aside from these basic personality traits, I was a young parent not only in years but in experience, emotionally immature, and sometimes tended to treat Jenny and Charley more as my siblings than as my children. Growing up I had been the eldest of three, with a sister (Gretchen) two years and a brother (Tim) four years younger—the same gender order and number of years between them as Jenny and Charley. The coincidental symmetry led to my sometimes getting their names confused, calling Jenny "Gretchen" and Charley "Timmy." And I sometimes tended to treat them accordingly, as contemporaries rather than small beings who were dependent on me. On the one hand this led to a kind of nonparental familiarity that seemed to bring us closer. Jenny and Charley called Lin and me "you guys," the same thing we called them, and never seemed afraid of or intimidated by us (on the contrary). But of course, my teasing, which I considered a kind of verbal roughhousing, could also be taken as aggressive and belittling if done wrong or taken in the wrong way by the person on the other end. Humor often contains an element of aggression. I was aware of this and tried to avoid stepping over the line. But my line may have been different from Charley's. Jenny didn't seem to take the teasing seriously. I would eventually wonder whether Charley, more fragile and skittish, did.

Or maybe it wasn't so much the teasing. There is another, different reading of the Woody poem and other expressions of Charley's discomfort with me— namely, that they were less about teasing and more about what he saw as my failure to listen to him or take him seriously. In a diary he kept when he was about eleven, a few months after Lin's and my divorce, he wrote a paragraph each about Jenny, Lin and me. The one about me went,

> My dad is very funny and humorous. I think my dad is kinda fun. But in a way I don't want to be around him. He isn't very understanding at all. I don't think he changes his mind very much when he makes a decision. It's '84 and I love my dad truly.

Some of this sense of disconnection may have resulted from my history of alcoholism. I had begun drinking sporadically in my teens, and by the time Jenny and Charley were born, I was a daily drinker. I never binged and rarely got sloppy drunk, but every day as a matter of routine I would drink at least a quart of beer, often two, when I got home from work. I drank hard liquor when I could, and there was no such thing as keeping alcohol around the house for special occasions; anything brought in would soon be gone. Nevertheless, I functioned. I never missed work or political meetings. What I may have missed, I eventually realized, was part of my life. I stopped drinking for good (on the third try) in 1980 at the age of thirty-one, less out of wisdom or moral sense than an instinct for self-preservation. Vanity, a vice that can be of more benefit than some virtues, also played a part—I was already getting fat and red-eyed at thirty. Once I stopped drinking I came to see from observing other people who drank that at a certain point alcohol removes us from where we are. Jenny and Charley were young enough (nine and seven) when I stopped drinking not to remember later that I had ever drunk at all, but that in itself may say something about the pervasiveness of my drinking and its effects during what were for them crucial years. Was Dad just a little less *there* than he might have been otherwise? Was that a kind of parental absence or rejection?

Something else happened a couple of months before Lin's and my breakup that may have added to Jenny and Charley's insecurities. I came down with a serious case of gastritis, caused, doctors thought, from years of taking aspirin to treat headaches I had gotten from working nights and drinking too much coffee. I went into the hospital intensive care unit and spent several days on an IV, a heart monitor and a respirator. I needed six one-pint blood transfusions; bleeding from my stomach had caused me to lose half my blood.

Lin brought the kids to visit me the second or third day I was in the ICU, when I was still flat on my back in bed and barely able to move, hooked up to various machines by several sets of tubes and wires, heart graphs spiking and needle gauges dancing, red and white lights flickering, beepers beeping, strange liquids undulating through clear serpentine tubing. This was my first time in a hospital, and the first time Jenny and Charley had ever seen me so vulnerable. To children, parents are giants. Now I'd been felled, and along with the fear and pity they no doubt felt for me there must have come a new and upsetting sense of how exposed and vulnerable their own lives were as well. Although I think both kids were affected, I wonder whether Charley's more tender years and particular nature might have made him especially susceptible to external insecurities, to the illness he was seeing in me now as well as to my past and future dislocations.

I have spoken about how hard he took the divorce a couple of months later. When I moved into my tiny bachelor apartment in a rickety old wooden duplex a half-mile away—Lin called it Dogpatch—I had no money and no furniture, and for a while I slept and ate on the floor, which was covered by an old shag rug. The apartment's bareness became a family joke. When Lin brought the kids over on Fridays for their weekends with me (they slept in sleeping bags) she would often stay while I made dinner and I would always say, "Okay, who's gonna set the floor?" I didn't mind having no furniture, but Charley seemed quite bothered by my lack of a bed, so he gave me a little child's stretching mat he had gotten from appearing on a Disney cable aerobics show, *Mousercise.* The mat was covered with pictures of Donald, Mickey, Goofy, Pluto, et al., who became my sleeping companions until Jenny and Charley gave me an army cot for Christmas. In the meantime they continued to sleep on the floor when they stayed with me. Why was Charley so concerned with my sleeping arrangements? Did he, the male child, identify with me, the exiled father? Did he see my (albeit consensual) eviction from the family dwelling, my lack of a bed, as a kind of homelessness or even metaphorical death that he internalized because nobody really talked about what was going on? His diary in the months after the divorce (he was not yet eleven) expresses great unhappiness, little or none of which I saw at the time. He talks repeatedly about wanting to go to a boarding school and about wanting to kill himself. For example:

> I just had a talk with my mother about a boarding school. She says she'd miss me and it's too expensive, and she said she'd think about it. I hope she says yes

or I'll kill myself. It's Dec. 19 and Christmas is near. I'm on vacation trying to relax. I got a fish yesterday and I named him Oliver. He's cute but I don't know if he is happy here. . . .

The next entry, written in a rare (for the diary) happy mood, talks about an interesting dream:

> I'm in a good mood right now. Don't ask why, I just am! I have a dream you know. I want to write it down while my ideas are fresh.
>
> It would be that I was in a movie that would be about a baby being born when his mother was pregnant and then in a car accident. And when I (the baby) was born, and instead of being deformed being gifted in the mind, you know, like having a super brain.
>
> And people would start being amazed by what I could read, write, have a reasonable conversation with a legal adult at three years old!
>
> I could do division, algebra, decimals, and see my mom's mistakes on adding her bills at five years old. And a few years later having amazing skills like winning every questioning game show around.
>
> It was just a thought. I'm going.

In this dream, described with such poignancy and charm, superhuman Charley is able to solve all problems, particularly his mother's. Is this a distant precursor to his grandiosity at Yosemite and after? The next diary entry is a return to angst:

> I am really frustrated. My sister just knocked the door broken. I might kill myself!

And finally:

> God Dammit! I'm so pissed at life I want to kill myself.
>
> I get into a fight with my sister! My mom throws me out in the rain! I take a little walk outside! Then, my dad gives me the third degree on how he hates my behavior, WELL F--- HIM!!! He's such a loser it could go into the Guinness Book of World Records. . . .
>
> My parents don't seem to UNDERSTAND that I'm unhappy. I try to tell them I want to go to a boarding school. But all they say is that they'll miss me and it's too expensive.
>
> I want to run away any minute.
>
> I'm going to my dad's in a few minutes and I wish I had a tape rec. to tape all the nasty things he'll say to me.

Diary, I'm trying to be happy 'cause it's Christmas Eve. BUT IT'S
IMPOSSIBLE!!!!!!

For Charley, all these things—a lifetime of family tension culminating in
divorce, his parents' insufficient communication about the divorce and attention to his wounded feelings and needs, "favoritism" toward Jenny, my teasing
or lack of understanding or "nasty" remarks—may well have appeared to him
as a lack of love even though Lin and I loved him, frequently told him we loved
him, and spent a lot of time with him. Perhaps in his mind we were talking the
talk but not walking the walk, not giving him the stability and security his
unsettled temperament desperately (although mostly silently) craved.

Along with all the family problems, his childhood discomfort may have
been worsened by the undeniably alienating qualities of Los Angeles itself.
Charley is not the first person who ever found L.A. "inimical to the soul." Part
of the discomfort was actually physical. Charley often complained about the
city's unremitting light, the assaultive desert sun Yeats called "blank and pitiless."
People with mood instabilities have been known to be particularly sensitive to
climate and season. L.A.'s endless sun may have been physically painful to
Charley. But he was seldom comfortable for long even in his beloved San
Francisco. A visit there while he was working in L.A. for the summer during
high school started promisingly:

> I am entering the city of San Francisco by Greyhound bus at this very
> moment. I feel I want to embrace it all: the cute little compact homes, the gusty
> winds, the azure sky, the pedestrians who make their way through. Ah, so beau-
> tiful, so real. I love it.

But by the very next page, still in San Francisco:

> What should a lonely, melancholy young writer write as he sits alone, disen-
> chanted at a table with only candle flames to accompany him. "Sometimes," he
> feels, "the pain is almost tangible as the world spins consistently. At times there
> is no definite, secure place he can depend upon, where love is abundant and
> warmth is overwhelming. And one cannot describe the hurting, one merely
> feels. And what can that boy do?" I'd feel so much better if there were only some
> way to express the pain, thereby releasing it.

Charley seems to be saying that the very spinning of the Earth is responsible for his pain and insecurity. You can't get much more insecure than that. No wonder it's so hard to describe. How do you describe, differentiate, define, the effect on you of something as fundamental as the turning of the Earth? And what do you do about it? Obviously, in the face of alienation this basic, being in San Francisco, situated as it is on that painfully spinning Earth, could not provide the answer to Charley's anomie. Soon he would transfer his hopes of finding a home from San Francisco to Reed College, the new oasis glimpsed from afar. Visiting the campus with his mother while still in high school he writes,

> I am among intelligent people right now. I feel the vibes of conscientious college students as I am staying at Reed College for the weekend with Mom. It is such an uplifting experience to be around young people who think and are aware of, just, what's around them. How could I have thought the whole world was mindless and infantile? . . . Ahh, so, so much to live for . . . and so many lovely girls. The Intellect is Divine.

The problem was that Reed, like San Francisco, was also situated on the spinning Earth.

The Rationalist

> I'm playing the piano a lot. In a way it keeps me from going crazy.
> *(Charley's journal, winter of his freshman year at Reed)*

The early journals revealed to me a side of Charley that I hadn't seen much of at the time, the volatile, emotional side. But they contain a more familiar side as well, the Charley I had known from early childhood for his clarity of mind, his critical sensibility, his irony—the Stendhalian, "brightest little boy in the whole park" side. My favorite example comes from the summer of 1989:

> A true writer must learn to live in harmony with others without looking down on them. He must learn to adjust to living among common people and avoid being an elitist. The word "common" is condescending when used to describe people, so the writer of these words is a hypocrite.

Not bad for sixteen. It could have been written by Stendhal himself: the mordant self-awareness, the epigrammatic dramatization of the dual sensibility—the grown-up taking to task the well-meaning but grandiose "true writer." It also demonstrates the complexity of Charley's inner life. It seems apparent that the "common" in sentence two was not meant ironically at first, that Charley really changed his view from the second sentence to the third after realizing what he had just written. Again the volatility, the pull between the desire to be special, a genius, and the desire not to be so lonely, to belong. There were times when he seemed to see clearly not only this rivenness but what was behind it. Earlier the same year, talking about his own sense of being above other people "in an incredibly absurd world, alone, afraid, and angry . . . too deep to fit into the simplicity that smothers society," he writes, "And why do I feel this need to judge others, analyze them and put them under me? Is my superiority complex really an inferiority one?"[2]

Another example of his more rational, objective side, as well as his understanding of its limits, is a journal entry from the spring of 1991, the end of his freshman year at Reed, a couple of months before Yosemite:

> I look around and I feel so many are closed, unapproachable, or am I the one who is closed? Another day has passed, and I am alive. Tolstoy is there when I need him, along with Chopin, [he then names two male schoolmates], Mom, and . . . on another level, Scott Joplin, Camel filters, Mozart, black coffee, Kit Henderson. Those who are unavailable are Ella (my aunt), [he then names a female student], Dad, Jenny, Ramona, Meighen, Grampa, and home-cooked meals. . . .
>
> One day I will have children, and a wife, and a career (or will I have a career?). I should also have a house I suppose and probably a car. I refuse to live in any town with less than 500,000 people. I must have a piano for I shall continue to improve. Books are in my future for sure. A television is hardly necessary, but then again renting movies is good. Do I have genius?? I could try a movie career, maybe not. I might play piano in Nordstrom or in some dark bar, or make falafels on a pier in Santa Cruz, as Mom always jests. I could go to New York and become a yuppie of some sort. Law school? Why do I scorn people who major in political science? Because they're indulging their intellect instead of planning to be useful. What could possibly be useful about a poli-sci major? Carpentry school perhaps. That's real work if there ever was any. Love will be obligatory, along with intelligence, kindness, and altruism if I can ever attain that. There is a lot of Mark Twain to read along with Shakespeare, Steinbeck, etc. etc. There is more Bach to listen to, more Schubert to play, and more

women to meet (must understand sexism better). Shall I stay at Reed four years?
Looks iffy. Two years I can take. I must go to France at some point. . . . I will
quit smoking some time. Right now it gives me solace. I must learn to meditate. I've got to see more Marlon Brando movies. . . . I must go to sleep. I'm glad
I love myself.

What is notable to me in this sort of mock self-inventory is its contradic-
toriness, grand ambition going hand in hand with an apparent scaling back of
that ambition. Nothing about being a concert pianist. "Do I have genius?" is
followed by the prospect, contemplated with seeming serenity, of playing the
piano in a department store or bar lounge. The mood does not seem to be one
of depression, as it is in the "Idle Thoughts of Distress" entry, where the whole
world is painted dull and gray by the verbal landscapist's brush of despair, or of
elation, which characterizes other entries in which the writer is convinced of
his genius. The entry seems to represent a kind of wistful balance, an at least
momentary equilibrium, a calm, self-aware, slightly self-mocking realism. Or is
it Charley's attempt to talk himself into these? The last section of the entry may
be a little *too* calm, the "I'm glad I love myself" a bit forced, especially since
within a couple of months the prospect of playing piano in a department store
would be forgotten and Charley would be having visions not simply of being
a concert pianist but of being Franz Liszt himself.

Department store. Cosmic concert hall. Somewhere in the chasm between
those two perceptions lies Charley's truth.

4

"One More Bloody Year of Reed"

Year Two—Two Immortalities

He lived with Lin in Santa Cruz until spring, taking some classes at the community college. They talked about his going back to Reed in the fall and worked on lining up enough financial aid to do it without putting Lin too much more in the hole. He came back to L.A. in May (1992) to live with me for the summer, working part time at Café Athens and at several other jobs he held for short periods. He got jobs easily and lost them just as easily. I didn't worry too much about this. Charley had always had a hard time staying employed, but at least now he was trying to work and stay engaged. He seemed sane but a bit hyper. I attributed that to romantic exertion. He had one serious love affair that spring and summer as well as several more casual ones. At one point he was dating two women named Jenny (like his sister) and flirting with one or two non-Jennys. Even with Charley's excellent hand-eye coordination, the concentration required to juggle so many Jennys would have made anybody a little nervous.

There were only a few reminders of the previous summer's breakdown. One was when Charley told me he was applying to Maharishi International University (MIU) in Iowa, which was connected to the self-realization institute in Pacific Palisades where he had started looking for god consciousness through transcendental meditation the year before. The idea that he was still interested in TM concerned me, but I didn't want to be excessively parental, and I doubted he would end up going to MIU anyway. Reed still seemed to be his first choice. So I pushed the Maharishi and his "unified field–based system of education" out of my mind.

He still talked occasionally about the piano as a career. The Franz Liszt dream or some variation was still alive, although how alive I wasn't sure. It was his business and I tried to stay out of it. I told him that if he really wanted to make music his career I was sure he would find a way.

Only once during the summer do I remember his indicating concern about having another breakdown. One night in my kitchen after dinner we were talking and he said something like, "I wonder what it would be like to take Navane again."

I tried to sound casual. "Why? Do you feel like you're at risk of having another episode?"

"No, not really," he murmured.

I let it go, not wanting to push it—not wanting to *think* about it. Later, I would learn that these casual remarks always meant something. Later still, when I read his journals, I would find out how *much* that something could be. Charley's writings in the spring and summer of 1992 are particularly revealing because they came at a time when his inner life was particularly complex. He was in love with one of the Jennys. He was also over his postbreakdown lull and entering an as-yet controllable upswing whose destination he couldn't clearly see. His journal indicates that he was for a while more serious about Maharishi International University than I realized at the time, for reasons that became clear when I found the draft of an essay he wrote in his application to the school. The essay talks about two types of education, "the channelled" and "the experienced," one being formal study, the other being the knowledge one gets through

working, travelling, interacting with more sorts of people. . . . From the experience

I've had with my TM teacher and TM center, I've gathered that students of MIU appreciate greatly both knowledge and experience in an ideal balance with each other. I believe that the approach which MIU takes toward a holistic education is both unique and visionary. . . . The school I am presently attending, Reed College, though well respected in its reputation for the pursuit of intellectualism, seems almost one dimensional in that the knowledge which the students come to grasp is not really incorporated into their lives. The students become surly, unkempt in their attire, and cynical toward life and ever finding contentment in what they believe is a hopeless world. They are continuously overloaded with work which to them seems generally pointless and impertinent.

It appears that MIU does not buy into this impertinence but has a healthy attitude toward finding happiness in life and education.

Even allowing for the college-application "Why MIU is right for me" tone, I think Charley's formulation of how he saw education (and life) was sincere. He wanted something less rigorously academic than the intellectualism offered by Reed, something more artistic, a better balance of structure and "experience." But he wanted more. Journal entries from the same period show that Charley was restless again and feeling nostalgia for the higher consciousness he had gained at Yosemite. Viewed in the context of this nostalgia, his continued interest in TM, which was the basis of MIU's "unified field" program, looks like a desire to regain the previous summer's god consciousness, but in a more structured and safe environment. MIU seemed to promise both god consciousness and safety.

But then, in his journal of May 13, 1992, Charley writes about being awakened that morning by a call from an admissions person from MIU who had read his application.

He had many questions to ask, and it was somewhat disconcerting so early in the day. He asked me what I've been doing for the past eight months. How can I tell him, nothing, since I've been recovering from a nervous breakdown? I felt he was prying almost cynically into my life. He then told me never to smoke marijuana again and that I must meditate regularly. He said he didn't want to dictate my life to me, then he did just that. His attitude wasn't that of one who wanted to welcome me aboard and just had to ask a few bureaucratic questions, but more with the intention of weeding out any individuals who are not pure enough to join the MIU community. Enough 4 2nite.

The school's finger-wagging probably marked the end of any genuine interest Charley had in MIU—even when it sent him an acceptance letter two months later that I found among his papers. As far as I know he ignored it. "Give me chastity, but not yet!" St. Augustine had written. Charley's version might have been, "Give me structure, but not yet!" The next journal entry, written late the following night (May 14), ranges far and wide. MIU is nowhere to be found.

> As the full moon approaches sleep does not come easily. What can I do? God knows I need rest after such a long day. Today I was at the clothing store unpacking boxes and boxes of packages of clothing. Now my mind wanders searching for fulfillment. . . . Does the moon's effect on me mean I have a lunatic's tendencies? I smoke, yet find little satisfaction lately. I have strange dreams these days about psych wards, nurses, and more madness. Will I devote my life to intellectualism or music or shall I meander about in search of meaning I will never find? What else is there besides what we perceive with our five senses? I'd give anything to know. Will I ever find my right therapist? How will it be when I return to Reed and all its impertinence, leaving Jenny behind? These questions trouble me tonight. My dad said he would buy me the watch I want next week. *I've come to understand little by little the root of my psychosis last summer. Having delved into the pit of my soul after a series of events I discovered there was nothing there besides pain, hopelessness, and a desire yet a repulsion for death. Having achieved for a brief while immortal consciousness, I wanted to transcend this piteous world, but was at the same time forced to stay here being undeniably attached to my mortal body.* (emphasis added)

Like other journal entries quoted earlier, the writing here, the jumping from topic to topic, indicates a heightened mood. It is caused or exacerbated by sleeplessness, and it expresses worry, even dread, of going mad again. The italicized passage is permanently obscure. The "psychosis" Charley refers to can only mean the breakdown at Yosemite, since in the days and weeks before the camping trip he had been rational, although perhaps teetering on the edge after weeks of sleeplessness. But clarity ends there. He does not explain the "series of events" that led to his soul-searching and desire for transcendence. Did it involve the girl he stood too close to at the campground? Did it result in the fear that made him crawl into his mother's sleeping bag at four in the morning? Not even the meaning of his attempt "to transcend this piteous world" is clear. Was closing his eyes while driving a conscious suicide attempt based on depression, or an attempt at transubstantiation based on elation? Or was it both? Charley himself had presented two versions of his state of mind at the time of the crash, one at St. John's and one at San Francisco General a few weeks later. Dr. Gray, in his discharge summary written when Charley left St. John's (and in conformity to his phone conversation with me while Charley was in the hospital), states that while at Yosemite Charley

> began to have delusions of grandeur and began to experience auditory hallucinations [hearing voices]. He reported being attracted to a young lady at the camp and felt "vibrations" that she was also attracted to him. He never spoke to her but he made a public disturbance at the camp which he thought would in some way attract this young woman and [make her] want his attention. Following this the patient had a single-car accident, totaling his vehicle because he tried to drive with his eyes closed, guided by his hallucinatory percept. Remarkably he was not injured.

But then Charley's San Francisco General medical records state:

> Initially, the patient reported that he was driving with his eyes closed and believed that the "force" would help him to drive the car and was experiencing auditory and visual hallucinations. . . . Upon admission to Unit 7A, the patient changed this report and claims that it was a suicide attempt and that he was actually trying to kill himself as a result of depression.

These two accounts of the crash correspond to two different versions of the psychosis itself that he wrote later, several months apart. One version is the May 14 "root of my psychosis" journal entry that I quoted above. In this version the crash seems to have been a conscious suicide attempt ("I wanted to transcend this piteous world") resulting from profound, even psychotic depression ("pain, hopelessness, and a desire yet a repulsion for death"). But compare this to another, undated entry written in Santa Cruz three or four months earlier when Charley was still recovering and feeling (in his words) "idle and withdrawn":

> I don't think I shall ever be fully content until I rediscover what I discovered in Yosemite in July '91. I don't wish to only find it once more but to understand

it. Yes, to understand how it was I had reached "God Consciousness," how I felt a [word missing] of energy when I heard the birds chirp, how when I put my hand to where the river flowed over the rocks it began to flow more strongly, how I was able to drive so fast through the winding mountain roads. How?

But why, when I went home to L.A. did I fall into a state of utter destitution?

In this version the "destitution" only came after, not at, Yosemite: At Yosemite itself there was no pain, no hopelessness, no desire to transcend the piteous world. No car crash. The author only remembers the sensation of driving "so fast through the winding mountain roads," not what came after.

There is no reason to think that either version was a lie. Rather, they probably expressed two very different memories of the same phenomena written in two different mood states, showing how complex and changing Charley's moods and thought patterns were, how closely the "no" was always entwined with the "yes." Viewed this way, the two versions of both the psychosis and the crash may not be as contradictory as they seem. Later, in examining the phenomenon in manic-depression known as "mixed states," we will see that such rapid shifts of mood and thought are not uncommon.

But for now let us return to Charley's May 14 journal entry, which continues without a break after the *"piteous world"* passage italicized two pages above:

What did I learn, what did I gain? I learned we are all stuck here and must endure the pain, however trying it may be. And the meaning? As one fellow at the hospital said, it is to establish a relationship with the Almighty and learn to work with it as best we can. Hmph!

Why the "Hmph!"? I think there is something fundamental being expressed here. For Charley, the experience at Yosemite hadn't meant establishing a relationship *with* the Almighty. It had meant *being* the Almighty—or at least the Almighty's infallible vicar, as illustrated in the card of the psychedelic pope he had sent me at Christmas. Like many others in the furthest throes of mania, Charley had come to believe, if only "for a brief while," that "I ha[d] the ability to see all the beauty in the world as if I were the Creator." Good work if you can get it, but how do you stay employed as God if pretty girls don't respond to your vibrations and their fathers report you to the authorities—or if your own father starts prying and "intervening"? What happens if, or when, such meddling and disrespect cause you to drift—or plummet—back to Earth?

The journal entry continues:

> I am coming closer these days to the conclusion that I must be a musician. One more bloody year of Reed College must take place first. There I will practice relentlessly to prepare myself for the audition for SFCM [San Francisco Conservatory of Music]. All the composers have left behind traces of themselves, and are therefore immortal since they are still played. Recognizing their love of humankind as I play their music I am exercising my sense of the commonality of man. Tolstoy learned late in life that one must live for man in order to serve God, instead of vice versa as he had formerly thought. He, however, was wealthy enough to explore all these ideas and learn them firsthand. I can only take his word for it.
>
> It doesn't make sense though. How can I live for man if I work at Banana Republic and Café Athens, which both cater to the indulgences of the affluent?
>
> I cannot find God through drugs. That is out of the question. Perhaps through meditation? introspection? exploration? starvation?
>
> Like many young men I am utterly lost (almost utterly), searching for a place in the world.
>
> Time, hah hah, plenty of time, so I say now. And it passes, so gently through our lives, going almost unnoticed.
>
> The latinos work so hard at the restaurant. They grow old working like mules, for rich men, who are satisfied and indifferent.
>
> I will see my psychiatrist soon.
>
> I make love to Jennifer and life is okay. Afterwards I eat and smoke and life is okay.
>
> I believe I have *manic* propensities.
>
> Adieu pour la nuit, Charley. (emphasis in the original)

There's a lot going on in this passage, written during a sleepless night, the full moon approaching. All of Charley's basic insecurities about his talents and his future—the roots of the Yosemite breakdown—are still present. He still feels the need to redeem himself, to find a "place in the world" that will give him status and solidity and allow him to avoid the fate of his Latino coworkers, a fate that is particularly scary because he can see its outline in himself as well—in the form of his parents' influence.[1] He had been counting on Maharishi International University to help him, to provide a safe haven in which he could meditate and reachieve god consciousness. But now that idea is discarded because they won't let him smoke pot. So the plan to go to music school reemerges. He will become a concert pianist and achieve immortality not by direct god consciousness—that is, by becoming God *("as if I were the Creator")*—but by artistic association with "immortal" composers *("Recognizing their love of humankind as I play their music I am exercising my sense of the commonality of man").*

I think this switching back and forth between achieving god consciousness through TM and being a great artist was a recurring pattern in Charley's psychology, a sort of path A and path B. The switch had already happened once after Yosemite when, failing to transcend the world after achieving immortal consciousness, his fantasy self-metamorphosed from being God to being Franz Liszt. Achieving god consciousness, in other words, was the preferred choice. When that failed, as it inevitably did, the only slightly less exalted but more labor-intensive path of becoming a great artist (first writer, then pianist, later actor), took its place. Taking the still more rigorous academic route, full of surly, unkempt youths and work overload, was path C. Below that was path D, "the proletarian lifestyle," being stuck forever unpacking boxes and busing tables. But this was less a real path than the absence of one.[2]

I have listed these four paths in what seems to be the order of Charley's own preference at this time in his life. In terms of his actual previous history, however—what had led him to this point—I believe the list needs revision. This is because path A—god consciousness—had not always existed, but had come into existence only at Yosemite. In a sense, the breakdown at Yosemite *was* path A, taken as the result of years of growing tension and doubts regarding his future, which he usually saw as one of being an artist.

As I have indicated, in the three years before Yosemite, starting with his visit to San Francisco and first episode of insomnia, Charley was periodically visited by the notion that he was a person of extraordinary talent, a genius, destined to perform extraordinary deeds in both art and life. But at the same time as he was convinced of his genius he was also plagued by doubts about it, afraid he was deluding himself, and unsure of how to realize his ambition and turn it into actual achievement.

Charley was still very young, only fifteen, when these severe mood swings (known as *cyclothymia*) began. Further, they came on top of a lifelong history of less obvious but nonetheless real instability that seemed to be inborn and may have been exacerbated by family instability: his difficulty sleeping, skittishness, impulsiveness, accident-proneness and difficulty concentrating—all things which, I believe, made it particularly hard for him to develop a firm sense of himself—a difficult enough task, of course, for *any* adolescent even under the best circumstances.

Charley's youth and previous history when his first episode of insomnia and hypomania occurred at fifteen may have been crucial factors in the later havoc his disorder was able to wreak. He simply was not old enough to have developed a sense of himself and his place in the world that was sufficiently strong or flexible to survive the increasingly powerful pummelings of his moods, which acted as a kind of psychological wrecking ball. Making the problem worse was that the same powerful nervous energy that gave rise to his extreme ambition also undermined his ability to focus or concentrate on realizing it. First he wanted to be a great writer, then a great pianist; later it would be acting. But his growing instability—the mood swings and the insomnia, as well as his attempts to deal with these through drugs, alcohol, coffee—made any kind of sustained effort difficult. Charley was a talented writer and musician, but actual accomplishment, at least to the extent he desired it and thought it would "save" him, remained elusive. He was a fine pianist; his music teacher at Reed said he was the most musical student on campus. He would play a piece—say, a Chopin impromptu—for hours, going back and forth, evening out the rough spots, showing concentration that seemed to elude him in other areas of his life. (As he said himself, playing the piano was a way of not going crazy: perhaps, like his various substances, it was a kind of self-medication, a calming influence.) But despite his intentions (*"I will practice relentlessly to prepare myself for the audition for SFCM"*) he showed little interest in doing the fingering exercises and long hours of boring work necessary to become a professional. As a result he was bound to fall short of his own expectations. So what to do? "Transcend" the norm through meditation and visualization and higher consciousness.[3]

I think Charley's growing fear of failure, and his attempts to surmount it, were what led to the breakdown at Yosemite, where all thoughts of pianos and such seemed to disappear during the romantic fixation on the girl camper and the attempt at suicide/transcendence that followed, only to reappear a few days later when he found himself still alive and still facing life choices about school, profession, money, etc. So the idea of going to Juilliard or the San Francisco Conservatory reemerged, only to dissolve in the "utter destitution" of anxiety and panic and hospitalization. The idea kept decomposing and recomposing. Charley had asked me while at St. John's whether he had to be Franz Liszt, and I said no. But once out of the hospital, and a few days before his trip to San Francisco with Kit Henderson that ended at San Francisco General, he matter-of-factly announced (in a conversation with me and a family friend) that he intended to become a concert pianist because "What else is there for me to do?" A couple of weeks after that, at San Francisco General, he disclaimed the piano dream entirely and even blamed his family for it. His SFGH medical records report that during a therapy session with one of the hospital psychologists, "Patient expressed feeling pressure from family to be a pianist *when in fact, he may not enjoy playing piano all that much.* When asked what other interests he may have, patient replied 'writing and acting.' *Patient has felt obligated to pursue piano because of family pressure,* and began playing piano after observing grandfather playing, whom he idealizes↑." (emphasis added) This is absolute nonsense. There was never any pressure on Charley to pursue the piano.

Still later, even after his recovery the following fall and winter, the thoughts (and doubts) about his genius were still there. In the journal passage where he talks about himself "as if I were the Creator," written in Santa Cruz the winter after Yosemite (see p. 22), Charley attributes his earlier achievement of god consciousness to the fact that "I am by nature a genius, though my brilliance has apparently been resting . . . the past few months. I *know* I have *genius* and I deserve to have what was rightly mine previously. God has granted it to me. I deserve love, fulfillment, contentment. My mental breakdown has been an educational process. *It is now time to move on.*" (emphasis Charley's) This comes a few lines after saying he practices TM twice a day.

But move on where? By the following May he is having heightened moods again and is trying to figure out how to achieve, or reachieve, immortality. But now there are two kinds of immortality, what I previously called path A and path B, alternating in his mind: the immortality of god consciousness (the ego as God achievable *"through meditation? introspection? exploration? starvation?"*) and the more human immortality of artistic achievement. But this second kind, decomposing and recomposing as it does, may be out of reach because it involves sustained effort that given Charley's instability is difficult or impossible.

Hence the tendency to look back toward the previous summer's god consciousness, which is ultimately the same as death—the end of all effort and suffering. A few weeks later in another journal entry, Charley expresses this identity obliquely.

Madness—a haiku

One vision, one thought
Come together forming naught
All things are the same.

In the end, that's what god consciousness seems to have come down to.

It was in this frame of mind that Charley faced his first post-Yosemite summer and the prospect of resuming his "surly, unkempt" real life.

Toward the end of summer, his return to Reed approaching, he seemed to be getting more antsy, but I wrote it off to nervousness. Lin came down from Santa Cruz and the three of us drove the eleven hundred miles from L.A. to Portland together. We hadn't done this at the start of Charley's freshman year, and it seemed like a delayed rite of passage.

Once More to the Underworld

I've returned to you, Reed
My precious dear Reed,
Without whom my soul would
*   be in great need.*
You missed me too? I could not tell
For during my leave you've held up
*   so well.*

I pray that this time your
*   babes be more girlie.*

And that the feminists be
just a little less surly.
Let the pot grow copious
and the beer flow free.
But spare me Iawaska,
and bad LSD.
Oh dear Reed, you're one
hell of a college.
With your stout old buildings
And abundant, sweet foliage.
I thank the good Lord that
I'm once again here.
To avoid the real world for yet
one more year.

("To Reed, with Thanks," Fall 1992)

But the real world would again encroach into the ivy halls of academe. Charley's edginess on the trip to Portland was more serious than I wanted to admit at the time. Along with the mood swings and nostalgia for god consciousness, which I did not know about, there had been more visible signs of tumult during the past months—some emotional volatility (he cried to me one night after his boss criticized him at work) and some drinking. Perhaps most serious was his ongoing infatuation with Jenny Lewis, one of the two nonsister Jennys. Jenny Lewis had been the main reason for his leaving Santa Cruz for L.A. the previous spring. Charley had met her while she and her brother Danny were visiting Lin in late winter; they were longtime friends of Charley's sister and acquaintances of Lin. Charley, smitten, had followed Jenny Lewis back down south, actually moving in with her for a while in March (she lived in Venice, just south of Santa Monica) before reinstalling himself in my apartment. The affair did not last. Jenny Lewis was ten years older than Charley and also very volatile, and after a few weeks of living together she wrote him a letter asking him to move out. Charley took the rejection hard. He talked to me about it several times, the last time by phone when he was back at Reed. My journal of September 7 discusses the conversation in depth, and I quote it here because I think it gives a sense of the complexity of Charley's and my relationship, the good and the bad, and of how, although I tried to be a good father, the role was not a natural one for me.

10:40 Labor Day night. Just talked for an hour to Charley on the phone. He's been at Reed for two weeks and is very upset about breaking up with Jenny Lewis. He thinks that she's heartless and cruel for not responding to his phone calls etc. and not being upfront with him. He got upset with me for being cold and objective in my analysis and trying to convince him just to let it go. After a while we started communicating better, I apologizing, partly tactically, for not being more sympathetic. Jenny Aurthur told me today that Jenny Lewis had changed her number to avoid his calls, and Lin told me last week that Danny had told Charley to stop harassing Jenny Lewis, so I was perhaps overreacting on the side of the harassment issue (how serious it is I don't know) than on the sympathy issue; i.e., more worried about Charley's potentially or actually obsessive and potentially dangerous behavior than I should have been. I'm not sure. We started to connect better later in the conversation when I talked about male romanticism and men's tendencies to set up impossible ideals for women and then be horribly disappointed when they don't live up to them; and how men (the corollary) also set up impossible ideals for themselves relating (as Charley said) to "providing" for women, saving them, etc., and then being crushed when those don't work either. He asked if that meant there wasn't a place for romance in the world and I used the analogy of banana splits: they're good once in a while but we wouldn't want to live on them. Then about Stendhal's dual perspective and how that can save us from going off the deep end. I tried to appeal to Charley's amour propre, asked him if he was writing in a journal, that that helps, that there are meetings available (Relationships Anonymous?) etc....The conversation got a little better toward the end.

He's obviously going through a very painful separation. I told him about my relationship with Claire [a youthful crush] and how similar it was, how it often happens that the other person is going through a completely different thing than you are and has no idea what effect she's causing or else doesn't care, and how we can't make them care. The only thing we can do is start the process of getting over it by admitting, first, that it's over. As Charley said, the hardest part. I have to think about this more and remember my own feelings in similar situations. It's not as easy as I sounded, I know that.

Nothing we can do will make them care; at least nothing actively. The sooner we realize that the better off we will be. Charley's into this whole thing of, She'll be sorry. But she probably won't; and if she is it won't matter anyway.

"This is not therapeutic," he said midway through the conversation when I was being too rough, and I had to change my approach. I just hope he doesn't go off the deep end of real active obsession and harassment. He claims that he won't. He resents the age thing being brought up all the time, people not taking him and his feelings seriously because he's young "and will get over it." He said that he felt neglected by her for most of the time he was in L.A. I asked if that didn't indicate that there was never a real equality of feeling. He said that she had indicated feelings for him, that they had a committed relationship, etc. I have no idea what really happened and, while sympathizing with him, don't want to appear to endorse his posture of self-righteousness and resentment toward her as the bad one. Hopefully some of the later discussion of male romanticism and our impossible expectations of women (which he seemed to react to as if it made sense) started to make a dent in that feeling of his. It was an interesting discussion. He's a very bright kid and extremely sensitive. There's no way I ever could have talked to my father (or anybody really) the way he talked to me; he's much more open and exposed and willing to be vulnerable than I ever was. I hope to the good.

But such talks did no good, and the summer's jitters soon bloomed into a full-fledged manic episode. I heard about it secondhand from Lin when Charley visited her in Santa Cruz in October and acted spacey—"psychotic," in her words, which I took seriously, knowing her dislike of psychiatric jargon. On November 18 he called me from school sounding very weird, and I thought about the call the previous year in San Francisco before his second hospitalization. This time was different, though. He was not dreamy and elegiac but manic, motor mouthed. He told me that David Bowie was communicating with him, that he was writing a note to an "Irish babe"—one of his campus crushes—on a dollar bill with his 1925 Underwood typewriter, and that he was practicing the piano to get into Juilliard. I asked him if he was getting ready for another trip to the psych ward. He became offended and told me I was "grilling" him. I felt entitled to be blunt, though, because he had written me the following letter a few days earlier:

Mon Cher Père: It takes an especial effort these days for a man to write his father. With no kings and queens and only ridiculous presidents it is difficult to know who is in charge. I can only say it is a son's duty and to aspire to greatness we must look to ancestry in sincere retrospection with the hope of learning through trial and error. If we look merely to the philosophers we shall only find that we prostitute ourselves.

When I suggested to my piano teacher that I play Gershwin as a form of nationalism during this country's dire condition he said queerly, "You wanna save Western civilization." I might have lied when I said I had no intention of doing so. I can also say I am tired of the trips to the underworld. I wrote to Brian Marsh that the voices therein are like parakeets in a stolen cave. I saw *Last of the Mohicans* the other day with two friends. I will grant that Day-Lewis was completely charmless and that the film was essentially a drag.

So, in reading books like *L'étranger* in one class and *To the Lighthouse* in another we students are bound to know corruption in a thousand ways. The Hum 220 lectures are fascinating, however, I have to tell you.

I promise to make it safely to L.A. by Christmas, et vous, attention à travers les rues sur la bicyclette. Votre fils.

I took this as a sign that he wanted me to know he was flipping out. Two days after the "Irish babe" call—Friday—he called again, telling me he felt "scared," that he had come from outer space like *The Man Who Fell to Earth* (a David Bowie film) or Superman. I told him the role of Superman was already taken. I also told him to try and get some rest over the weekend. The following week was Thanksgiving and he would be able to get away from school for a few days.

I wasn't being completely callous. Between the two phone calls I had tried to contact the school's medical staff to see whether they knew that Charley was flipping out. The school psychologist was out of the office, and her secretary told me that yes, they were aware of Charley's situation but for confidentiality reasons couldn't give out any information. On Sunday night I got a call back from the school physician, not the psychologist. He told me almost apologetically that Charley was back in the hospital.

Again the path to the psych ward had started with a romantic fixation, although it was no longer Jenny Lewis. Sometime in the past few weeks she had stopped being the object of Charley's romantic longing, and he had replaced her with one of his female professors. He had decided that the two of them had a mystical psychosexual kinship (later he wrote that he felt intense sexual longings for her), and during an after-class conference he tried to kiss her on the cheek. A little later he grabbed the faculty office keys from a campus cop and tried to get into her office (she wasn't there at the time) to gather evidence of their kinship. He was picked up by campus security. Security called the school psychologist, who convinced Charley to go with her to the local psychiatric ward and admit himself voluntarily to avoid being arrested and taken in by the police. He agreed, and the two of them went to Portland Adventist Hospital, where he was locked up and put back on Navane. A couple of days later he demanded to be released and was put on a five-day hold.

The next day, the Monday before Thanksgiving, I talked on the phone to the psychiatrist at Adventist and got an idea of the hospital's plans, which were largely determined by economics. Since I hadn't put Charley in the hospital—hadn't even known he was going in until two days afterward because of the school's confidentiality concerns—I wasn't financially responsible, and Charley had no insurance of his own. There was no one who was going to pay, in other words, so Adventist wanted him out as soon as the hold was up (the following Monday), sooner if possible. There were two places Charley could go, the psychiatrist said: the state mental hospital in a town south of Portland or a local county psychiatric facility in Portland called Ryles Center. Later that day I talked to a court evaluator, a woman with a private agency contracted by the county mental health system and in touch with Adventist. Her job was to figure out what to do with Charley when and if he had a hearing to get the hold released. The tentative plan was to keep him on the hold as long as possible and see how he did back on Navane, then send him for a week or more to Ryles Center, avoiding the state mental hospital. Meanwhile, the evaluator would talk to Reed about granting him a medical leave.

It all sounded very abstract to me. The prospect of a state hospital somewhere outside Portland didn't bode well, and I had no idea what Ryles Center was like. But at least Charley wasn't going anywhere till after Thanksgiving, three days away, so I had a little time. I told the evaluator I would be in Portland by Wednesday. I called Lin in Santa Cruz. She said she would meet me in Portland Thanksgiving morning.

I still didn't have a car, so I decided to go by bus, partly because airfare was very expensive booked on such short notice and partly because twenty-three-hour bus rides can be very calming, at least if you have a window seat and you're not all that anxious to get where you're going anyway. Why rush? Charley was safe, and I knew the kind of reception I was going to get. The evaluator had said that when she interviewed him in the psych ward he was paranoid and suspicious. He had also apparently freaked people out in his Reed dorm the week before being hospitalized, talking on the phone to parties unknown about when he was going to be crucified and whether he'd be able to eat a final meal beforehand. Yeah, I could wait an extra day before dealing with all this.

I arrived in Portland early Wednesday afternoon, rented a car and drove to Reed to meet with the school psychologist and dean of students. Even now, after all the disruption Charley had caused, they both told me how fond of him they were, what a great kid he was, and how they would even be willing to take him back after winter break if he got better and kept up with his assignments at home. The next morning I picked Lin up at the Greyhound station; to save money she had also come by bus. We drove to the hospital to visit Charley (I for the second time; I had already seen him Wednesday evening). He was in his imperious mode: haughty, superior, contemptuous of the hospital, the staff, humanity in general and his parents in particular. He was planning a lawsuit against the hospital for not letting him smoke.

This was what I had come eleven hundred miles for. I had expected the imperiousness but it was still hard to get used to. It was part of the mania, I knew, although he didn't appear manic. It was also a defense mechanism to try to deal with his essential helplessness. A few days ago everything had been great—well, at least intermittently great, between phone calls about last suppers and crucifixions. He had been at school writing love letters to "Irish babes" on dollar bills and communing with David Bowie, feeling mystical bonds with good-looking women professors, his mind and libido in turbo drive. Now, suddenly, he was back in the psych ward on the hated Navane, monitored, prodded, asked "How are you doing?" and "So . . . what's going on with you?" by condescending shrinks and clueless parents. Who wouldn't be pissed off? But it was still always hard for me to feel sorry for Charley when he was in his imperious mode. I preferred feeling sorry for myself.

After visiting hours, Lin and I had Thanksgiving dinner at Carrow's, a regional chain restaurant near the Motel 6 where we were staying. The dinner, counterintuitively, turned out to be an antidote to self-pity, the midwestern blandness of the restaurant and its dry white meat and gluey gravy comforting rather than depressing. I felt at home among the other diners, mostly older Anglos who resembled my mother's family. Mom's parents had been

small-towners from Missouri and Iowa who had moved to western Idaho—
only a few hundred miles from where I was now—in the 1920s when the west
was still almost frontier. I had spent several summers with them in Idaho when
I was a kid, and I was reminded of them now as I looked around. There was a
kind of unself-pitying grit about these people. I was eating Thanksgiving dinner at what was essentially a coffee shop because I was in a strange city and my
kid was in the local nuthouse; what was *their* excuse? I think Lin, also with roots
in the midwest peasantry, felt the same way. You look disaster in the eye with a
kind of fishy stare and then, if you're still standing, continue on your way.

Friday brought a turn for the better. The evaluator and the hospital had
decided Charley would go to Ryles Center rather than the out-of-town state
mental hospital, and he would do so today. Ryles was free because it was
county run. When Lin and I got to Adventist in the morning for visiting hours
Charley knew he was about to leave and seemed much better.

We weren't prepared for how much better how fast. Ryles was located in a
residential part of town about a half mile from our Motel 6 and not far from
Reed. We knew Charley was due to arrive there via hospital transportation
sometime in the afternoon, so around midday we decided to take a walk by
the place to see what it looked like. It was a sunny, chilly, leaf-blown fall day,
and we felt reenergized as we strolled in the pleasant old neighborhood, soon
arriving at Ryles, which consisted of two one-story wood structures that could
have been houses. As we walked past we saw Charley through the front window. He had just gotten there himself and was at the admissions desk. He saw
us and gave a big smile and wave. He seemed totally himself. It was as if Mom
and Dad had just dropped him off at summer camp and he was watching us
go. We kept walking—it wasn't visiting hours yet—shaking our heads in
amazement. When we went back later that evening for a real visit he still
seemed fine. As we got ready to leave, the staff person who had admitted him,
a young man named Jeff, walked us to the locked front door to buzz us out.
"How does he seem to you?" he asked.

"He seems like his old self," Lin said.

"So this is his baseline?"

"Yeah," I said. "That's Charley."

Lin took the bus back to Santa Cruz the next day. I stayed through the

weekend to see how long "the ol' rugrat" was going to be at Ryles. My upbeat
mood was tested when I talked to the staff head, a woman named Gayle who
uttered the "S" word for the first time, the mental illness equivalent of the Big
One. Schizophrenia. Aside from being unnerved I was surprised, since another
staff member, a young guy who was Charley's main caseworker and himself
manic-depressive (or "bipolar"), was convinced Charley was bipolar as well. I
was getting two diagnoses from two people in the same facility, although
Gayle's wasn't definitive, she admitted: A diagnosis of schizophrenia required
that the symptoms—hearing voices, delusions, paranoia and so on—last for six
months. But there was a subtext of certainty under the disclaimer. College
might not be the right place for Charley, she added. Too much stress. She talked
about his resistance to being asked questions, his irritability. "Something's going
on in his head that he's afraid to tell us" (echoes of Dr. Gray at our first meeting). He needed to stay at Ryles at least another week, maybe longer.

It sounded good to me. I had to get back to work. Charley actually seemed
comfortable—borderline happy. His mood was calm, at least with me, and he
and his bipolar caseworker had seemed to hit it off. The other patients were
mostly young folk he might actually relate to. I told Gayle I would go back to
L.A. and return to Portland for Charley's release.

Ryles was a locked facility but with some flexibility. Patients were considered voluntary—no 5150 holds—which seemed to make the place a little
less asylum-ish. They were often allowed out on three- or four-hour community passes, so the next evening, Sunday, I picked Charley up and we drove
across the Willamette River into Portland's downtown to have dinner at an
Indian restaurant he liked. He seemed miraculously better compared to a
week—even three days—before. During dinner and after—when we went
back to the motel and hung out for the rest of our three hours—he also
opened up to me more than he ever had before. Again, beyond the immediate
fixation on his professor, there had been a sexual (or "gender") aspect to his
latest episode. "I felt like the battle of the sexes was going on my head," he said,
using the phrase Lin had heard during the first breakdown. The two sides of
his brain had been at war with each other. "It was totally schizophrenia, Dad,"
he said, using the word himself, adding that his Aunt Ella had called him a
"paranoid schizophrenic" during his "sojourn" at San Francisco General the
year before.

Despite it all, it was a wonderful evening, one of those eye-of-the-hurricane times when all conventional ideas of what happiness and accomplishment and everything else mean—what *meaning* means—go out the window. Here I was in a cheap motel in a city I didn't particularly like, faced with a twenty-three-hour bus ride the next morning, with a possibly schizophrenic son whom I was about to take back to his locked facility—and, oh yes, I'd just realized that I'd left my credit card at the restaurant, which was now closed. But I felt great. I was having a great time with my kid.

I decided to start reading up on schizophrenia.

"A Nice Birthday Present for Sis"

February 24, 1993

Three months later. The phone was ringing at work again. The same office, the same desk, the same time of day, a year and a half after the call from the California Highway Patrol. This time the voice was Lin's, from her office a couple of miles away (she had moved back to L.A. a month before). Charley had just phoned her from my apartment. He had slit his wrists with his Swiss army knife and wanted to know what to do.

I still didn't have a car, so we agreed that she would go get him and take him to the St. John's Hospital emergency room; I would meet her on my bike in a half-hour. Before leaving I called Charley and asked him how he was. He didn't sound like he was dying, but he said he'd swallowed pills too, his lithium. (Dr. Gray had put him on lithium in December.) He said he had already thrown up some of it.

"Swallow some soap, Charley," I said. "Swallow some soap. Get it all up. You're gonna be okay, okay? D'you understand what I'm saying?"

"Yeah. Swallow some soap. . . ." He sounded very subdued. I told him to wait for Mom, not to go anywhere. He said he'd wait. We hung up. I told my supervisor what had happened and took off. It was three in the afternoon, the day before his sister Jenny's twenty-second birthday.

As I pedaled toward the hospital I castigated myself for not having seen this coming. Charley had been living with me since getting out of Ryles in mid-December, working at Café Athens again, trying to take classes at Santa

Monica College. Two nights ago we had sat up almost till midnight, side by side on his futon as he poured out his anguish over the wreck his life was becoming. He had been very depressed for weeks, although he had tried to hide it. "Oh Father, Father, why did you beget me?" he asked in a stricken voice, and it broke my heart. He grasped my hand, talking about how he was holding on by a thread, how he felt his life was slipping away. He cringed with mortification as he talked about how he had acted like a jerk at Reed while he was having his breakdown over the professor, going around insulting people, acting arrogant. "I described myself to my dorm advisor"—a female student—"as a Greek god. Jesus, Dad . . ." He said he felt old. "He's caught in purgatory now," I wrote in my journal that night, "can't go back, can't go forward . . . also expressed fear of not being in control of internal processes—that illness could recur at any time—sense of uncertainty, the shapelessness of his opponent—unable to fight something so amorphous. . . ."

When I got to the ER Lin was already there, sitting in the waiting room. Charley was inside having his wrists treated and his stomach pumped. Dr. Gray had been paged and was on his way. "I can't help thinking this has something to do with Jenny's birthday," Lin said.

"Yeah, nice birthday present for Sis," I replied. Charley was always comparing himself to Jenny—her relatively sanguine temperament, her wide social circle, her devoted long-term boyfriend, her ability to finish school and hold a job.

"I feel pissed off," Lin said. Her voice was tight. "I feel manipulated."

"Yeah, I know . . . ," I said. "I feel like that a lot myself. Although right this minute I don't. I know how miserable he's been." I told her about the discussion on the futon two nights before. Why hadn't I listened better?

After a while, Lin was let in to see him. He didn't want to see me. That night I wrote in my journal that the suicide attempt didn't seem completely serious. "When I came home . . . all I found of the attempt, beside wet towels hanging off the shower glass, was a trace of blood on the edge of the tub—a forlorn little trace. It's so sad! . . . Poor little fellow! I feel so *sorry* for him. Helpless . . . I should've asked him if he was thinking about suicide. . . ."

He spent a day in the intensive care unit, then back to the hospital's psychiatric wing, the unlocked ward this time. Then home with me again, now on even more medication. Since Ryles, he had been taking Navane, Cogentin to counteract the side effects of the Navane, and Klonopin for sleep. Then Dr. Gray had put him on lithium in late December. Now he added an antidepressant, Wellbutrin, because even though lithium is supposed to treat both mania and depression (and suicidality!), it obviously hadn't worked for the latter two.

All this witches' brew of medication made one thing clear, at least: Nobody knew what Charley "had." The day after he cut his wrists, Lin and I met Dr. Gray and we all visited Charley in the ICU to tell him everything was all right and that we were going to try to do a better job of helping him. After we left his room I asked Dr. Gray if he had a moment to talk. "Sure," he said, "let's have a family meeting." He found an empty conference room nearby and he, Lin and I met for almost an hour in an atmosphere that was fairly relaxed; Charley was safe just yards away, being baby-sat—because of the suicide attempt—by a nurses' aide. I asked Dr. Gray what he thought Charley's illness was, saying I was totally confused. During the first breakdown Dr. Gray had theorized that Charley might be manic-depressive. Then, after the Thanksgiving breakdown at Reed, when I had asked him whether I should call UCLA's Affective Disorders Clinic, which treated manic-depression, he had said no, he didn't think they would take him—Charley didn't have an affective (mood) disorder—in other words he *wasn't* manic-depressive. Now, three months later, Charley was on schizophrenia medication (Navane) *and* manic-depression medicine (lithium). Plus Dr. Gray was starting him on Wellbutrin for depression, the third major mental illness. By now he had been treating Charley off and on for a year and a half and had come to know him fairly well. So?

Dr. Gray shrugged. "Well, he could be both schizophrenic *and* manic-depressive. The rule of thumb is that one out of a hundred people are schizophrenic and one out of a hundred are manic-depressive. So one out of a hundred times one out of a hundred are both."

I looked at Lin. "Well, we always said Charley was one in a million."

"Strictly speaking, one in ten thousand," she replied. We all laughed hollowly.

Lin and I talked about what we thought were the shortcomings of the purely psychiatric approach, the fact that it hadn't stopped Charley from trying to kill himself. She, as always, expressed her especial dissatisfaction with the purely physical treatment he had been getting, the emphasis on medication, and the fact that locked psych wards didn't seem to be the best approach to helping people in crisis. Didn't they need love? To my surprise Dr. Gray didn't disagree. He mentioned something that had been tried in France during the eighteenth century, when the standard of care for the mentally ill was literally to chain them in asylums. A physician who was a reformer—Dr. Gray thought his name was Morel—had hired an entire village to take in insane people— "for money"—absorbing them into village life and treating them with love. Nothing like it existed now, as far as he knew.[4] We talked further about the psychological aspects of Charley's condition, saying that there were clearly other levels besides chemical imbalance. Again, Dr. Gray, who practiced psychoanalysis as well as psychiatry, agreed, saying he thought Charley had a narcissistic disorder and needed more than medication. "If you folks were millionaires, I'd recommend intensive psychoanalysis for Charley—four or five times a week. The kind where the patient becomes so dependent on the therapy that he has to be hospitalized when the therapist goes on vacation."

Lin and I weren't millionaires. We weren't paupers, either. Between the two of us we earned more than $100,000 a year. But the kind of therapy Dr. Gray was talking about would cost $30,000–40,000 a year, with at most a few hundred covered by even the better types of mental health insurance. In Dr. Gray's mind, any really effective treatment for whatever Charley had was only accessible to millionaires. Short of that we could keep doing what we were doing, which was to have him see Dr. Gray once a week for talk therapy. One session cost $150—a lot for us, but affordable. Or he could go to a less expensive shrink for talk therapy, a psychologist with a masters or Ph.D.; their going rate was $100–110 per hour. Meanwhile, Dr. Gray would continue to see him for a half session every two weeks ($85) to monitor and represcribe his medication. We decided on this new approach, and Dr. Gray gave us the name of a woman Ph.D. he knew.

Charley's depression didn't let up right away when he got out of the hospital, wrists bandaged. He wanted to return to Café Athens immediately, and we had an hour of black comedy preparing for his first night back at work, trying to figure how to hide the bandages under the cuffs of his white busboy's dress shirt so they wouldn't pop out when he reached across a table to fill a diner's water glass. A pair of gloves seemed to work, although at least one of Charley's coworkers saw through the ruse. "When Cado saw the bandages around my wrist," Charley wrote in his journal, he said, "You didn't do this stupid thing. You're so pretty and intelligent. . . ." Cado is a waiter and a guy I know. Sweet fellow. My sister told me on the phone when I was in the hospital that she was angry at me for my selfish behavior. Two black security guards were hounding me in the ER. "Why do you wanna do yourself in for? The women get much better as you go on." I guess that's nice to know. The scars I suppose will be a problem for a little while.

There were a couple more rough weeks as we waited for the antidepressant to start working. When it finally did, it worked in a way it wasn't supposed to. Rather than cure the depression, the Wellbutrin gave Charley a severe rash on his arms, which made him even more depressed. It was like some biblical curse. How had my son become like the Egyptians, inflicted with "blotches and blains" by an angry Jehovah? I began worrying that he was going to kill himself for real now, and I stayed home from work several days to watch over him when he seemed particularly despairing. When I did go to work, Lin and I called him several times a day.

But then another seeming miracle. I took him to my regular doctor to treat the rash, and he prescribed a steroid, which got rid of not only the rash but the depression. Steroids contain hormones, and apparently the one prescribed for the rash jump-started Charley's neurons—"It's all electricity, anyway," as one of his therapists said—and kicked him out of the down mood. Or maybe it was his recovery from the rash; convalescence can be a sort of resurrection. Whatever it was, within a few days he seemed fine. "I'm feeling a lot better, Dad," he said when I hadn't even asked, and with a smile I knew was genuine. He started seeing the therapist recommended by Dr. Gray, a doctorate in psychology with a license in marriage and family counseling named Barbara Blum whose office was only a few blocks from my apartment. He continued having half sessions with Dr. Gray every two weeks to adjust his medication. Dr. Gray put him on another antidepressant, Zoloft, to replace the Wellbutrin and sent him to St. John's every month to check his lithium level. The bifurcated therapy seemed to work. Charley now had a second set of parents taking care of him, Lin and I commented to each other—Dr. Gray his therapeutic father, Dr. Blum his therapeutic mother. With so much parenting he would have to get better, if only in self-defense.

A Layman's Guide to Major Mental Illness

Sertraline: Brand name: *Zoloft*

Pharmacology: Antidepressant. The antidepressant effect of sertraline *is presumed* to be linked to its ability to inhibit the neuronal reuptake of serotonin. It has only very weak effects on norepinephrine and dopamine neuronal reuptake. At clinical doses, sertraline blocks the uptake of serotonin into human platelets. . . . Like most clinically effective antidepressants, sertraline downregulates brain norepinephrine and serotonin receptors *in animals.*[5] (emphasis added)

Charley's sudden recovery thrilled me, and made me think I knew what his problem was. By now I had observed his behavior for more than two years. I had seen him crazily manic (more than seen, I'd *felt* the mania, the buzz the weekend after Yosemite). More recently I had seen him in his "postpsychotic depression" (Dr. Gray's term), which had come after Christmas when the autumn mania abated; Charley had been suicidal, but "rationally" suicidal. And now I had seen his sudden emergence out of the depression. None of this sounded to me like schizophrenia, which I had read is marked by steady, long-term deterioration. Charley's condition was just the opposite; it was all over the place. Further, the symptoms seemed to be mood driven, coming and going with his ups and downs. The psychotic thinking was not "autonomous," in other words. He didn't think he was Franz Liszt when he was depressed, only when he was manic. Similarly with his romantic fixations; they came with his grandiose highs and went away with his lows. So even though Dr. Gray was unwilling to diagnose Charley as one thing or the other, I thought I was starting to get a clearer picture of what was wrong.

To explain my thinking at the time I need to discuss, briefly, some current psychiatric theory. For those who wish to go into the matter more thoroughly, I have written a fuller account and added it as Appendix C.

Presently, psychiatry distinguishes three major mental illnesses: (1) schizophrenia, (2) manic-depressive (or bipolar) disorder, and (3) major depression, that is, unipolar depression (depression without mania). Lately, (2) and (3) are tending to be lumped together into a single category, major mood disorder, as opposed to the *thought* disorder schizophrenia. This axiomatic distinction between thought and mood (also called "affect") is important in psychiatry. Schizophrenia, which until the 1920s was known as *dementia praecox* or premature dementia, is characterized by long-term disordered thinking—delusions, hearing voices, hallucinations, paranoia, severe "cognitive dysfunction" (inability to process sensory information), etc.—which exist independent of the relatively short-term changes in how a person feels. Manic-depressive illness, the theory goes, is different[6] in that it is characterized by wide swings in feelings ranging from extreme elation to extreme depression.

The theory has problems, however. For one thing, the distinction between thought and mood and their respective malfunctions is often not clear-cut. The way people feel affects how they think as well as the other way around, and it is not always clear which comes first. In practical terms, people with mood disorder often manifest the same kinds of disordered thinking as people with thought disorder. For example, people with extreme manic-depression often present exactly the same psychotic symptoms as schizophrenics do—delusions, hearing voices, thoughts that one is Jesus Christ, being talked to by God. The difference, psychiatric research has determined, is that for manic-depressives these symptoms are mood-driven and temporary, changing with the cycles of mania and depression. Also—this is another important distinction—people suffering from mood disorder experience periods of spontaneous recovery and normality and more or less regular functioning, whereas symptoms of schizophrenia last six months or longer. Untreated schizophrenics, and even some treated ones—treatment here referring to antipsychotic medications—are considered doomed to a permanent deterioration in their mental state and quality of life. This is because, more and more, psychiatry defines major mental illness and even many secondary personality disorders (attention deficit disorder, obsessive-compulsive disorder, phobias, alcoholism and so on) as "brain diseases," neurological disorders caused by (probably genetic) malfunctions or imbalances of brain chemistry or even brain structure. This view of mental illnesses as physical brain diseases that can be treated (although not cured) with antipsychotic drugs has achieved the status of conventional wisdom.

Even if the brain-disease theory is true, however—and for a long time I accepted it as true—there are holes in it. For one thing, there is no direct physical way of observing schizophrenia or manic-depression, no germ or virus or damaged gene that can be seen under a microscope or through X rays or blood tests. Although certain patients diagnosed as schizophrenics have (often minor or subtle) physical brain abnormalities of various kinds, others don't. In the case of manic-depression, even though researchers think they are getting close to discovering observable physical and testable signs of manic or depressed brains (such as abnormal brain scans), they haven't yet. No clear "underlying pathology" for mental illness has been found yet, no physical "lesion" or other abnormality that has been proved to *cause* (rather than accompany or even be caused by) delusions or mood swings or paranoia. "Imbalances" in brain chemistry (neurotransmitters) have been put forward as possible causes, but research into the hugely complex soup of brain chemicals and their interactions is still too primitive to prove anything, and no one knows yet whether changes in brain chemistry, even if they are related to mood swings, delusions, etc., as they seem to be, are the cause or the effect.[7]

A good indication of how little is still known about mental illness is what the research establishment itself says. Recently I read a document on schizophrenia on the National Institute of Mental Health Web site. NIMH is the mental health division of the federal government's National Institutes of Health, the prime public funder of mental health research. To the question "Is schizophrenia caused by a physical abnormality in the brain?" NIMH replies:

> Many studies of people with schizophrenia have found abnormalities in brain structure (for example, enlargement of the fluid-filled cavities, called the ventricles, in the interior of the brain, and decreased size of certain brain regions) or function (for example, decreased metabolic activity in certain brain regions). It should be emphasized that these abnormalities are quite subtle and are not characteristic of *all* people with schizophrenia, nor do they occur *only* in individuals with this illness. Microscopic studies of brain tissue after death have also shown small changes in distribution or number of brain cells in people with schizophrenia. It appears that many (but probably not all) of these changes are present before an individual becomes ill, and schizophrenia may be, in part, a disorder in development of the brain.[8] (emphasis in the original)

Notice the tentativeness of the language, the qualifications: "Quite subtle," "not characteristic of all," "nor do they occur only," "small changes," "it appears," "may be, in part," etc. The language gets even more tentative in answer to the next question, "How is it treated?" The answer begins, *"Since schizophrenia may not be a single condition* and its causes are not yet known, current treatment methods are based on both clinical research and experience."[9] (emphasis added)

"Since schizophrenia may not be a single condition and its causes are not yet known . . ."This seems to indicate a fairly gaping hole in the conventional wisdom that "everybody knows" that schizophrenia is a brain disease. So if it "may not be a single condition," what is it? It is the diagnosis of last resort, the diagnosis arrived at after all other *observable* and *verifiable* possibilities have been ruled out. Before arriving at a diagnosis of schizophrenia, NIMH says, "It is important to rule out other illnesses, as sometimes people suffer severe mental symptoms or even psychosis due to undetected underlying medical conditions"—like brain injury or tumor, certain vitamin deficiencies or allergic reactions, sleep deprivation, and so on—which, by implication, schizophrenia is not. What is it? A skeptic might say that "schizophrenia" is Greek for "none of the above." It is the abominable snowman of illnesses. It *must* exist—we've heard the stories and seen the footprints—but, well. . . .

Much of the uncertainty surrounding schizophrenia also goes for manic-depression. It too is a condition that exists not in any kind of concrete, verifiable form—virus, bacteria, lesion, damaged gene, chemical imbalance (such as too little insulin in diabetics)—but as a collection of symptoms. Some of them, like cyclicity, are a little less amorphous than the symptoms of schizophrenia. Some of them, like hearing voices and hallucinating (in the more extreme manias), are exactly the same, which is why the two conditions are often mistaken for each other.

The theoretical uncertainties regarding mental illness have practical consequences. In the absence of positive medical tests for the various disorders, they are still defined (and diagnosed) not as specific physical conditions but as complexes of symptoms (for example, heightened mood, irritability, hallucinations, paranoia, obsessive behavior) as observed by clinicians or described by the patients themselves. And because many of these illnesses have overlapping symptoms, making a differential diagnosis (for example, telling schizophrenia from manic-depression) is a two-step process. First a psychiatrist makes a preliminary diagnosis by observing a patient's symptoms and behaviors and trying to match them against lists of criteria for the various defined mental illnesses in the bible of psychiatry, the *Diagnostic and Statistical Manual of Mental Disorders.* Then he or she prescribes a medication that matches the preliminary diagnosis: an antipsychotic if it looks like schizophrenia, lithium or an equivalent if it looks like manic-depression, Prozac or another antidepressant if it looks like unipolar depression. If the medication relieves the symptoms, the preliminary diagnosis is confirmed. If it doesn't, the psychiatrist tries something else and then changes the diagnosis based on what medication does work. If lithium or carbamazepines (lithium substitutes) mitigate the wild mood swings, the person is determined to have manic-depression. If antipsychotics work, he or she has schizophrenia. If neither of them work by themselves, the person is both manic-depressive and schizophrenic or else has a hybrid condition known as schizoaffective disorder (which, in fact, was often how Charley was diagnosed). If nothing works, the person has refractory schizophrenia with poor prognosis.

Diagnosis of mental illness, in other words, is made by reasoning *backward,* from treatment to disease. This is the reverse of general medical practice. Usually the disease determines the treatment. In psychiatry the treatment determines the disease. I saw this in the way Dr. Gray treated Charley. "This is not rocket science," he said once to Charley and me as we were trying to figure out what medications to give him. "It's mainly a process of trial and error." Trial and error based on observation over time—and a lot of drugs. For long periods, Charley took medications for all three major mental illnesses simultaneously, which seems to reduce to absurdity one of the big selling points of the brain-disease model, its supposed scientific precision—namely, that by defining mental illnesses as physical conditions and then "differentially diagnosing" which one a person has, psychiatrists can prescribe specific drugs for the specific disease and cut out unnecessary treatments—not only other drugs but labor-intensive and pricey talk therapy as well, which supposedly doesn't help with brain diseases.[10]

In the spring of 1993, however, when Charley's suicidal depression suddenly lifted, I thought I had grasped the essence of his illness—that it was mood driven—and was thus in a position to help him and his doctors focus on how to deal with it.

Delirious Mania

Convinced that his condition was a mood disorder, I decided to read up on manic-depression. I put aside my materials on schizophrenia and bought the most complete book on mood disorders I could find, a 938-page text called *Manic-Depressive Illness,* by Frederick K. Goodwin and Kay Redfield Jamison. Dr. Gray approved. "Yes, that's the party line," he nodded, mentioning that he had known Kay Jamison when they were both teaching at UCLA (where she started the Affective Disorders Clinic). Kay Jamison had a particular interest in artists, Dr. Gray added, and had made a series of educational TV shows on the relation of mood disorders and creativity.

As soon as I started reading *Manic-Depressive Illness* I felt a sense of relief. Yes, this was Charley, I thought. He wasn't schizophrenic, whatever that meant. I was particularly excited by the early, descriptive parts of the huge book, which included first-person accounts of people's experiences with mania and depression, experiences that included the most extreme psychotic symptoms: hearing voices, having delusions and hallucinations, thinking one was God. Much of the description matched almost exactly what had happened to Charley, and I kept underlining passages and showing them to him, hoping they would register with him, too, and make him see that what was wrong was not as shapeless and mysterious as he (we) had feared, that he was not floating alone in some indefinable nebula. Wouldn't knowing that he had a serious but *knowable* condition—and one shared by other valuable, creative people like Robert Lowell and Byron and van Gogh—strengthen his resolve to go on? One passage in particular impressed me. It is attributed to "a patient" but was actually written by coauthor Jamison herself, who a few years after *Manic-Depressive Illness* was published wrote an autobiography, *An Unquiet Mind,* in which she came out of the closet as having herself suffered from manic-depressive illness for years. The writing sounds very much like passages in Charley's journal blended with the expressions of despair ("Oh Father, Father . . .") uttered as we sat on the futon in late February, two nights before he cut his wrists:

> There is a particular kind of pain, elation, loneliness, and terror involved in this kind of madness. When you're high it's tremendous. The ideas and feelings are fast and frequent like shooting stars and you follow them until you find better and brighter ones. Shyness goes, the right words and gestures are suddenly there, the power to seduce and captivate others a felt certainty. . . . But, somewhere, this changes. The fast ideas are far too fast and there are far too many; overwhelming confusion replaces clarity. Memory goes. Humor and absorption on friends' faces are replaced by fear and concern. Everything previously

moving with the grain is now against—you are irritable, angry, frightened, and uncontrollable, and enmeshed totally in the blackest caves of the mind. You never knew those caves were there. It will never end. Madness carves its own reality. It goes on and on and finally there are only others' recollections of your behaviors. . . . What then, after the medications, psychiatrist, despair, depression, and overdose. . . . What did I do? Why? And most hauntingly, when will it happen again? Then, too, are the annoyances—medicine to take, resent, forget, take, resent, and forget, but always to take. . . . And always, when will it happen again? Which of my feelings are real? Which of the me's is me?[11]

A few pages later Goodwin and Jamison describe a particularly extreme condition, Bell's mania, also known as *delirious mania,*

a relatively rare, grave form of mania characterized by severe clouding of consciousness. When Bell described the syndrome in the mid-19th century, he noted its sudden onset, severe insomnia, loss of appetite, disorientation, paranoia, and extremely bizarre hallucinations and delusions. . . .[12]

They cite other authorities on delirious mania:

Consciousness, which is clear in the less severe states [of mania], becomes clouded, illusions and hallucinations may be observed, and the condition may resemble a delirium. These states are seriously debilitating and may endanger life. *Sleep* is severely disturbed in these graver psychoses, but it is also shortened in the milder forms. Another bodily symptom is the exhaustion which supervenes on months of hyper-activity and reduced sleep.[13] (emphasis in original)

They also quote Emil Kraepelin, a pioneer researcher of mood disorders, on delirious mania:

The state is accompanied by a dreamy and profound clouding of consciousness, and extraordinary and confused hallucinations and delusions. . . . Consciousness rapidly becomes clouded; the patients become stupefied, confused, bewildered, and completely lose orientation for time and place. . . . At the same time dreamy, incoherent delusions are developed.[14]

Kraepelin, I thought as I read this, could have been describing the more extreme forms of Charley's god consciousness. And I wasn't the only one who thought so. Back at college the next year, Charley wrote me a letter accompanied by a photocopy of the above pages from *Manic-Depressive Illness*, which he had found himself in the school library, having forgotten that I'd shown him the book the previous year in Santa Monica. He wrote, "I found the description of 'delirious mania' in a large book on manic depression. I thought it was interesting 'cause it seems to describe exactly my condition in 7/91 [the time of Yosemite]."

I wanted to cry out in thanks as I read this—not (obviously) because I was glad Charley had an extreme and life-threatening condition, but because we finally seemed to know what it was. Most important of all, as his library search showed, Charley finally seemed to be doing his own independent investigation, taking charge of his own life.

The encouragement I got from reading Goodwin and Jamison's book didn't end there. Another one of their findings, which corresponded to what I had observed in Charley, is that mania and depression are not as opposite and mutually exclusive as the idea of "bipolar" might indicate. Rather, they accompany each other in what psychiatry calls "mixed states." Another description attributed to "one patient" but in fact written by Jamison herself talks about this:

> I have felt infinitely worse, more dangerously depressed, when manic than when in the midst of my worst depressions. In fact, the most awful I have ever felt in my entire life . . . was the first time I was manic.[15]

As I read this I began to think back on Charley's anxiety attacks after Yosemite, how different they had seemed from what one normally thinks of as mania or elation. Now I was beginning to see why. In one particularly clear passage that I not only underlined but double-asterisked and showed to Charley, Goodwin and Jamison quote other researchers as follows:

> It would appear that the traditional conception of mania and depression as representing "opposite" pathologic extremes of affective expression is simplistic and reductionist in several ways. While most depressive states share the common affect of sadness, mania appears to be not as well characterized by elation but rather by a state of heightened overall activation, with enhanced affective expression together with lability of affect. *The co-occurrence of severe depressive thought content and*

behavior (e.g., crying) with elation and heightened anger and other affects in varying inten-
sities in the same manic individual suggests that the equation of elated mood with mania
represents an oversimplification of the varied phenomena of mania.[16] (emphasis added)

Yes, exactly! It sounded so much like what Charley had manifested the weekend after Yosemite: the elation turning to anxiety, the panic attacks, the crying, the descent into near immobility. They were all part of the same manic episode. Mania didn't mean merely elation. It meant extreme sensitivity, over-worked nerves quivering at the edge of their functioning, crackling and quiv-ering, then suddenly going dead as the circuit breaker flips off. Years later, when I read his journal, many passages (some of which I quoted earlier) seemed to speak to the same mixed states: elation and a sense of his own super-nal talent, his genius, existing at the same moment with fear and self-doubt. (*"My talent, hah! How can I flatter myself so? Where is the proof?"*)

The final proof for me that Charley was manic-depressive was the connec-tion Goodwin and Jamison draw between manic-depression and creativity—the fact, known and written about at least since Plato, that there is some kind of link between madness and artistic talent, particularly poetry and music. Throughout history, a disproportionate number of artists and other important historical figures—too many to be explained by the laws of probability alone—have suffered from mood disorders of varying severity, either manic-depression or unipolar depression. Artists, particularly musicians and poets, have also suf-fered from a larger than normal incidence of suicide. Although many of these creative people who went insane (like van Gogh) used to be called schizo-phrenic, Goodwin and Jamison and others now claim that historically schizophrenia has been overdiagnosed and manic-depressive underdiagnosed, and that actually van Gogh and other "madmen" were manic-depressive.

Exactly, I thought—Charley, too! He too was initially assumed to be schizophrenic—by Gayle at Ryles and Dr. Gray, among others—because of his "thought disorder" symptoms. But they had been wrong. I was sure of it.

From the time of Yosemite, when I thought Charley was in shock from the car crash, until now, I had been sure that his breakdowns were the result of a physical condition. I didn't know whether it was caused by temporary insomnia, drugs, some underlying instability or chemical imbalance, or a combination. But it was *something* real, something material that had happened suddenly. Part of my thinking came from my own "prosaic" temperament. Part of it came from my not knowing about his earlier episodes, his *chronic* insomnia and his mood swings. And part of it came from the undeniable physicality of his condition—the buzz, the tension in the air when he was manic, the palpable pall when he was depressed. Whatever other emotional or spiritual elements may have been involved, I thought, the problem was more than adolescent angst and uncertainties over the meaning of life. Other people—even I!—had experienced angst and uncertainty about life without flying off mountain roads or telephonically planning precrucifixion meals. There had to be more to it, and now my readings were showing me what that "more" was: a diagnosable and treatable mind/brain disorder with an old and even hallowed history, the disease of artists.

This both comforted and inspired me. Scary and life-threatening as manic-depressive illness was, especially the extreme form Charley had, compared with schizophrenia it was by far the lesser of two evils, especially because it was treatable by the relatively benign lithium (one of the natural elements) rather than the hated Navane or other neuroleptics. Everything is relative. If you have to have a major mental illness, I thought, better manic-depression than schizophrenia. All Charley had to do was take his lithium and he would have a long and almost normal life.

The Muse Is a Harsh Mistress

Artists are the raw nerve ends of humanity.

(*My godfather, the painter Jimmy Ernst*)

Selling the idea to Charley, however, was not as easy as selling it to myself.

Especially since the early nineteenth century, the links between mood disorders and creativity have given us the popular image of the artist dying young, the suffering and tormented youth hanging from a cross whose vertical beam is genius, the horizontal beam disease, arrayed against a backdrop of societal misunderstanding. In the United States the doomed young artist or rock musician too sensitive for this world—the James Dean or Janis Joplin or Jim Morrison or River Phoenix or Kurt Cobain, our modern-day Byrons and Shelleys, shooting stars who streak across the sky with a burst of glory and then disappear, but not before eclipsing the dimmer, longer-lasting stars around them—has become a cultural fixture. Was Charley fated to be one of those streaking comets?

I hoped not, and I argued the opposite position with him using all the reason and rhetoric I could muster. Although talent and mood disorder, or even madness, coexist in some artists, I said, whether one *causes* the other, and, if so, which causes which, is less clear. Many great artists are not manic-depressive, and most manic-depressives are not great artists. You can have one without the other. An artist can still be an artist and take medication if it's necessary to keep him alive. He can live a healthy life of good nutrition and exercise and minimal booze and dope and still be creative. Look at Michelangelo, or Bach, or Robert Frost, or Mark Twain or your beloved Tolstoy, I pleaded. They all died old. You can have your cake and eat it too. Stick around, boy.

But while I was mouthing one bakery metaphor he was hearing another: "half a loaf." I sounded like a dull old father who'd had his fun and now wanted to spoil everybody else's, especially his son's. And when years later I looked at his journals, particularly the early ones in which he was writing under the influence of his pre-Yosemite hypomanic flights of fancy, I could see why. His proclamations about being a genius, a great writer or concert pianist, seemed inextricably bound up with his highs. It was as if the highs gave him not only the energy but the self-confidence, the emotional propulsion, that he needed to strive to create. Like many people who experience mania, Charley was always worrying that what he called his "excursions" were connected to his talents, particularly in music and poetry, and that if he took his lithium (which, as we shall see, flattened out his moods), if he became "normalized," his talent would disappear.

"Your talent will also disappear if you're *dead*," I kept replying.

Like so many irrefutable arguments, this one made no impression whatsoever. Charley's condition—his illness or (as he himself called it) his "affliction"—seemed too basic to not only his artistic but his human identity to give up easily, even if such a thing was possible. Can a comet decide one day to become a fixed star? Like all metaphors, this one threatens to hide more than it reveals, with perhaps fatal consequences. But let us keep it in the back of our minds anyway, as I think Charley did.

And not just Charley. "Which of the me's is me?" Kay Jamison asks, echoing the plaint of the person buffeted by wild swings of feeling and experience. This basic, *Ur*-question cuts to the very heart of the "ontology" of manic-depression. Is manic-depression in fact an illness at all, or is it a fundamental part of one's being that cannot be removed without destroying that being, or at least altering it beyond recognition? How can something that produces great works—or at the very least is inextricably bound up with the production of great works—be a disease? And not just great works. How can something that unleashes such positive *life* forces—creativity, mental strength, sexual power, *joie de vivre*—be bad?[17]

Like the equation of madness with love and poetry, the notion that madness is divine, a kind of higher sanity, also goes back at least to the time of Plato. In its modern form of romanticism, the cult of individual sensibility originating in the Enlightenment, madness is equated with nonconformity. The madman is a variant of the noble savage, Rousseau's natural man driven to extremes by bourgeois tyranny and convention. He only seems mad; it's really the world that's mad. Weren't Byron or Beethoven thought to be mad? and Galileo? How many times have we heard that "So-and-so"—fill in the name of some genius—"was thought to be mad in his day"? In this view, calling eccentric or rebellious behavior "mental illness" is a way of marginalizing and delegitimizing rebellion or innovation—or of contemptuously dismissing those who psychologically implode under the pressures of "success" and the demands of the rat race. The pseudoscientific vocabulary of psychiatry is the enabling ideological legislation a repressive society uses (verbally, at first) to isolate and quarantine its rebels and denigrate its "weaker" members—those people, often the raw nerve ends, who short out under the power overload of a system that purports to be natural (as social Darwinism and its modern variations claim) but is really totally unnatural. But from the "psychiatric" *words*—mental illness, brain disease, genetic defect, gravely disabled, danger to himself and others—the psychiatric *wards,* with their locks and straitjackets and forced medication and electroconvulsive therapy and lobotomies, are soon constructed.

In a society that has elevated buying not only to a state religion but to a moral imperative ("Economists fear that a slow Christmas season could lead to recession"), a society that only half-jokingly refers to the workings of the stock exchange—the state church—as the battle between "fear and greed," such arguments are not entirely unconvincing.

Who's Crazy?

A January 7, 2000, article in the *Wall Street Journal* titled "Hey, Baby Boomers Need Their Space, Okay? Look at All Their Stuff" talks about how there was a 10 percent growth in the size of the average American home during the 1990s bull market. "Like the American waistline, the new American home is getting larger,"[18] the article reports, citing the luxury home market in particular, which has among other things produced twenty-foot-high ceilings and double-decker walk-in closets with clothing racks ten feet above the floor. "If you're ten feet tall they're great," says Diane Bean, a woman "of average height" who has such a closet (and a hard time reaching her own clothes).[19] Others with similar homes acknowledge that they don't really need all the stuff. A forty-three-year-old New York garment executive named Michael Levine, for instance, bought a five-thousand-square-foot house with a conservatory "as well as a spacious, well-appointed kitchen. 'Not that anybody cooks, but it looks impressive.'"[20] Musical instruments, as well as gourmet stoves and refrigerators, have become status symbols. Levine "wants to put a piano in his living room, though the room otherwise won't see much use. 'Do I need one? I don't need one,' he says."[21]

Even the people who build the luxury homes are becoming queasy. The *Journal:*

> "Does anybody need all this? No," says Robert Toll, chief executive officer of Toll Brothers Inc., the nation's largest high-end homebuilder. . . . To Houston architect William Stern, who builds just two or three large homes a year, the trend is appalling. The bigger-is-better trend is about "showing off to neighbors," he says. "People are saying, 'I can be a 1920s tycoon like everybody else.'"[22]

This excess—excessive even to the people providing and indulging in it—is taking place in a country which, with 4 percent of the world's population, already consumes 35 to 40 percent of the world's resources. Meanwhile a billion and a half people, one-quarter of humanity, live on a dollar a day. More than half the world's population live on two dollars a day. Is it really unfair to ask who is crazier, the guy covered in newspapers muttering in the alley or the guy who wants twenty-foot-high closets and two stoves even when he doesn't use one? Who "lacks insight" more, the guy dressed in rags talking to himself on the street or the Internet entrepreneur who builds an old-growth-redwood deck on the back of his house so he can have a better view of nature? But which of them is the social outcast and which is the role model for the adults of tomorrow—or *was* the role model, until the NASDAQ dot-com bubble burst on Friday, April 14, 2000, thirteen weeks after the *Wall Street Journal* article was written, setting off a soapy, iridescent explosion of burst bubbles that ended up drenching not only the dot-commies but the energy and telecom billionaires and countless other paper *nouveaux riches*—as well as many, many 401(k) retirees and other ordinary people along with them. But don't worry! The next bout of economic mania will produce a new crop of "1920s tycoons" to rival past crops in both grandiosity and self-delusion. It is no accident that our culture gives tacit recognition to the parallels between mental illness and "the free market economy"—capitalism—by the parallelism of its vocabulary: stock market mania, euphoria, depression, or Alan Greenspan's famous phrase, "irrational exuberance."

Given these parallels, the "brain-disease" model of psychosis, whatever else it may or may not be, is certainly a useful social bulwark against the temptation to analyze that parallelism too closely. After all, the guy in the alley has a brain disease, the entrepreneur in his twenty-foot-high closet doesn't.

Right?

Madness: Divine or Not? Two Views

Soon after Charley's first breakdown I came across a book called *The Loony-Bin Trip,* by Kate Millett. It was at a time when Lin and I, and Charley, were wrestling with the question of how to treat his condition, whether it was physico-chemical or spiritual, and particularly whether he should take medication or not, I taking the position that he should. The description on *The Loony-Bin Trip*'s back cover said that its author was a diagnosed manic-depressive, and the blurb on the front described the book as "the courageous story of a fiercely independent mind" and a "radical call for new tolerance toward mental states that are 'at the margin'—from flights of artistic inspiration to states of altered consciousness."

I bought the book, read a few pages, and put it back on the shelf for six and a half years. I had thought I wanted to hear opposing views to mine, but when I started reading, I realized that I really didn't.

The Loony-Bin Trip is Kate Millett's account of her decision to stop taking lithium in 1980 after being on it for more than six years following an episode diagnosed as manic-depression in 1973. Going off lithium led to a resumption of her mania—which she basically refuses to call an illness (and which, in fact, sounds like a much milder type than Charley's). Millett's refusal to resume taking lithium resulted in conflicts with family and friends, and later in her forced hospitalization. Eventually freed, Millett fell into a major depression, and out of desperation went back on lithium voluntarily. Later she went off it again and when she wrote *The Loony-Bin Trip* (published in 1990) she had not suffered any further breaks.

In *The Loony-Bin Trip,* Millett, a lifelong radical with a particularly strong interest in civil liberties, argues that the idea of mental illness is a social construct developed and used by a repressive society to control people who are different or who pose a threat to the sociopolitical hierarchy. In the book's preface she says she is telling her story of hospitalization and coerced medication to "help all those who have been or are about to be in the same boat, those captured and shaken by this bizarre system of beliefs: the general superstition of 'mental disease,' the physical fact of incarceration and compulsory drugs. . . ."[23]

Millett's decision to stop taking lithium had both a personal (physical) component and a sociopolitical one. She made the decision even though taking the lithium had helped her get out of the prison of psychiatric hospitalization. "Then why quit taking lithium? Six years of diarrhea. Six years of hand tremor in public places, on podiums, at receptions, at the moment one is watched and observed."[24] Later she talks about the shame and humiliation of forced hospitalization, the feeling of helplessness it engenders in the imprisoned person, especially since those doing the imprisoning—loved ones and doctors—are convinced they are doing it for the person's own good. Such benign tyranny can be especially hard to fight because it engenders doubt and guilt in the mind of the prisoner, a sort of Stockholm syndrome whereby the prisoner begins to collude in the imprisonment and the medication regimen that comes as a condition of release. For Millett, lithium "represented collusion; when I stopped I was no longer cooperating in some social and emotional way."[25]

Millett defends mania and a person's right to experience it, claiming that the

ill effects that often seem to come from it—paranoia, irritability, arrogance—
are not really a result of the mania itself but of the hostile environment created
by those around her who have been taught to fear madness.

> For we could enjoy mania if we were permitted to by the others around us so
> distressed by it, if the thing were so arranged that manics were safe to be manic
> awhile without reproach or contradiction, the thwarting and harassment on
> every side that finally exasperates them so they lose their tempers and are cross,
> offensive, defensive, antagonistic—all they are accused of being. A manic per-
> mitted to think ten thousand miles a minute is happy and harmless and could,
> if encouraged and given time, perhaps be productive as well.[26]

Millett's demedicalization of mania extends to depression also. It is not some
disease of the brain, but an internalization of the world's disapproval, "a hang-
over of penitence and self-renunciation, that complicity with social disapproval. . . ." But, she says, "Wait a moment—why call this depression?—why not
call it grief? You've permitted your grief, even your outrage, to be converted
into a disease. You have allowed your overwhelming, seemingly inexplicable
grief at what has been done to you—the trauma and shame of imprisonment—to be transformed into a mysterious psychosis. How could you?"[27]

Although I didn't (and don't) agree with all of Millett's views, it was still impossible for me to read *The Loony-Bin Trip* while Charley was alive. Her angry, pity-
ing accounts of her well-meaning but clueless friends, relatives and lovers who
loved her so much they couldn't wait to stick her in the nuthouse and drug her
up reminded me too much of myself at the times when Charley was breaking
down and I was forced, or thought I was forced, to become his jailer. Her position, like Charley's, basically boiled down to, I'll be okay if you just stop bother-
ing me. And I was answering him with exactly the same mix of concern and
condescension that Millett's family and friends had used on her. At the same time,
though, Charley had very nearly killed himself, and would again, for reasons that
had nothing to do with parental or psychiatric meddling, so he was not simply a
"happy and harmless" eccentric wandering amiably in the sun-dappled gardens of
his own mind. Thus I continually felt wind-sheared between my inclination to let
him alone and my fear of what leaving him alone might lead to. No wonder *The
Loony-Bin Trip* made me uncomfortable.

Soon after I finally read it all the way through more than a year after

Charley's death, I read Kay Redfield Jamison's memoir, *An Unquiet Mind*. I was of course already familiar with Jamison as the coauthor of *Manic-Depressive Illness*. But her memoir is very different from her textbook. It is her coming-out party, where after twenty years as one of the world's leading authorities on manic-depression she admits to being manic-depressive herself. In a strange way, Jamison's story mirrors Millett's, both in its differences and similarities. One could almost say that Jamison is Millett's twin—whether the good or evil one depending on one's opinion of mainstream psychiatry.

At first glance the two women couldn't be more different. Millett is dark-eyed, black Irish, left-wing, and a lesbian, a defender of Northern Irish political prisoners and other marginalized groups, strongly antimedication and antihospitalization. Jamison is the Establishment candidate, a blonde-haired scion of an upper-middle-class WASP military family, the good daughter who literally wrote the book (cowrote it, anyway) on manic-depressive illness, apolitical and openly heterosexual (with a predilection for slim and handsome upper-crust Englishmen). Whereas Millett hates lithium, Jamison credits it with saving her life. Whereas Millett condemns psychiatric hospitals as instruments of social control, Jamison worked in such a hospital for years before becoming a professor of medicine at that East Coast bastion of straightitude, Johns Hopkins University.

But scratch the surface and commonalities appear. Millett is an artist, both a writer and a creator of pen-and-ink drawings. Jamison is also a writer, one whose particular interest is in art and the creative process, particularly the link between mood and creativity. Although she swears by lithium and credits it with saving her life, she also suffered years of demoralizing side effects at least as bad as Millett's—"severe nausea and vomiting many times a month," occasional ataxia (inability to control muscle movements), slurred speech, and, most important, a loss of concentration and memory.[28] From the '70s to the late '80s the standard of medical practice changed, however (Jamison does not explain why), and psychiatrists found that patients could be maintained on less lithium, with correspondingly milder side effects. This led her to reduce her own dosage—very carefully, because she was terrified of having a recurrence of mania.

> The effect was dramatic. It was as though I had taken bandages off my eyes after many years of partial blindness. . . . I realized that my steps were literally

bouncier than they had been and that I was taking in sights and sounds that previously had been filtered through thick layers of gauze. . . . I felt more energetic and alive. Most significant, I could once again read without effort. It was, in short, remarkable.[29]

Not exactly a panegyric to lithium. Jamison is even more ambivalent about psychiatric hospitalization. Although she herself worked in a psych ward for years and routinely locked people up, she refused to be locked up herself during a severe depression that followed a manic episode caused by going off lithium. Her psychiatrist, afraid she was about to attempt suicide,

> repeatedly tried to persuade me to go into a psychiatric hospital, but I refused. I was horrified at the thought of being locked up; being away from familiar surroundings; having to attend group therapy meetings; and having to put up with all of the indignities and invasions of privacy that go into being on a psychiatric ward. I was working on a locked ward at the time, and I didn't relish the idea of not having the key.[30]

Jamison resisted being locked up, in other words, for exactly the same reasons anybody, including Kate Millett and Charley, resists being locked up. Not exactly a ringing endorsement of current psychiatric practice. A sense of irony is not one of Jamison's strong points, and she does not seem to notice the "do as I say, not as I do" nature of her position. A cynic could simply term it hypocrisy and ask how comfortable one would be going to a restaurant whose owner prefers to eat somewhere else. But that may not be entirely fair. Where Millett dwells on the liberating possibilities of mania, Jamison, speaking of research she did while coauthoring *Manic-Depressive Illness,* says,

> Time and again, because of both personal and clinical experiences, I found myself emphasizing the terrible lethality of manic-depressive illness, the dreadful agitation involved in mixed manic states, and the importance of dealing with patients' reluctance to take lithium or other medications to control their moods.[31]

Despite her own problems with lithium and resistance to being hospitalized, Jamison is openly contemptuous of the antimedicationists. She has no tolerance, she says, for those individuals—especially psychiatrists and psychologists—who oppose using medications for psychiatric illnesses; those clinicians who somehow draw a distinction between the suffering and treatability of "medical illnesses" such as Hodgkin's disease or breast cancer, and psychiatric illnesses such as depression, manic-depression, or schizophrenia. I believe, without doubt, that manic-depressive illness is a medical illness; I also believe that, with rare exceptions, it is malpractice to treat it without medication.[32]

There is, then, an irreducible difference between Jamison and Millett's positions. Still, Jamison is hardly some Orwellian lobotomist, some clanging sledgehammer of patriarchy. She has spent years researching and writing about the links between mood disorders and creativity, delving into what she calls the "positive features of mania and cyclothymia."[33] In the epilogue to *An Unquiet Mind* she even refuses to say that she would have been better off not being manic-depressive. "I have often asked myself whether, given the choice, I would choose to have manic-depressive illness," she remarks (imagine asking a similar question about Hodgkin's disease or breast cancer!), then continues,

> If lithium were not available to me, or didn't work for me, the answer would be a simple no—and it would be an answer laced with terror. But lithium does work for me, and therefore I suppose I can afford to pose the question. Strangely enough I think I would choose to have it. . . . I honestly believe that as a result of it I have felt more things, more deeply; had more experiences, more intensely; loved more, and been more loved. . . .[34]

Not so utterly different from Millett's defense of mania. How many other diseases would one choose to have under *any* circumstances?

And how hard to treat. The positive side of manic-depressive illness is more than an intriguing philosophical question. It becomes a practical matter when a person is faced with having to take medications that alleviate the worst aspects of depression but also tamp down the highs, the bursts of creativity, the enhanced sexuality, the feelings of oneness with the world. Imagine trying to convince a person to have chemotherapy not for a short time but every day for the rest of their life when their cancer, instead of making them feel awful, either has no symptoms at all most of the time or else makes them feel good— or better than good—a lot of the time. How long would the person put up with the nausea and hand tremors and hair loss? Continuing to take lithium becomes especially hard during the times when both the mania and depression have disappeared. The person feels normal—*except* for the drug's side effects, the flatness, the shakes, the diarrhea, the cottony feeling in the head, the humiliation of being dependent on medication. Why do I have to take this stuff? they ask. Why do I have to have my arm stuck every month and have blood taken when I'm obviously fine? No wonder I can't play the piano as well as I used to.

And no wonder the issue of lithium (and, generally, medication) compliance is such a huge one. Even Kay Redfield Jamison, with all her education and medical background and broad support network, waged a "war with lithium"[35] that almost killed her. "Psychological issues ultimately proved far more important than side effects in my prolonged resistance to lithium," she says. "I simply did not want to believe that I needed to take medication."[36] It was only after years of conflict and bouts of mania and depression that she finally realized that for her the choice "was between madness and sanity, and between life and death."[37] Contrast this with Millett's account of going off lithium entirely. It points, I think, to the enormous variability of people's individual situations and experiences, their psychologies and physiologies and needs. Brain chemistry and the problems of the mind simply do not exist on the same plane as tumors or clogged arteries or diseased lungs or kidneys.

If Kay Jamison's "it's a matter of life and death" starkness does not correspond to Kate Millett's experience, however, it does I think speak to Charley's, at least as his life was evolving after more than two years of breakdowns and recoveries. If there was ever any doubt that his condition and treatment problems were life-and-death matters, that doubt would disappear for good the second spring after his Thanksgiving breakdown, the spring of a year that started with such promise.

5

M. Butterfly and Mr. Lithy

Getting Back on the Horse

We thought we had it licked that year, 1994. Charley's postdepression recovery during the rest of 1993 had seemed complete, as much rebirth as convalescence. He continued to see both his therapeutic parents, Dr. Blum and Dr. Gray, and took his lithium as prescribed, 900 mg per day. He was doing so well that I became only mildly hysterical when, in late spring of 1993, he told me he wanted to go back to Reed, and that both Mom and Dr. Blum thought it was a good idea.

I thought it was a terrible idea. I didn't like the prospect of his being eleven hundred miles away, for one thing. For another, I still didn't think it made financial sense. One of the causes of Charley's first breakdown at Yosemite had been guilt over the financial stress that paying for Reed had put on Lin (and indirectly on me). Although he would be getting financial aid from Reed, the out-of-pocket tuition was still high, creating internal pressure to perform, and Charley didn't need more pressure. Finish college, sure. But why Reed?

California has the best state university system in the world. He could do what his sister had done, go to Santa Monica College for a year or two, then transfer to UCLA or another University of California campus.

But it wouldn't be the same thing, Charley said. He had to get back on the horse that had thrown him. So he, Lin and I met with Dr. Blum. Lin and I even met with her a time or two without Charley, ex-couples therapy, to see why we kept clashing, particularly over Reed. I convinced no one. Lin said she would pay the tuition not covered by financial aid, which meant I had no real veto power.

Reed also was leery. The school dean was prepared to take him back—Charley had a way of worming his way into your heart, he would say later—but made him sign a contract. Charley agreed to take lithium according to Dr. Gray's instructions and get a blood test every month to verify compliance. If he started acting strange at any time between regular tests, the school could demand a blood test on the spot. He also had to see a school counselor every week. No more "confidentiality" constraints, either: The school had permission to contact Lin and me if Charley began to show "unusual behavior." His refusal to comply with any of these conditions would be grounds for dismissal. All in all, a pretty tight leash—a tighter one, I realized, than Lin or I could keep him on if he stayed in L.A. against his will. At least back at Reed he would have no excuses; it was where he wanted to be. So what the hell, I thought, let's give it a try. Maybe he did need to get back on the horse. The kid had guts. He'd tried Reed twice before. Maybe the third time would be the charm. In the end, not wanting to be the perennial Dr. No, I gave in.

Once I decided to support the decision, I did it wholeheartedly. I didn't crab or cavil or sabotage. "Dad says I'm much more mature this summer than last," Charley wrote in his journal two days before flying to Portland in August, adding, "It's hard for me to tell. I pray this year at school will go smoothly and successfully. I feel so much better, immeasurably better than I did in February. It's amazing what six months, not a lot of time, can do for one's health. 180°. I thank God for the recovery I've made."

A few pages earlier (July 21) Charley had written the following poem, called "Mortification":

Were Time not so finite
The hand of Fate not so strong

I might erase all contrite
Recollections like a song.

Like a jarring song unwanted
On memory's cassette
It plays itself undaunted
With the rhythm of regret.

So Muse, take or borrow, my
Repentance and my weeping
I ask surcease of sorrow
And leave them in your keeping.

"What is done cannot be undone"
Once a wise woman stated
The forgiveness has begun
If contrition is abated.

The prospects looked good. Charley's situation as he went back to Reed was as promising as one could ask for under the circumstances (always that qualifier). His "affliction," awful as it was, appeared to be treatable. He would be at the place he wanted most to be, highly motivated to keep to his treatment regimen, which included the relatively benign lithium, not the hated Navane or other antipsychotics. He would be surrounded by a support network of people who cared about him.

What could go wrong?

For months, nothing. In midautumn, things were looking so good that I decided to visit him. This was a stretch for me. After two numbing bus trips to and from Portland the previous year and a trip to the deserted, frozen campus the past January (during winter break) to pack up Charley's room, I had sworn never to let my gaze fall on the city or on Reed again. But now, at the beginning of November, delighted that Charley was well and wanting to show my support, I flew up for the school's annual parents' weekend. We attended parent-kid events and wine-and-cheese receptions and bagel-and-croissant breakfasts where I talked to Charley's counselor and a number of his teachers and the school president. I met a number of his friends, visited his new dorm, and sat in on classes on modern German philosophy. We ate Greek and Cajun food and saw Peter Weir's movie, *Fearless,* about a man who survives a plane crash and decides he's immortal. We both loved it. Charley said it reminded him a lot of what he had been through, which I had somehow known even before he told me. I told him I could not have been more proud. He had gotten back on the horse.

M. Butterfly

Shizuko, or "Juko," was just a name to me while Charley was alive, at most a slightly exotic female voice on my phone when she called asking for him. He had mentioned her to me a number of times with a kind of uncharacteristic reverence, and I had the impression she had played a different role in his life than most of his other girlfriends, who, once they were gone (like Stephanie) were really gone, cast off into the netherworld of disillusion and betrayal, or else remained just beyond his inner horizon, only their auras still visible, like suns already set. From the way Charley talked, Shizuko seemed to fit into neither category, neither Hadean shade nor afterglow. For a time I wasn't even sure they had been a couple.

It was not until I actually met Shizuko in March 1998, about a year and a half after Charley's death, that my scattered impressions began to come together. She had long since finished Reed and was back home in Japan, occasionally in touch with Lin by letter or phone. One day she called Lin from Boston. She had been visiting friends and was stopping over in L.A. on her way home, and she wanted to meet "Charley's parents." Lin invited her to stay with her for two days before continuing on to Japan, and she made arrangements to meet Shizuko's plane when it arrived from Boston. I got a slight preview of what "Juko" was like when Lin told me about the phone conversation arranging the pickup. The two had never met and neither knew what the other looked like. "How will I know you?" Lin asked.

"Well, I'm Japanese," Shizuko replied.

So I was prepared for the wit. But I wasn't prepared for the beauty, for the slim, willowy figure that floated into my apartment, accompanied by Lin, the first evening of her stay. She was twenty-six (a year older than Charley would have been), of medium height, with an oval face and clear, dark eyes and gleaming shoulder-length black hair. She spoke nearly perfect English. Her manner was one of calm intelligence, although not the eyes-averted, self-obliterating calm of the mythological "Asian woman." Charley himself had grasped her layeredness in an early letter that Shizuko later copied and sent to me. It was from when they first became friends, in October 1993, shortly before my parents' weekend visit. "Juko," he wrote, "Was ever such serenity manifest in one person? One who has such insight and depth, yet without pretension or imprudence. Of the temporal world she is, but the ethereal world is her close ally. What's more she has great taste in friends! C."

When Lin introduced us, I told her I was glad to meet her finally, after all this time, and was slightly embarrassed when she told me that actually we had met once before, under a ficus tree near the Reed library four and a half years ago, during my parents' weekend visit to see Charley. I could feel myself blushing as I apologized for not remembering (how could I have not remembered this beautiful creature? I really *was* getting old!), saying that I had met a lot of people that weekend and didn't know at the time that she and Charley had a special relationship. She laughed—it was her turn to blush—and said that at that time, early in the school year, their relationship wasn't yet that special.

They had formed a very close, Platonic friendship that October, she told Lin and me over dinner, and that's how it remained for most of the year. She spent six hours a day with Charley, who was living in a dorm, she off campus. They would get together around four every day at the student union, where he would play the piano while she kept him company doing her organic chemistry homework, preparing for the medical school she was now, in 1998, attending in Japan. It was part of a deal she had made with her parents. She had wanted to be a painter, they wanted her to be a doctor (her father was a urologist). They compromised. She went to art school for one year after graduating from Reed, then transferred to medical school. Charley hadn't wanted her to go to med school, she told Lin and me, and he couldn't understand why she would do it just to satisfy her parents. We all chuckled as she talked about Charley's complete inability to understand the concept, central to Japanese culture, of duty to one's family.

We talked for several hours. The next evening Lin had a previous engagement, and dropped Shizuko off at my apartment around six. We spent the entire evening sorting through Charley's papers—letters, schoolwork—and talking. I fed her some homemade lentil soup—she looked so thin—as she described an ongoing crisis in her family. Her mother had tried to kill herself about two years before and was currently hospitalized with severe depression. Her father had been having a long-term affair with his secretary, a woman about ten years older than Shizuko, and wanted a divorce. Shizuko had become her mother's main caretaker since the latter's hospitalization. Medical school was about three hours by train from Tokyo, and she had spent the last year or so coming back to Tokyo every weekend to take her mother home from the hospital for two days, then back. She also worked a couple of part-time jobs. All that and a full load of med school courses. I was getting exhausted just listening.

Juko's role as the eldest sibling and, for the past several years, essentially her mother's mother and the head of household may partially explain her and Charley's attraction. Several of Charley's girlfriends or "muses" had come from backgrounds where mental illness and caretaking were familiar. Aside from Shizuko herself, another girlfriend had a manic-depressive sister, another's whole family was torn by severe depression and alcoholism, another had a mother who was a therapist, and Charley may have seemed familiar territory to these young women. Juko herself described their relationship as at least partially her taking care of him. She had cooked, ironed his shirts (she mentioned ironing several times), kept him company for hours every day. In some respects their relationship sounded almost like a traditional marriage.

As we went through a large box of Charley's papers, Shizuko sorted them into files marked "Girlfriends," "Family," "School," etc. She said she thought one of the things that had brought her and Charley together was their common condition of being culturally or psychologically in two places at once. She was in a sense riven into two cultural halves: a very traditional Japanese half—dedicating herself to family, training to be a doctor like her father, taking care of her mother, speaking a language of indirection (there is no second person in Japanese grammar—you talk to people in the third person); and a more individualistic American half. She said that she had sensed a similar division in Charley: caught uncomfortably between the physical world, in which he was never fully at home, and an internal world, part illness, part music and poetry.

She and Lin and I had talked about some of this at dinner the night before, trying to figure Charley out, to grasp in death the shimmering mirage that had eluded us in life. Since that discussion I have done further reading about one of the common features that artists with mood disorders have seemed to share historically, particularly poets: a tendency to be mercurial and chameleonic, to change form and color with light or season. A friend of Byron talked about the poet's "chameleon-like character or manner," and Byron himself said to the same friend that "I am so changeable, being every thing by turns and nothing long. . . ."[1] Charley had increasingly seemed to me to be like this after his first breakdown. I told Shizuko my theory of Charley's inborn skittishness, a lack of solid grounding in the world that had caused, among other things, his accident-proneness and mood swings. A lifetime of being somewhat unsettled internally, not quite at home in the world, had made him unable to develop a solid ego, a sense of himself. As he reached adolescence and developed chronic insomnia, the instability got worse and graduated first into hypomanic and later extreme manic episodes accompanied by full-fledged psychosis.

Shizuko, Lin and I compared notes. Charley had had a fascination with acting, with role playing, with the external accoutrements of character. I thought it was significant that his models for acting were not the internal American "method" school of the Actors' Studio, but rather the British classical school that stressed speech and technical training, working from the outside in. His favorite actor was Laurence Olivier, who had reportedly said "Give me a hat and I'll give you a character." Charley loved such props. He had an Anglophile side, and liked to wear an old tweed golfer's cap and smoke Benson and Hedges. He refused to wear polyester, only cotton, and hated wire clothes hangers. He didn't like computers. His most prized possession was a 1925 Underwood typewriter, with its clackety-clack and crooked old letters. He loved being "an entertainer," as Lin said when he was still little. He liked doing animal imitations. Once, when he and Lin and I were driving through northern California going to Reed, we passed a field of cattle. Charley was in the back. Suddenly I heard a low rumble. "Moooooo . . . !"

"That was great, Charley," Lin said. "Do a sheep."

"Baaaaaaaaah . . . !" A horse and goat soon followed. A regular backseat barnyard.

His love of the changeable, of metamorphosis, extended to art. His favorite artist was Magritte, the painter of the surreal *trompe l'oeil,* the visual pun. He loved Poe and Oscar Wilde, two misplaced characters if there ever were any. His favorite musician was "that English singer—I forget his name," Shizuko said.

"David Bowie," I replied. I said that I thought Charley's powerful affinity for Bowie was significant. It had gotten so I almost knew when a manic episode was starting because Charley, who usually listened to classical music, would suddenly start playing Bowie albums, sometimes standing up close to the stereo, as if listening to something on the other side of the music. He told me more than once—for example, during his Thanksgiving breakdown—that Bowie actually spoke to him directly. It may have been Bowie's own epicene, chameleonic character that created this affinity. Bowie was "the man who fell to Earth," Ziggy Stardust, always metamorphosing, in flux, androgynous, wearing weird makeup, changing his appearance and persona with each album. It was as if he was a role model for Charley, giving him permission to be like that himself, the battle of the sexes fought to an amicable draw. Shizuko added that Charley himself talked about how everybody wears masks, and how he had liked to put on makeup and cross-dress. This surprised Lin and me at first; we hadn't known. But it fit into the picture of Charley's fluidity, his "qualities of androgyny," his love of costumes and props. It was as if he was always seeking to build an external form, a mold into which he could pour his quicksilver self and then solidify. But solidity was elusive. He was like mercury, a metal but without metal's cohesiveness, constantly threatening to break into shimmering drops.

Except in his music. His piano playing—the thing that "keeps me from going crazy," he had written—gave a form and direction to his mercuriality. When he played his favorites—Chopin, Beethoven, Schubert, Scott Joplin— the jittery quicksilver of his nature seemed to stream out through his fingertips, through the keys and strings and into the air, for a while leaving his inner self relaxed.

Shizuko, herself a talented pianist, talked a lot about Charley's playing, particularly in the Reed student union, a charmless building whose drafty, wood-floored common room reminded me of an old summer camp. She thought Charley played the clunky old piano in the SU rather than the better ones in the practice rooms in Prexy, the music building, because there were other students hanging out in the SU. Charley's playing was at least partly for them, a way of trying to reach them in a way he couldn't reach them verbally despite his sophisticated vocabulary. Or because of it. As Charley got older and his breakdowns increased in number, he tended even in periods of relative normality to adopt a rather stilted manner and archaic word usage that, although doubtless a protective coating which, like a hardening shell, grew more and more inflexible as the inner thing it was protecting grew more and more delicate, appeared to outsiders as mere conceit. Reed was a small school, about fifteen hundred students, where everybody knew everything about everybody. During Charley's third try in 1993–1994, the other students must have known about his history, particularly the November 1992 on-campus breakdown, the weird phone calls, the obsession over the woman professor and the fugitive kiss, the hospitalization, the medical leave. And this history, together with his eccentricities and sometimes off-putting manner, had the effect of making a lot of people upset with him, unable or unwilling to see behind the physical and verbal façade—what he called the mask. He was "too beautiful" for Reed, Shizuko said, and came across as pretentious. Because of the nature of the school and its curriculum, its heavy academic emphasis (the dean once described the school to me as an "academic boot camp"), students tended to take refuge in intellectualism, frowning on feelings. Charley, by contrast, often expressed himself nonintellectually. This was especially true in his relationship with her, Shizuko said. Their communication and the intimacy they established was largely nonverbal, expressed through music. For all his well-read intelligence, Charley was not basically an academic intellectual. He was an artist, a raw nerve end, not at home in the drill sergeant environment of Reed. Shizuko thought that his playing in the student union was a way of bridging the intellectual-artist gap, of giving something to these other students, to reach them in a way he couldn't reach them directly because of his alienating manner, a manner whose real content he had recognized years earlier (*"Is my superiority complex really an inferiority one?"*) but which he couldn't, despite this understanding, alter—except when he played the piano. Shizuko said that in Charley's playing, particularly of Chopin, he achieved a directness and purity of expression that otherwise eluded him. When he played—and I had seen this myself—all his irritating, alienating mannerisms melted into air, the false self (or selves) falling away like the old, cast-off shell of some molting crab. He was able for ten minutes or thirty minutes or an hour to shake off that dead integument, that protective rigidity, and reveal his basic tenderness and craving for connection that he wrote about in his journal during that sleepless May full-moon night as he worried about more madness: *"All the composers have left behind traces of themselves, and are therefore immortal since they are still played. Recognizing their love of humankind as I play their music I am exercising my sense of the commonality of man."*

Hard as he tried, though, Juko said, Charley's efforts to break through his isolation fell largely on deaf ears. Most of the other students *("overloaded with work," "surly, unkempt in their attire")* weren't interested in classical music, and even when they were, the piano in the SU was old and out of tune and didn't sound very good even when played well. So even when Charley was himself being sincere and expressive, it was in an arena and in a way that did not particularly appeal to the people he wanted so much to reach. But he did try.

That was their relationship for most of the year: Juko sitting and studying, Charley playing (often when *he* should have been studying). As spring approached, however, things changed. Shizuko explained the change to me somewhat sheepishly, as resulting from the coming of spring itself: the rising of the sap, the reigniting of the torch of life by the warming sun, the burgeoning of new green after long gray winter.

I didn't hear all of this from Shizuko herself during her two days in L.A. Some of it came from her letters to Charley that I found among his papers after she left, some of it came from later e-mails and conversations. Earlier in the year, she told me, before they established their musical friendship, Charley made some advances, trying to kiss her a couple of times, but she had a boyfriend and rebuffed him. Charley accepted that, and their relationship settled into its Platonic, shirt-ironing routine. Then, in early spring, that original dynamic reemerged, but reversed. Shizuko's feelings for Charley seemed to grow more intense. Or perhaps she had harbored them for a while and now they finally burst out. Whatever the case, she wrote him a passionate (undated) letter in late March or early April of 1994.

> It is now the time to tell you how I feel since I am unable to deceive myself into thinking that I only want to be friends with you. Continuous conflicts stir my mind and throw me into confusion whenever I see you. Although I don't want to lose the friendship we have, I am faced with the despair of not knowing anything anymore. I thought that if I can convince you that I am just a good

friend to you, eventually I will convince myself that that is in fact what I want. So, I will keep this emotion hidden within, carefully so no one can detect it. I can bear it no longer!

This tone continues for two pages, one of both longing and fear, fear that her declaration will upset the precarious balance of friendship. But her feelings are too intense to hide. "Understand that this letter comes from the bottom of my heart," she says near the end. "I rather feel naked since I exposed my feelings so much."

"Shizuko dear," Charley writes back,

I don't know if you expected some response of some sort, oral or written or with body language or whatever (now *my* English is faltering) so I'm giving you a note. You know already that I'm very fond of you and that I value our friendship a lot. So I figure why clutter it with notions of love, etc., things which are more precarious than friendship? A while ago Cedar [a girlfriend for a brief time] asked me what I had with you. I told her there were no sexual ties in our relationship and that's why I valued it. She of course looked at me strangely and made me rephrase my thoughts. You didn't want to talk about our relationship before, so you've forced it to come to this prosaic (look it up) candor. I am somewhat flattered by your flustered state but you need not stay in it much longer.

This is not a blowoff letter you know. I will continue to like you as I have before. If you want to be aloof that is your option.

In the paper I'm writing on Descartes I talk of the freedom which boundaries allow, how enhansive they can be. You understand. Time will tell all I suppose, so don't test him.

With the knowledge that you're going to be alright, Charley.

Shizuko's response to this non-blowoff blowoff letter was, at least on the surface, a brave expression of acceptance and relief. No doubt we have all felt it in similar circumstances: Well, at least *that's* over. The hot, torturing blister of infatuation had burst—or been punctured; the self-enslaving chains of obsession had suddenly been loosed. "How pleased and relieved I felt after I received your letter!" she writes back. "Now things have settled, although I may not like the outcome, I feel free again."

Why Charley's rejection? His journals and my talks with Shizuko indicated that he was carrying a torch for someone else at the time—Cedar, possibly—

and that if Shizuko had been Pallas Athena and Aphrodite combined it wouldn't have made any difference. Or maybe, after her initial rebuffs the previous fall, he had reframed his vision of their relationship as one of friendship, and as far as he was concerned that was that.

So matters stood for a time. Thus far their relationship, and this latest twist in it, was nothing that unusual—two good people in a slightly mismatched friendship in which one wants more, the other doesn't. Too bad, but that's life. And if Charley and Juko's story had ended there, or if they had merely reverted back to their former state, I would not recount it in such detail.

But they didn't.

Mr. Lithy

Lithium Carbonate

Pharmacology: Antimanic agent . . . The mechanism whereby lithium controls manic episodes and *possibly* influences affective disorders *is not yet known.* . . . The primary *toxic effects* in man appear to be on the central nervous system [CNS].

Indications: Acute manic episodes in patients with bipolar affective disorders. Maintenance therapy has been found useful in preventing or diminishing the frequency of subsequent relapses in bipolar manic-depressive patients (with a history of mania).

Adverse Effects: *The following adverse effects have been reported usually related to serum lithium concentrations:* Gastrointestinal: *Anorexia, nausea, vomiting, diarrhea, thirst, dryness of the mouth, metallic taste, abdominal pain, weight gain or loss.* Neurologic: *General muscle weakness, ataxia, tremor, muscle hyperirritability (fasciculation, twitchings, especially of facial muscles and clonic movements of the limbs), choreoathetotic movement, hyperactive deep tendon reflexes.* CNS: *Anesthesia of the skin, slurred speech, blurring of vision, blackout spells, headache, seizures, cranial nerve involvement, psychomotor retardation, somnolence, toxic confusional states, restlessness, stupor, coma, acute dystonia* . . . Dermatologic: *Dryness and thinning of the hair, leg ulcers, skin rash* . . . Miscellaneous: *General fatigue, dehydration, peripheral edema.*[2] (emphasis added)

> *They say you are a worthy friend, Mr. Lithy,*
> *The medical salvation of the warped mind.*
> *But let me tell you, and I may be pithy,*
> *I'm not sure you are so kind.*

Ere I made your acquaintance, Mr. L.,
I with tattered soul and shattered nerves,
Though I lived beneath a demon's spell
I KNEW MYSELF WELL, if memory serves.
And thanks to those MD's, eternally omniscient,
Who know many terms and made you a sacred entity
And put the broken life on a course more efficient,
At the dear cost of IDENTITY.
> *(Untitled, written by Charley in L.A., early January 1994, 3 A.M.)*

I dreamed—recently—such a dream of flight. Those flying dreams many of us know. Most are pleasant, but to be suspended in the skies, somehow guiltily, over fields and trees, evading the scope of others unable to descend; 'tis a frightful prospect.

> *(Charley's journal, two pages after the*
> *Mr. Lithy poem, winter 1994)*

When Charley wrote the Mr. Lithy poem one sleepless night, he was staying with me in Santa Monica on his winter break, taking his lithium without complaint. During that month, which included the big L.A. earthquake of January 17, 1994, he was his rational self. When he went back to Reed on the twenty-first he seemed stable, and my journal for the entire period makes no mention of any problems. Up to then and for some time afterward, as far as I can determine now from various sources, Charley had been keeping to the letter of his bargain with Reed, seeing a counselor every week, taking his lithium and getting his blood tested for compliance every month. As of February, the time of his first blood test after the winter break, his lithium level was 0.7, comfortably within the therapeutic range of 0.5 to 1.5.

But in life as in nuclear weapons treaties, the devil is in the details. Details like one's sense of self, one's autonomy, the coffee one drinks and the cigarettes one smokes and the other substances one takes to counteract the flattening effects of psychoactive medications. Charley's journals for the period indicate that he was doing various things to unflatten himself. In an undated, pre-Christmas entry he talks about trying (unsuccessfully, thank God) to get a prescription for amphetamines from the Reed school physician. Then: "I started doing TM again and it seems to help a great deal. It gives me truly an advantage in life." He may also have been titrating his lithium—taking less or none for periods between blood tests, then taking more to get his level back up to therapeutic. I have no direct evidence for this, but a poem in his journal in late January when he was back at Reed expresses his depression (which lithium is supposed to mitigate) at one moment frozen in time:

> *The January mist blends smoothly with cigarette smoke*
> *Dragging slowly I feel I've befriended death.*
> *But it's on the stale taste of life I choke.*
> *As the smell of salt tears exudes with my breath*
> *In this sour day the Earth has no charm*
> *No one clear thought that propagates hope.*
> *And each complex soul that once seemed warm.*

A note in the margin says "must finish." Around the same time:

> This wine and pot lifestyle is becoming tedious. I could not nod off until after 4 last night, after a Xanax. I have the disadvantage of being hypercontemplative when I take (most) drugs. . . .
> I bought some hashish today to boot. Must I be such an adolescent? That's my excuse—I'm an adolescent, thus I must be asinine. I am turning over a new leaf. I have recognized my transgressions. Is that not the first step? to fully appreciate one's errings? In less than a year I will quit smoking *for good* on my 22 birthday.[3] Thence I shall be able to achieve physical perfection. From hereon I will limit cannabis intake to six puffs per week—at the most.

Despite everything, Charley kept himself under control into spring. He came to L.A. on a five-day visit during his March break and stayed with me; my journal doesn't indicate any problems. He was writing film reviews for the Reed student newspaper and mentioned a movie he had recently seen and liked a lot: *M. Butterfly,* with Jeremy Irons, an ironic retelling of Puccini's opera, *Madame Butterfly,* about the Japanese concubine (a male transvestite Chinese opera performer in the film version) who, cast off by her American lover, commits suicide by hara-kiri. I later found in his journal a draft of a letter to Irons complimenting him on his performance and wondering—"It's a terrific longshot that you'll respond"—if Irons might be interested in taking him on as a pupil. "I do possess some acting potential. And I should be honoured to meet you; if not soon then perhaps by chance some other day. Yours humbly . . ." Shades of path B here, the writer/pianist/artist path to immortality, although for the moment expressed with moderation.

There is nothing more about Charley in my journal until a few days after he got back to Reed in late March. Then came a phone call one night to talk about a scare he had had the night before, an "intense physical reaction" while playing Beethoven's last piano sonata, the C-minor opus 111. He had telephoned Lin after it happened, "scared." But my journal reports that he "sounded okay tonight. Somewhat chastened."

It should have been a warning: Being overwhelmed by Beethoven (as in the car at Yosemite before the crash), the fear—code terms for heightened mood. But I was taking the glass-half-full approach. My journal:

> Re: Being scared. There are, or can be, positive aspects to fear. Fear of what is dangerous or threatening, fear when you're at risk, as Ch. is re: mood disorder, has historically played a positive evolutionary role. The ones who walked up to the saber-toothed tiger and said, Hello, Kitty, didn't make the evolutionary cut. . . . Healthy fear is okay.

Wishful thinking. The saber-toothed tiger was coiling, fangs bared. Charley's journal entries for the period—the following are from the end of March and mid-April—are like an encroaching low-pressure weather system, not the storm yet, but the calm before:

> In my small dorm room I have a strange solitude, for I could stay here indefinitely to think without interruption. With a bedpan I could accomplish much. The other two places where I spend most of my time are Prexy [the music building] and the library. The library I've decided is the converging point for lost souls, those souls of course which have not shed yet the human form. Now I make presumption. Yes, but the books which I see on those these desks can be only for souls who have made already much inquiry. Now at the impasse frustration resides. Coffee and cigarettes become fuel to lead over disheartenment. And now that spring is here distraction becomes easier to find. Prexy, however, is the building in which the living interact with the dead, actively rather than passively. It rains now. 3/30/94.
>
> 4/19/94, 4 A.M.: Some days are for sleeping and some days are for living. Sunday was for sleeping and Monday was for living. I went to all my classes including Nat Sci lab. I played three sports vigorously, read and ate and also had sex, not to mention sending a picture to David Bowie [uh-oh!—JA]. Indeed a certain madness has

come w/April. Everything has been put to nature's disposal. The terrific thing is that one must succumb to her flow or else die. Could it be?

As spring progressed, sometime between late April and mid-May, Charley stopped taking his lithium. By late May, when I learned what was happening, his blood lithium level was 0.2, below the minimum therapeutic level of 0.5. The lowered lithium level, added to the effects of the drugs, coffee, sleeplessness, meditation and other stimulants he had been using for months—including crystal methamphetamines and synthetics like XTC, Shizuko told me later—began to push him toward the edge. Shizuko thought the reason for Charley's taking uppers and going off lithium was the pressure of schoolwork, particularly his end-of-year papers (he was having special trouble with Milton). Writing papers wasn't easy for Charley; he preferred playing piano.[4] When it came time to do the reading and writing, Juko thought, he needed to be able to concentrate better, to be less mentally flat. This is a common reason for going off lithium. Both Kate Millett and Kay Jamison talk about it. It is not just nostalgia for the highs, but also frustration over "Mr. Lithy's" dulling, slowing effect, like weights around a runner's ankles—tolerable for practice, maybe, but not for the actual race.

We have seen how all of Charley's breakdowns were marked at the beginning by a romantic fixation: standing too near the girl at Yosemite, thinking the young woman in San Francisco was "Allison," becoming obsessed with the humanities professor at Reed. This is typical of budding mania, one of whose symptoms is hypersexuality, the feeling of erotic omnipotence in which (as Kay Jamison says) "the power to seduce and captivate others [is] a felt certainty." It is possible that Charley's romantic fixations were particularly intense because of his own sexual doubts, a form of overcompensation, of trying to win the "battle of the sexes" which, like the romantic obsessions, also characterized his breakdowns.

Whatever the case, when one is feeling irresistible the word takes on a literal meaning, and the notion that the object of one's longing may not share that longing becomes unthinkable. Here we arrive at the very essence of what mental illness, at least in its most extreme form, is all about, and why I think Kate Millett and the other defenders of madness as a valid form of self-expression or social criticism are in the end wrong. That essence is solipsism, or what one author of a book about his own manic-depression called "ego-centricity," the belief that no one but oneself really exists as an autonomous being.[5] For the mad person, not only is all the world a stage, but he or she is the only live performer. The other inhabitants are props in a solo show that is so magnificent it doesn't even need an audience; the performer provides his own. Of course, in many ways this is not so different from how everybody thinks or acts at times; we all (well, most of us) have a tendency to "objectify" other people, manipulate them, not to feel empathy and so forth. But in a way, that is the whole point. Madness (whether called manic-depression, schizophrenia or whatever) is not some unique, inhuman condition, but an extreme form of ordinary human behavior. Hence the great difficulty (if not impossibility) of categorizing and isolating madness as a structural deficiency of the brain or some other foreign pathogen. *"Everybody, Dad, is just a little bit crazy,"* Charley had written me from San Francisco General, a formulation that I saw (I believe correctly) as a sign of his recovery. What gives psychosis its special look or feel is that whereas in supposedly sane people ordinary self-centeredness is blended with and moderated by empathy and feelings of commonality (not to mention shame and guilt), in psychosis it separates out from those countercurrents and stands alone at one pole of the personality, the top-of-the-world psychopathic side, triumphantly waving the flag of pure ego.[6]

One of the forms this egotism took in Charley in the spring of 1994 was a change in his behavior toward Shizuko. For whatever reason—frustration over the failure of other infatuations, simple erotic tension, or something deeper and more indescribable—Charley, having so recently rebuffed her, decided that he and Shizuko should become lovers after all and began, in yet another inversion of their relationship, to pursue her again. But because this change was more of mood than of heart, his behavior now seemed to her odd and, particularly in light of his recent (albeit diplomatic) blowoff, insincere. And in a sense it was. The hypersexuality of growing mania is characterized by conquest and manipulation, not sympathy and affection, and being pursued in this suddenly avid but strangely unloving way by someone who had recently rejected her felt artificial to Shizuko, artificial and hurtful. Doubly hurtful, because not only did it feel impersonal, it felt almost like a parody of the passion she herself still felt.

That was how she experienced Charley's sudden pursuit of her: inexplicable, disconcerting and insincere. Despite her doubts, however, she gave in to him. Charley could be extremely pushy when he was like this, and she did, of course, still care for him. Their sexual relationship was brief, but with consequences that were painful for her and nearly fatal for him.

Three on a Honeymoon

"Life is what happens while you're making plans to kill yourself," I wrote in my journal on Friday morning, May 20, 1994, after the latest coffin nail arrived from Portland.

I don't know whether I had felt more than ordinary trepidation when the phone rang ten minutes earlier, or whether I made the trepidation up afterward. But after ten years of having teenage kids, and almost three years after Yosemite, I tended to feel the same way about phone calls—especially Friday phone calls!—that football coach Woody Hayes felt about the forward pass. "When you throw a pass," Hayes said, "only three things can happen, and two of them are bad."

"Hi. This is Joe Jaspers, from Reed?" the voice said when I answered the phone. "We met last fall?"

It wasn't the California Highway Patrol this time, but it wasn't good either, I knew that right away. Joe Jaspers was Charley's school counselor, the one he had been seeing once a week. I had met him during parents' weekend. He was an ex-hippie, a little younger than I, decent enough, a little touchy-feely for my taste. Charley had mentioned with a trace of condescension that Joe once told him he'd taken 250 acid trips when he was younger, which of course thrilled me. The perfect mentor for my kid. Still, Charley had continued to meet with him as agreed in the Reed contract, so what did I know? Now school was over. Charley was due to fly to L.A. the following morning for ten days, then go back to Portland to work for the summer, subletting an apartment near campus from a fellow student. I had spoken by phone to "the ol' rugrat" four days before and he sounded good, a little stressed and breathless, maybe, but happy to be through with school, triumphant at having gotten back on the horse, finished the race, fulfilled his contract, conquered Reed College. His only worry had been completing a paper on Milton. As far as I could gather—or had gathered till fifteen seconds earlier—everything was fine.

"Hi, Joe. What's happening?"

"Well . . ." His voice had the slightly bedside heartiness I have learned to associate with certain kinds of psychotherapists and auto repairmen. "It seems that Charley has had a little slip."

"What kind of a slip?" I could hear my own voice getting high and flutey.

Joe proceeded to tell me, his own voice reassuring and no-big-deal-ish, that Charley had stopped taking his lithium a few days earlier—"apparently as kind of a celebration of the end of school." This, along with a "small amount of speed," had precipitated a manic episode that had included, among other things, Charley's crawling through a bramble bush and swamp in the canyon near his dorm. He had apparently scratched himself up rather badly and shown up at the infirmary Thursday morning, confused, frightened and covered with mud. "But showing up at the infirmary was a good sign," Joe assured me. "It shows that he knew he needed help."

I asked what had happened next.

"Well, Dr. Newhall"—the school physician and somebody Charley truly liked—"gave him some Klonopin and that seems to have brought him down off the high. He seems a lot better this morning. He's at home, resting."

Joe had spent the previous morning after the infirmary with Charley, bought him refills of his medication—the Klonopin and some more lithium—taken him to breakfast and generally looked after him most of the day. I thanked him and said I would reimburse him for the drugs and the food. Joe said he thought that if Charley got back on the lithium regularly and kept taking the Klonopin—a sedative that can act as an antipsychotic—he could make a quick recovery.

Great! I was in the early, grasping-at-straws stage. The guy was a professional, right?—a veteran of 250 acid trips. If he thought everything was going to be fine, who was I to argue? More profuse thank-yous, wishes for a good summer, thanks for helping Charley. Good-bye.

Hang up. I stared dully at a large painting of mine on the wall in front of me, a ballerina I had started seven years before and worked on periodically since. She stood tall and sturdy, perfectly balanced on her right toe, left leg raised parallel to the floor, both arms extended, fingers arrayed like feathers glowing in the light of a window behind her. A phoenix rising. At least that's what I had tried for. I had painted her at another time, when my own life was unbalanced; maybe being able to paint balance could save me. I looked at her for a while longer, sipping lukewarm tea, postponing for a minute the call I had to make.

It had been too good to be true, of course, the idea that Charley had stabilized permanently, that after two major breakdowns and near-suicides in two years he had bought into his recovery. The minute his contract with the school had run out—possibly even earlier, I didn't know for sure—he'd ditched his lithium. And so his prospective arrival the next day to visit, which I had been looking forward to as a "hail the conquering hero" coronation, was about to become something quite different. Even if Joe was right and he was restabilizing quickly, what he had done—going off the lithium and taking speed, the latter a new and potentially fatal wrinkle for someone prone to mania—was raising issues which, fool that I was, I had convinced myself were over and done with.

But he was only twenty-one, I thought as I looked at the ballerina and scribbled the "Life is what happens" line in my journal. A twenty-one-year-old Anglo male, and in certain respects a young one. How could I expect him to act like a grown-up? When I was twenty-one, I was in many ways as big a basket case as he was, a budding alcoholic, a drunken driver, a twit. My only virtue was that I wasn't "mentally ill," so my failings and stupidities hadn't melded with psychotic breakdowns or led to conscious suicide attempts, although at least a couple of times my drunken driving put me and others at risk and my male supremacist behavior while drunk and stoned on marijuana led at least once to groping a woman at a party (or so I was told later; I was blacked out when I did it) in a way that would nowadays probably be prosecutable as sexual assault, although at the time (1969) it was merely considered uncool. How, I wondered as I sat and stared at the ballerina, not wanting to dial the phone, could I judge him more strictly than I had been judged?

"Hullo?" He answered after the third ring, his voice druggy.

Trying to sound normal: "Hi, Charley. It's Dad. How's it going? I got a call a little while ago from Joe Jaspers."

"Oh, yeah . . ."

"Are you okay? He said you had another episode."

"Another excursion, yes."

A bad sign, the word "excursion." "Episode" was the shrink's, or the recovered crazy person's, term for a breakdown. "Excursion"—nonmedical, poetic—was insider talk, the positive spin. Using it meant that Charley was looking at what had happened—or was still happening—in a positive light. He was still inside whatever mental spaceship he had flown off in. Out there. But how far and for how long?

I wanted to believe Joe Jaspers, that this was just a temporary downward blip on the generally upward line of recovery. But I had already learned that the insanity of others, if we love them, tends to be mirrored in an insanity of our own. Sometimes that mirroring takes the form of contagious bad mania—the ugly buzz of negative synergy I had felt before when Charley's solipsism and imperiousness and my frustration and sense of helplessness caused me to become angry and cruel. But sometimes it takes the opposite form: a delusion of normality that corresponds to the mentally ill person's denial that anything is wrong, a denial that we desperately mimic to stave off the enveloping chaos. And we keep pretending for as long as possible. Sometimes even longer.

When I picked him up at the airport the next day he let me know right away how crazy he was. "Dad," he whispered to me with a tone of unalloyed triumph, leaning over to put his mouth close to my ear as I steered Lin's car—she was on vacation in Italy till the following Wednesday—out of the airport tunnel into the sunlight. "I threw away the Tissot!"

The Tissot was a pricey watch Lin and I had gotten him the previous Christmas, its face full of calendars and little dials that turned into stopwatches or told you the time in Moscow. He had picked it out himself; he loved his Tissot. And now he had thrown it into the swamp—along with his wallet, he told me proudly—during his little ramble in the bramble near his dorm. I could see the scratches on his face and arms.

I didn't bother to ask why he had thrown away the watch. Either he would say, "Dad, you just wouldn't understand," or else it would be something about divesting himself of the finite and transient. Throwing away watches was a Charley favorite. The now-swamped Tissot hadn't been the first, after all. He had tossed his watch away during his freshman-year Halloween "iawaska" seed episode, and he had bought and then immediately given another one away to the homeless man the weekend after Yosemite. Discarding watches had something to do with obliterating time, which had something to do with having god consciousness.

"Oh, great," I merely said.

I drove on, still in semishock from Joe Jaspers's call because I really hadn't seen this one coming. What was more, it caught me at a bad time. I had quit my job two and a half months earlier to write, living first off four thousand dollars in accrued vacation pay and cashed-in company pension money and lately on credit cards. Taking time off had been a luxury I had allowed myself precisely because I'd thought Charley was okay and wouldn't be needing me. But after a promising start my writing project had gone sour, and I had been on the edge of a creative and personal slump even before Joe Jaspers called.

All these subjective weaknesses would for me make this new crisis the worst so far. The hours and days that followed with Charley were like an imprisonment, solitary confinement without solitude. It wasn't that he himself did anything particularly awful. There were no suicide attempts, no really crazy behavior. He was simply oblivious, unconcerned about what had just happened—flipping out at school, ditching the lithium and the Milton paper and the Tissot, dooming his relationship with Reed forever. His sole concern seemed to be to get rent money from me and Lin for the apartment he had sublet in Portland, to which he wanted to return as soon as possible. I was reduced to support staff for his one-man show, a backstage technician at best, an insentient prop at worst. He dealt with me when he had to, patronizingly. I asked him whether he had a job lined up for the summer. Well no, he didn't have one yet, but no problem—when he got back to Portland he would "formulate résumé," he wrote on a wish list presented to me toward the end of his stay (note the correctly accented *e*'s). I felt like the third person on a honeymoon, some misplaced chaperone whose only function was to keep the champagne glasses filled for the happy couple (Charley and his mania), otherwise discreetly disappear. Normally I would have shrugged it off, but in my own defeated mood I was needier than usual and took his condescension more personally than I normally would.

There was also the constant underlying concern for his physical safety, the fear that he was capable of hurting himself at any time even when he wasn't suicidal—like the time he had started out into traffic at the Castro Street fair. Even tennis could become a white-knuckle sport with Charley. He suggested one day that we play, but once on the court he began doing a disappearing act in plain view, forgetting how many games were in a set. bending down to talk to birds in the middle of a game, and hitting balls over the fence onto the busy boulevard next to the court, which meant going out into the street to retrieve them. Should I let him go, or would he dart out into traffic and get killed? I could go instead, of course—and did, a couple of times—but was this what my life had become? Retrieving my son's tennis balls because I was afraid he would get killed if he tried doing it himself? As I stood on the court watching him be more attentive to a sparrow than he was to me, I became so freighted down with misery that I thought, wouldn't it be great if *I* could just disappear, if the cement under me could just open and swallow me up? Or maybe *I* could dart out onto Wilshire Boulevard in front of a truck, do an Anna Karenina. It would look like an accident and I'd be dead before I felt a thing. Anything was better than this.

But then he would look at me with a sweet smile—particularly after communing with one of the sparrows flitting around the court—and I knew I couldn't kill myself, I had to keep *him* from killing *him*self. He was still my kid, and I loved him, and I was responsible. I couldn't walk off the job now.

A few days later I did, in a sense, walk off the job, or allow the job to walk off from me. With a little help from Southwest Airlines.

Fight and Flight

Clonazepam: Brand name: ***Klonopin,*** Rivotril
Pharmacology: Anticonvulsant
Indications: Alone or as an adjunct in the management of myoclonic and akinetic seizures and petit mal variant (Lennox-Gastaut syndrome). May also be of some value in patients with absence spells (petit mal) who have failed to respond to succinimides.
Adverse Effects: *CNS:* Alterations in behavior, which have been variously reported as ***aggressiveness, argumentative behavior, hyperactivity, agitation,*** depression, ***euphoria, irritability,*** forgetfulness and confusion. ***These behavioral reactions are particularly likely to occur in patients with a prior history of psychiatric disturbances*** and are known to occur in patients with chronic seizure disorders.[7] (emphasis added)

Charley was adamant about going back to Portland; it was not even a matter for discussion. Naturally, I was totally opposed as things now stood; he was clearly psychotic, despite occasional periods of apparent sanity, and letting him out of my albeit tenuous grasp would be parental malpractice of the worst kind. So I tried to work out some compromise, and I actually wheedled him into postponing his return from May 31 to June 2, promising that I would then let him go if he was okay. I didn't really mean it; I was playing for time. But short of putting him in the hospital—which wouldn't have been easy since he was not flagrantly psychotic and I didn't have insurance anymore anyway—negotiation and cutting him off financially were the only arrows in my quiver.

I shot off both. On May 31 we had a joint session with Dr. Gray, and Charley agreed to go back on a small dose of Navane together with the lithium. All the while I kept trying to talk him into staying in L.A. longer. But June 2 came and he was insistent. Lin and I told him we still didn't want him to go, and we thought we had him boxed in. The airline required an additional thirty-five dollars to change his return date, and he had no money or credit cards (they were in the wallet at the bottom of the Reed swamp along with the Tissot). The evening of his flight he told me I should give him the thirty-five dollars since it had been my idea to change the return date. This was of course true, but I refused to give him the money anyway. He accused me of going back on our deal, which was also true. He called Lin and asked her to drive him to the airport. She refused. He asked me for money for a cab or shuttle. I refused. He then silently packed his bags, gave me a contemptuous glance and stalked out of the apartment toward the nearest bus stop, where for fifty cents, which he had, he could get a Santa Monica bus to the airport.

After he was out the door I called Lin and told her what had happened and to expect a call in a couple of hours from the airport, a final plea to give him the thirty-five dollars followed by a demand when she said no to come and get him. He called exactly as I'd predicted, but when Lin refused to give him the money and asked if he wanted to be picked up he said no, he could take care of himself. She and I then talked again, convinced he was stuck at the airport and would call us later that night or the next morning. He might stay at the terminal all night to scare us or save his pride, then come home.

He called the next morning—from Portland. He had talked the ticket agent into rebooking his flight for free.

Lin and I were by now exhausted—exhausted and fed up. Fed up with Charley, fed up with the airline, fed up with ourselves for not being tougher.

What to do? Go up and get him? But how? We had no legal standing. Charley was as tall as Lin, taller than I; we couldn't handcuff him and carry him back to L.A. What if we just left him? He had no money to live on. He didn't seem suicidal (I had convinced myself I could read his moods). On the contrary, he was determined to live, to find a job and work the whole summer, so maybe he wouldn't do anything self-destructive for a couple of weeks till we got our strength back and figured out what to do next. We decided to let him stay in Portland, keep in frequent telephone contact, see what happened. Lin even ended up sending him money, which of course contradicted our "starving him out" strategy, but we didn't want him to become malnourished aside from everything else. Our periodic attempts at "tough love" were just too tough— on us.

"I'm Sorry to Have to Tell You This, Sir . . ."

The next three weeks added new meaning to the concept of *sturm und drang,* and not just for our family. About a week after Charley went back up north, Nicole Simpson and Ron Brown were murdered and the whole O. J. Simpson drama erupted. My birthday came a few days later, June 15. Lin took me, Jenny and her boyfriend Jim to dinner, and we all talked about O. J. and tried to enjoy ourselves while silently wondering how the person not at the table was doing. At the end of dinner Lin gave me my present, a brightly painted wooden Oaxacan dragon, about two feet long, with a little spit of fire coming out of its smiling mouth. "Lin and I worried about Charley," I wrote in my journal that night. "Yesterday had thoughts seeing myself (& her) almost preparing ourselves psychologically for losing him—a kind of distancing process—not whole story of course but there's an aspect to it—like we're trying to buffer ourselves." Our contact with him had been minimal since his flight back to Portland. So, it turned out, had everybody else's. Much later I pieced together an account of what had gone on, mainly from Shizuko.

When Charley arrived back in Portland on June 3 he was at least intermittently psychotic. He took to wearing dark glasses and seemed confused, Juko said, often not knowing where he was. One day he got a bottle of Guinness Stout and told her they had to do something together. He took her on the bus to downtown Portland, where they walked to the Willamette River. He wrote some romantic words and phrases in Japanese on a piece of paper, then asked her to write romantic things in English. He put the paper in the bottle and launched it into the river, saying that if she retrieved the bottle in Japan it meant they would be a couple.

She saw him a few other times that week. They would have cappuccino at a coffeehouse near his apartment. He cooked her dinner one evening, a dish I taught him, caramelized broccoli and garlic sautéed in olive oil over pasta. He was difficult to deal with, arrogant and aloof in his dark glasses, talking about how everyone had masks. When Shizuko asked him to remove *his* mask he became agitated, saying there was nothing behind it. On June 9 she wrote him from Northern California, where she had gone for her sister's college graduation. The letter is full of confusion and anguish:

Dear Charley, Greetings to you from hot and sunny Santa Cruz. Thanks again for the delicious dinner. Too bad the atmosphere got hostile toward the end. I have all your notes and letters with me right now. I re-read them at least twenty times. You remain dear to my heart and your letters are valuable to me. . . . Why are we being so hostile to each other? I meant to tell you at Papocino's why I did not return your phone calls. Perhaps you might rip this letter into pieces but I will say why this time.

The night you came to my house and had Chinese rice and tea, you left me to go to Safeway at the empty SU. I felt so used and disposed. This is why I didn't return your phone calls. This is also the reason why I was annoyed when you took the cigarettes from me. It was not the fact that you took the cigarettes, but the way you took them. I'm sure you know what I am talking about. You've caused me to feel petty and used, in the same way that I felt when I was left in the SU. I couldn't speak this discomfort to you for the fear of upsetting you. But, you are puzzled, so this is an answer. I am not going to be passive this time. At one point when you were away to L.A. I thought of not being friends anymore. But, I read a passage in one of your notes which said, "Without music life would be a mistake." I agree. You are dear to me. Sometimes you make me feel so intimidated because of my horrible English. Thanks to you, my vocab. increased (I am not being cynical). I love your metaphorical ideas and projects. The way you are sensitive to light, smell, taste, and noise makes me aware of different perspectives. I noticed the impressive glance you had when I touched your face before I left (perhaps this is why I touched it). The way which your eyelashes fell and the smiling edges of your mouth are aspects of yours that are imprinted in my mind. I love the way your mouth slightly curls up. I have not realized this before, but you are very attractive.

I want you to know that I am in this flustered, as you might call it, state because I like you and I don't know what to do with these rude actions (i.e. leaving me in the SU). Please, don't do things that you don't want other people to do to you to me.—This is all I ask. If you are going to use me, do it wisely. Do it in a subtle and vague manner. Don't let me know that you have used me. Please let me know what is upsetting you. I really cannot go on like this, being confused and disturbed.

The confusion reminds me of my own confusion after Yosemite. Shizuko had never seen Charley psychotic before. Anything she knew of his history of breakdowns was abstract and vague. Till now he had been a slightly off-kilter youth who played Chopin and was too beautiful for Reed, his less desirable qualities—a tendency to be self-centered and arrogant—smoothed out in her view not only by her love but by her understanding: she could see his aloofness for the shield it was. Now, suddenly, he was acting in a new way, odder and more demanding, thoughtless and importunate, his diamond-in-the-rough, tough-tender persona gone, only the rough and tough remaining. And when she called him to account, hoping for some acknowledgment of her feelings and needs, it didn't come.

At least it didn't come directly—not yet, anyway. But it would soon come indirectly. It would come because it was both Charley's blessing and his curse that he never remained alone at the top of the world for long, at the pole of pure ego. His basic decency and human feelings always reemerged, but in the wake of his manic outbursts in which he had treated others badly (or behaved "inappropriately") these feelings often took the form of profound embarrassment and self-disgust. The summer before, writing in his journal about his fall 1992 obsession/breakdown over the humanities professor, he had made a list of "Associations" with her. They included "ancestral connection . . . identity fulfillment . . . psychosexual dysfunction . . . romance, fantasy fueled by primal urges, maternal, nubile qualities (shudder) [the "shudder" is Charley's interpolation, not mine—JA] . . . incoherently primal forces . . . *the fiendish influence of mania . . . contrition resurfaced . . . delusional cancer . . . histrionic tendencies.*" (emphasis added)

Although I am taking some liberties in claiming that these same associations now came into play regarding his treatment of Shizuko—especially the "incoherently primal . . . fiendish . . . delusional . . . histrionic . . . contrition resurfaced"—subsequent events would show that something similar and perhaps even more extreme was at work. We would soon see the results.

But not quite yet. For the time being there was silence. Charley didn't answer Shizuko's letter or return her phone calls, and finally, exhausted by his behavior and feeling her own integrity under attack, she gave up on him. During the same period that they lost touch, the second and third week of June, he was mostly out of touch with Lin and entirely out of touch with me. The ten days after Shizuko's letter of June 9 are largely a void.

On June 19, Sunday, I was due at Lin's for a family evening; she had invited Jenny, Jim and Jim's father for an early dinner and asked me to cohost. When I got to her place around three, the first to arrive, she told me she had been on the phone with Charley in Portland and he sounded very weird. Apparently he had "lost" his lithium and Navane. He wanted more, but didn't know how to get refills.

This was extremely ominous for several reasons. Normally Charley took medication under a kind of permanent protest, going along with the program because I (or his doctors, or the school) wanted him to, not because he believed he needed to. For him now to be actively trying to get medication was uncharacteristic, and it probably meant that he was very scared. The survival part of him was sending out alarms. It also meant that he was obviously disoriented; otherwise he would have been able to get the prescriptions refilled without us.

I dialed his number and he answered. He was so vague that it took me a while just to figure out what his problem was getting the refills. It seemed to involve some sort of miscommunication with his pharmacy; possibly he was calling the wrong store entirely. I tried to help him get focused enough to find out whether there was an open pharmacy in his neighborhood that he could get to without a car. After a couple of calls he gave me the name of one and I called it to make sure it would fill a prescription over the phone from an out-of-state physician or psychiatrist (Charley had told me that his regular school physician, who normally wrote his prescriptions, was out of town). Yes to both questions, the pharmacist said, although they were closing early—in an hour, since it was Sunday. Would they accept payment from me by credit card? Yes again. I hung up and called Dr. Gray to ask him to call Portland and talk to the pharmacy. Naturally, Dr. Gray was also out of town for the weekend, his voice mail announced, referring emergency callers to a colleague I had never met. I called the colleague's number and got *his* voice mail, which gave an emergency number to page. I punched it in, left my (I hoped not totally incoherent) SOS message, then hung up and waited, trying not to panic. The colleague (bless him) called me back in minutes, calming and helpful. He phoned the pharmacy in Portland and authorized them to fill the prescription, then phoned me back to let me know. I called Charley and tried to communicate to him which store had the medication and where it was located so he wouldn't go to the wrong one, find it closed and give up. I told him he had less than an hour.

When I hung up for the last time I didn't know if any of what I had done would actually help. Even though Charley wanted the medication, he was so confused and at times combative, at one point hanging up on me when I started getting too pushy and parental, that I wasn't sure he was capable of getting to the store quickly enough, or at all. It was obvious that other things—"internal stimuli"—were vying for his attention. One time while I was talking, trying to get him to focus, he lost touch with me completely and started mumbling about "the serpent . . ." Instead of making me more sympathetic and determined to see him through this—clearly he was in need of immediate, serious help—it just made me mad, although I suppressed it. *The serpent!* I thought. *What next?!* It was like some bad teen horror movie (my Stephen King son!). Because of this, by the time I finished giving him the information about where to pick up the refills, my feeling was "good riddance." What more could I do? There were people coming and I had food to prepare. It would be rude to burden our guests with all this drama. My idiot notion of having to be a good host even under the most dire circumstances, together with my accumulated anger and frustration, were overcoming whatever shreds of sense I had left. In my mind, the two tasks of restoring Charley's sanity (and perhaps saving his life) and not overcooking the spaghetti seemed of equal weight. Actually, the spaghetti was weightier, since it was there and Charley wasn't.

Fortunately, at this point Jenny stepped forward. When she and Jim arrived after the flurry of phone calls, Lin and I greeted them with what we hoped was hospitable calm, but Jenny saw right through it and asked what was going on. I, the all-wise, all-powerful father who wanted to spare his daughter any discomfort, assured her that everything was okay. We had been having a problem with Charley but we had worked things out. Stressed? Me?

Jenny didn't buy it. As I marinated the salmon she took Lin aside and prodded her for more details. As I cooked and played host to Jim and his father, mother and daughter gulped down their food and resumed huddling in the next room with the door closed. Like me, Lin had temporarily lapsed into the belief that Charley was okay—hadn't the calls solved the problem?—but Jenny the skeptic continued to work on her, questioning and prodding and demanding that we do more to help her pain-in-the-ass but beloved "widdiw wudduh"—little brother. I will always treasure her for this. It could not have been easy to breach the blank parental wall. For all our mistakes, Lin and I had for the most part been reasonably sane parents, and it would have been easy and natural for Jenny to let the matter drop. But she didn't. This was how the family operated during these years of crisis. When one of us—or two—faltered, another would pick up the banner. This time it was Jenny. By the end of dinner she and Mom had decided that Lin would fly to Portland on the next available flight.

The decision would end up saving Charley's life for another two and a half years.

But it wasn't saved quite yet.

By the next day, Monday, my journal reports, everything seemed to be working out. Lin flew to Portland in the morning and found Charley alive and apparently well in his apartment. He hadn't known she was coming and tried to keep her out at first, but she mothered her way in and eventually got him to go with her to our home away from home, Motel 6. When I spoke to her around seven in the evening she said Charley seemed okay, mentioning only in passing that there were some blood stains in his apartment. They had come, she thought, from a cut on his ear that he had shown her; he didn't manifest any other signs of injury. I shrugged mentally and said it didn't sound like a big deal, and the discussion moved on. I didn't even mention the remark about the blood in my journal entry later that night. There were more important things to think about—for example, should she bring him back with her to L.A. or try to get him help up there?

The whole horrendous drug-refill experience of the day before—Charley's helplessness, my incompetence—had roused me from my months-long writers' block torpor. When Lin and I hung up, I called Ryles Center, remembering how well Charley had done there a year and a half before after getting out of Portland Adventist Hospital. I asked for the staff member I remembered, Jeff, the young man who had buzzed Lin and me out after our visit the day Charley was admitted. Amazingly, Jeff was there, and yes, he said, he remembered Charley. I explained the situation. He said he would call the motel (only blocks away!) and talk to Lin. "I felt somewhat better after talking to him," my journal reports in the entry that doesn't mention the blood, "since for the first time in this present crisis I had taken some initiative." I also called Dr. Gray and, for the first time ever, got the actual human being rather than the voice mail. (Wow! Could there be a better omen than that?) We talked about possible places for Charley to go once Lin brought him back to L.A.

By the next morning my restored sense of reality was taking other forms. I decided to go back to work, and I quickly lined up a new job. If I couldn't write, at least I could proofread; I wasn't incompetent in everything. In fact, given the family chaos, ending my sabbatical without having written anything worthwhile could be seen as necessary rather than an admission of defeat. In a horrible kind of way, these family crises provided a refuge and excuse, a chance to stop worrying about my creative failures. They certainly made the time pass. "Almost this whole day from 1 P.M. on spent sitting/lying semicomatose from lack of sleep last two nights and worry/anxiety," my journal reports.

They were good for my waistline, too. "Appetite zero—in weight loss mode per first two episodes of Ch.'s psychosis. The first one I lost about ten lb. in one week. Who needs dieting?"

By the next morning I was sure my renewed resolve had helped save the day. Jeff had called Lin at the motel just as he said he would. "Talked to Lin 11-something last night," my journal says Tuesday morning. "Ch. in Ryles—yay!! We get to go to Mississippi after all—hopefully for the whole five days unless I have to fly back to Portland in emergency. He actually was willing to go to Ryles."

The "Mississippi" reference was to a trip Lin and I had been planning to Jackson for the thirty-year reunion of Freedom Summer voter-registration veterans, of whom Lin was one. She had asked me months before if I wanted to go with her, and I had said yes. We had planned to leave L.A. early Wednesday, June 22, and come back on Sunday, but the crisis with Charley had put all those plans on hold, and when Lin went to Portland on Monday we figured Mississippi was probably out. But now on Tuesday, thanks to Jeff and Ryles, Charley would be in Portland for at least a week or two, so there was no reason not go to Mississippi after all. Lin flew back to L.A. Tuesday afternoon, the day after she took Charley to Ryles, and we got ready to leave the next morning. I asked her how he had seemed. She said that once he finally let her into his apartment he had become subdued, almost docile. She mentioned the bloodstains and the ear injury again, and said that when they were at the motel he had wondered out loud whether he might need to go to the emergency room. She had thought about taking him—she had assumed he was thinking about psychiatric hospitalization, since he seemed okay physically except for the ear—but then Jeff had called from Ryles and she had taken Charley there instead.

I spent Tuesday evening at my apartment packing for the trip, then went to Lin's to sleep on her couch, which would simplify getting to the airport the next morning. At around ten she went upstairs to a neighbor's to say she was leaving and ask her to feed the cats. I was relaxing on the couch, thinking about going to sleep.

The phone rang. It was Jeff from Ryles, asking for Lin.

I told him who I was and said she was out for a minute. He sounded very subdued. He asked if we had gotten his earlier messages. I said no, Lin's answering machine wasn't working. Was there something wrong?

He spoke haltingly. He must have picked up on my cheery tone; as far as I knew everything was fine. He seemed disappointed that I hadn't heard whatever message he'd left earlier that day.

"Mr. Aurthur, when Charley's labs came back we—"

"I'm sorry—what are 'labs'?"

"His lab tests. We take routine lab tests when patients are admitted. When the labs came back there were some weird readings of his blood work. They pointed toward the beginning of kidney failure. We didn't know why. So we took your son to the emergency room at Portland Adventist and he was given a complete physical. The doctor found two punctures in his chest that were causing internal bleeding. So he was taken to another hospital—Providence Hospital—where he's undergoing open-heart surgery right now." Pause. "His chances are fair." When I didn't answer: "I'm sorry to have to tell you this, sir . . ."

"Oh my God . . ."

"I'm sorry to have to tell you this, sir," he repeated in a tortured voice. (It didn't sound like he thought Charley's chances were "fair" at all.) Another few seconds of silence. Then: "Sir?"

"...Yes ... ?"

"Would you stay where you are for a few minutes while I call Providence? I want to verify what I just told you and get any more information I can. Will you stay there?"

"Yeah, sure ..."

"I promise I'll call you within five minutes."

He hung up. I sat staring ahead, the life seeping out of me as if there were a puncture in *my* chest, feeling the way I had always imagined Willy Loman felt in *Death of a Salesman*—sagging shoulders, a ruin. I felt as if I were out of my own body, observing myself—a lifeless hulk—looking dully out the window. Charley was dying—or already dead. Jeff had said as much. Emergency Room Charley had hit the wall at last.

Then a thought almost as frightening. *How was I going to tell Lin?* Charley was eleven hundred miles away but she was here, upstairs chatting with her friend, telling her where the cat food was, as lighthearted as I had been five— no, three—minutes before. How was I going to deal with her? I felt like a little boy who had misbehaved and now had to tell his mother before she found out on her own. I stood, staring, a rabbit caught in the cosmic headlight. Couldn't I just stay like this? Maybe if I just waited here, absolutely still, something would happen—a major earthquake, a giant asteroid striking the earth and bringing about mass extinction. I could die out, like the dinosaurs. Anything to avoid having to tell Charley's mother.

But no earthquake came, no asteroid. I remained standing and staring for another minute or so, first surrendering to and then trying to shake off the overwhelming fatigue, the sense of utter futility that had engulfed me. But nothing was going to save me now.

Then it did.

The phone rang. Oh yes, I remembered, Jeff had said he'd call me back within five minutes. Had it been five minutes? I had no idea. I looked at the phone as it rang. It would be bad news, of course, I had no doubt about that. But at that moment even bad news would keep me from having to go upstairs for another minute or so. I picked it up and said hello.

"Hello, Mr. Aurthur?"

But it wasn't Jeff. It was a new voice.

"Yes . . . ?"

"This is Dr. Duane Bietz, Mr. Aurthur." A confident voice—warm, hale, with a kind of robust calm, a midwestern farmer's voice talking about a good crop. I'd been expecting death. This voice was life, streaming into me over the phone. "I'm the cardiology surgeon at Providence Hospital in Portland. I wanted to get back to you right away because the fellow from Ryles Center just called me and told me what he'd told you, and what he said wasn't accurate. I wanted to clear it up."

"Yes . . . ?"

"Mr. Aurthur, your son was brought in here a few hours ago with two punctures in his chest. I don't think they've punctured the heart but there's been some internal bleeding. Your son isn't really able to give us a very good account of what happened, so I'm going to do exploratory surgery. As I said, the chances of his having punctured the heart or the pericardium—that's the membrane around the heart—are very remote since his other vital signs are good."

"You mean they didn't puncture his heart?" I was two sentences behind.

"I can't be sure, that's why we're doing surgery. But I'd say the chances of his having punctured his heart or the pericardium are extremely small, about one in a million."

"Oh my God. You mean he's going to be okay?!"

"I'm almost positive. Listen, I need to get into surgery."

"Of course, of course . . . !"

"The surgery is going to take about three hours. It's very routine. I'll call you when it's over and I know what's going on. What time is it now, about eleven?"

"I think so. . . ."

"I'll call you by two."

After I hung up I continued to stand, staring, trying to absorb what I'd heard. I felt like a man who in three minutes had been arrested, tried, condemned to death, strapped in the chair, heard the switch starting to be thrown, and then been reprieved by the governor's call at two seconds after twelve. I still had to go upstairs and tell Lin, but now it would be easy. The boy was okay, I knew it. There was no way Dr. Bietz—that voice, that assurance!—would let us down.

He called back at five after two. I had spent the three hours lying awake on the couch. Lin and I had talked. Charley's chest! *That's* where the blood had come from, obviously, not his ear. But he hadn't said a word to her about his chest in Portland. He'd stabbed himself in the chest—probably Sunday night after he and I talked and tried to get his medication refills, or the day after. Then he had walked around for one or two days and not said anything to anybody. No wonder he'd seemed pale and a little weak and docile, Lin said, short of breath walking up the stairs of the motel. He'd been bleeding in his chest. Jesus Christ.

But that wasn't all, Dr. Bietz said when he called back. The surgery had been successful, but it hadn't been routine. Not only had Charley punctured the pericardium, he had lacerated the heart as well, not with a puncture but with a three-quarter-inch gash in the right ventricle. The one-in-a-million occurrence had occurred, and then some; even Dr. Bietz sounded a little surprised. He said he was glad he'd done the exploratory, overriding the ER physician at Portland Adventist, who had wanted to observe Charley overnight before doing anything, since the chances of the two punctures going anywhere important had seemed so low.

I asked how Charley had survived for two days. Dr. Bietz said that the placement of the gash had saved him; there was not a lot of pumping pressure in the wounded ventricle, which meant that the blood had seeped rather than gushed through the cut. In addition, the wounded tissue had apparently flopped over on itself like the gill of a fish, partially closing the wound.

But it was still miraculous, to survive this kind of injury—and to walk around for two days. This after surviving the car crash at Yosemite. How much more could Charley take?

Instead of flying to Mississippi the next morning I flew to Portland—by myself, since Lin had already gone once that week.

When I arrived at Providence Hospital's cardiac care unit in midafternoon Charley was sitting up in a chair in his critical-care room, hooked up to every machine known to man, sipping at a container of juice through a straw. A new-fangled self-adhesive wound dressing ran vertically from just under his throat to beneath his solar plexus, binding his chest together. He had had full open-heart surgery.

I walked over to him. "Hey, what's happening, Homes?" I said as I leaned over, fought my way gently through all the tubing, and gave him a kiss on a slightly stubbly cheek. He smiled wanly. Even though he was sitting up he looked very logy. He was on tons of morphine. "Hi, Dad," he said as I grasped one of his hands. "I was going to write you about what's been going on. . . ."

I sat with him, holding his hand, saying little. Occasionally, I would give it a squeeze, or he would squeeze mine with his long, spidery fingers—good, strong squeezes—or else give me a wink. He always amazed me. Sitting up in a chair twelve hours after open-heart surgery. How could such a powerful will to live and will to die exist in the same person? The cardio staff couldn't believe it either; they weren't used to such vigor. Most coronary care patients were at least fifty years older than Charley, their hearts used up. One of the nurses showed me a Polaroid of Charley's heart taken during the operation. It lay exposed in his chest pan, purplish red, paler than I thought a heart would be. There was a dark red line on the lower part: the wound. The nurse said that Dr. Bietz had been showing the photo around. Nobody had ever seen anything like it.

At four-thirty a nurse and orderly got Charley out of his chair and walked him around, trying to make him breathe deeper, get his oxygen circulating to clean out his lungs. He was feisty enough to get irritated when one of the nurses mentioned the stabbing. "Yes?? And—??" he demanded. "Like it was her fault," I wrote that night in my journal. "What a little putz." He still seemed psychotic, although he was so doped up it was hard to tell. Most of the time I spent with him that afternoon we just sat quietly holding hands. I tried to get him to drink more juice and eat something. When he periodically dozed off I came and went, talking to the staff and wandering around. I spoke with the nephrologist about possible kidney/liver problems caused by the several days of inadequate blood flows, but apparently recovery was good there, too; another bullet dodged. I asked for Dr. Bietz, but he had already left when I arrived, so I would meet him tomorrow. I would also talk to the psychiatrist, I hoped. The nurses had told me that nobody from the psych unit had yet appeared, which concerned me, since Charley's mental condition was still obviously grave. After a while I got ready to leave. When I asked a nurse where the nearest motel was—Providence was on the other side of town from our Motel 6—she said I didn't need one. The hospital had converted its old nurses' quarters into a dormitory for the relatives of patients; a room cost fifteen dollars. Mine was tiny and monastic but spotless. A crucifix hung on the wall over the narrow single bed. There were showers and toilets down the hall. It was like being back in college.

After unpacking I left the hospital. It was early evening, still bright and sunny out, only a day past the summer solstice. Before getting dinner I went to Charley's apartment to make sure nothing was on—gas, lights—and that it was closed up properly. Part of me dreaded doing it. I had been thinking about the apartment on the plane, I wrote in my journal, having lurid fantasies of blood everywhere, the place a "metaphor for my failure as parent, human being, etc. Melodrama."

The actual experience was both less melodramatic and stranger than I had imagined. Portland is very green, and the apartment, which was near Reed, was in a particularly green part, an old neighborhood overhung with large old trees. The apartment was not in a building; it was a rental unit over the garage of a private house in an isolated little canyon off the street, reached by going down a steep and bumpy one-lane dirt driveway so totally canopied with thick, tall trees that it was dark even in the daytime. It was like a green birth canal, Lin said, the feeling going down it one of depth and removal. The house and garage at the bottom were made of rough brown wood, like some rustic hunting lodge. The small rental unit itself was fairly ordinary. It contained much less evidence of carnage than I'd feared, and I could see how Lin, finding Charley apparently all right, could have believed the cut-ear story. There were a couple of fair-sized blood stains—now dry and brown—on the living room rug and couch, not much more. Cigarette butts littered the wooden outside stairs, which were covered with pine needles, and I shuddered thinking of him here for two weeks by himself, psychotic, more and more isolated, brooding on whatever he was brooding on. (At this point I knew about nothing except the "serpent" remark.) As I looked around, I hated myself even more for having let him come back up here alone. If I had known what this place was like I would have done more to stop him—tied him to a fire hydrant, anything. The idea that he had wanted to be here alone was the most frightening thing of all.

Despite my shudderings and self-scourgings, when I got back to my little monk's cell I slept well for the first time since Monday, when I had thought Charley was safe at Ryles. My only concern, now that Dr. Bietz had saved him physically, was his mental state. Why hadn't a psychiatrist seen him and put him back on his medication? Look what he'd done to himself when he was off it. Might he wake up in the middle of the night and decide to pull all the tubes out? Who knew?

Even at my most patriarchal, pro–Western medicine worst, I never had much hope for Charley's recovery through periodic hospitalizations and medication, although I advocated both when I thought they were necessary. I reminded myself of Margaret Thatcher, one of my least favorite people in the world. When Thatcher became the British prime minister in the late 1970s, the story went that whenever she proposed some particularly mean-spirited, anti-labor policy as part of her "revolution" and was criticized for it, she would intone in her toothy, round-voweled way, "There is no-o-o-o alternative . . . !" She said this so often that reporters nicknamed her TINA—the acronym of the endlessly repeated phrase.

Was it true? Was there really no alternative to hospitalization and medication for Charley? I saw none, at least in the short term. What I called his illness and what he called, at various times, his crisis or affliction, was obviously life threatening and now, it appeared, chronic. At least two of his three suicide attempts (the car crash and now the stabbing) had happened when he was not on medication. He had called the antipsychotics "chemical straitjackets," which sounded rhetorical although it was no doubt partly true. But what *was* the alternative? Real straitjackets? Or should we just write him off and let him kill himself? Virtually everybody Lin and I dealt with in our attempts to get him treated, from holistic psychiatrists to humanistic therapists, told us that medication was a necessary evil. It was not until this trip to Portland, however, almost three years after Yosemite, that the lightbulb would go on over my head telling me what these medications, whether necessary or not, really were. It would happen the next day.

My Drug Epiphany; or, The Morphine Connection

I got up early after my good night's sleep, went back to the cardiac care unit, greeted Charley, and waited to see Dr. Bietz and the psychiatrist. The nurses agreed with me that Charley was still psychotic. So, I asked, trying not to sound anxious, was he back on his antipsychotic medication yet? No, they said, that required a psychiatrist's okay, and still no psychiatrist had appeared. I continued to fret. Charley wasn't being baby-sat, as he had been in the intensive care unit of St. John's after the wrist cutting. Why still no medication?

Dr. Bietz soon arrived, a round-faced bear of a man who looked like his phone voice had sounded and made me think of a Breugel peasant, earthy and kind, with just the trace of an antic gleam in his eye. I wondered as I shook his large paw of a hand how such a hand could perform the intricacies of surgery, manage the tiny tools it took to rearrange the tissues of a damaged heart. We chatted about Charley's physical condition. Dr. Bietz assured me that it was excellent, that he would recover fully without any organ complications. I thanked him again for saving Charley's life, not just by the surgery but by overriding the ER doc's decision to wait till the next morning before doing anything. Charley could have died during the night or at least suffered irreparable kidney failure. Dr. Bietz just shrugged. "When I see two punctures like the ones in his chest, my training tells me I want to know where they go."

What about Charley's mental condition? I asked a little cautiously, not wanting to step on interdepartmental toes. Was it okay that he still hadn't been seen by a psychiatrist and put back on antipsychotics?

"I've had a little difficulty dealing with the psychiatric staff on this whole matter," Dr. Bietz said with a bit of a twinkle. "I had to do a little talking to them to convince them to deal with the situation with the requisite seriousness." Apparently the problem was that Dr. Roth, the psychiatrist in charge, had been out of the office the previous day when Dr. Bietz had called the psychiatric unit, and he hadn't shown up since. Dr. Roth, the amazing disappearing man. I was beginning to dislike him intensely.

What a disappointment, then, when my impression upon actually meeting him—he soon arrived in the cardio unit and, after a brisk greeting, led me into a small conference room down the hall—was completely favorable. He was the exact opposite of Dr. Bietz in every way, a slim, balding but still youngish man with a salt-and-pepper goatee that made his already long and narrow face look sharp as a pick axe. He sounded like he was from New York, like me, his manner intense in the way New Yorkers' manners are, their mental and physical machinery ratcheted up a notch from everybody else's.

"Were you surprised when this happened even though he'd tried suicide before?" he asked across the conference table, and I felt ashamed. But his tone wasn't accusing, and he nodded when I answered lamely that I hadn't thought

Charley would do it in this part of his cycle, "I guess I was wrong, huh? Now he's tried to kill himself in every phase: when he was manic, when he was depressed, and when he was in mixed states." God.

I asked what would happen when Charley recovered enough from the surgery to get out of the cardio unit. He'd go to the psychiatric ward, said Dr. Roth, for as long as he needed.

For as long as he needed? But who would pay? I was wondering. At this point I was thinking that, as Charley's father, I was responsible. Would I be getting a bill in a month for—what?—fifty, sixty, seventy thousand dollars? The heart surgery alone must have been thirty to forty. I was broke and in debt. "But won't that be very expensive?" I said out loud.

Dr. Roth shrugged and gave a slight New York smirk. "Doesn't matter," he said. "Look," he continued, when he saw me fidgeting nervously. "This is a nonprofit hospital. It's tax-exempt. Taking care of patients like your son is part of the deal."

I felt a warm flood of relief. Not only was I not expected to pay but I wasn't even expected to feel guilty about it! If Dr. Roth didn't have any Jewish guilt, why should I? Charley was over twenty-one, no longer my dependent. He would be classified as indigent. Indigent, shmindigent. Who cared about labels?

Dr. Roth's dismissal of my money concerns gave me the courage to ask. "He was taking Navane before for his psychosis," I said as diplomatically as I could. "One of the reasons he stabbed himself was that he'd gone off his medication, and he's been off it for probably a couple of weeks at least. I'm a little worried about him now. Were you . . . planning to put him back on the Navane?"

"Yeah, when he recovers from the surgery enough," Dr. Roth answered, sounding totally unconcerned. He looked at me and again smiled slightly as he saw my latest fidget. "Don't worry. He's on morphine for the pain. The morphine is taking care of the psychosis, too. That's why morphine was originally developed. It was the first antipsychotic."

That's when the lightbulb clicked. So that was it. I'd been dimly aware before that antipsychotics didn't "cure" mental illness, they "treated" it. Now for the first time I was finally seeing what that meant. Navane and all the rest— "tranquilizers," the dictionary says—were clubs more than straitjackets. Basically they were just heavy, brain-deadening drugs, like morphine. They doped people up to the point where they were too zonked out to be crazy—

or, in the case of people who were suicidal, too indifferent to life to have the energy to end it.

The fact that even after metabolizing this knowledge—after hearing the click of the lightbulb—I would still want Charley to take these drugs (because they seemed to give him a fighting chance of staying alive, if you could call it living) is testimony to the still-medieval state of psychiatry.

"Some Failed Romantic Relationship"

It would take me a while—years in the case of some details—to find out why Charley had stabbed himself, although I got the gist fairly soon, not from Charley directly but from another psychiatrist at Providence, a woman named Sandra Fischer, who took over from Dr. Roth and treated Charley when he was transferred from the cardio unit to the psychiatric unit. I talked to her by phone the week after the surgery. I was back in Santa Monica. Lin and I had ended up going to Mississippi after all. We had caught the last two days of the reunion and come back to L.A. Monday morning, almost exactly a week after she had flown to Portland and spirited Charley out of the blood-stained apartment. "He admitted to some failed romantic relationship," my journal says Dr. Fischer told me, "that lined up cosmic forces in such a way as to lead him to cut himself (Sun. night?). When he woke up he felt differently."

At this point I knew nothing about his connection with Shizuko, so I had no idea what the "failed romantic relationship" referred to. Charley didn't seem to want to talk about it, and within a couple of days he got mad and stopped talking to me for several weeks anyway. The reason was that during my phone conversation with Dr. Fischer, which included giving her Charley's psychiatric history, I had mentioned that a letter to him from Reed College had arrived at my apartment and that I had opened it. I hardly ever opened Charley's mail, but in this case, given his current condition and where the letter was from, I had made an exception. The letter stated very diplomatically that the school was through with Charley. This would have been apparent to any rational person anyway, but at this point of course, Charley wasn't rational. Some part of him still believed he could go back, and when Dr. Fischer told him about the letter he called me from the hospital and assailed me bitterly for opening his mail and talking behind his back. He dissolved in tears and I felt awful. His latest fall, and now Reed's permanent rejection of him, were terrible blows. So he simply ignored them. The stabbing? Not worth mentioning. "I tried to be independent. I tried to get a job. I didn't get it," as if that explained things. He "ran out of lithium," a little slip that just happened to cause him to stab himself in the heart. It could happen to anybody.

"Did I do the wrong thing?" I asked my journal after the phone call.

> I hate to see him miserable ("I want to rest now"), but it seems to me he's going to have to be pretty miserable at some point when it sinks in about Reed, not going back, etc. . . . Is it possible to help him take realistic stock of the situation but *without* making him completely lose faith in himself? How do you help somebody "de-grandiosize" without going to the opposite extreme of self-loathing? I feel so sorry for him, but am unable (or was just now) to resist communicating to him what some of what has happened has done to me and to rake him over the coals for not taking any responsibility for his situation.

The next day he called to ask me to deposit his allowance in his checking account. "He still seems to think he might stay in Portland," I wrote in my journal. "Me: 'You're not staying in Port.' He: 'That's not entirely clear.'"

It was to me.

We didn't talk for two weeks. No doubt he had cast me into hell, along with his other betrayers, and maintained an angry silence. It was a silence I decided I could live with for a while. I checked up on him indirectly, calling Providence every couple of days and talking to his psychiatrists. At the same time, Lin and I tried to figure out what to do with him once he got back to L.A., and the next half dozen pages of my journal consist of notes about different resources, free and fee, private and public, inpatient and outpatient, ranging from the local "county psych ward"—for us this meant Harbor-UCLA Medical Center, about twenty miles away from where we lived—to places that were closer and we hoped less institutional. Since Charley was no longer legally our dependent we also started the process of getting him on Medicaid (Medi-Cal in California) and SSI (Supplemental Security Income), which is similar to disability and given to people who are chronically unable to work for physical or mental health reasons. Also, again because Charley was now legally an adult, Lin began going through the steps of becoming his conservator, a kind of legal guardian.

Over the Fourth of July weekend he was moved from the Providence Hospital psych ward back to Ryles. Two Fridays later, a little more than three weeks after his surgery, Lin and I flew up to Portland to get him released and drive him back to L.A. in a rental car loaded with as much of his stuff from the apartment as would fit. The rest we would send UPS.

The process of closing out Portland took place over three extremely difficult days. Lin and I were on a tight schedule when our plane landed late Friday morning, July 15. She was an urban planning consultant working as an independent contractor, without sick days or vacation; if she didn't work, she didn't get paid. She had already taken a lot of time off recently because of Charley's crisis and needed to get back to L.A. as soon as possible to deal with a growing backlog of work. I needed to get back too; my new proofreading job was scheduled to start on Monday. We had to get Charley out of Ryles, buy boxes and other shipping materials, pack and clean his apartment, get everything to the UPS office before it closed at noon Saturday, then start the twenty-something-hour drive back to L.A. to arrive at a reasonable hour Sunday evening. I was so preoccupied that when Lin and I picked up our rental car at the airport I couldn't seem to open the trunk to load our bags. I kept trying to fit the ignition key into the lock. I didn't notice that there was a second key on the key chain.

It was going to be a long weekend.

It was still less than a month after the stabbing, and Charley was still in a very bad way when we picked him up at Ryles, not floridly psychotic but "unresponsive, sullen, preoccupied, uncommunicative," my journal says. Not a word of acknowledgment to his mother for saving his life, or to us for spending an entire day, with minimal cooperation from him, cleaning up his apartment, which included washing the blood stains out of the rug and couch and doing his laundry. He was back on Navane, but it didn't seem to be working. The staff person at Ryles who released him to us strongly recommended that we take Charley directly to the Harbor-UCLA psychiatric unit when we got back to L.A.; he was still at risk, she thought, and needed round-the-clock professional supervision and protection. Lin resisted the idea (as did Charley, of course), so uncertainty and contention were piled upon the present stress of having to do a lot in a little time. Neither Lin nor I could have gotten through this weekend alone, but togetherness was taking its toll, too, and our never completely united front was beginning to show cracks.

The endless drive back to L.A. was a mostly silent misery. Charley was so withdrawn the entire trip (highlighted by an overnight stay in a mosquito-infested dust trap of a motel in the alkaline midsummer hell of the Sacramento Valley) that my heart leapt when he whispered to me at dinner back in L.A. Sunday evening, "I'm sorry I've been such a pain in the ass." He "seemed to show signs of life," I noted in my journal that night. Later, as he drove with me to drop off the rental car, the same entry continued,

> we actually had a conversation in car—first time since—when? late May—certainly 1st on this trip, where he acted like zombie most of time. Told me he feels that "something's been lost between us—maybe I'm just getting older." I said I thought he was mad at me for May, opening his mail, etc.—that I'd betrayed him. He said, "It's like you used to say: 'I love you, I just can't stand you.'" Few minutes later: [He:] "We can be intimate enemies." He said "he made some dangerous moves 1st half of year. . . ."

One can imagine what the previous three days had been like if the above interactions constituted welcome improvements.

So what now? The immediate problem was familiar. Lin and I couldn't just leave Charley by himself while we both worked. In fact, the problem was even more acute now than it had been a year and a half earlier when he'd swallowed his lithium and cut his wrists. Even then it had not been completely clear how chronically suicidal he was. The car crash had been ambiguous, after all, and the wrist/lithium episode could have been the proverbial cry for help. The stabbing, however, had not been a cry for help; it showed that Charley was capable of anything. More than that, we now knew there was no way of reading him for suicidality. He had tried to kill himself when he was up, when he was down and when he was in between; before he ever started taking medication, when he was on it and when he went off it. The only times he had been safe were when he was locked up. But St. John's was not an option; I had no insurance anymore and Charley didn't have Medi-Cal yet. The nearest free hospital, the county's Harbor-UCLA, twenty freeway miles south, seemed infinitely far away and very abstract, even assuming that Lin would agree to his going. So far she was not convinced.

There was another possibility. Before flying to Portland she and I had checked out a private facility I will call Tender Loving Care in West Los Angeles, not far from our respective dwellings. I had heard about it from Dr. Gray, whom I had talked to while Charley was at Ryles. TLC provided psychiatric care, individual and group therapy, and various other activities for a predominantly youthful clientele, Dr. Gray said, adding that he had a young male patient there now who was doing well. The director was a family therapist named Rob Klein whom Dr. Gray talked about enthusiastically.

The place sounded worth investigating, so the week before Lin and I flew to get Charley we went to TLC and talked with its admissions director, a friendly woman named Kimberly who was about eight months pregnant. The organization had both an inpatient and an outpatient program, she said, which meant Charley could live there during his stay or attend day sessions and sleep at home. Or he could do a combination, beginning as an inpatient and becoming outpatient as he stabilized. Kimberly quoted us a price of about thirteen thousand dollars for a two-month package, which included two weeks inpatient and six weeks outpatient.

That was a lot of money for us. TLC didn't take Medi-Cal or SSI (neither of which Charley had yet anyway), so if Lin and I enrolled him it would be entirely out-of-pocket. We were both broke and in debt, mainly from kid-related expenses, but of course there were always credit cards. Seeing that we were both still upright after hearing the price tag, Kimberly invited us to come back the next evening for "family night," a weekly meeting attended by clients and their families (and prospectives like Lin and me), half group therapy, half question-and-answer, presided over by Rob Klein, the therapist Dr. Gray liked. We would be able to get a feel for how the place worked, Kimberly said. Why not? Looking was free, so Lin and I decided to go.

I have very few absolute rules in life, but one of them is, Never trust anybody over fifteen, male or female, with a ponytail. It is testimony to my marginal mental state during this period that I almost forgot my own rule, and it almost cost me. Charley would save *me* this time.

Rob Klein, TLC's director, baby-faced and forty-something, was impressive in the way he presided over family night the next evening, smooth and affable, a no-nonsense, commonsensical kind of therapist, humanistic and empathic, full of good advice about making "I statements." His clients, mainly young people, seemed to like him, although before the meeting started and everybody was sitting in a big circle of chairs in the common room waiting for Rob to arrive, one young male client mentioned, his voice tinged with irony, that Rob *always* did this, always arrived between twelve and fifteen minutes late—made, in other words, an entrance. Still, Lin and I came away from the meeting wanting to be impressed. Our only (mainly unspoken) misgiving—aside from the fact that TLC didn't accept Medi-Cal or SSI payments—was that Rob Klein had the manner of the charismatic leader. Under the quiet, humble-sounding tone, under the deferential way he waited for other people to talk before he came forth with the right, sensible answer to some difficult-seeming question, under the we're-all-equal circular seating arrangement, he was full of himself. He made entrances. And he had a ponytail.

Charley saw it all right away. At noon on Monday, the day after we got back from Portland, we dragged him to TLC for an interview with Kimberly (Rob himself was unavailable, she told us, due to a previous appointment). Actually, Lin dragged him. It was my first day at work, so I biked over from my office to meet the two of them at the TLC admissions office on my lunch hour. Charley was hostile and refused to cooperate. He had no intention of staying at this place, he said, so why answer all these intrusive questions? Kimberly, who was soon no doubt kicking herself mentally for not having gone on maternity leave sooner, could see that the interview was going nowhere. I asked whether Rob could join us. I was remembering his easy mastery on family night, and Dr. Gray's recommendation. Maybe by some miracle Charley would like him, too. They would bond. Kimberly was dubious. Rob was in an important meeting in his office upstairs, she said. Still, Charley (who was edging toward the door) was a potential paying customer, so she decided to call Rob and, after a quick conversation, announced that he would come down and talk to Charley briefly. He arrived soon after, looking less mellow than on family night. It must have been a pretty important meeting upstairs.

"So, what's going on?" he asked Charley after he sat down, the world's worst question to ask a person in mental crisis. He seemed uptight, not the lord of the manor I'd expected.

Charley barely acknowledged him. "I refuse to be a caged bird," he said, turned on his heels and stalked out of the room.

Rob and Lin and I looked at each other. I asked Rob what he thought. He asked whether Charley was on medication. I said yes. He said it didn't seem to be working. "He needs to be hospitalized. Something needs to be done to deal with the psychotic ideation." The sudden shift in vocabulary startled me. Gone, suddenly, was the touchy-feely "So, what's happening?" stuff, the family night populism. "Ideation" was no-nonsense shrink talk. He could do that, too.

Rob and I kept talking while Lin went out into the hall to look for Charley. I asked whether TLC could handle him in this condition or whether we should take him to Harbor-UCLA first and maybe do TLC later, when he'd stabilized. No, Rob said, TLC could handle him. This was what the inpatient program was designed for.

How long and how much? I asked.

"We can work something out," Rob replied.

I stared at him with a mixture of disbelief and incredulity. Did the guy think I was going to hand over my kid *and* my credit card, blind?

How much? I asked again, and again he refused to give me a figure. We could work something out.

At that precise instant, Lin came back into the room and said Charley had disappeared from the building; somebody had seen him striding out, they didn't know where. I thanked Rob Klein, said we'd be in touch and left. I never spoke to him again.

Charley was nowhere to be found, so Lin went home and I went back to work and we kept in phone contact for the rest of the day. She called the police a couple of times, reporting a missing kid, but a couple of hours later he turned up at her apartment. He had taken the bus home.

He may well have saved me thousands of dollars that afternoon. To this day I'm not sure what would have happened if he hadn't disappeared when he did. Even after my bullshit detector started clanging I might very well have handed him along with a figurative blank check over to Rob Klein, so desperate was I to do *something*. From that day forward, whenever Charley cost me money, I always tried to factor the TLC episode into the asset side of the ledger.

I arrived home after work utterly spent, disgusted with myself and angry at Lin for continuing to resist putting Charley away. Our relationship was beginning to crumble under the pressure of the past month—the past three years, really. There were reasons we weren't married anymore, and here we had just spent almost the entire past three and a half days together in conditions that would have tested the conjugal mettle of Beaver Cleaver's mom and dad. My journal of Monday evening—Charley was back at Lin's—indicates my mood:

> I'm totally exhausted emotionally . . . the prospect of forcing him to be institutionalized again, even though I know it could save his life, is so horrific . . . thinking of Charley physically resisting, crying in total despair (as he has in my house when the whole weight of his misery crushed him)—that I also hesitate. . . .
>
> Lin & I unable to reach real agreement on where to put him—she wanting his approval, I unable to fight both of them. . . . The prospect of him being permanently deranged (even if he doesn't kill himself) looms. I was fantasizing before about getting a powerful gun, getting in the bathtub, closing the sliding door and, after leaving a message on Lin's machine that by the time she got this I'd be dead, shooting myself through the heart. (This is *only* fantasy, mind you, I'm not seriously thinking about it. . . . I'd never leave Lin, Charley, & Jenny in the lurch like that. Too cowardly.)

Ten minutes later Jenny called, "worried as hell," my journal says, wondering what was going on. She was at her place and had just talked to Lin, who had cut the conversation short because Charley "was doing something." Jenny asked me what we intended to do. I was worried too, I said, and told her I would call Lin and we would arrange something. It was like the infamous Sunday "serpent" dinner all over again, Jenny again prodding us into action.

Lin called back soon afterward; she'd had it too. We would take Charley to Harbor-UCLA. I biked to her apartment and found him lying on her couch under a sheet, undressed. "Charley, we're going to take you to the hospital," Lin said.

He looked up, vaguely. "Which one?"

We told him. Why that one? Because it was free, we said, we couldn't afford anything else. His look and tone of utter hopelessness were almost too painful to bear; I almost would have preferred him manic and combative. Almost. What had he done to deserve this? Yes, yes, he'd screwed up, gone off his medication, "hadn't taken responsibility" for his life. But what *kind* of a life? He was just a kid. What kind of a hand was this to be dealt, what kind of an enemy—shadowy, cowardly, treacherous—was this to face?

He didn't even fight as we put a few pieces of his clothing in a bag and got ready to go. It was almost a rerun of that misery-soaked first drive to St. John's three years before when he had thought he was going to work, except now we were going twenty miles to a public hospital, not ten blocks to a private one. Again Lin sat with him in the back, his head on her lap, stroking his face. Traffic was light on the freeway and we got to the hospital in half an hour. We led him to the emergency room. He began to rally a little as the reality of where he was and what was happening began to sink in. He kept veering toward the exit as I steered him into the mostly empty ER waiting area and sat him down to wait to be interviewed by the triage nurse, a sweet-tempered young blonde who spoke to the people she was interviewing with kindness and respect. A couple of times he got up and started to walk away. I followed him and steered him back. A firm grasp and some reassuring words were enough; he didn't fight or run.

"What's the problem?" the blonde nurse asked when it was our turn, and I handed her a stapled stack of papers, Charley's medical records from Providence and Ryles that explained his recent medical history. She started to skim the text. Then she stopped, focusing on the second page, which contained a diagram of Charley's chest and a description of the surgery. She looked at it intently, then at Charley.

"You had chest surgery recently?" she asked.

"Yes."

"Is your scar giving you any problems? Is it leaking at all? Hurting?"

"A little."

She glanced at me and then back at him, still friendly but now all business. "You come right this way with me, okay?" she said, coming out from behind her desk and taking his arm like an older sister. She led him into an examination room where he was looked at, then taken to psychiatric admissions on the other side of the building. Lin and I followed and sat outside the admissions office and waited while he was evaluated. After a while, the admitting psychiatrist, a young Asian woman, emerged through the office door and introduced herself. We gave her a history of Charley's illness, I doing most of the talking. She went back inside and reemerged a few minutes later, saying they were admitting him to the psychiatric ward, Eight West; he was already on his way upstairs. She gave us the phone number of the 8W nurses' station. We left without seeing him.

Once we were outside in the warm, furry summer night air, Lin started bitterly attacking me for being so cheerful during the interview, for talking so easily about Charley's history of accident-proneness and other eccentricities, for deriving such apparent enjoyment from detailing his problems and weaknesses. "This is just great cocktail party talk for you, isn't it?"

I didn't answer—I *had* blathered a lot to the doctor inside—and neither of us said anything for ten or fifteen minutes until the car was on the street heading back to the freeway. Then she started in again. By now, I'd had it. "F--- you, Lin," I said. "Just f--- you, okay? Yeah, I really love all this."

As I said, our relationship was showing signs of stress. The rest of the drive home was spent in oppressive silence, occasionally broken by similar eruptions of half-hearted bile. We were "like two over-the-hill fighters," my journal reported the next day—I was in my Norman Mailer mode—"slugging away with comically exaggerated roundhouse punches without any real force behind them. As I said to her, twenty years ago I would've cared about what she was saying."

Eight West

Risperidone: Brand name: *Risperdal*

Pharmacology: Antipsychotic Agent. Risperidone, a benzisoxazole derivative, is a *novel antipsychotic drug* which binds with high affinity to the serotonin type 2(5-HT(2)), dopamine D(2), and alpha(1)-adrenergic receptors. . . .

Indications: For the management of manifestations of schizophrenia. In controlled clinical trials, risperidone was found to improve both positive and negative symptoms.

Adverse Effects: The most frequent adverse reactions observed during clinical trials with risperidone were insomnia, agitation, extrapyramidal disorder, anxiety, and headache. . . . *In some instances it has been difficult to differentiate adverse events from symptoms of the underlying psychosis.*[8] (emphasis added)

Charley had two stays in Eight West in the summer and fall of 1994. The first lasted from July 19 to August 5, during which time, he told me a month after he got out, the voices went away. But after being released he fell into another serious depression and made another suicide attempt—again swallowing his lithium—on the morning of September 13 while I was at work. In the evening he told me rather sheepishly what he'd done, saying that, like the first time, he'd had second thoughts and thrown up the pills. He was okay now.

Sure he was okay. Over his and Lin's objections—she had known about the pill swallowing before I did but hadn't told me, which made *me* psychotic—I insisted that he go back to the hospital. Who knew if he had thrown up all the pills? At the very least he was at risk of lithium poisoning, which could ruin his kidneys, and he'd already had so many miraculous escapes I couldn't take chances. So back on the freeway we went, back to the Harbor-UCLA ER where Charley's stomach was pumped and he was put on suicide watch in restraints, then back in the psych ward after a short stay in the hospital's medical wing, cuffed to his bed with leather straps. This time he stayed for more than a month even though he wasn't crazy anymore, just very depressed. "That was the worst time," that second stay at Harbor-UCLA, he wrote me later, "when they had my left hand in restraints. I couldn't even piss right. Can you imagine trying to pee into a cup with one hand? You can't quite get it in. What d'you do, ask someone to come help you?"

Like San Francisco General, Charley's first "county psych ward," which was connected with UC San Francisco medical school, Harbor-UCLA Medical Center was a public teaching hospital. Although it was clean and professionally run, it had none of the amenities and cachet of St. John's or especially Providence Hospital in Portland, where Charley had been only weeks before and of which he always spoke highly. Many of the Harbor-UCLA psychiatrists were newly out of UCLA Medical School and relatively inexperienced. Worst of all for Charley, the hospital didn't permit smoking. "Dad: It's either write letters or make paper airplanes," he wrote in an undated letter during his first stay: "I absolutely detest this institution. UCLA Harbor. I don't like harbors and I don't like UCLA. So what? I would probably smoke if I could. Now I'm forced to quit. Is that what this was all about? Giving up cigarettes? I pray it goes somewhat deeper."

Nevertheless, despite the tedium of the place, or perhaps because of it, Charley got better during each of his two stays at Harbor-UCLA, shedding his psychosis during the first and his depression during the second, although it was hard to know how much the hospital contributed to these recoveries and how much they were simply a natural part of his cycle of manic-depression. What the hospital did do, as all the others had done, was provide a safe haven, and not only because of the physical security it offered. Not even the most secure psych ward is suicide-proof. Many, many mental patients have killed themselves in locked wards, strangling themselves with dental floss or hanging themselves with shower curtains or cutting themselves with broken lightbulbs or drowning themselves in toilet bowls. But for some reason, as prone to suicide as Charley was, he never tried it in the hospital. It was as if the locked ward, for all its indignities (or because of them?—viz., the regular schedule and structure and monitoring of medication, the withholding of alcohol and other substances), gave him permission to go easy on himself. "I tend to believe that I'm inclined to hospitals because I need thinking space," he wrote me, clear-headed at last, in another undated letter from late that summer. "They provide a place where random, *excess* thoughts can take form. Why I should need that space more than the next guy is another question." (emphasis added)

The problem was, of course, that no one can (or should) stay in a psych ward forever; such respites or "sojourns," life-preserving as they may be, are not themselves life, and eventually become life draining. Charley was being preserved but not replenished in these periodic warehousings. Talk therapy was sporadic, carried on by psychiatrists and psychologists who came and went and generally saw their role as trying to get Charley to develop "insight" into his supposed (*DSM*-defined) chemical condition. He was like a World War I soldier, repeatedly wounded, repeatedly sprayed with sulfa drugs and patched up and sent back to the trenches, a little weaker each time. How long could this go on? Harbor-UCLA was his fifth psychiatric hospital, not including Ryles. The cycles had been going on for three years now, and Charley was showing signs of mental and spiritual exhaustion. One who has not experienced them can only imagine how wearing such yearly pummelings of the psyche must have been, how the white-heat friction of mania must have worn away at his being, especially when each extreme, hot expansion was followed by the rigid contraction of icy depression. Even the finest metal will grow brittle when exposed to such extremes of temperature and torsion, and like a steel bar repeatedly bent back and forth will become soft and mealy and eventually break. It was as if Charley's life was being used up at double or triple speed. He seemed to feel this himself, even more than in earlier years when (as we have seen) he spoke about growing up too fast and knowing too much too soon. The exhaustion comes through in a letter to me from Harbor-UCLA sometime in the fall:

> It's hard to believe I once thought I had a superiority complex. I guess being so self-assured in the past led me to my falling. But if the confidence was with me before it shall return. If only there was some method of proving my illness, my jaded state, was temporary.
>
> A gypsy palm reader told me (a couple of years ago) that I had the hands of an old man, and that I would be in a hurry to establish my place in the universe. I guess my curiosity for death is (or was) part of that longing. That such a curiosity should grab someone so young seems abnormal, not to mention unfair; that I should become so weary of the material world so soon.
>
> But thank God for modern surgery, anesthetics, etc., that my life was saved. However, I do not trust the antipsychotics, for fear of becoming a vegetable.

And what about the antipsychotics? What were *they* contributing to the gradual sapping of his will? I was increasingly worried about this, especially after the morphine discussion with Dr. Roth. During Charley's first stay at Harbor-UCLA he was, at Dr. Gray's suggestion, taken off Navane and put on Risperdal, an "atypical antipsychotic," one of the new miracle drugs— Clozapine (or clozaril) is another—periodically touted as the dragon slayer, more effective than the previous dragon slayers. But the Risperdal didn't work, so Charley was put on the antipsychotic Haldol and eventually back on Navane, along with Cogentin for the side effects of the antipsychotic, plus lithium, plus an antianxiety drug for sleep. Later an antidepressant would be added again. How many different heavy medications can one person take without being completely thrown off balance?

My dissatisfaction with the emphasis on medication increased when Lin lent me her copy of Peter Breggin's *Toxic Psychiatry* a few days after Charley's second admission to Harbor-UCLA. I skimmed the book, which is a bitter attack on psychopharmacology and mainstream psychiatry in general along the lines of Kate Millett's *The Loony-Bin Trip*. Breggin himself is a psychiatrist, and his attack, from the inside, is even angrier than Millett's. He takes special aim at neuroleptics, calling them chemical straitjackets (that's where Charley had gotten the term). I didn't agree with everything Breggin said (and still don't), but his account of the short- and long-term dangers to the brain of antipsychotics seemed well documented and worth worrying about, and my journal of September 18 notes that Lin and I talked for a long time on the phone the same day that she gave me the book. Even before looking at it I had been thinking of getting Charley off the Navane, and my journal reports that I called him at Harbor-UCLA and said I would support him if he refused to take it, which he had begun doing anyway.[9]

The same day, stimulated by *Toxic Psychiatry* and wondering what good the neuroleptics really did, I sat down with my journal and tried to make a chronology of Charley's episodes going back to Yosemite, including their durations and the medications he had taken during each episode. After listing all the information I could remember, I taped some sheets of paper together and drew a time line from July 1991 to the present, September 1994. The episodes seemed to last from two to three or three-and-a-half months regardless of what medications Charley was taking or not taking. His recent experience at Providence and Ryles—the fact that when Lin and I came to Portland he was still psychotic after a month of hospitalization and daily medication—made me think the psychotic episodes had a life of their own. The psychosis, the voices, the mania, could be beaten into temporary submission by the drugs, as we had seen after Yosemite when Charley had a relapse in San Francisco a few days after he went off Navane upon leaving St. John's. But they still remained, crouching in the shadows like a whipped but still-ravening dog determined to eat its fill, beatings or no beatings, meds or no meds. As an example of the opposite situation—recovery without medication—I remembered how he had recovered from the first episode on his own while staying at Bob and Meighen's and then at Lin's in the fall of 1991, off medication entirely.

Aside from my growing doubts about the neuroleptics, I was starting more and more to question the nature of Charley's illness itself, whether it really was just a chemical imbalance and whether, if brain chemistry was involved, the imbalance was the cause or the effect. As he recovered from his latest episode, he was opening up to me more. At the beginning of September, between his two stays in 8W, he for the first time began describing to me what his voices were like—they were a collection, male and female, one with an English accent, hectoring him. Sometimes they cursed him, he said with a sheepish smile, "saying things like 'F--- you.'" He "injured" himself, he said, to get the voices to stop. From my journal:

Later he talked about feeling of unworthiness & I asked him about "serpent" remark on phone the day he stabbed himself, saying I had a feeling he hurt himself as a way of purging himself of pestilence, possibly letting the poison out through the wound. He said I was very perceptive, so maybe there's something to it. . . .

Question: Where is the point of intersection between the mental illness, giving rise to the voices, and whatever neurotic feelings Charley has? I.e., Why are the voices mean and abusive & disruptive rather than nice & helpful? Assuming that the voices are caused by the illness, and also positing that the form the psychosis takes is somehow related to the general mental state, what does this indicate about Ch's psychology? How can he be helped with neuroses, self-dislike, weak ego, etc.? Where did neurotic problems come from or, more relevantly, how can they be mitigated? Or are the voices etc. not related to rest of his mental state, but autonomous unto themselves?

As Charley began talking a little more—the most recent psychosis and stabbing had been so awful, I think, that he needed to unburden himself—I began to see that the voices and other "internal stimuli" weren't arbitrary. They had something to do with the "failed romantic relationship" Dr. Fischer had mentioned to me on the phone in June. Later that summer Charley used the phrase "sleeping with the enemy" while talking about the stabbing to Dr. Gray. Then, in a conversation with Lin and me while we were visiting him during his second stint at Harbor-UCLA, he said that in May–June he thought he had been a Nazi concentration camp guard in a previous life. A few evenings later, when I visited him alone, he volunteered even more. "He remembered being 'mean to me during that time,'" my journal says, "thinking I was a Jew." A Jew? I asked. Did it have something to do with me being cheap and pushy (the stereotypical "Jewish father," so to speak), not wanting him to go back to Portland and not giving him the thirty-five-dollar change fee for his ticket? I had noticed once or twice before that Charley sometimes became anti-Semitic when he was manic, and I wondered why. My journal reports that I asked now whether it "had something to do with his 'Nazi war criminal' self-image. He smiled. 'This certainly is the season for psychoanalysis, isn't it?' . . . He says the day he stabbed himself, he jumped off the stairs & lay on the ground, naked, praying for 'God to come & take me.'"

My main reaction upon hearing this was horror at the act (and at my having in a sense made it possible) rather than curiosity over the reasons. "The more I hear the worse it gets," my journal notes, "and the weaker and more inept I feel for having let him go back up" to Portland alone.

I wondered about the "sleeping with the enemy" remark. What did it mean? By now I had inferred from things Charley had told me that "the enemy" was Shizuko. I decided it must have had something to do with World War II. Japan and Germany were Axis powers. Shizuko was the enemy Charley had slept with, their intimacy turning him into a fellow Axis-member, a Nazi, which made him want to kill himself. Is that what the voices had been telling him?

That was as far as I got, at least then. After our few fragmented discussions he said little more about the whole matter, and I didn't ask, not only because I didn't want to pry but because I wasn't sure I really wanted to know. Now we had Nazis along with serpents. My Stephen King son, indeed.

This interpretation turned out to be wrong in one important detail, which I learned from Shizuko during her visit to Los Angeles in 1998; she had learned it from Charley. In the days after June 9, when they parted on such bad terms and she wrote to him expressing her hurt at his behavior, Charley retreated into the isolation of his sublet apartment at the bottom of the green birth canal. The voices he was hearing were angry and accusing (as he had also told me). One of the voices was Shizuko's. He decided that he had exploited her and because of that deserved to die—and not merely die, but die by stabbing himself. He had gotten the idea from *Madame Butterfly* (indirectly, via the movie *M. Butterfly*), but with one major alteration. In the Puccini opera, it was the cast-off Asian woman who stabbed herself. In Charley's case—as in the movie—the ending became inverted, with the male European exploiter rather than the oppressed Asian paying for the European's behavior. That's what the stabbing meant to him, Shizuko believed: a corrected ending of the movie and performance (Irons's) he had admired. It was Charley's repudiation of his role as the imperialist—"the enemy." This was, I think, the detail I had gotten wrong in my interpretation of his "sleeping with the enemy" remark. It was not Shizuko who was the enemy. *He* was the enemy. He had not become a Nazi by sleeping with her. He had been one already. He had violated her trust and their musical relationship and now had to pay the price.

I still don't know if all this is exactly right in every detail. Was the stabbing an approximation of hara-kiri (disembowelment), or an attempt to kill "the serpent" he mentioned to me on the phone, or both? Was his heart itself "the serpent"? Charley never said much more about the stabbing to me or, I believe, to anyone else except Shizuko, always referring to it in terms like "cut myself" or "hurt myself" or "injured myself." While at Harbor-UCLA he resumed contact with Shizuko, who was back at Reed. In an undated letter that I think was from his second (clear-headed) hospitalization he wrote:

> During my crazed state, when I stayed at Maxim's [the sublet apartment], I could hear you speaking to me. How can I not believe in a surreal world when I hear voices that cannot be real? I can't understand why I have been allowed to experience, or rather endure, the *strange* phenomena of the universe within the psyche (if that makes any sense). It's next to impossible to verbalize the things I've gone through. (emphasis in the original)

This is not the only time Charley voiced an inability to describe in words at least the most extreme parts of his episodes, so it would be presumptuous of me to try. But it seems indisputable that there was a link between his psychoses and what was going on in his life, and that the voices and visions—Shizuko's voice, the English voice saying "F--- you," the serpent, perhaps—all evolved out of the extreme psychic stress he was suffering owing to his manic episode combined with his perceived betrayal of a beloved friend. There was, in other words, both a physical aspect to the crisis (the mania potentiated by his going off lithium and taking stimulants) and a psychological one (guilt). Both aspects were obviously deeply intertwined, perhaps leapfrogging each other in ever-mounting intensity, but they were not the same thing, they were not reducible simply to a chemical imbalance. It's all brain chemistry, the post-Freudians tell us. But if brain chemistry explains everything it explains nothing. The taste of a carrot stick is brain chemistry, too. Why did Charley's voices badger him about exploitation and betrayal, and not about, say, carrot sticks or brussels sprouts?

As I tried to understand the link between psychosis and one's life circumstances, I remembered something a college classmate of mine had said thirty years before. I had tried LSD—which induces psychosis—a few times and found out that she had too, so I asked her what her experience had been like. "It's what you already have, only more so," she replied, and I had to agree. The mental effect of LSD is to lift the haze of familiarity that normally hangs between us and the world. In our everyday lives we see but we don't observe, as Sherlock Holmes said. Once the haze of habit and routine lifts, we look at things as if for the first time, newly vivid and alive, pulsating with previously unseen meanings and interconnections. The same effect can be achieved by staring at something for a long time; eventually it starts to vibrate and change. LSD or other hallucinogenics make this happen to an extreme degree and without any effort on our part, thus seeming to be magical. I believe that it was this kind of extreme intensification of experience and accompanying loss of perspective that possessed Charley during his May–June mania, the exponentially heightened sensitivity of the mania turning what ordinarily would have been merely guilty regret over bad behavior into a life-threatening catastrophe. (Imagine "obsessing" over some bad deed or humiliation, as we all have done at times, but then not being able to stop.) Later, when the mania subsided, he was able to see his treatment of Shizuko in less-earthshaking terms. He wrote to her from Harbor-UCLA:

> June of this year turned out to be the worst month of my life (more or less) when considering the inner turmoil I suffered I simply flipped out, and ended up hurting myself badly. So now I'm finished with Reed and will be taking a few months to recuperate before returning to any school.
> I tend to have periods where I fall down. It's just the way I am. I didn't keep in touch because I felt some guilt over our intimacy, but it doesn't bother me any more. I'm going to go to sleep now. Best wishes, Charley

The periods of falling down, however, were adding bruise on top of bruise. "Even though I'm only twenty-one and a half," he wrote Shizuko soon after the above (in September), echoing his "hands of an old man" letter to me,

> I feel my life has been lived to its full extent. I'm afraid it may be boredom from here on. . . .
> I'm resolved that life is just very hard, and that my carefree, confident attitude in the past is what caused me to take a fall. Anyway, things can only get better. Perhaps I can see you some time in San Francisco or even Portland. I'm sorry I can't be there at Reed keeping you company. Think good thoughts for me and I will be relieved from my condition. ♥ Charley

Although they continued to correspond and occasionally talk on the phone,

Shizuko was coming to realize that Charley was in truth gone from her life, and in fact they never saw each other again. The last time they talked—long distance during one of his later hospitalizations—he said "I love you, Juko," and she answered, "I love you, too, Charley." For her, that exchange was the coda of their duet. When she heard about his death a year later, awful as it was and bad as she felt, it was a kind of anticlimax. We talked about the meaning of that death the evening she visited me in 1998, and I summed up her view in my journal: "Shizuko: Charley couldn't understand why he had been marked with this curse—his illness. Shiz. thinks that's why he killed himself—to get back at the illness or whoever had cursed him—tit for tat—denying it/them that triumph of seeing him suffer."

Perhaps the "it/them" was the serpent he was trying to expunge, in his very heart.

Charley and Shizuko's correspondence makes it clear that their connection was genuine. When she spoke to me years later, she could still say that in some ways Charley had been the person closest to her in her life, and she wasn't alone in this. Other friends of his would tell me the same thing, again and again, unsolicited, long after such statements could be written off as consolations to a grieving parent. Charley really had influenced them profoundly and, selfish as he was in certain earthly ways, he was not selfish spiritually (except during the extremities of mania), and he was able to connect with people who got to know him in ways they considered profound. The problem, though, was that all of them without exception—Shizuko was only the saddest case, because she cared the most—ended up having to pull away, and he always ended up alone. Take Brian Marsh, the friend from freshman year who had called me from New York after Yosemite to tell me about Charley's "iawaska" episode and about how in a school full of depressed people Charley had been the most depressed. Charley talks about Brian in his journal at Reed in the spring of 1994, a month or so before the stabbing. "He's so far away this year," he writes, and continues,

> He has become tall indeed, a real Nordic survivor, and with such sensibility. Why, why, why should he be so estranged? As if the world were not harsh enough without the ones we cherish being inaccessible. Perhaps that is the beauty of our friendship. We keep our affection *in our spirits*. It may sound like bullshit *but it is all I know*. I must leave before I come to despise myself. (emphasis added)

"I must leave," in this particular entry, merely meant leaving Portland; school was almost out. Later it would mean leaving life. One by one, the people Charley cared about pulled away, exhausted. In the end he, too, even more exhausted by his own self-devouring self, would need to pull away. But how do you pull away from yourself? And if in the end we're alone anyway, if living "in our spirits" is *all we know,* and if those same spirits are consuming us, why stay around to be periodically lashed and beaten by an unseen, unfair, and merciless foe? Such steadfastness could begin to look like masochism, each exhausted recovery an ever-diminishing return.

Jonathan, Lin and five-month-old Jenny on our Brooklyn stoop, summer 1971, me with a bottle of Colt 45 Malt Liquor in one hand, an unfiltered Camel in the other. When Lin saw the photo she exclaimed, "Oh my God, I gave birth to a little pig?!"

"The brightest little boy in the whole park." Lin and six-month-old Charley, summer 1973, at Jonathan's father's house in East Hampton, New York.

Chicago, Lincoln Park Zoo, winter 1974–1975.
Note tiger in background. I had just made the
remark to Charley about how the tiger looked
hungry.

Thanksgiving, 1981. "They never met
a camera they didn't like."

Mom and her boy, 1982, on our
Chicago stoop shortly before we
moved to Los Angeles.

Emergency Room Charley and Mom and Dad, Chicago, 1979–1981.

Charley as Dracula, Halloween, 1982 or 1983, biting Jenny's neck.

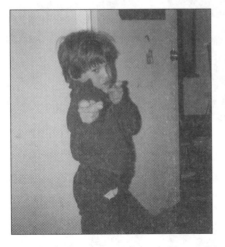

Jenny and Charley in front of our bookcase, 1980 or 1981. The white volumes behind Jenny's head are part of the collected works of Karl Marx and Frederick Engels. Jenny, whose middle name is Marx, was named after Karl's wife, Jenny von Westfalen Marx.

Charley the martial-arts hero. I nicknamed him "Bruce Flea."

School photo, 1988,
I believe at Uni High
in West Los Angeles.

Charley in Culver City, spring 1987, shortly before
he went to England and Germany for part of the
summer in a family exchange program.

Shizuko, Prague, 2001.

The four of us at a Christmas party, probably 1985, possibly 1986.

Jenny in 2000.

Portrait of the artist, San Francisco, probably
Charley's final year of high school, 1989.

Mom, Grandpa Bob and Charley at Bob's house in San Francisco,
where Charley was living, Bob's birthday, January 1990. When
Charley sent me the photo he labeled it "The Gruesome
Threesome."

Charley, age fifteen, in Marin County, with San Francisco in the background, 1988.

"The Battle of the Prints," Castro Street gay pride fair, October 1991, during Charley's recovery from Yosemite and his first two hospitalizations. Charley is clearly "present and accounted for," although a few minutes earlier he had started to wander off the curb into traffic after the walk light turned red.

Christmas 1995.

Dad and Charley, summer 1996, a few months before Charley's death, on my balcony in Santa Monica. We photographed each other.

Self-portrait, early or mid–1990s.

READER/CUSTOMER CARE SURVEY

We care about your opinions. Please take a moment to fill out this Reader Survey card and mail it back to us.

As a special **"thank you"** we'll send you exciting news about interesting books and a valuable **Gift Certificate.**

Please PRINT using ALL CAPS

First Name [_____] MI. [__] Last Name [_____]

Address [_____]

City [_____] ST [__] Zip [_____]

Phone # ([__]) [__] — [__] Fax # ([__]) [__] — [__]

Email [_____]

(1) Gender:
___ Female   ___ Male

(2) Age:
___ 12 or under   ___ 40-59
___ 13-19   ___ 60+
___ 20-39

(3) Marital Status
___ Married
___ Single
___ Divorced/Widowed

(4) Did you receive this book as a gift?
___ Yes   ___ No

(5) How many Health Communications books have you bought or read?
___ 1   ___ 2-4   ___ 5+

(6) How did you find out about this book?
Please fill in ONE.
1) ___ Recommendation
2) ___ Store Display
3) ___ Bestseller List
4) ___ Online
5) ___ Advertisement
6) ___ Catalog/Mailing
7) ___ Interview/Review (TV, Radio, Print)

(7) Where do you usually buy books?
Please fill in your top TWO choices.
1) ___ Bookstore
2) ___ Religious Bookstore
3) ___ Online
4) ___ Book Club/Mail Order
5) ___ Price Club (Costco, Sam's Club, etc.)
6) ___ Retail Store (Target, Wal-mart, etc.)

(9) What subjects do you enjoy reading about most? Rank only *FIVE*. *Use 1 for your favorite, 2 for second favorite, etc.*

	1	2	3	4	5
1) Parenting/Family	O	O	O	O	O
2) Relationships	O	O	O	O	O
3) Recovery/Addictions	O	O	O	O	O
4) Health/Nutrition	O	O	O	O	O
5) Christianity	O	O	O	O	O
6) Spirituality/Inspiration	O	O	O	O	O
7) Business Self/Help	O	O	O	O	O
8) Teen Issues	O	O	O	O	O
9) Sports	O	O	O	O	O

(14) What attracts you most to a book?
(Please rank 1-4 in order of preference.)

	1	2	3	4
1) Title	O	O	O	O
2) Cover Design	O	O	O	O
3) Author	O	O	O	O
4) Content	O	O	O	O

TAPE IN MIDDLE; DO NOT STAPLE

BUSINESS REPLY MAIL
FIRST-CLASS MAIL PERMIT NO 45 DEERFIELD BEACH, FL

POSTAGE WILL BE PAID BY ADDRESSEE

HEALTH COMMUNICATIONS, INC.
3201 SW 15TH STREET
DEERFIELD BEACH FL 33442-9875

FOLD HERE

Comments:

6

Weaving the Shroud

"A Desire Leading One to Death"

"I asked my father if he believed in an afterlife and he told me no," Charley wrote Shizuko while at Harbor-UCLA. "Remember Glenn Gould said it was more plausible than oblivion. I favor that argument. I feel I've made a muck of my present life."

Note the wording: "*present* life." Aside from my lifelong inability to embrace religion, my reason for telling Charley I didn't believe in an afterlife was that I didn't want to give him any ideas. The more people told him there might be something better ahead, the more quickly he might decide to see for himself, like some early Christians in the days before "the Everlasting . . . fixed his canon against self-slaughter," as Hamlet, another blond youth plagued by melancholy, put it. If God is love and heaven is waiting, why not make the journey sooner rather than later, especially when life down here is mostly Romans and lions and growing frustration at having made a muck of life, a muck that deepened every year as Charley saw his classmates graduating and moving on, getting careers and making lives while he was stuck in yet another hospital after yet another fall? Eventually, as the poet (and diagnosed manic-depressive) Robert Lowell put it, "the breakage can go on repeating once too often."[1] Or as an offbeat psychiatrist named Edward Podvoll puts it, speaking of the aftermath of psychosis,

> One wakes up, looks around, and, unlike in the dream when asleep, one has to take responsibility for the actions and reactions committed during the delusion. One feels at that point like King Lear, who recognizes that he has made a monstrosity out of his life and that his authority and even his love were destructive to other people. At such a point, people frequently say, "I am getting out of this before I do more harm."[2]

These lines, from a book called *The Seduction of Madness* that Charley himself discovered, seemed to describe his condition as the years wore on and defeat followed defeat, disappointment followed disappointment, and his élan vitale, that wobbly mercury, seemed increasingly to seek escape. But it was the paragraph directly after these words of Podvoll's that Charley himself seemed struck by, because he underlined it in red—one of only four marks he made in the book. The underlining reads:

> It is not just that the consequences of psychosis lead to death, but also that death itself is inherent in the urge for transformation. Because death is the undercurrent of the pleasure and the freedom being courted in the psychotic transformation, it requires the death and eventual freedom from the body, from relationship to the world and from the workings of one's mind.[3]

This passage speaks to the strange unity of elation and self-destruction that Charley had expressed in his May 1992 journal entry about his breakdown at Yosemite: *"Having achieved for a brief while immortal consciousness, I wanted to transcend this piteous world."*

But why would immortal consciousness, which seems so life affirming (particularly in Charley's case: birds chirping, the flow of a stream controlled by the waving of one's hand), lead a person to try to kill himself?

Podvoll is not satisfied with purely biochemical answers to this question—for example, that the neurotransmitter agitation and resulting mental discomfort of extreme psychosis (particularly mixed states) can be so overwhelming that the sufferer simply must escape. This may be true as far as it goes; no doubt something like it was occurring during the June 1994 *M. Butterfly* episode when Charley stabbed himself to silence Shizuko's voice. But Podvoll doesn't simply stop there and (so to speak) write out a prescription for neuroleptics (rather than Swiss army knives) to stop the voices. He believes there are psychological rather than purely physical reasons why some people go mad, reasons having to do with "psychic predicaments" they find themselves in, life crises that they are unable to handle through ordinary means and that seem to require extraordinary or superhuman leaps to overcome. Very often, people in such predicaments use some kind of substance (drugs, stimulants like coffee) or physical routines (meditation, staring at candles, sleep deprivation, exertion), or both, to alter their mental states and propel the leap. Whatever the means of transformation, Podvoll says, the need to transform originates in a personal crisis that may have been "cooking" since an early age. It is not simply a sudden burst of "adolescent" or "adult onset" manic-depression or schizophrenia that erupts out of nowhere because of some yet-obscure maturation of the brain, as I thought Charley's breakdown at Yosemite had been once it became clear (after his second episode) that the first had not just been a nervous breakdown.

"Urge for transformation . . ." "Freedom from the body . . ." But why? It seems to make no sense. Charley was handsome and athletic, not some deformed, self-loathing Richard III or Quasimodo. But for some reason he was not at home in his body. Thinking about this reminded me of a Michael Jackson video from the late '80s in which Jackson turns into a spaceship in order to carry some children away from danger. When I watched it—this was before accusations surfaced about Jackson's alleged pedophilia—it occurred to me that his transformation into an inanimate object represented some deep wish fulfillment; after all, he had been attempting to change his actual physical appearance for years anyway. When the pedophilia scandal broke I wondered further whether turning himself into a rescuing spaceship—a body that saved children rather than abused them—represented Jackson's attempt to sublimate desires he couldn't otherwise control; pure metal, like pure spirit, does not feel lust. Whether this analysis was right or wrong, it seemed clear that Michael Jackson was one of those people, like Charley, who are not comfortable in their own skin. But Jackson wasn't suicidal; Charley was. And unlike most of us, for whom death is distant and very abstract and very undesirable, he saw it as familiar and

personal and often not undesirable at all. Lin once said that Charley lived in a chronic existential crisis; every day he woke up thinking, in effect, Should I kill myself today, or look for a job? Should I kill myself, or make coffee? His life operated on the edge of Occam's razor—the principle that we should always look for the simplest explanation first. For all his intelligence and complexity, Charley lived life at its simplest and most basic, in a place where the fads and frills of medicine and talk and ideas and even the most empathic interventions by others were like fleas on a dog. His suicidality was not just a function of his depressed states; it was an "undercurrent"—Podvoll's word—in all of them.

How true this was became clear to me when I read his journals. One particular entry, from the summer of 1995, about a year after the *M. Butterfly* stabbing, expresses his sensibility in an unforgettable way. Before presenting it, however, I need to give it context by telling a family anecdote. When Charley was living in Santa Cruz with Lin in the winter of 1991 and 1992 and recovering from his first breakdown, she took him to see a Native American shaman (this was a different shaman from the Sacramento shaman Charley talked to sometime later about feeling unloved as a child). I heard about it a few months later when Charley, Lin and I were having dinner back in Los Angeles. I was curious. I knew that he was interested in Eastern religion and Native American warrior mythology and that she had also done reading in pre-Christian, goddess-based nonpatriarchal religions. Although a skeptic myself, I was also trying to keep an open mind. Western medicine certainly hadn't done that great so far. Who knew what worked and what didn't? Charley certainly seemed better since being in Santa Cruz. "So what did the shaman tell you?" I asked.

Charley looked at Lin with a slightly abashed grin. "He told me not to worry so much about god consciousness. He said I needed to get a job, a car and a girlfriend."

This became family folklore. "O great Guru," I would intone when I told the story, "I have given up all my earthly possessions and spent the last twenty years crawling on my hands and knees up to this Himalayan peak to humble myself and be worthy of you and your wisdom! Tell me, O Guru, what must I do to achieve enlightenment?"

"Get a job, a car and a girlfriend, my son. . . ."

There was at least one period during these few years when Charley actually had all three. It was in the summer of 1995, after he recovered from the stabbing and the two stints at Harbor-UCLA. He was living with me, getting SSI (almost eight hundred dollars a month), and fairly stabilized once more on lithium. He had a job "slingin' lattes" at a coffeehouse a short walk from our apartment, he had a car (he bought an old VW Bug in June, which he loved) and he had a girlfriend named Lysa. He seemed to be successfully talking my brother, Uncle Tim, into helping underwrite a trip to Paris to study French. His journal reflects a fair amount of contentment and even a return of self-confidence. Then, sometime in late June or early July, he writes:

> After my 5½ hour shift today I came home, had a bite, took a Xanax and a nap @ 1.45. Woke up @ 5.00, and took a shower.
> I tried to watch an old Japanese film with my father, *Red Beard*. Not interested really.
> Tim called yesterday to discuss plans for Paris, and said I should go to study intently if I go at all. I'm not sure how much he'll help financially.
> Off to retire.
> I'm not afraid of Death—CA

The Suicidologist

Was there a person or a thing that could end this intimate preoccupation? I had great hopes for one person in particular, Max Freulich, a therapist Charley saw in late 1994 after getting out of Harbor-UCLA. Max was a suicidologist. I first heard about him from Katie, a friend of mine, one autumn day—I think Charley was still at Harbor-UCLA—as she and I were taking a Saturday morning walk on the beach and I was expressing my frustration at not being able to find anyone—therapist, psychiatrist, caregiver, whoever—that he could really talk to. Katie replied that she had learned, particularly from people who are prone to suicide, that one possible route to saving someone is to find a person they can bond with—a kind of mentor with whom they can form an emotional link stronger than the link they are forming with death. She said she had heard that Max, who was a founder of the suicide hotline and the American Association of Suicidology, was a specialist in treating suicidal people.

This was an interesting idea to me. I had never thought of it quite this way—that somebody like Charley, who has tried suicide repeatedly, is in the process of forging a link with death (or Death), each failed attempt making the link stronger rather than weaker. Is there a way of reversing this process?

I spoke to Lin and we decided Max was worth a try. As usual, it was a chore getting Charley to talk to yet another shrink, and he agreed to go with us to meet Max more out of obligation than conviction. (Lin and I had a long-standing policy that as a condition for living with one of us, Charley was required to have some kind of talk therapy in addition to either working or going to school, or both.) Max turned out to be a man in late middle age with grizzly gray hair and moustache and a strong New York accent and New York directness. As Charley, Lin and I introduced ourselves I made an educated guess and asked what part of Brooklyn he came from, saying that we had been living in Brooklyn when Charley was born. Brownsville, Max said.

Perfect, I thought. *That* was who he reminded me of: the Brownsville doctor played by Paul Muni in the movie *The Last Angry Man,* which I had seen when I was eleven; Muni's mensch-y performance as the tough-tender inner-city doctor ministering to the lost and oppressed had made a lifelong impression on me. Now, this evening, Max's appearance and strong Brooklyn accent and manner were as familiar and comforting as the Ben Shahn–type prints on the walls of his homey office and the volumes of Freud in his bookcase; the office reminded me of the apartments of the left-wing Jews I had grown up with in New York. Maybe Max was the mentor Charley needed!

The session itself buoyed my hopes further. Max asked about Charley's background, and we talked about the history of suicide attempts. When Charley described the February 1993 wrist slitting he mentioned that there hadn't been much blood, which was one of the reasons he had given up the attempt and called Lin and me. Max asked him to describe the actual cuts, and Charley said they had been across the wrists. Max nodded and said that often such types of incisions don't lead to much bleeding.

"So how do you make yourself bleed more?" Charley asked.

Max smiled and shook his head. "I don't give pointers." We all laughed.

We talked about the therapy Charley had had the previous year with his therapeutic mother Dr. Blum, which was less psychoanalytical and intellectual than emotionally supportive. Max said he didn't work that way; his method was more to challenge the person he was working with, to dig deeper. He seemed to be of the old, more psychoanalytical school, dismissive of the eclectic, nurturing kind of therapy currently in favor. That was fine with me. I thought Charley needed an intellectual challenge. Aside from Dr. Gray, whom he respected but couldn't afford for in-depth therapy because his folks weren't millionaires, Charley's view of therapists tended to be that they were shallow and clueless, not intellectually at his level, and I had the impression that because Max seemed to have some depth as well as breadth of practical experience, Charley wouldn't be able to dismiss him so cavalierly. My optimism grew when in the course of the discussion Max made a couple of seemingly wild guesses about Charley's history and condition (unfortunately I can't remember what they were) that were so uncannily accurate that even Charley seemed impressed. I could barely contain my excitement. Was this the guy who would finally gain his respect and help break the death chain he was forging?

No. As with his other therapists, after a few sessions Charley announced to me that going to Max Freulich was a waste of time and Mom's and my money, that Max just didn't understand what was going on and never would. Which made sense when I thought about it later. Charley, after all, had never heard of Paul Muni and couldn't have cared less about the Ben Shahn–type posters and the mensch-y Brooklyn accent. *I* was the one who had bonded with Max.

The (Almost) Smoking-Gun Pamphlet

September 30, 1995

Almost a year later, a Saturday morning, clear and warm. I was home alone cleaning my apartment. Charley was back in the hospital, St. John's this time, and I was feeling the guilty sense of freedom and security that always came when I knew that somebody else was responsible for him and that if he wasn't actually getting well he was at least safe. His Medi-Cal had kicked in, which meant that St. John's—like Providence Hospital in Portland—had to take him if he was flagrantly psychotic; it was part of the tax-exemption deal. We had gotten through the past year without a suicide attempt, but Charley, after cutting down his lithium again, had had another breakdown the last week of September after acting more and more hyper over the summer. Lin and I had taken him to the ER two nights before. For the first time ever, he had gotten violent and had to be handcuffed by hospital security before being led to the psych ward.

Charley's yearly "excursions" had begun to seem almost routine. But that sense of routine was about to end. As I cleaned my living room, which doubled as Charley's room, I noticed as I straightened papers on his entertainment center a pink State of California pamphlet outlining the steps required to buy a handgun.

I felt a cold flutter in my stomach, then a nauseating sense of doom. Charley had never shown the slightest interest in guns, either as a little boy or as a teenager. Why now? But given his history of suicide attempts, two of which had failed only by miracles, did I really even need to ask? He was going to make sure he did it right this time, obviously. At least that was my immediate reaction—which was bad enough, especially since I couldn't help thinking that I might well be the one to find him; he had been living with me for the past year.

But then, out of nowhere, I thought of something else. Given his sudden violence at the hospital two nights before—understandable as it had been (he had erupted when I tried to take his credit cards out of his wallet in case I needed to pay for the hospitalization)—might he be going through a personality change, becoming capable of shooting somebody else?

This was a new idea. Bad as things had gotten over the past four years, Charley had never resisted me physically, and I had never been afraid of him. He was taller than I and probably stronger, but he had been gentle even as a little boy, rambunctious but not a fighter. It had never occurred to me that he could be capable of premeditated violence toward others. Things involving handguns—murder-suicides by jealous husbands or boyfriends, rampages by paranoid schizophrenics, postal workers blowing away their supervisors, high school massacres by disaffected classmates—none of those were Charley. Our family had its share of weirdness, but murder?

Now, suddenly, I was thinking about new possibilities. Aside from his suicide attempts there was the question of his girlfriends, his ex-girlfriends and his would-be girlfriends, and his evolving—or devolving—relations with women. From his early teens, Charley had been chased by girls (and boys). He had never been without girlfriends in junior high, in high school, in college or even—until recently—during his years of illness. But as his breakdowns had become more chronic, with shorter periods of recovery, his relationships had suffered. Even women who loved him, like Shizuko, eventually had to retreat.

I remembered that just a few days earlier, before he became psychotic, he had mentioned that the phone hadn't rung in two days. He had wondered whether it was broken.

And the romantic obsessions. Aside from his pursuit of the woman professor at Reed, I remembered Charley's harassment of Jenny Lewis after she broke up with him; he had called her repeatedly until she threatened (reluctantly, because she still cared for him) to call the police. Lately, perhaps as a counterbalance to his growing difficulties with real women, he had begun fixating on actresses and models like Linda Fiorentino and Claudia Schiffer, buying Schiffer's exercise tape and taking it to be autographed when she came to a local bookstore. No big deal in itself, of course, but he had also started trying to contact these women and writing them "why don't we get together?" letters, asking his sister, who worked for a talent agency, if she could help him find their addresses. Jenny had reacted with distaste. "God, Dad," she said to me, "doesn't he know what happens to letters like that? The women don't even get them. The guys in the mailrooms open them and pass them around and laugh over them!"

Was Charley becoming just another isolated loser sitting alone, fixating on fantasy women, or worse (the letters really worried me), forgetting they were fantasies? Was my beautiful, affectionate son, who at seventeen played the *Well-Tempered Clavier* and read Camus in French and enthused over Tolstoy's "What Is Art?," who still on occasion would come up to me and hug me, then pick me up off the floor to show me how strong he was—was my little Chopin and David Bowie aficionado really sliding into such emotional vacuity and poverty of thought?

And what if the lonely fantasizing turned to anger at the women for not responding to him? What if he decided to go after them? What if *that* was what the gun was for?

I called Dr. Gray and left a voice mail. Then I went to see Charley at St. John's—in the familiar locked ward—and told him I had found the gun pamphlet and demanded to know what was going on. He told me he had gone to a pawnshop in downtown Santa Monica and put a deposit down on a .38 handgun pending the waiting period the state requires. I asked why. "Protection," he said dismissively, and he refused to talk about it any more. When Dr. Gray called me back later I told him about the gun and asked whether

Charley's attempt to buy it, given his history of suicide attempts and unwanted attentions to a number of women, could be grounds for a longer-term hospitalization than the three- or fourteen-day holds that psychotic patients are normally put under when committed involuntarily. No, probably not, Dr. Gray said, since he hadn't used it yet.

When we hung up I sat staring at the entertainment center. For the first time it occurred to me that at some point I might be faced with having to stop Charley physically from doing violence to somebody besides himself, possibly me. (Me? Might he be thinking about shooting *me* if I got in the way of his doing whatever it was he was planning on doing? Would I have been safe in my own house with him and a gun?)

It had come to this. I was sitting and thinking about being maimed or killed by, or maiming or killing, my own son.

I felt a warm shiver of self-pity, again nauseating but—this was so strange—comforting at the same time, as I have heard heroin is. Until this moment, despite my many moments of exhaustion and frustration since Yosemite, I had always been sure that Charley, assuming we could keep him alive, would recover, that Lin and I could help him outgrow or at least adapt to his mysterious and virulent affliction, that we could save him and ourselves and Jenny. I had also believed that until that happened I would be able to tell, at least in broad outline, when he was crazy and when he was sane and as a result know how to deal with him at any given time. True, I had failed the year before to read his incipient suicidality when he came down to L.A. from Portland and then went back up and stabbed himself. But at least I had known he was crazy. His moods determined his thought patterns, and the moods, the manias and the depressions, were observable. Weren't they? Suddenly I wasn't sure. The gun pamphlet was forcing me to consider the possibility that even when his mood appeared to be stable he was thinking and doing crazy things—trying to buy a gun, at the very least—that I knew nothing about. What if the struggle between insanity and sanity that often seemed to go on during his psychotic breaks—where literally from one moment to the next he would appear rational and then irrational, as if two equal forces were struggling for control of his mind like two big basketball centers elbowing each other under the basket—what if it was not that at all, but a state of near-permanent insanity that he was simply able to disguise better some times than others? What if he was not, in other words, a relatively harmless (at least toward others) manic-depressive? What if he was becoming (or always had been!) a paranoid schizophrenic, capable of God knows what? For the first time ever I felt not merely concern, helplessness and sorrow, but real fear.

But even as I was feeling it, this fear was becoming something else, and something happened as I sat staring vacantly at the entertainment center where the pink gun pamphlet again lay. My mind, and in a strange way my morale, seemed to rally in a kind of adrenaline rush—around the organizing principle of protecting innocent people. I could not let him harm somebody else. That was a given. Like it or not he was my responsibility, since nobody else who could really stop him seemed up to *this* task. (As much as I leaned on Lin, I could not imagine her taking Charley on physically.) The idea of somebody being hurt or killed because I had knowingly let a sick person—even some-one I loved—run loose was worse than the thought of hurting or even killing him. It was so simple. And tragic. And noble.

But my noble and tragic thoughts were not altogether pure; I could feel that even as I thought them. There were bits of anger and resentment mixed in. It was as much a desire for revenge as a righteous indignation that was fueling my seemingly cool calculation. It was anger—not only at what Charley might do to Claudia Schiffer but at what he had already done to me: he had put me through the ringer, ruined my life, caused me anxiety, dread . . . and inconvenience. I had periodically felt anger and resentment the past few years—and had felt guilty because of it. But now the guilt was being replaced by a sense of sullen triumph, because finally I had a righteous hook for my resentment. Wouldn't it be better if he could just be gotten rid of? Not because he was an inconvenience to me, of course, but because he was really and truly a danger to others that I could with impunity neutralize—a word with the same root as *neuter*—by any means necessary. The ultimate Oedipal revenge fantasy: Get rid of the troublesome son—my hold on immortality, sure, but also younger and handsomer and more desirable than I. And do it in such a righteous way that no judge, not even his mother, could convict me.

My conscience recoiled from these limbic thoughts seeping up from some mindless, reptilian part of my brain, even as I thought them in that sunny, mote-filled Saturday room. But they were there, I had to admit it. And my con-science recoiled even more as it watched the reptile (or serpent?), as in some cheap horror movie, metamorphosing into the human and seemingly rational. Shamefully, despite myself, I watched myself sit, coolly going over recent events and possibilities, including the possibility of maiming or killing my son, like an accountant perusing a balance sheet. The liability side of Charley's recent signs of aggression and the gun literature was that I was losing all hope for his recovery. The asset side was that, well, maybe the gun angle was a way of getting rid of the problem altogether.

The new hospitalization was particularly difficult, partly because of my own growing fears and partly because of Charley's growing frustration. He fought with the staff several times, kicking one male nurse in the groin and grabbing another's keys. Several times when I went to see him he was strapped to his bed in leather restraints or else locked in the scuff-walled surveillance room next to the nurses' station, the same room where he had spent his first days of confinement, talking French, four years before.

What was new about this breakdown, aside from (or related to?) the gun business, was that Charley had acted as if he wanted to be hospitalized. He had seemed almost to goad me into taking him to the St. John's ER, and when he started getting better I asked him whether that was a fair interpretation of his behavior. He said it was fair. Why? I asked, thinking of the gun. Had he been afraid of what he might do to himself or someone else? "To someone else— not myself," he said, but wouldn't say anything more.

The Monday after he was hospitalized I biked to the pawnshop where he had put the deposit down on the .38. I wanted to cancel the transaction and if necessary tell them about Charley's history in case he ever tried to buy a gun there again. The clerk I spoke to remembered Charley and the transaction and said there hadn't been anything unusual about him or it; the fourteen-day delay to complete the deal was routine. He showed me the gun sitting in the layaway area sheathed in a black holster. When he picked it up to put it back on the display shelf, the gun's physicality and the awfulness of the whole situation hit me again. If things had gone just a little differently, by now Charley would have owned a handgun, for what fathomable or unfathomable purpose I could only guess.

River Community

As I was leaving [the ward] at 7 P.M. last night a kid [a fellow patient] named Jason whom Ch. has become friendly with said, "Sir?" (He was standing near TV in main sitting room.) I turned to him. He continued. "He's just lonely. He needs a friend." I said something like, "Be one." He said he'd try.

(My journal, October 8, 1995)

Depakote: Valproic Acid (Valproate; Divalproex Sodium)
Drug Class: Anticonvulsant
Principal Uses: To control certain types of seizures in the treatment of epilepsy and other disorders. *Also used to treat acute mania in the treatment of bipolar disorder.*
How the Drug Works: Valproic acid *is thought* to depress the activity of certain parts of the brain and suppress the abnormal firing of neurons that cause seizures.
Side Effects: *Serious:* Severe abdominal pain and vomiting, muscle weakness and lethargy, yellow discoloration of the skin or eyes, etc. *Common:* Nausea and vomiting, heartburn, diarrhea, cramps, loss of appetite and weight loss, increased appetite and weight gain, hair loss, tremor, dizziness, clumsiness or unsteadiness, confusion, sedation.[4] (emphasis added)

By the middle of his second week of confinement Charley was getting ready to leave, but again with no real resolution or plan for what to do. He "thinks he can drive again for livery service—it's as if nothing happened," I wrote in my journal of October 10 (he had been working for a limousine service when the new episode started). "He didn't get any sleep, that's all—wants to sweep the latest episode under rug—[he claims] I can't understand him—I don't realize what it's like to be him." He had spent much of this latest hospitalization in a very bad state—foggy, miasmic, visibly psychotic, very depressed—and when he was discharged from the St. John's psych unit on Saturday, October 14, fifteen days after going in, he was still very shaky, "heavily medicated," my journal says, "40 mg Navane per day, 1500 mg lithium, 1500 mg Depakote (this is new—we're trying to switch from lithium because of incipient thyroid problems), Klonopin, Artane, Zoloft—top of fridge looks like drug store shelf." The only thing missing was powdered toad testicle.

Now what? The perennial question. Two days after his release Charley called me at work and said he was putting a dimmer on the kitchen light. I asked him whether he'd turned off the electricity. He said no. I told him to stop working immediately until I got there. I hurried home and saw that he had dismantled the wall switch for the kitchen light; the bare ends of three live wires were sticking out and he had no idea where any of them went. He seemed unconcerned. This was an extreme example of the kind of impulsive, dangerous behavior he had been engaging in since he was old enough to walk. How could I leave him alone, much less concentrate on my work? "I became very agitated & started berating him," I wrote in my journal,

> in a mean, contemptuous tone for endangering himself etc. We cursed at each other. . . . Overwhelming feeling of frustration and put-upon-ness. Projecting outward a feeling of anger at myself for having to leave him alone, for not watching over him more effectively, etc. . . . I keep advising Jenny to take him with a grain of salt, cut him slack, etc., but then don't follow my own advice. I need to stop getting angry because it really does hurt me more than it hurts him.

Then, a possible solution. The previous summer when Charley was at Harbor-UCLA, Lin and I had visited a treatment facility called River Community, a converted forest-ranger camp in the mountains about fifty miles from L.A. It was "dual-diagnosis," meaning that it treated people with both mental illness and drug/alcohol problems based on the Alcoholics Anonymous twelve-step model. The community's staff and the mostly youthful clientele were multicolored and predominantly working class, and when Lin and I were led through the camplike common room we saw prints by Diego Rivera and Frieda Kahlo and posters of Rosa Parks, Malcolm X, Emiliano Zapata and others we admired hanging on the walls. I told Lin that if Charley didn't enroll in River Community, I would.

He didn't show any interest in the place when we told him about it, though, so River Community was forgotten. Then suddenly, a year later, a couple of days before his latest hospitalization, Charley had mentioned it during an emotional argument in which he tearfully accused me of not taking care of him properly. Why hadn't I sent him to River Community the previous year? he demanded, as if he had wanted to go and I hadn't let him; obviously he wasn't a priority in my life. It was nonsense, of course—this was the same kid who was always accusing me of hovering—but it pushed all the parental guilt buttons nonetheless. Did he have a point? Was I really not doing everything I could?

I thought about what my own father would have done. When I was three or four he and my mother and I were visiting relatives who lived in a second-floor walkup. As we started down the stairs to go home Dad took my hand. Then one of us tripped on the first step and we both started to fall. As we tumbled down the stairs Dad somehow maneuvered his body under mine so that he would hit the bottom first and not land on top of me. We both ended up all right, and from then on his behavior was my model for how a parent should be. I have always liked to think (and I told Charley this) that if I had been faced with a simple, definitive choice—my life or his?—I would have willingly given my life to save him. When I say "willingly" I don't mean I would be happy about it, or particularly courageous. I would demand a lot of tranquilizers and my last meal would have a lot of courses. But I always felt, as a parent and a good Darwinian, that it is only natural and right for the older generation to protect the young so that the young can someday protect their young, and so on; otherwise, what's the whole thing all about? And within the limits of my material condition and flawed understanding and sometimes flagging spirit, I tried to protect Charley as much as I could, to lay the conditions for his survival. His mention now of River Community intrigued me. Was it an emotional club he had grabbed to beat me with (there had been others), or was he actually, finally, signaling real interest in taking control of his life?

It was a question worth answering, so he, Lin and I visited River Community (Charley for the first time) after he got out of St. John's in mid-October. He had misgivings about the dual-diagnosis aspect of the treatment, insisting he wasn't an alcoholic or drug addict. I told him not to let that be a deal breaker. I had never been an AA or twelve-step devotee myself, although I knew they had their uses and saved some people's lives. Charley definitely had a problem with pot and alcohol. Was he an addict? I had no opinion on the matter, and I said so. I told him that he was a smart guy; if he liked the place he could find some way of finessing the program. Go to the twelve-step meetings and listen. Nobody could force him to talk or admit anything.

The visit, including an interview with an attractive young woman who was the admissions person and whom Charley seemed to take to, went well. (Hey, if it took a little feminine pulchritude to get him to go to a place that could help him . . .) Money was more problematic. River Community was partially funded by L.A. County, but its payment structure was such that the first month of his stay would not be subsidized; I would have to pay out-of-pocket the full rate, which came to slightly less than six thousand dollars. After that, if he stayed on, the county subsidy would kick in and River Community would accept his monthly SSI check (about eight hundred dollars) as payment in full.

I told Charley I was willing to put the six thousand dollars on my credit cards for the first month if he agreed to stay at least one additional month, and on the drive home we negotiated a deal. He would stay a minimum of two months. He would obey the community's rules of no dope or alcohol, attend twelve-step meetings (no matter what he thought about them secretly), take his medication (River Community used lithium and neuroleptics and had psychiatrists on staff), and generally make a good-faith effort to make the place work for him. After two months we would see. I said I hoped he would stay for at least a third month, but I promised not to pressure him. He agreed, and a few days later I rented a flatbed truck and Charley and Lin and I filled it with his things, including electronic keyboards and a bicycle, and headed for the mountains. The day was rainy and nasty with a cold winter wind, and I'd had to jerry-rig a tarp over the back of the truck and tie it down with rope so that Charley's stuff wouldn't get soaked. The tarp snapped and crackled the entire long, slippery drive up the gray mountains. We got a flat tire a quarter mile from the camp, and by the time we had unloaded Charley and his stuff and I headed home after dropping Lin at her place I was a quivering wreck. But mission accomplished! Charley was in a safe place that might actually do him some good. And I, for a mere six thousand bucks, had bought two months of peace and quiet.

Or so I thought.

Another Nail

I could hear my phone ringing as I climbed the stairs to my apartment after returning the rental truck, and more out of habit than reason I hurried to open the door. Charley was safe in the mountains, wasn't he? It couldn't be bad news.

There was a male voice on the other end of the line. "Is this Mr. Charles Aurthur?" I said no, his father. "Mr. Aurthur," the voice went on, "this is Detective Holt of the Poughkeepsie, New York, police department."

Poughkeepsie . . . ?! Poughkeepsie was three thousand miles away. Even riding a Minuteman missile Charley couldn't have gotten from River Community
to Poughkeepsie in two hours. (It was a measure of my general mental state
that something like that actually flipped through my mind.)

"How can I help you, Detective Holt?" I said, genuinely curious.

"Mr. Aurthur, do you know where your son is?" Detective Holt was a
pleasant-sounding fellow whose broad, flat vowels sounded slightly New
Englandish.

"Yes, I do," I answered. "He's in a recovery facility about fifty miles from Los
Angeles. I took him there myself just now."

"So there's no chance he's in the Poughkeepsie area?"

"None at all. He's in California. Why do you ask?"

The detective told me that Charley had for the past few months been making unwanted communications to somebody named Jane Davis.

I was still totally confused. Who was Jane Davis?

"She's a former professor of your son," said Detective Holt. "She used to
teach at Reed College and she's now at Vassar."

Oh, my God. I was starting to get it. Jane *Davis*. The humanities professor.
The obsessed-over recipient of the fugitive kiss. The mystical relation whose
office Charley had broken into during his second big breakdown three
Novembers before.

The detective kept explaining. Charley had somehow gotten her phone
number and since the beginning of the year had made a number of nuisance
calls, hanging up when she answered. He had sent her letters and a package.
And today she had received a second "threatening" package from him, as yet
unopened. The bomb squad had been called in.

"The *bomb* squad?!"

The first package, Detective Holt told me, had contained a watch and a
cryptic note—he didn't have all the details—that Jane Davis had found threatening. So they had called in the bomb squad to deal with the new package.
They were also worried that Charley was in the Poughkeepsie area, stalking
her.

I assured Detective Holt again that Charley wasn't, and wouldn't be,
anywhere near Poughkeepsie. But as we talked I was having flashes of the
attempted gun purchase a few weeks before. Had *that* been what it was

for? Had Charley been planning a trip back east?

After Detective Holt and I hung up, I sat for a while in my now-familiar numb, staring-forward state. Then, rousing myself, I looked through recent phone bills and saw that there were indeed a half dozen short (one- or two-minute) calls to Poughkeepsie starting the previous January. What had Charley been doing? How, and why, had he tracked Jane Davis down? She had departed Reed on some kind of stress leave the spring after he had broken into her office, partly, we were told, because of the experience; Charley had really upset her. Her leaving, in fact, had been what allowed him to go back to Reed the next fall; if she had remained on the faculty and objected, the school would never have let him back, and he knew it. One of the conditions of his return was that he would not try to contact her, and that if she came back and wanted him gone he would go, no questions asked.

So what was going on now? Charley's tracking Professor Davis down—the phone calls, the packages—looked to me like an escalation of his pattern of fixations. Was it now going beyond mere weirdness and nuisance calls and letters into actual intent to do harm? "More homicidal stirrings"—of my own— "after Davis call," I wrote in my journal that night. "Thinning the herd etc.— thinking about story of a father forced to kill his homicidal/paranoid schizo son—what could be worse than filicide?"

The main immediate reason for Detective Holt's call had been to find out whether Charley was in New York State stalking Professor Davis, and when I assured him he wasn't, his immediate concerns were allayed. In subsequent weeks I spoke to him again and got more information. The postmaster of New York also became involved, as did Vassar security. I called the school to tell security to tell Professor Davis that Charley was not, and would not be, in the area. The head of security was an affable fellow. "Oh my God, you don't have any idea the excitement your son caused around here!" he exclaimed cheerfully when I told him who I was. "I mean it was quite something! We called the bomb squad, we had bomb-sniffing dogs around here, there was really quite a commotion!"

When the second package was finally opened, he went on, it contained a reddish fabric, a box of wooden matches, a can of Mace, and a couple of other items including a rather puzzling note saying something like, "Sorry about Thanksgiving; Christmas is ahead," which, along with Charley's other communications, had led Professor Davis to think he might be coming to the area to find her. It was possible, I figured. The "Sorry about Thanksgiving" remark could have meant he had been planning to go back to New York but had his plans preempted by River Community. (Later, when I questioned Charley himself, he said he had sent Professor Davis the Mace as protection against other attackers, not him. He was acting as her guardian, not her assailant, he assured me in the tone one uses with a slightly dull-witted child.)

In a further discussion with Detective Holt, I got a better picture of the other written communications Charley had been making to Jane Davis. In January 1993 he sent her a card apologizing for breaking into her office. In March 1994 he sent her a letter. In February 1995 he sent her a package of preserves with a note in French saying "Sweets for the sweet." There was also a tape cassette, although Detective Holt didn't know what was on it. Sometime between February and August there was a package containing a necklace with a key attached, as well as a figure of a person and a chalice and a note saying, "You are not forgotten, my dear," which of course could be interpreted as a threat.

The more I heard, however, the more I began to feel that Jane Davis, although quite understandably, had misread Charley's communications, which were crazy, true, but harmlessly crazy, more sad than threatening. But of course this could be my own wishful thinking. And it wasn't the point anyway. The point, as I said to Charley when I told him about the call from Detective Holt, was that he had promised two years earlier that he would never again have anything to do with Jane Davis. He seemed to agree and said he would never contact her again. But of course he had said that before.

More than a year after his death I found among his papers a copy of one of the items Detective Holt had mentioned, his March 1994 letter to Professor Davis. Charley had written it from Reed two months before the May–June *M. Butterfly* breakdown and stabbing. The "last letter" that he mentions in the first sentence is lost:

> Dear Ms. Davis, I am writing to you now, for the sake of professionalism, a counterpart to the last letter I sent you which was more a restless and lame attempt to vindicate myself. The correspondence I sent in Jan. '92 [he means '93—JA] was written before I fully regained my bearings and realized my deep humiliation. I am almost finished with what has been a sober and stable year, that is, one without any dramatic mood swings. My psychiatrist in Los Angeles

informed me that if you had not taken a sojourn from Reed this year I would
not have been permitted to re-enroll. As I have been led to believe it is your
intention to return next year I am impelled [to] offer at least some promise of
mental composure. If and when you resume your teaching position I assure you
I will not try to contact you or seek your society in any way. If you are still not
content with this and believe your performance here will be taxed by my being
present I am prepared to leave the school and continue my education elsewhere,
and will do so quietly. No one knows so far that I am writing you. I am trying
to address the issue before it finds me, yet if it does find me it will go through
our dean, Jim Tederman.

This has been the most prosaic letter I've ever written, probably because,
after all, I really don't know you. I can't imagine what you think of me. Nor can
I fully comprehend my absurd behavior that fall. As bizarre as it may have been
it is in the past and I am happy to keep it there. Please accept my most grave
and sincere apologies, and know that I have endured much contrition.

Yours respectfully . . .

*(". . . One wakes up, looks around, and, unlike in the dream when asleep, one has
to take responsibility for the actions and reactions committed during the delusion. One
feels at that point like King Lear, who recognizes that he has made a monstrosity out of
his life and that his authority and even his love were destructive to other people. . . .")*

Home Alone

It had been gratifying to be able to tell Detective Holt that I knew exactly
where Charley was. Didn't it show that I was a responsible parent acting
responsibly? Charley was safe in the mountains, out of Jane Davis's and
Detective Holt's—and my—way, for two months minimum. That was the
agreement. I was counting on Charley to keep it. For all his problems he was
a good kid. He would have a hard time at first. I was expecting daily "Dad, get
me out of here!" phone calls for the first week or two. But a deal was a deal.
And it would work out in the end. Dr. Gray himself assured me of that when
I told him Charley was at River Community for two months. "After two
weeks he'll hate it. After a month he'll still hate it but see that it may be, um,
doing him some good. After two months he'll want the whole world to be a
River Community."

So I hoped. But recent revelations had shaken me. The idea that Charley had been quietly seeking out Jane Davis and trying to buy a gun during a time when he appeared normal continued to unnerve me. More than two years before I had convinced myself that he was manic-depressive, meaning that his periods of recovery were genuine and that they could be made permanent with the proper care and self-discipline. But what if Dr. Gray's casual remark to Lin and me so long ago—that Charley might be both manic-depressive *and* schizophrenic—had been right all along? What if the schizophrenia was of the paranoid variety? I had long since become skeptical of all this labeling—even when, as now, I found myself using it—but labels or no labels, the question was a real one: What if I was faced with the prospect of having not only a long-term crazy person on my hands, but a long-term *dangerous* crazy person? Were things like sending him to River Community merely ways of throwing money at the problem to delude myself that I was "doing everything I could"? Was money acting as a substitute for good sense? On the Saturday after I dropped Charley off I wrote in my journal:

> My feelings about Dr. Gray, hospital, River Community etc., the manipula-tive way in which the parents, not the patients, bond with the Dr/institution becomes the important thing. Then we talk/cajole the patient into coming up to our comfort level rather than the other way around. For it is in a certain sense we, not the patient, who are the true "consumers" of the medical care, since we, not they, are paying. I.e. the whole thing is geared to satisfying & serving us, not the sick person. . . .

The hospitalizations, the medications, the periods of "tough love" alternating with wishy-washy oversolicitousness, my practice of making sure Charley took his medication at the same time that I was tolerating, if not condoning, forms of behavior (drinking, pot smoking, excessive caffeine consumption) that were designed, consciously or unconsciously, to negate the effectiveness of that very medication—how much of it all really made any difference to Charley? How much of it just made matters worse? In a sense we were dealing with someone who was indifferent to life as that word is commonly understood; this had become increasingly clear since the Yosemite crash. Given that fact, and given his lifetime of self-destructiveness, what was the point of "trying to keep him alive until he decided to keep himself alive," as Lin and I defined our role as parents? Were we in the end merely ripping apart, piece by piece, the one thing he had left—"his own reality," his inner life?

Still, Charley had gone to River Community voluntarily, and our first few phone conversations gave me grounds for optimism. He didn't seem to hate the place. Three days after he arrived (the same day as the above journal entry) he called asking me to send him some good coffee, and I happily agreed. The matter of getting used to the new regimen came up, and my journal records that we argued about the pronunciation of the word *acclimated,* he saying *ac'*-cli-mated, I saying ac-*cli'*-mated. ("Great scene," I wrote in my journal—"arguing about pronunciation of a word in the middle of some horrible crisis—shows that father is just as crazy as kid.") Two days later, Monday, I wrote him a chatty letter inside the requested care package of decaf coffee (and cigars). The same day he was writing me a note that would cross my package in the mail:

> Dear Father, I've got all the drugs I need: caffeine (even instant coffee); nico-tine, Zoloft™, Klonopin, etc. No Booze No Booze. That's why you put me here. You really fear I shall be an alchy, huh? Well I got news for you. If this is your idea of de-tox you must be joking. I'll write a real one soon. C.

Not blissed out, exactly, but sounding like he was settling in (what else could "I'll write a real one soon" mean?). That same day, we talked on the phone at around 6 P.M. He sounded okay.

About four hours later I got a call from a River Community staff person, Mike. Charley had been "discharged" because he had "attacked two residents," Mike said. "We're a peaceful community here. We can't tolerate physical attacks." Charley had been arrested by county sheriff's deputies. "The ol' rugrat" was on his way to jail.

This was a little after 10 P.M. It took another couple of hours of phone calls by me and Lin to find out exactly where he was. The jail he had been taken to was about fifty miles away. I was tempted to leave him there, but of course I didn't. Lin and I left in her car at about midnight, squinting at maps in the dark all the way, and finally found the jail at about two in the morning. It took another hour to get Charley released. He came out of the lockup to meet us in his casual mode, nonchalant, slightly superior. We drove home in mostly toxic silence.

I had been furious since getting the call from Mike—primarily at Charley, secondarily at myself and tertiarily at River Community for being the bearer of bad news. I soon reordered my fury, but it took a couple of days. In the meantime, I was so exhausted and dispirited the morning after getting Charley out of jail that I called in sick to work and "took to my bed," my journal says, like a Victorian valetudinarian. I had decided—again—that I'd had it with him. He would have to move out, I told him and Lin that night at dinner at my apartment. She could take him if she wanted, or he could go to a board-and-care or to a motel and pay with his credit card, I didn't care. Charley shrugged fatalistically and made some gestures toward packing his stuff. He would leave the next day.

My "new" resolve didn't help my mood, and I woke up the next morning as miserable as I have ever been in my life. My anger at Charley was quickly wearing off as I thought more about what had happened. Why had I been so quick to take River Community's side? Maybe Charley had been wrong, but why had I automatically assumed it? I dragged myself to the gym in the early morning to stretch and lift weights, my daily prework workout. Normally the exercise gave me energy for the day, but today I felt worse with every abdominal crunch, and I arrived at work more dead than alive. But then, as the morning wore on, I started feeling better. It was becoming obvious that I couldn't kick Charley out in his condition. It just wasn't right. Or maybe it was right. It didn't matter. All my intellectual musings of the previous weekend about why we do things—for our kids or ourselves, out of rationality or guilt— slipped away. I couldn't live with myself knowing that he was crazy and alone in a motel somewhere, it was that simple. I could not and would not make him move out, I realized, and immediately started to breathe again.

Other than improving my mood, however, the decision solved nothing. Charley remained in a kind of mixed state, alternately manic and depressed, sometimes both. I thought he belonged back in the hospital. Lin wasn't sure. We called a few locked board-and-cares that accepted SSI as payment, but they only took patients directly from hospitals. In order to get into a board-and-care, Charley would first have to go back to St. John's, and I didn't think they would take him. He wasn't acting crazy enough to be put on an involuntary hold, and Medi-Cal wouldn't pay for him if he went voluntarily, which there was no chance of his doing anyway. I called a local county mental health facility called

Santa Monica West, a few blocks from my apartment, and asked if they could funnel him into St. John's. They told me that he would have to come in himself for an evaluation, which was about as likely as Moby Dick leaping into Captain Ahab's lap in the *Pequod*. I asked about state mental hospitals, but the man I was talking to said they were basically for the criminally insane, not merely the insane, and unless Charley committed a serious crime he would never get in. "It didn't used to be that way, but things have fundamentally changed in the last few years," the man said. It was basically a good change. I understood that. It was good that people couldn't be put away forever like Jack Nicholson in *One Flew Over the Cuckoo's Nest*. But it also meant I still didn't know what to do.

Meanwhile I was getting madder and madder at River Community. In a series of phone calls I learned that they had purposely (they claimed for some kind of liability reasons) not sent Charley's medications along with him to jail, possibly endangering him (even antimedicationists advocate that people going off medication do it gradually). Then came an argument over the refund. I asked, I believed reasonably and fairly, for my six thousand dollars back minus one thousand dollars, which would cover the five days Charley had actually been at the facility. No, River Community said, they were entitled to keep fourteen days' worth of the six thousand dollars (about twenty-eight hundred dollars) for administrative expenses—it was in the contract. Yes it was, I saw when I looked. What was *not* in the contract was anything about River Community's having the right to call the cops and drag my kid off to jail without any prior warnings or discussions with me, the payer. Like hell they were going to keep half my money.

I got unexpected ammunition the following weekend when I rented another truck and drove with Charley up to River Community to get his things. His bike was locked to a post and the staff, who ranged from hostile to merely unhelpful, claimed (wrongly, it turned out) that they didn't have the key and refused to look for it. I was not leaving without the bike, so we waited while a locksmith drove up from the nearest town and broke the lock. The delay turned out to be a good thing. As we sat outside waiting for the locksmith, a couple of residents who had become friendly with Charley during his five-day stay came over to say hello. The four of us chatted, and when Charley wandered off to talk to somebody else, one of the two residents, a thirty-ish

Iranian named Emir, told me the other side of the story. The incident that had led to Charley's expulsion and arrest had not been all that serious or even all his fault, Emir said. An older, larger resident had taken a dislike to Charley because of his haughty attitude and refusal to "share" at twelve-step meetings. The personality clash had led to a shoving match in the common room Monday evening, which had been broken up by staff and appeared to be over until the older resident started up again later.

Why wasn't this other guy expelled and arrested, too? I asked Emir. Because the staff and some of the other residents looked at Charley as a spoiled rich kid, Emir said. He didn't act grateful enough to be there.

Well, they were right about the "spoiled" part, I thought, madder than ever at River Community and at myself for having automatically blamed Charley for everything. Sure, he was a pain in the ass, but they'd known that when they took him and my six thousand bucks. Wasn't his pain-in-the-assedness the whole point? He had gone to River Community because he was seriously troubled and needed help. "They want to be counselors, so let them counsel," the pretty young intake coordinator had said, referring to the staff, when I warned her about how tough Charley was to treat. They'd counseled him, all right—straight to the county jail. So I resolved to get not only the whole six thousand dollars back but the charge for the locksmith and the cost of the lock as well. Which I did, although it took me a couple of weeks of phone calls and threatening letters. It was all good fun, actually, the fighting and threatening, a welcome distraction from more intractable problems. Still, Charley's inability to get help from River Community was a real blow. The place, with its Malcolm X and Frieda Kahlo posters, had almost seemed like a last hope: relatively humane and nonasylumish, no locks or fences, with a social conscience and a clientele not possessed of the looks of walleyed hopelessness the mentally ill so often wear— or acquire. Affordable, too, sort of. But now just another burned bridge, and I still didn't know what to do next as this beast of a year, which had started so smoothly and become so rough, slouched toward Bethlehem, to die.[5]

When T. S. Eliot said April was the cruelest month, he obviously had never heard of November. I forbade Charley to drive when he came back from River Community, and to make sure he didn't, I disabled his car by disconnecting the distributor wire. After about a week I relented and let him drive. I hated treating him like a child. His life was joyless enough without being humiliated further.

But of course he shouldn't have been driving. He promptly had an accident on his way to a date with a woman he had met through the personals. The accident was entirely his fault. He wasn't looking where he was going and rear-ended a car stopped at a light, barely avoiding injury to a man, his pregnant wife and child. Charley smashed the front end of his Bug and bruised his chest on the steering wheel, causing trauma to the scar from his open-heart surgery, which meant another trip to the emergency room. The car he had hit suffered major rear-end damage and I started getting phone calls from the driver, who thought I was liable because Charley was my son and didn't have insurance.

A week later I got a call from Dr. Gray at work, which surprised me, since he had never called me before except when I had left him a message first, which I hadn't. He told me he had been contacted by the (apparently somewhat older) woman from the personals Charley had been on his way to meet when he had this latest accident. They had hit it off at first, she told Dr. Gray, and after a couple of dates had gotten as far as some hugging and kissing. But then Charley had "freaked her out" by announcing—I think on the second date—that he and she were everlastingly linked together, at which point she moved expeditiously albeit diplomatically to terminate the date, which involved agreeing to have sex with him if he didn't commit suicide by age twenty-five (he had already given her an account of some of his previous attempts). The next day she also changed her phone number, investigated restraining orders and called Dr. Gray, whose name Charley had apparently given her.

Dr. Gray reported all this in his usual calm way. But then at the end of his account he made clear the main reason he had called. He wouldn't be able to treat Charley anymore, he said. He was no longer on staff at St. John's and there was no point in his being Charley's private psychiatrist since Charley didn't see him regularly for real therapy anyway, only for sporadic half-sessions whose purpose was medication monitoring. He referred me to the new assistant medical director of the psychiatry department at St. John's, a man named David Breen, who unlike Dr. Gray took Medi-Cal and whose practice would be more suitable for Charley. Dr. Gray had heard good things about him. "Not all the heads of the psychiatry department have been good, but, um, this one is."

I was surprised at first, but I shouldn't have been. Charley had told me during his most recent hospitalization that Dr. Gray had told him he "was full of shit" and threatened to send him to the state mental hospital. ("Good for him!" I had written in my journal.) That degree of countertransference should have been an indication that Dr. Gray had about had it, and the call from the woman from the personals and his own unfamiliarity with Medi-Cal gave him a way to bow out gracefully. "There's still a piece missing," he had said of Charley the year before, after the 1994 stabbing and hospitalizations. Over the years, Dr. Gray had made a number of references to how hard Charley was to treat because on some basic level he didn't accept the psychiatric version of what was wrong with him, at least long enough to collaborate in his own recovery. He was always self-medicating, trying to find what Dr. Gray called "the sweet spot"—the right combination of medications, dope, alcohol, sleep deprivation, sleeping pills, TM, music, literature, romantic obsession, and all the other things, legal and illegal, that would relieve his restless anxiety and allow him to transcend his mundane (and "piteous") self and soar into the jet stream, crazy but not too crazy. The problem for Charley was that there were just too many volatile elements working on an already unstable temperament. When Beethoven and relaxation techniques and full moons become risk factors for mental breakdowns, how can any balance stay balanced for long?

And the problem—not just in treating him, not just in keeping him alive, but in giving him a reason to live—went even deeper than that, as implied by his underlining of the passage in *The Seduction of Madness* about "death itself" being "inherent in the urge for transformation . . . the undercurrent of the pleasure and the freedom being courted in the psychotic transformation." Charley, having achieved god consciousness at Yosemite, a consciousness that was bound up with death as closely as Siamese twins who possess two heads and one heart, could never be permanently satisfied with anything less than god consciousness. The vision of himself as "the Creator" was always beckoning to him from just beyond the edge of the cliff. Thus, life after Yosemite was a race: Would he outlast his grandiosity or would it kill him? As we saw with Kay Redfield Jamison's war with lithium, it often takes years, if it happens at all, for a person with a mood disorder to achieve the maturity—or degree of exhaustion—necessary to give up the periodic space flights, to opt for life on earth. Death, especially if one's pattern includes extreme suicidality, may very well come before maturity. Slow and steady may not win this race—especially when one's fellow relay team members (friends and therapists) are dropping out.

Dr. Gray's decision to end their relationship was yet another blow to Charley, a further sign (as Lin put it later) of what Charley must have seen as his declining fortunes. Tom Gray was not only his first therapist but also the only one who had been with him, if only in the background at certain times, since his first breakdown. He was a classy guy with a nice office who dressed well, with a slightly tweedy Anglophile elegance that Charley could identify with. He could see through Charley's bullshit, but respectfully (until lately), and their relationship, despite Charley's resistance to treatment, was real. Its severing now was a severing of the thin but till now unbroken thread that Charley had been unraveling on the dark and chaotic forest path behind him, as characters in fairy tales do to find the way home.

Groundlessness, Common Ground and the Future of Psychiatry

As polarized as the currently out-of-fashion psychological and the *au courant* physicochemical models of mental illness are, there are some (to me) interesting areas of common ground, as I learned while trying to understand what happened to Charley, why nobody helped him, and whether anybody could have.

Although Edward Podvoll, for example, the author of *The Seduction of Madness,* falls into the psychological camp because of his objections to medication and hospitalization, his analysis of "groundlessness" and theories of how manic episodes come about correspond in some ways with the brain-disorder view. In *Manic-Depressive Illness,* Goodwin and Jamison also talk about how "environmental causality and biological vulnerability need not be viewed as opposing hypotheses,"[6] and speak positively of theories "that postulate that *instability is the fundamental dysfunction in manic-depressive illness,*"[7] particularly instability in sleep patterns (insomnia) and moods (daily and seasonal) caused by biologically based disruptions in circadian rhythms. They present a chart entitled "Clinical Implications of Instability Models," which outlines measures for preventing manic episodes. These include the careful maintenance of "circadian integrity" by a "regular schedule of sleep, meals, exercise, etc.," intervention "under special circumstances" (including "stress or event-related insomnia"), and the avoidance of "substances which disrupt rhythms (alcohol, cocaine, etc.)." The chart also recommends that persons at risk of mania "avoid intermittent stressors (including substances) with kindling potential, including episodic alcohol and drug abuse."[8]

When I read this I thought how familiar the chart's list of "do's" looked, and for good reason. They represented everything that Charley *didn't* do from early adolescence on. Charley was a veritable template of risky behaviors. But of course this was no accident. The "kindling potential" of the frowned-on substances and behaviors—those "excitants" or "accelerators," as Podvoll terms them, that "fuel the momentum of the coming transformation"—is precisely why people like Charley use them. Thus, for mental-health professionals simply to advise vulnerable individuals to avoid such risky substances and behaviors as a purely medical matter without addressing the psychological and temperamental reasons for their attraction to these behaviors seems naïve in the extreme. It's bad enough when parents like me do it. Cut out stuff like pot and alcohol and cigarettes and too much coffee that screw up your sleep, I would say to Charley. Get plenty of exercise, eat healthy food, take vitamins, keep a stable schedule. I said it all till even *I* was sick of listening to me. But I was unable, along with everybody else who tried to help him, to hook into his psychology as well as physiology, his need—at least in the absence of a better course that he could believe in and embrace—to keep engaging in patterns that would keep kindling his "excursions." More important than my inability, of course, was Charley's inability. He was aware of the dangers of his behaviors, especially his use of drugs, and his journals are full of accounts of trying to give up cigarettes and pot in particular.[9] But the daily anxieties of life, most of all (I think) the awful, demoralizing problem he had sleeping (and then functioning after not sleeping), made relinquishing his substances too daunting a task in the absence of a different type of help than he was getting.

Whether anything else would have worked—such as the intensive psychoanalysis Charley could have had with Dr. Gray if we had been richer—is not clear. I have never been a big fan of psychotherapy, particularly traditional psychoanalysis and other forms of "deep work." When I was fourteen my father, thinking I was more than normally silent and depressed, talked me into going to a Freudian analyst several times a week. The sessions lasted a few months before I quit, and I have only been to a therapist a couple of times since. In pressuring me to go into analysis, my father of course broke the most basic rule of psychotherapy, which is that it must be voluntary. Otherwise it is at best an expensive waste of time, at worst a type of coercion. In Charley's case, Lin and I broke the same rule when we insisted that he see a therapist (of his choice) as a trade-off for living with us. We knew we were breaking the rule when we broke it, but we were desperate. The thing that was perhaps most disturbing about Charley's illness (aside from his suicidality) was his increasing social isolation, and we hoped that even if he went to therapy under duress he would get something out of it. So in addition to medication he had a fair amount of talk therapy over the years, from psychiatrists to psychologists to college counselors to shamans. He could have had more if he wanted, within the limits of Lin's and my nonmillionaire status; we would have been delighted. But again, our efforts were wasted because they were *our* efforts.

One rare instance where Charley tried to find treatment himself was with Vern, the Sacramento shaman whose letter about Charley's feelings of not having been loved as a child I quoted earlier. I never met Vern. Charley found him on his own and never discussed their relationship with me, so everything I know comes from three letters from Vern that I found among Charley's papers together with an application (not filled out) for a course in shamanism (Vern thought Charley had great potential as a healer). The final letter, written about a month after Charley slit his wrists in early 1993, begins:

> My Dearest Friend Charley, First of all I want you to know that what I am going to say is out of Love. The Scriptures say "we are to Love [one] another in deed (actions) and truth (sincerity). I can't heal you unless you want to BE HEALED. If you wanna DIE, then die! I feel that dying is easy, LIVING IS HARD! If you want to take the easy route, then DIE! Personally, I feel that you are AFRAID of living so you are constantly sabotaging your life through pain, depression, committing suicide, loneliness, apathy, etc. These are all sabotaging elements to give you reasons to die! To be blunt, you are already DEAD! You WANT me to RAISE you from the DEAD! I can't RAISE You from the DEAD unless you WANT to be RAISED! I can't Help you crawl if you don't try to make a move to crawl. You didn't want to do what I ask you to do because you WERE AFRAID what I ask you to do would WORK! MAKE You ALIVE! Raise yourself from the DEAD. Oh, no! Can't be HAPPY! Wouldn't know what to do with myself, then, etc.

The letter continues in this vein for four more pages—interspersed with advice about getting exercise, dancing when depressed and drinking special herbal teas. Reading it, I couldn't help but find some morose satisfaction in the fact that it wasn't only Western medicine and prosaic fathers who were unable to deal with Charley. It was everybody. Vern's non-Western, holistic exasperation *("If you wanna die, then DIE!")* at least equaled Dr. Gray's (and my own) more mainstream variety *("Dr. Gray said I was full of shit and he was going to send me to the state mental hospital"; Me: "Good for him!").*

The new psychiatrist, Dr. Breen, had a different kind of practice from either Vern or Dr. Gray. We found this out the week after Dr. Gray "fired" Charley. Dr. Breen's office suite consisted of a tiny, always-full waiting room and two inner rooms connected to it by a single door. Every ten or fifteen minutes Dr. Breen would open the door from inside, poke his head out, and announce a name; the person named would then get up and follow him into the inner office, never to reappear. Where were they going? When our turn came, we learned that departing patients left through a second door in the inner office leading out into the hall. The two-door system made for maximum efficiency and turnover, allowing patients to come and go quickly and efficiently, without the arrivals and departures bumping into each other and slowing the flow. With this system a psychiatrist could process three or four appointments per hour.

Dr. Breen was a thin-faced, good-looking man of perhaps forty-five with a deadpan expression. After calling Charley's name he led us—Lin and I had come as well—into a small, cluttered consultation room, more like a shipping clerk's office than a doctor's. After we introduced ourselves, he sat Charley in a soft chair about six feet to the side of his desk, beckoned Lin and me to sit nearby, then sat down himself, half-facing Charley and half-facing a laptop computer on his desk. He tapped away at the laptop as he asked questions about Charley's history of breakdowns and hospitalizations and especially medications. I had never heard of a therapist typing on a computer during a session; it was as if, in case his deadpan physiognomy and flat voice and angled-away body weren't distancing enough, he needed the thin, vertical laptop screen in front of him to serve as yet another little wall between him and the patient. When we questioned him about his approach to therapy he said

unblinkingly that he was a psychopharmacologist, his specialty was treatment
with medication, he didn't do talk. He wrote out some prescriptions, scheduled Charley's next appointment in two weeks, and showed us out the back
door. We couldn't have been there more than twenty minutes—and this was
the meaty, getting-acquainted session. Charley's reaction to all this—Charley,
who didn't do particularly well even with warm and mensch-y therapists—can
be imagined.

It was now about two months after his latest breakdown and he was still
very unstable—from the mood swings themselves, from the soup of medications in his system, and from his various recent setbacks. Dr. Gray had put him
on a high dosage of Navane in the hospital and had only lessened it a little
since, and Dr. Breen actually lowered the amount during their initial session.
Within a few days Charley seemed to spiral downward, I think because the
episode that had started in September had not run its two- to three-month
course, which meant that he would tend to be psychotic unless tranquilized
with the drugs, which Dr. Breen had now cut back. He was having trouble
sleeping, muttering and laughing to himself, "smiling at whatever," I wrote in
my journal, as bad as I had ever seen him. When I told him he seemed "almost
zombielike"—partly I was just lashing out, partly I was trying to get through
to him on *some* level—he became furious and asked if I liked *Psycho.* "Do you
want to be like Janet Leigh? Or the investigator?"

I didn't take these particular threats seriously. They seemed almost theatrical
(Lin said more than once that she thought a lot of Charley's behavior during
his psychoses was acting). And at least he was communicating.

But mostly he wasn't, so I called Dr. Breen and left a message, then didn't
hear back that day (or the next). Charley was becoming so unresponsive that I
decided to adjust his medication on my own. I raised the Navane dosage back
to where Dr. Gray had had it (30 mg per day), which seemed to help almost
immediately. Something did. Charley slept that night and was much better the
next day. When Dr. Breen finally called me back two days later I told him what
I'd done and what the results had been. He said I'd done "exactly the right
thing" to increase the Navane. I expressed doubt. Had Charley's deterioration
really been caused by lowering the Navane? The past few days had been so
crazed and confused that it was hard to know what caused what.

On the contrary, Dr. Breen replied, what had happened showed exactly what caused what. It showed that the 30-mg dosage was the correct one, and that "he should stay on the medication for ten to twelve months."

I didn't like the idea. Based on past experience, I thought that Charley would eventually recover on his own and then wouldn't need Navane. "What about the medication masking the natural cyclicity of the disorder?" I asked.

I could almost hear Dr. Breen shaking his head on the other end of the line. "No. Ten to twelve months."

Charley continued to be nervous and jumpy, but that had been the trough and he got steadily better after that.

Footnote to 1995

Years after this latest episode, as I read Charley's journals, I found a possible explanation for why he had tried to buy a gun, an explanation that, while bad enough, was a lot less bad than the various scenarios I had conjured up when I found the pink State of California pamphlet. After buying his own car in June, the old VW Bug, Charley had, without telling me of course, taken to going into the black and Latino parts of town while I was at work, looking for marijuana (possibly other things as well, but his journal only mentions marijuana). He had decided that he needed protection during these expeditions—and in fact, we will recall, "protection" was the one word he uttered to me in the hospital when I demanded to know why he wanted a gun. Protection from what? I had asked, genuinely curious (our apartment had never been robbed or threatened), but he didn't answer, so I assumed he was lying and continued worrying about what I thought the real reason or reasons were.

So I was glad, if glad is the right word, when his journal seemed to bear out the "protection" story. As nerve-racking as the idea was of Charley driving his rickety old Volkswagen into the 'hood with a .38 illegally hidden in his glove compartment looking for drug sellers on street corners, it was a much more comforting explanation for the gun than the others hatched by my feverish brain, and I like to think the true one.

7

The
Final Year

"A Place of Stopping, Not of Recuperation . . ."

If the last part of 1995 was mostly a disaster marked by evictions from therapeutic communities, jailings, leather restraints, auto accidents and an unrequited love affair that brought in its wake threats of restraining orders and the end of Charley's relationship with the one psychiatrist he related to, his last year, 1996, began with the promise of better times. In early January we took a trip together to San Francisco. I had heard about a large exhibit of the late works of Willem de Kooning at the San Francisco Museum of Modern Art, and I decided to go up north to see it and asked Charley if he wanted to go with me. He said yes, so the first week of January I rented a car and we went.

De Kooning took only a couple of hours. I had hoped the exhibit would be interesting, perhaps even redemptive. I had always had a warm spot for de Kooning and considered at least one of his paintings, "Excavation," done in 1950, a masterpiece of the highest order. He had moved down the road from my family in The Springs near East Hampton, New York, in the early 1960s, and I used to see him pedaling his clunky old bicycle past our house on Fireplace Road almost every summer day, head bowed, getting his daily exercise. I also saw him around town, and he seemed like a great guy. He was also a big drunk for many years, and when the booze caught up with him in the late 1960s and 1970s he went through a long artistic decline. In the early '80s, however, he began painting again in a new style, turning out a very large number of big canvases that began as recognizable evolutions of his earlier style—dense, complex, highly worked—but soon became increasingly unrecognizable as de Koonings, the famous layered, brushy style evolving into a thinner use of paint consisting of a small number of primary colors stroked lightly onto a white ground, transparent as water colors. Controversy swirled around these paintings, because as he was painting them he was also showing signs of mental deterioration that was eventually diagnosed as Alzheimer's disease (although this was never proven). The progression of his dementia corresponded to the increasing simplicity of the paintings. Their defenders termed the simplicity haikulike and "achieved minimalism," the serene musings of a Zen master. Their detractors called the paintings simplistic, the mindless doodlings of a helpless old man cynically exploited by greedy handlers.

I had seen book and magazine reproductions of a few of these late works and some of them looked beautiful on the page, so I went to San Francisco wanting very much to like them. How nice it would be if despite de Kooning's encroaching dementia his talent had run so deep in the preverbal, oceanic depths of his brain that masterpieces could still float to the surface in a kind of final eruption of creativity, the way volcanic eruptions on the ocean bottom send life-giving heat and renewal up through the cold water. How wonderful if these last paintings really were the serene musings of a sage, a last gift to himself and the world, a kind of creative dessert.

But no. The paintings, arranged chronologically in the big airy rooms of the gorgeous new museum, went from intermittently interesting (1980) to bad (1985) to worse (1990), following de Kooning's declining mental state. So there was, after all, no free dessert. What had seemed beautiful on the slick pages of coffee table books and art magazines now seemed at best pretty. Charley, who had a keen eye and critical sense and no sentimental attachment to de Kooning (any more than he had to Paul Muni), saw through the hoax even faster than I did. He took one look at one of the newer, emptier paintings, made a face

and said, "Later, Dad," and disappeared to look at other things in the museum.
I couldn't blame him. Later I would wonder whether there was a commonality of wishfulness in my hopes that the de Koonings were great paintings and
that Charley had finally turned the corner, that his life, despite a crippling crisis of the mind not totally unlike de Kooning's, could also find some creative
equilibrium of volcanic mineral heat and cool ocean depths, and thus achieve
some sustainable mixture of energy and serenity.

Charley didn't write in his journal much in 1996, but the few things he did
write are revealing. His handwriting had changed almost completely from the
first journal (1989), becoming increasingly angular and emphatic, the letters huge
and spiky and overlapping from line to line, ascenders and descenders crossing
each other like sabers. The first entry of the year—January 14, about a week after
our return from San Francisco—reads, "Last night I dreamt of ants ravaging my
kitchen. There were fish in the sink. I dreamt last night that I was back in Hi
School forgetting the classrooms I was supposed to be in." In late February or
March:

> I find myself thinking about the "nurses" in the psyche [sic] wards, and I've
> come to the conclusion that what attracted them to their jobs is the superiority
> they feel over mental patients. Where they can always feel on top of things
> because their lives are never as bad as those that they watch over. At least at
> UCLA Harbor. I can't imagine the "nurses" ever realized the miracle of a soul's
> healing, one of the merits of nursing. Because all of the patients at Harbor
> seemed damned in some way or another to eternal confusion.... To recount the
> experience leaves a bad taste in my mouth. It exists as a long moment of horror
> in my earthly existence. It was a place of stopping, not of recuperation....

Charley wrote this at a time when he was working sporadically and seeing
two psychiatrists. One was Dr. Breen, whom he went to once or twice
a month for fifteen minutes. We also started sending him to a Dr. Leo Sobel,
a Jungian talk therapist Lin had found through a friend. Charley didn't like
either of them, so I investigated the Menninger Clinic in Kansas, one of the
best-known psychiatric facilities in the world; its catalog said it had a
program for "refractory patients" that seemed designed for Charley. Lin and
I began investigating whether Medi-Cal or SSI covered Menninger's

one-thousand-dollar-a-day cost. Meanwhile, I monitored his medication by measuring out his pills in the little white paper cup twice a day and watching while he swallowed them, like a nurse. Not a foolproof method. Some psychiatric patients grow adept at tucking the pills under their tongues or performing other evasive maneuvers. Anything to avoid swallowing the hated "meds."

In mid-February Charley got fired from a bagel shop a few blocks from my apartment after only a couple of shifts; he had dropped a bagel on the floor and then tried to serve it, thinking the customer hadn't seen. By this time I was less insistent than in the past that he either work or go to school (as well as see a talk therapist) as a condition for living with me (Lin had also tried to enforce this rule), so he stayed home most of the time or wandered around Santa Monica while I went to work. Sometimes he stayed at Lin's. His journal of March 27:

> Last night, in my sister's bed at Mom's place, I had another "back in school" dream, where I was at Uni High. Only it wasn't really like Uni because the corridors were maze-like. I had a locker, the combination of which I couldn't remember at the end of the day. I recall now mostly just a sense of disorientation, where I couldn't find my classrooms and I would forget those classes I had.
>
> "Why," I ask myself, "am I having this series of dreams, floating from one former school to another?" I would guess it's some sort of wish to be in that structured environment, or to have a chance at the past—to do it over again. I also have had dreams recently that I have the option of returning to Reed again. I know that consciously I really miss that place.

By the beginning of April he was having entirely sleepless nights, always a sign of impending mania. At dinner a couple of weeks before the sleeplessness started, he had wondered out loud in a sort of general way whether he might go back to the third floor of the St. John's mental health center (the locked ward) "sometime," but when I asked whether he needed or wanted to go now he said no. The eternal battle: part of him wanted help, part of him didn't. And even if he had gone to St. John's they probably would have turned him away because he was a Medi-Cal patient and Medi-Cal wouldn't reimburse for hospitalization in his current condition; he wasn't dangerous or gravely disabled enough yet. So things merely deteriorated for a couple of more weeks.[1] One day during that period I took him to his acupuncture appointment, normally something Lin did, but today she was busy. I had never met his acupuncturist, Dr. Pan, but knew about him from his pills. He had been prescribing two types of Chinese herbal medicine for Charley—tiny black pellets and larger yellow ones—and I had started adding them to the little white paper cup as part of my twice-daily ministrations.

It was a nasty, rainy day and Charley, sleepless for at least one night, was distracted and hyper. At the end of the session I told Dr. Pan that we needed refills of the herbal pills. He turned to Charley and asked him what dosages he was taking. Charley didn't answer; he just looked vague. I jumped in. "He takes three yellow ones and eight black ones twice a day."

Dr. Pan turned to me in surprise. "Why do *you* know that?"

"Because I'm the one who gives them to him."

"But *he* has to do that."

And another lightbulb clicked on. The next day I wrote in my journal:

> Last night (early this A.M.) . . . I had a small epiphany that I can't keep nursing him—it doesn't do any good—I was lying awake listening for his sounds of being awake and thinking about how I was probably going to spend another sleepless night—then realized how ridiculous the whole thing was—and untenable—letting my life be controlled by his craziness and *it not doing him any good*—all my oversolicitousness and cooking etc. having absolutely no effect whatever—at which point I relaxed and went back to sleep fairly quickly—seeing I have no real control over the situation.

So I decided not to give Charley his medication anymore; I merely made a list of what he was taking and gave it to him. My insight deepened a few days later when I went with him for his (now monthly) fifteen minutes with his one remaining psychiatrist, Dr. Breen (he had ditched the Jungian weeks before). Charley had never much liked Dr. Breen to begin with. Today, jittery and truculent, he was openly uncooperative, and when Dr. Breen asked whether he had been drinking or doing drugs Charley pulled out a hip flask, opened it and started swigging. Dr. Breen asked for the flask, smelled the spout, announced briskly that Charley could no longer be his patient, and led us out of his office by the familiar back door.

Out on the street again, cast off yet another planet in the mental health firmament! But as mad as I was at Charley and his histrionics, I also felt a sneaking admiration for him—for his *beau geste,* rear-guard rebelliousness, so self-destructive and yet self-preserving at the same time. That night I wrote in my journal that Dr. Breen's office "reeked of Irish whiskey and countertransference."

Still, I was through being his nurse and keeper. After almost five years of psychotic breaks and suicide attempts that always began with sleeplessness, for him to say things now like "I've stayed awake all night before—it's okay" was not okay with me. As we biked home, I told him yet again that he couldn't live with me anymore since he was obviously not willing to take care of himself and I couldn't live his life for him. By the next weekend he was back at St. John's, this time going on his own, a first. I wanted to see something good in this, my journal reports: "Ch's going to St. John's on his own is interesting. . . . Does this mean he's finally taking some initiative . . . ?" Or did it just mean that he needed a place to sleep and eat, so that he could *avoid* taking some initiative for a while longer? (And another thought: since "initiative" for Charley often seemed to involve knives and overdoses and cars going off mountain roads, how anxious should I be for him to take some?) In any event, when St. John's released him after a few days, he moved in with Lin, who had a much larger apartment than mine. Jenny had been living with her, using the spare bedroom, but she had just flown to Japan to travel and work for a few months as an Osaka bar girl (every father's fondest wish), so there was plenty of space now for Charley.

His journal of the next few weeks indicates a kind of limbo. April 14: "The day has dragged and dragged with no apparent end. I played tennis with Dad for about forty minutes. I took my medicine early, just to shut everything out. But no luck. Last night I started reading Lawrence's *Women in Love,* and that had no apparent end." April 16: "I find myself now at the Westside Pavilion. Just bought some clothes and cologne. Now I'm off to see Charlotte Brontë's *Jane Eyre* on film. That book which Jane [Davis] haunted me with." April 19: "Another day finds me at the Novel Café, where this book began. So many books, too much time." April 22: "Woke up at 9 A.M. precisely. Had an Export 'A' then made some coffee with a ceramic French Press. Two cups. Played the gourd [short for 'gourdalin'—a mandolin-like stringed instrument made from a gourd—JA] with the Stones' *Stripped.* My hand is tightened from strumming. Don't feel like writing owing to that."

"So many books, too much time." Lin and I were both working, so Charley was spending most of his days alone with nothing to do. This was a continual worry, not merely because of his at-home suicide attempts in 1993 and 1994 but because we were afraid that left to himself he would sink further and further into isolation and anomie. Whatever physical or psychological causes mental illness may have, it is also a habit, a lifestyle, characterized by a growing isolation that can take on a life—if that's the right word—of its own. A person who begins by only being troubled and eccentric may, through self-isolation and (as he grows increasingly "weird") rejection by others, become truly crazy. Neurotransmitters don't just affect psychology; psychology affects neurotransmitters. This was why Lin and I had tried to enforce a work-or-school-plus-therapy rule in exchange for letting Charley live with us. But we didn't always succeed, and he was often alone and idle. Part of the problem was that it was becoming harder and harder for him to go to school or hold a job, as the recent bagel-dropping episode illustrated; his last extended period of employment, at the coffeehouse, had ended almost a year before. So what was worse—letting him sit idle at home or pressuring him to get jobs which he would lose after only a day or two, causing further demoralization? Charley's journal of May 2 alludes to one such failed attempt to work, this time at a coffee and pastry house where he had made a good initial impression, at first even being considered for management duties. But then he was let go after only a couple of shifts:

> What went wrong at Sweet Dreams L.A.? I'm really not sure. It all lies in the structure of management I believe. If I could have been my natural "mellow" self (that being the ultimate reason for my termination), I would have gotten along fine with the clientele. But night managing must call for more "aggressiveness," as Joe M. pointed out to me. So the question lies, "How shall I find gainful employment in this world of lost opportunity?"

Lin was curious about why he had been fired after the initial high hopes, so she went to the store's owner and asked. The owner told her that Charley, despite being obviously personable and intelligent, had made the customers uncomfortable because he didn't perform the ordinary social behaviors—making eye contact, carrying on small talk—that put people at ease. It was becoming increasingly difficult for him to perform ordinary social functions, even at a time when he was not psychotic.

So he idled about, mostly alone, going to movies and reading at cafes. Looked at from one angle it was the life of a spoiled, indolent youth, mental illness or no mental illness. Charley himself saw his own failings clearly. "I feel overwhelmed by my own laziness," he wrote later in the summer, "and I have a fear that I shan't overcome it. To be content with idleness seems altogether disgusting."

Looked at from another angle, though, such brief periods of indulgence can be seen as minor consolation prizes to someone who had already lost most of what was valuable to him. And, to be fair, Charley's laziness was not all his doing. Aside from the alcohol and pot, he was doped to the gills with other, *prescribed* medications that he took regularly or semiregularly: one or more antipsychotic and antimanic drugs, an antidepressant, plus other drugs (powerful in their own right[2]) to counteract the side effects of the antipsychotics, plus powerful sedatives for sleep. Most of these medications act as tranquilizers or mood flatteners, so it is hard to tell how much of the responsibility for Charley's lethargy, and even his social difficulties, was really his. Even their defenders admit that psychotropic drugs, while alleviating the "positive" symptoms (voices, hallucinations) of mental illness, tend, because of their tranquilizing effects, to worsen the "negative" symptoms, including passivity, lack of motivation, difficulties relating to others, etc. Since I was the main person who had introduced him to this hobo stew of drugs and then continued to feed them to him—I, who didn't even like to take aspirin—I never felt comfortable criticizing him too much for his funks and lack of drive.

But I did worry. Something I had seen the previous summer haunted me. It was during a period when I was fighting with Charley about smoking dope and generally not taking care of himself. I was riding my bicycle about a block from my house, and when I stopped for a light a young man crossed the street in front of me. At first he seemed to be just another stereotypical Southern California surfer type: twenties, reddish tan, handsome, long blond hair bleached by the sun. But then as I looked closer, I saw that he was dressed in rags, his bare feet dirty and bruised. He was also carrying on an animated conversation with himself, wide-eyed, grinning, gesticulating. As I watched I felt a stab of panic: This could be Charley in a few years. In fact it could have been Charley now, if Charley hadn't had parents he could live with and some sort of support system to allow him room for error. But what if he outlived us? What if something happened to Lin or me? Even if we continued to prop him up indefinitely, something—our morale, our sanity, our physical selves—would eventually give out, and he would be on his own. Then what?

In mid-June Charley had to be hospitalized again, and this time he didn't go quietly. Lin and I had to take him to Santa Monica West, the county mental health office near my apartment that I had phoned the year before, and when he tried to walk out he was restrained and taken to St. John's in handcuffs. Once there, he told me a couple of days later, he fought with some male orderlies and fell and hit his head and needed fourteen stitches. He was put in leather restraints under a fourteen-day hold.

By now Lin was at the same level of frustration I had reached two months earlier, after my Dr. Pan epiphany. Living with Charley was extremely difficult for her. Until recently he had stayed mostly at my apartment during the past two years, and Lin had not felt the full effect of living with a person who, at least when he was ill, tended to turn those around him into nonpersons. But if he didn't live with one of us, where would he go? He refused to consider a board-and-care, a kind of boarding house for the mentally ill that accepts SSI checks as rent and provides a room, food and medication monitoring. I looked into one, Ocean View, on a sunny street in Santa Monica near the beach about ten blocks from my apartment, and I asked Charley to walk over and look at it with me. But when we approached the building, a homeless-looking man, one of the residents, was standing outside smoking, looking as if his life was one long, random wait, and as we got nearer we could both see, through the front window, the blue ghostliness of the TV. "No, Dad," Charley said, and turned and walked away. How could I blame him?

NAMI

The question of living arrangements had been one that I had thought about a lot since the stabbing and months-long psychosis two years earlier, when it had become clear that Charley's problem was not going to be chased away by a little lithium, at least not yet. While he was at Harbor-UCLA I had gone to a few meetings of the National Alliance for the Mentally Ill, a support group for families going through crises like ours. I had actually known about NAMI for some time and had first contacted the group in 1993 after Charley slit his wrists. A St. John's social worker gave me the name of the local NAMI facilitator, a woman named Sharon Taney, and I called her to find out about programs he might be able to hook into once he got out of the hospital. "How old is he?" Sharon asked after I'd briefly described his episodes.

"Twenty."

"Oh, poor thing," she replied. "Then he's just starting out." I don't remember the rest of the discussion, only the pity in Sharon's voice, the pity and the certainty.

I was chilled and vaguely offended by this certainty. There was an arrogance in it, as if, after knowing me for a total of fourteen seconds, and Charley not at all, Sharon already knew more about his life and future than he or I did. As a result—and also because Charley soon returned to Reed—I didn't contact NAMI again for a year and a half, till he was at Harbor-UCLA. By then our situation had changed. He was no longer a minor and my dependent, which meant that even though I had a new job with new health insurance he wasn't covered. Also, he was stuck in L.A. indefinitely, and Lin and I needed to find out about possible places and programs for him here. That was what NAMI was for, I had been told, so I put away my memories of the first encounter and called Sharon Taney again. The local NAMI group met twice a month in downtown Santa Monica, and I went to three or four meetings over the next couple of months. Lin went with me to one of them, I think the second.

Sharon, who was still the local NAMI head and chaired the meetings, was a quietly authoritative woman in her sixties whom I liked immediately when I met her. She was a layperson, not a doctor or academic, and had gotten into the field, I found out later, because she had a mentally ill child. The meetings were attended by anywhere from ten to twenty people, most of them parents of children diagnosed with schizophrenia. Despite its name—National Alliance for the Mentally Ill—NAMI is actually a support (and advocacy) group for *families* of the mentally ill, people like me who, like flash-flood victims, suddenly find ourselves up to our necks in a crisis that is completely incomprehensible and uncontrollable. Some attendees seemed to be regulars, people who knew Sharon fairly well; for them the meetings were like group therapy. Others, like me, were there to get information about the confusing and fragmented mental health system. For this Sharon was enormously helpful, a wealth of experience and practical information about hospitals, government programs, board-and-cares, clinical trials for new medications, criteria for getting SSI and Medi-Cal, how much a person could earn from outside work and still qualify for SSI, the process of becoming an adult child's conservator, and anything else you could name. My notes from my first meeting (two days after Lin and I took Charley to Harbor-UCLA for the first time) consist of a page and a half of names Sharon provided of places where he could live or programs he could participate in.

Any port in a storm, any rooftop in a flood. Aside from her broad knowledge of the mental health system and how to navigate it, Sharon had her own ideas—gained partly from her experience as a mother—about what parents should and should not do with and for their kids, and her calm and assured voice, the voice of experience, gave her words weight. "Sharon: Kids need to live on their own when they're adults," say my notes from the first meeting. She firmly believed that mentally ill children need to learn independence, and that parental oversolicitousness is a kind of sentimentality that can do more harm than good. How could anyone argue with this? The problem was that for our kids, living on one's own usually meant being warehoused in a board-and-care or similar facility (sometimes locked, sometimes not) that was essentially a kind of residential hotel for the mentally ill with a low level of treatment, mostly medication monitoring, added on.

Medication was the core of the treatment regimen NAMI represented. "Is he taking his meds?" was typically the first question Sharon would ask when a distraught parent finished his or her account of an (often adult) child's latest mishap or instance of refractory behavior. Yes, the answer often came, but then the parent might add that the medication (usually an antipsychotic for schizophrenia like Risperdal, Clozapine or Haldol) wasn't working properly, or *had* been working but wasn't anymore. Or the child was gaining weight, or had become increasingly lethargic since being on the medication. In virtually all cases Sharon's response could be characterized as, Get them properly medicated and out of the house. This was not said cruelly or uncompassionately, and because it wasn't, because Sharon spoke in a calm, no-nonsense way, her voice smooth bronze like blind justice, and because she was saying what many of us had been at least semiconsciously thinking, it was easy and natural to accept her approach, at least after an initial period of resistance. Of *course* Charley had to live on his own. Lin and I had never really put it that way before. Our idea had always been that he could stay with us (one or both) as long as he worked or went to school, did *something* other than lie around the house. But after a NAMI meeting or two even this approach seemed to me inexcusably soft.

I saw how this thought process worked when a new person showed up at my second or third meeting, the mother of a troubled adolescent girl. She gave her distraught, confused presentation of her problem, as we all did the first time. When she was finished, Sharon gave her brief, convincing talk about self-sufficiency, board-and-cares, and the necessity of the child's living on her own. The new woman looked at Sharon in amazement. What? she asked. Was it simply okay to throw the kid out? What about parental love and family bonds?—all things I had said or thought at my first meeting a month before. But now as the new woman said them I could hear myself thinking, "Stop whining." I was even more hard line than Sharon, who when she did reply, did so in her calm, rational way, a lot nicer than *I* would have been if I had been in charge. Part of my new "realism" flowed from the undercurrent of resentment I tended to harbor toward Charley, accompanied by an almost sadistic satisfaction I sometimes felt—less often than the resentment but more often than I like to admit—at seeing him disciplined by institutions or people (other than me) who in theory were doing it for his own good. Maybe this time he'll get it, I would think. Maybe this time he'll wake up and realize he has no alternative but to get better; no alternative, that is, except board-and-cares or residential motels or the street; Lin and I couldn't care for him forever. But this cold-water-in-the-face approach never worked with Charley—if for no other reason than, given his penchant for suicide, he always had at least one other alternative available! Rather than rouse him, the slaps of "cold reality" just made an already fragile soul more fragile. I always fought my resentment, and of course wish now I'd fought it even harder—but, I also wish I'd had better options for real care.

I don't know how often and how consistently the parents at the NAMI meetings actually followed Sharon's advice. Perhaps those who didn't, or couldn't, simply stopped coming. I stopped after about three meetings. My immediate reason was that the meetings had a kind of in-groupy feel to them that made me uncomfortable. But on a more basic level I just didn't agree, the more I thought about it, with the NAMI philosophy, which in *Toxic Psychiatry*

Peter Breggin characterizes as the parental rallying cry of "We are not to blame."[3] When I first read this characterization I thought it was unfair, as I did Breggin's implication that much if not most of mental disturbance is the result of bad parenting. "Overt outrage and hatred toward their parents is a frequent characteristic of most people who get labeled crazy," Breggin says. "Often they attack their parents emotionally, and frequently their communications portray their parents in seemingly irrational fashion as agents of the devil, the FBI, or other feared authorities. With obvious metaphorical meaning, they literally may describe seeing horns growing out of their parents' heads."[4]

Breggin actually understates things here. Some children do more than attack their parents emotionally. One parent at a NAMI meeting I attended, a late-middle-aged woman, told of how her "paranoid schizophrenic" son had tried to kill her, and that she was now living in hiding from him. She loved him, she said, and he loved her, but he wanted to kill her anyway. Of course I had no idea why. The woman seemed nice enough, and as I listened to her I couldn't believe that she could possibly have done anything to warrant her son's murderous rage. But of course, I was hearing only one side of the story.

And that is just the way NAMI wants it, I found out years later when I went to the NAMI Web site and began reading a document called *NAMI Consumer and Family Guide to Schizophrenia Treatment*. Section three, "The Right Kind of Psychotherapy," states:

> The right kind of psychotherapy, together with medication, can help you better understand and manage schizophrenia and can help reduce symptoms.
>
> - Psychotherapy aimed at providing information about the illness, managing symptoms and treatment, providing support, and helping with problem-solving skills should be provided to all individuals with schizophrenia.
> - Psychotherapy aimed at understanding unconscious drives or getting at the psychological roots of schizophrenia is *never* appropriate.
> - Family members in regular contact with a patient as well as others who help the patient day-to-day should receive at least nine months of education about schizophrenia, support, crisis intervention, and problem-solving skills.
> - Family therapy based on the premise that family dysfunction caused schizophrenia should *never* occur.[5] (emphasis in the original)

I have read a lot of strange things in my time, but bullet points two and four really stopped me in my tracks. "*Never* appropriate"? "Should *never* occur"? My immediate response was, How do *they* know? And, *What are they trying to hide?* The flagrant conflict of interest expressed by the last point in particular—a parents' group prohibiting children from discussing the role of parents ("family dysfunction") in mental illness—was truly amazing to me, and again revealed who the primary consumers of mental health care really are. Even on the most self-serving day of my life, it would never have occurred to me to discourage Charley from complaining about me or anything I had ever done. Lin and I begged him to get therapy, any kind he could relate to, to talk about anything he wanted to talk about. Anything was better than silence.

To be fair, there may be a kernel of good intention, at least, in discouraging discussion of "psychological roots" or "family dysfunction"—namely, the notion that if troubled people spend their entire lives blaming others for their troubles they will never get beyond the essentially passive posture of being the victim, and their lives will continued to be poisoned as a result. This is true even if a person really has been mistreated. Even in cases of real abuse, assuming that the wrong cannot be righted (the perpetrators are either dead, otherwise out of reach or merely indifferent), at a certain point the wronged person begins wronging himself by continuing to dwell on the past. We all know this. But moving beyond such self-torture cannot be accomplished by forbidding discussion of its causes, so even here NAMI's refusal to discuss psychological roots and family dysfunction is wrong.

Not that family therapy, or any therapy, is a magic solution. There are ways of cutting off discussion under the guise of encouraging it, such as in the dynamic where a family tacitly "assigns" one member—the person designated mentally ill—to be the problem, the repository of the family dysfunction, the lamb whose sacrifice ensures the survival of the rest of the family. Under such a polarity, family therapy becomes a ritual of the "healthy" members "helping" the sick one. This is a sort of microcosm of the broader disease model of mental illness, in which the healthy society ("healthy" despite a history of genocide, ethnic violence, class and national hatreds, militarism, religious bigotry, exploitation, egomania, and the utter lack of self-awareness that underlies all of it) quarantines the sick person to keep him from infecting it.

Even given the broad mainstream acceptance of this disease model, however, there are countercurrents propelling some theoreticians and clinicians to think about mental illness in new—actually old—ways. "Obviously there is no sharp dividing line between health and disease," says the writer George Engel, adding that "even when there is gross and manifest disability, we must recognize the relative integrity of other systems or modes of function, permitting us to speak quite correctly of the 'more healthy' parts of the body or the person."[6] This more integrated approach relies on the healthy—both within the individual and outside—to combat the unhealthy. It is like Dr. Gray's eighteenth-century French village, which absorbed the mentally ill into it, as opposed to the asylum, which herds all the unhealthiness together and lets it feed on itself, roped off from normal human contact. The disease model absolutizes the disease and equates it with the person who has it. "You're a schizophrenic. It's a brain disease. It can't be cured. You're going to be on medication for the rest of your life. Get used to it"—or, in softer tones, "Oh, poor thing, he's just starting out." And this approach advertises itself as taking away the "stigma" of mental illness! Is it any wonder that some people don't want to be part of a system that "destigmatizes" them this way?

As I look back on my mostly failed attempts to understand and help Charley, I cannot emphasize enough the importance of, and I believe the harm done by, the idea of a sharp dividing line between mental illness and normality and, following from it, the idea (never said directly, and hence more insidious) that the person *is* the illness, not a person who *has* an illness (or some condition that manifests itself as illness) but also healthy parts as well. How much this absolutism permeated my thinking even after I began doubting the existence of schizophrenia and manic-depression as discrete disease entities only became clear after Charley's death when I began looking at alternative views. I remember, for example, how struck I was by Edward Podvoll's notion that even the minds of the most psychotic people contain healthy parts, what he calls "islands of clarity" which can, with the proper help, be built on and expanded and eventually grow into continents. Some of these alternative views have begun to form the basis of alternative practical models of mental illness treatment, models that during Charley's life I was completely unaware of.

Treating the Disease or
Treating the Person? The Rehab Model

I first read about the Village Integrated Service Agency—which is where I got the George Engel quote—in a fall 1998 newspaper article, a roundtable on mental illness. Of the five participants, three were L.A.-area mental-health program administrators and one was on the board of directors of NAMI. The fifth was a psychiatrist named Mark Ragins, but Ragins didn't sound like an ordinary psychiatrist. Although as an M.D. he was the only "scientist" in the discussion, he was also the only speaker who didn't proclaim as a God-given truth that mental illness is a brain disorder. The first speaker, an administrator for a mental-health institute, immediately defines mental illnesses as "neurobiological illnesses" that are different from "everyday mental-health problems" in the same way a sore leg is different from a broken one. Ragins, speaking second, says,

> I only partially agree, actually. I work in a place where a lot of people have become seriously disabled or are homeless, and although I do see a number of people with biochemical disorders, with many of the people I meet it's less clear what's going on, less clear that it's a brain disorder. I meet the person who was that weird-looking kid in third grade who used to go in his pants and hit the girls. He has now grown up to be a homeless person. Society is saying, "You're a medical specialist, and that's not a medical disorder. He's got some sort of personality problem, so don't deal with him." Or if I meet someone whose mother was murdered by his father when he was three and he ran away and was homeless and using drugs by nine, I can argue that his problem really isn't a mental illness, that it's a mental-health issue and so he shouldn't be in the public system. But he's still homeless, still suffering. I think a lot of the people that we should be helping do not actually have biochemical disorders, or have other issues on top of their biochemical disorders.[7]

After Ragins comes the NAMI representative, eternally on the lookout for the heresy of thinking that parents (like fathers murdering mothers when patients are three) cause schizophrenia. "Mental-health issues are social problems," she lectures Ragins, "but severe and persistent mental illness, such as schizophrenia or bipolar disorder, is a physical brain disease. And we have to accept that and start from that point. . . ."[8]

The discussion, thus polarized, goes on from there. The further I read, the more I wanted to talk to Ragins. After a lot of hassle—neither the newspaper that printed the roundtable nor the phone company had any idea where Ragins or the Village Integrated Service Agency were located—I tracked them down in Long Beach thirty miles south of L.A. I called and told them about my book, and was invited to attend a daylong immersion on the organization's philosophy and practice.

The Village inhabits an old three-story brick building in a rather dilapidated part of downtown Long Beach. It was established in 1989 as an alternative, "integrated" method of care for the mentally ill, I was told by the organization's head, Martha Long. It is based on a treatment model begun in Madison, Wisconsin, called Program of Assertive Community Treatment. PACT came into existence in the wake of the "deinstitutionalization" movement begun in the 1960s. Its aim was to bring the psychiatric hospital environment into the community. A similar model is the "clubhouse" approach of Fountain House in New York City, according to David Pilon, the Village's director of training and consultation.

When I made my visit (spring 1999), the Village had 276 "members"—it rejects the terms *patients* or *consumers*—who ranged from the poor and homeless to middle-class, almost all with long-term major mental illness. Approximately two-thirds were diagnosed as schizophrenic, 16–17 percent were bipolar, 6–7 percent suffered from major depression, and 15 percent were "other"—borderline personality disorder, etc. (A few months after my visit, the state of California funded the Village to handle an additional population of mainly indigent and homeless persons with mental illness—many of them "dual diagnosis"—and as of 2002 the number of members was a little less than 500.) The membership is ethnically mixed, with a roughly three-to-two ratio of men to women. About 20 percent work, either short term at the Village, which runs several businesses onsite (a restaurant, mini-mart and janitorial service), or at outside jobs. About 10 percent attend school. All live offsite in a variety of situations ranging from their own apartments to staying with family to sober-living homes to board-and-cares. In keeping with its philosophy of being a link to the outside world rather than a refuge from it, the Village has neither inpatient residency facilities nor day programs, instead encouraging members to work or go to school during the day. The onsite businesses employ members only for a limited time, as training for getting jobs outside.

Now, the PACT notion of bringing the hospital environment into the community could mean a couple of things. It could mean doping up the mentally ill with neuroleptics to the point where locked wards are no longer necessary because patients are so sedated that they can be safely let out into society. Or it could mean making the community itself a place of recovery. The Village tries to do the latter. Although it uses medication and so is not in the militant antipsychopharmacology camp of Kate Millett, Peter Breggin, et al., medication is not the basis of treatment. The core concept is psychosocial rehabilitation rather than psychopharmacology, or, as Mark Ragins expressed it, "treating the person rather than the disease."

I asked Ragins, a shaggy-haired, youngish-looking man of early middle age who is the Village's head psychiatrist, to explain. "Sometimes an approach that's good for the person may be bad for the illness," he said. "If we're doing community outreach and give a guy sleeping under a bridge a sandwich and try to spend time talking to him, that may be good for the person but bad for the disease, since we're not giving him medication to treat the voices he's hearing. On the other hand, let's say a psychiatrist pressures a woman who's clinically depressed to have electroconvulsive therapy that makes the depression go away. That could be good for the illness but bad for the person. She might say, 'I feel better but I'll never forgive my doctor for putting me through that.'"

Or let's say a prospective member comes (or is brought) to Ragins, who would ask him why he's there. The man might say, "I'm hearing voices."

Normally a psychiatrist would then question the man about the voices. How long has he been hearing them? Are they mood congruent (indicating bipolar disorder) or mood incongruent (indicating schizophrenia)? Whose voices are they? What are they saying? All the unwelcome, prying questions people like Charley hate.

Ragins takes a different approach. "So?" he might ask instead.

The man: "What do you mean, 'So?'"

"Why is hearing voices a problem?"

"Huh?" No one, particularly a psychiatrist, has ever asked that before.

"What would you be doing if you *weren't* hearing voices?"

This approach has several aims. First, it is designed to lessen the distance between the doctor and the person in crisis by making the former less intrusive, less "up there," less interested in the usual psychiatrist's agenda of getting rid of the "positive" symptoms like hearing voices. Psychiatry has proven it can often (although by no means always) treat the positive psychotic symptoms of mental illness fairly well—the voices, hallucinations, delusions. But doing so doesn't necessarily make the person better. At least half of Charley's suicide attempts, including the successful one, took place when he was not psychotic.

A second aim of Ragins's approach is to shake up the person in crisis, make him think about what his real problems are. "What are your goals?" Ragins might ask.

"Goals?" the man might reply. It's been so long since he thought about any goals other than staying out of the hospital or off the street, or getting the voices to go away by taking his medication, or feeling better by using dope or alcohol. Now Ragins is asking him to think about what *he* wants, not what the psychiatrists (or the family) want for him.

So the guy might think a while and say, "I want to get laid. I haven't gone to bed with a woman since I got sick."

Ragins: "So what's keeping you from getting laid?"

"Well, whenever I try to have a conversation with a woman the voices start telling me I'm fat and ugly and no woman would want me."

It would go on from there. Once the member has determined his goal or goals—getting laid, holding a job, returning to school, learning a profession—the Village staff do whatever needs to be done to prepare him to achieve them. In a 1994 article in the *Journal of Psychosocial Nursing,* two Village nurses, both with M.N. and R.N. degrees, describe their work as "personal service coordinators" (PSCs), a term preferred to "case manager":

> [Members'] goals are diverse and lead us, as PSCs, into a diversity of activities. Our day may include accompanying them to the social security office [but not calling the office *for* them—JA] and waiting in line, doing side-by-side job coaching, going with them to the veterinarian, or teaching them how to use a travel agent. We also attend social events together in the community. At first we wondered why, with all our education, we were involved in such mundane activities. The answer is simple: because it works.[9]

The idea of simply spending time with mentally ill people and encouraging them to be active is not new. In fact it sounds a lot like Dr. Gray's eighteenth-century "love village," or the Belgian town of Geel, whose townspeople adopt the mentally ill into their families and treat them with ordinary human kindness. It also sounds a lot like what Edward Podvoll calls "basic attendance," the core of his non–medication-oriented treatment philosophy, although when I asked Ragins if he had ever heard of Podvoll or "basic attendance" he said no. (This is not the first case of people in the alternative mental-health field working along similar lines but unaware of each other.) Podvoll says that the skills of basic attendance

> are really only an extension of how people might naturally come to care for each other. For example, Manfred Bleuler [the son of the inventor of the term *schizophrenia*], after a lifetime of experience in caring for people recovering from psychosis, succinctly expressed this spirit of basic attendance when he said that there were only three essential therapeutic interventions that are of benefit: expand the community of people with whom they are involved; increase their level of individual responsibility; and help them to relax. These, I believe, capture the simplicity and directness of the work of basic attendance.[10]

Ragins and the others at the Village are aware that the strategy of doing things with people but not for them entails risk. The mentally ill are often very fragile and easily frustrated, and the best personal service coordinator in the world can't guarantee that the guy who hasn't gone to bed with a woman since he got sick is suddenly going to become Warren Beatty; even many of us who fall somewhere in the "normal" category have problems with romance. But that's the whole point. Psychosocial rehab's aim is to bring the mentally ill person's problems back into the realm of more or less ordinary human problems: love, work, friendship, personal satisfaction, finding a purpose to life. The Village operates on the principle of "high risk, high support" rather than "reducing stress." Staff help members prepare for challenges and then are there when the inevitable failures happen, helping to pick them up and dust them off and try again. The idea is to help the person become an active participant in his or her own life—always, I thought during Charley's last years, the root problem we had with him. He was becoming a wallflower at his own party.

A distinction between the Village model and the Podvoll "basic attendance" model is that the Village is not antimedication as a matter of philosophy. (This distinction may not be as great as it appears, however, since in their clinical work, Podvoll and his colleagues have also used antipsychotics, although as sparingly as possible and not as the basis of their practice, as the psychopharmacologists and brain-diseasers in general do.[11]) The Village uses antipsychotics as a routine part of treatment, including the new, more expensive ones. This means members and the organization have to deal with their side effects, and in fact, the day I was there Ragins was monitoring the situation of a member hospitalized in intensive care with a rare and potentially fatal condition known as "neuroleptic malignant syndrome" (I was later told she had recovered). When I asked Ragins what he thought of antimedicationists like Peter Breggin he said he hadn't read him and didn't believe that medications cause brain damage, adding, "Of course, I don't believe that mental *illness* causes brain damage either." His approach is to give members a list of what medications are available and what their side effects are.

Basic to the psychosocial rehab model is the idea that a lot of people with serious mental illness can and do get better. Ragins and the other Village staff talked a lot about this. One unintended but pernicious consequence of the NAMI "it's nobody's fault, it's a brain disease" philosophy is that a subtle or not-so-subtle defeatism may be generated among family and physicians, even a hidden desire for the mentally ill person not to recover. After all, recovery would mean that the illness was caused not by a shrunken brain or enlarged brain ventricles or bad genes but by human agency—possibly even family dysfunction or bad medication or physician incompetence. In contrast to what I would call the "mitigated hopelessness" of the brain-disease model and psychopharmacology, Ragins mentioned one study by Dr. Courtenay Harding and other researchers for the University of Colorado in the late 1980s. Harding et al. did a comprehensive longitudinal study of mental patients let out of mental hospitals in the 1950s. Two-thirds of them got better when they had psychosocial support. "Ten world studies have found," Harding et al. say, "that the long-distance outcome for schizophrenia is widely heterogeneous." It is determined by culture, the individual's environment, the individual's own attitude toward his or her condition, and the level of psychosocial support.[12]

Could the Village have helped Charley if I'd found out about it in time— something that would have been difficult enough in itself, since the mental health system in this country, even within metropolitan areas, is tremendously

fragmented and often hard to find? (It took me weeks of fruitless effort, followed by a burst of sheer luck, to locate the Village even after I knew about its
existence.) I don't know how Charley would have reacted. The place itself has
a pretty proletarian, utilitarian look and feel to it, and many of the members I
saw the day I was there would have been looked at by Charley as "dregs" and
"lost souls." I mentioned this to Martha and David with some trepidation during our end-of-the-day wrap-up discussion, not wanting to sound elitist. The
disclaimers were unnecessary; they both nodded in understanding. "Yes,"
Martha said, "he'd probably just say, 'This has nothing to do with me. I'm not
as sick as these people are.'"

He probably would. I had heard it so many times, especially when he was
stuck in the "county psych wards" at San Francisco General or Harbor-UCLA.
It was Charley's perennial excuse for not taking part in treatment programs
(even River Community); he just didn't relate to most of the people he found
himself among. He didn't fit their "profile," partly for reasons of background
and education, partly because most of them were older and more beaten down
than he was—and partly, I suspect, because it was a good excuse not to deal
with his own pot and alcohol problems. In one of his last journal entries he
speaks about a treatment facility he had tried, at Lin's and my urging, that has
some things in common with the Village:

> Today Mother and I visited Step Up on Second in Santa Monica, an insti-
> tution for the mentally unsound. If I were to engage myself there it would no
> doubt be a step *down*. For to put myself under their scrutiny would be to class
> myself w/the worthless misfits who live there. The man whom we met with,
> Chuck Lennon, was a decent enough sort, though I couldn't help but to sup-
> pose he himself had a history of mental problems. How else would he have cho-
> sen that job? I tend not to trust those who work with the mentally diseased
> because I see that line of work as a remedy for their own psychic discomfiture.
> Plus, they tend to have a patronizing aspect toward their "patients," or is it
> "clients" . . .

I was always of two minds about this dismissive attitude toward both other
mentally ill people and their helpers. On the one hand it was a dangerous form
of denial. It enabled Charley to continue thinking that he was basically okay
and that his periodic crises—including several near-miss suicide attempts—

were due not to some internal problem but to other things outside himself: parental meddling or incompetence, the solstice, running out of marijuana, prying, idiot doctors, and so on. But there was another, healthy side as well, an instinct for self-preservation. Denial is not always a bad thing. It is part of our evolutionary equipment, the thing that allows us to keep on going in the face of circumstances (the most basic being the certainty of death) which, if we looked at them squarely, might quite well paralyze us and render us incapable of doing anything. Charley's refusal to see himself as a sick person was the form his resistance took to being reduced to an institutional personality—*a* schizophrenic or *a* manic-depressive—by psychiatric labeling and ware-housing. It was the way he maintained his courage and his "himness" under the blows of a crippling, cruel fate, an implacable enemy that would, perhaps—we'll never know—have beaten him even if he had humbled himself before it. In that case, the defeat would have been even worse because it would have taken not only his life, but his pride.

His dilemma, a dilemma that reflected the way our culture deals with mental illness, was that he was forced to choose between his self-respect and his survival. Current psychiatric practice, with all its good intentions and attempts to "destigmatize" mental illness, tends to accomplish the opposite by robbing people of their complexity and denying the validity of their subjective experience under the guise of diagnosis, diagnosis that itself is by no means as objective and scientific as its practitioners claim. What self-respecting person would want to have his or her inner world reduced to a list of symptoms, and not even a firm, fixed list at that? Mental disorders come and go from edition to edition of the *Diagnostic and Statistical Manual,* the criteria of even those that remain changing from edition to edition. Homosexuality used to be a mental illness. So did "neurasthenia" and "hysteria." Who hears of them anymore? Can anyone be sure that "schizophrenia" will not suffer a similar fate? The glory that was Greece burns eternal, but made-up Greek words have a way of ending up in history's ashtray.

In contrast, the psychosocial rehab model practiced by the Village and simi-lar organizations shows promise because, with its "treating the person rather than the disease" philosophy, it respects the person's inner life and integrity and lets him or her determine, or at least be a participant in the dialogue about, what is illness and what is not. It is less concerned with defining and getting

rid of symptoms (a practice involving prying and intrusion) and more concerned with helping the person function according to his or her own definition of what "functioning" means.

As mentioned, I often wonder whether having a Village-type organization
in my area would have helped Charley and me during his first breakdown and
thus set a different, healthier tone for both his recovery and our subsequent
relationship. Would a more low-key, interactive approach rather than fatherly
panic (ending in a locked ward) have allowed him to avoid, or emerge more
quickly from, the utter "destitution" he fell into after his descent from the
mountain? Some years after Yosemite I heard about an organization in West
L.A. that sent teams of two mental health workers to people's homes when
they needed help. But it was private and cost fifty-five dollars per hour. The
Village provides the same service as part of its case rate.[13] I'm not sure what the
long-term benefits of such intervention would have been for Charley, but if I
had known about the Village or something like it in my area when his crisis
erupted, I would at least have gotten some short-term help. A couple of experienced staff could have come to the apartment and talked with us (or even just
me), using their clinical education and experience to try to relate to Charley,
evaluate the situation, and go from there. Even if he had refused to cooperate
they could have spelled me, allowed me to get some rest. I wouldn't have
felt so totally alone and helpless, feelings that, along with my concerns
for Charley's personal safety, contributed to my willingness to have him
hospitalized.

The Village uses psychiatric hospitalization as little as possible. Part of the reason for this is economic: psych wards are expensive, ranging from more than five
hundred dollars per day for public hospitals to about one thousand dollars per
day for private. But the main reason hospitalization is not used much at the
Village, Martha and David said, is that it is usually not necessary. Most of
the time, staff can manage a member's crisis short of hospitalization. Nor does
the Village automatically support families who are trying, often out of exhaustion, to involuntarily commit Village members. "It's a terribly thorny issue,
involuntary commitment," Martha said (how well I knew!), and Village staff deal
with it case by case. "Very often you'll have the family write something like
'caretaker exhaustion' on the commitment request in the space asking for
'reason for commitment'—meaning it's for the family, not the member."

How well I remembered!—the feeling of burnout and exhaustion, the desperate wish to have somebody else, *anybody* else, responsible.

"We don't trust the system," Martha continued. "We trust what *we* do."

Good Minutes, Good Hours

One of the compensations of facing a long-term, possibly irremediable crisis is that once our hopes are ground into dust and our plans shown to be the vain fatuities they are, we learn to live in the present. When I think of my visits with Charley in the hospital, or of the periods when I was trying to take care of him before or after the hospital, I think not so much of large chunks of time but of days, hours, even minutes. "That was a good hour," I would think after visiting him in one of the psych wards—even though, if I thought about the hour in its total context, it would be as merely a very small area of peace in a very large nexus of anxiety. But I learned, not consciously but by a kind of erosion of expectation, to adapt in the way a plant adapts to a dark room, growing more sensitive to less light. Robbed of well-being as a quantity, I began to experience it as a quality.

A Sunday visit a week into Charley's latest hospitalization in June 1996 was one good hour. It was a warm, sunny day that brought cheer even into the locked ward. We sat in the common room and had a nice, easy talk, occasionally glancing up at the supermodels in bathing suits on *Baywatch* on the TV hanging from the ceiling like a totem. Charley told me he was getting out in two days, long before the fourteen-day hold was up, and was feeling good about it. We talked about old times—how concerned he had been for his mother when she and I split up in 1983, how he had tried to look after her (he was ten at the time), and how worried he had been for me in my tiny, furnitureless Dogpatch apartment. He said he didn't really understand his mental processes. He guessed he was manic-depressive and that his last breakdown had been a result of the summer solstice. "The sun is very powerful," he said, causing sleep deprivation. He recalled that he had stabbed himself (almost exactly two years before) on June 20. I reminded him that a few days earlier he'd said he thought he'd outgrown his illness and didn't need medication anymore. "Oh, yeah," he replied.

"Why do I have such a sense of well-being?" I wrote that night in my journal. "Maybe because I've never really lost hope for Ch.—still think he can make it."

As I look back now on these good minutes and hours, I wonder whether there was a quantitative as well as a qualitative aspect to these times that I failed to grasp, whether what I thought of as good hours or minutes corresponded to what Edward Podvoll terms islands of clarity (not only Charley's but mine), that could, under different circumstances, have been built on further and not just enjoyed.

"And I Believe I Shan't Ever Return" (The Quiet Hell of August)

At the beginning of August, Lin and I went to a daylong symposium on schizophrenia in Santa Monica that we had heard about from some local mental health people. It was partly sponsored by drug companies, a fact that did not escape Lin or even me; that she went at all is testimony to how desperate we had become. Neither of us really believed in the existence of schizophrenia anymore, and in fact Charley had never been diagnosed as schizophrenic. His most recent psychiatrist, Dr. Breen, had said he was schizoaffective, a garbage-can term that means some combination of schizophrenia and manic-depression. By now it was all just words to us anyway; nobody knew what Charley "had." Nevertheless, Lin and I both stayed at the symposium the entire day, looking for something. Anything.

Soon afterward, Charley flew by himself to Portland to visit Reed, an event that may have represented the beginning of the end. Here is his account of the trip, from his journal about a month after his return to L.A.:

> A few weeks ago I made a visit, to Portland, OR, to visit my former place of schooling, Reed College. In the cab on the way from the airport I became very nauseous (from the plane food) and had to ask the driver to pull over so I could vomit. This omen set my appetite for the duration of my visit, for throughout the weekend I could barely digest a thing.
>
> I arrived at my old school friend, Alec's, that Friday night, a rundown house in South-East Portland, and immediately asked for marijuana to cure the

queasiness. Alec was a poor host, having neither food nor drink to offer. He was quiet, and seemed rather isolated. That's the effect, I suppose, that staying in one's room for hours upon end and playing with a computer has. Plus he was a psychology major at Reed, which is enough to make anyone a trifle strange.

The following morning, after a disturbing sleepless night, I made my way to the campus to see how this institution, filled with so many memories, was holding up. The walk there was less than pleasant; what with the sun blazing and cars roaring through streets empty of pedestrians, I was alone and exposed. I ventured through the cross-canyon dormitories that lie remote from the central part of the campus. They were empty and unclean, and the grass surrounding them was dry from the summer drought.

After roaming through the rhododendron gardens, a muddy wood adjacent to the school, I went to Eliot Hall—an old brick building containing many offices and classrooms. I went there to use the piano in the chapel. After this I went to the student union, which was dusty and haunting.

Back at Alec's a group of alums came over to share beer and small talk. Two guys—Doug and John—and a girl whose name I can't recall. She kept laughing for no reason. Eventually we drove over to the house of another former Reedie where there was gin and cable TV. Then we went to Hawthorne St. to some seafood dive where I couldn't touch a morsel. The thought of food during this trip was assaultive, so I subsisted on beef jerky.

Sunday passed by uneventfully but Monday was memorable. The campus was now functioning with the library open along with the student-run Paradox Café. At the library I went to the Thesis Tower, which held a vast collection of music books. I looked into Beethoven's letters, but I felt I was being intrusive and soon left. The piano in the chapel was locked. And there was a man who came in to ask what I was doing, if I was a student, and told me to use the piano in the student union.

While [I was] playing some of Chopin's Preludes on the beat-up, out-of-tune piano in the SU, a female security guard (a lesbian) interrupted me to ask if I was a student. Since I wasn't at present I was taken to the security building where they pulled my file, informed me that I was trespassing, asked if I had been in the hospital recently, then told me if I visited the campus again I'd be arrested. None of this made much sense to me since former Reed students were often seen on the grounds and were not unwelcome. Anyway I was glad to be escorted off the campus. And I believe I shan't ever return.

I then went downtown to the café at Nordstrom where I ate finally.

What remains most in my memory about this luckless voyage was the condition of Alec's house, the mindlessness of Portlanders, and what a cultural wasteland the city seems to be.

Another shattered hope. Charley's relationship with Reed had never been smooth, but even after the final separation in 1994 he had continued to think of the place longingly, as a difficult but fond former lover, perhaps. More recently, and without any rational basis, he had even seemed to believe that he could reignite the dead embers *("I also have had dreams recently that I have the option of returning to Reed again. I know that consciously I really miss that place").* Instead, coldness and nonrecognition were followed by too much recognition, files pulled, "lesbian" security guards warning him never to come back. A "luckless voyage" indeed, the sour-grapes reproaches at the end of his account a more heartbreaking testimony to the depths of his disappointment and humiliation than the most piercing cry. Now even memory was tainted forever. But forever would not last much longer.

Lin and I hadn't wanted him to make this trip to Portland, of course. After the summer of 1994 the very idea of the city made me shudder. On the other hand—parental hope springing eternal—there was the tantalizing possibility that making the "you can't go home again" journey might finally awaken him to the real conditions of his life.

And perhaps it did, although not in the way we wanted.

He returned safely to L.A. but soon sank deeper and deeper into mute isolation. By the third week in August he was verging on catatonia, and on the night of the nineteenth I got a call from Lin—he was back staying with her—saying that she was going crazy because Charley refused to talk to her at all. By the next day he was even worse. He came to my apartment for dinner because Lin had a business meeting in Culver City. He was as bad as I had ever seen him—vague, preoccupied, probably hearing voices. For the first time, also, I was struck by his deteriorated physical condition. He was thin and sallow. "He looks like he's wasting away," I wrote in my journal later. I would ask him a question and he would smile kind of sweetly and seem to be thinking about answering, then lose focus and lapse back into reverie. Psychotic depression? Who could say, but obviously he was extremely sick. After a while I asked what he wanted to do. Could he go home? I said yes. He gave me a kiss on the neck and said "I love you very much" and left.

I knew he had to go back in the hospital; our sentimental notion that he would get better at home had again proved wrong. As I tried to get a hold of Lin I wondered what to do once the immediate crisis passed. We had found out that the Menninger Clinic in Kansas, the gold standard of psychiatric care, didn't take Medi-Cal or SSI. I actually considered using all my available credit cards to send him anyway for a month; it would cost thirty thousand dollars, the extent of my credit. But a month wouldn't do anything. Stick him in a locked board-and-care? He would have to go into the hospital first anyway. But, I asked my journal,

> How much worse can he be than he was this evening—cadaverous, virtually catatonic, dying—or appearing to be. It's as if over time we careen from one faulty perception to the next, doing everything we can to avoid doing what eventually will have to be done if Charley is to survive long enough, *maybe*, to get well. Every time we put off the inevitable he is put at risk of perishing—through suicide, car accident, or whatever—one more time. So far our luck has held—barely. But it could run out at any time. . . .

I called Lin when she got home and told her we had to take Charley back to St. John's. She agreed. She drove him to the ER and called me from there; I biked over to meet them. Charley was totally noncommunicative with us, but when the ER doc finally questioned him he became conversant enough to say he didn't want to be admitted, which was good enough for the ER doc. I could have killed the guy, but it wasn't really his fault; again, Charley had been able to appear quasinormal long enough to satisfy legal criteria for not being gravely disabled. But then, once out of sight of the doctor, he lapsed back into total noncommunicativeness. Lin took him back to her place and I went back to mine. We were both close to despair.

The next day I went to work as usual, but rather than ride my bike I drove Jenny's Bug (she was still bar-girling as well as teaching English in Japan) because I had a feeling I'd be needing it. Lin again had business meetings all day in Culver City. At around two Charley called me in distress, saying he needed Cogentin, the medication he took to counteract the stiffness caused by the Navane. He was so stiff he couldn't move, he said. Could I get him a prescription?

The situation reminded me of the Sunday two years earlier when I was trying to get his lithium refilled by phone and he was imagining serpents in his chest. Now, at least, we were in the same city. I left work immediately and drove to Lin's, trying to understand the implications of what Charley had told me. He had probably been off the antipsychotic for some time, which was possibly the reason for his recent almost catatonic behavior. I had seen the same thing the previous December when Dr. Breen had lowered the Navane dosage at their first session; Charley had quickly gotten worse and had to be put back on the higher amount. Now, as in Portland before the stabbing, he was again in such bad shape that even *he* was panicking. I guessed he had started taking the Navane again but had either thrown away the Cogentin or run out of it some time earlier and not bothered to get more. Whether my guesses were right or wrong I had no intention of merely getting the prescriptions refilled. He was going back in the hospital if I had to carry him there myself; which, as it turned out, I did.

When I got to Lin's he greeted me at the door "looking like death," my journal reads—"soaking wet with sweat in his white bathrobe, claiming he couldn't move and wanting me to call Dr. Gray (!) and get Cogentin." Any doubts I had about his mental state went away when he mentioned Dr. Gray. Dr. Gray hadn't been his psychiatrist for nine months; he had gone through three others since. Beyond that, Charley's appearance touched me to my marrow. He looked as if he were in the final stages of a wasting disease: thin, almost skeletal, his skin pale and lifeless, his body clammy and morbid; he looked spectral. Nevertheless, I was determined to do what I could to help him. I decided not to go to St. John's directly after what had happened the night before; even now they might not admit him strictly on my say-so. So I called Santa Monica West and asked to talk to John Quincy, a clinical worker who had seen Charley two months earlier when Lin and I brought him in for a consultation. Charley had tried to escape and been manacled by the security guard, but as awful as things had gotten, I had thought John acted compassionately under the circumstances. Now on the phone he remembered us and told me to bring Charley in and present him to their emergency services person, a woman named Sarah. When I hung up I told Charley to get dressed; we were going to the hospital. But he just stood where he had been, half bent over, in his bathrobe, soaking wet.

"Come on, Charley, we have to go."

"Dad, I can't move. It's the Navane. I need the Cogentin."

"Charley, we have to go. Try to walk." I took his hand and tried to lead him. He didn't move.

"Dad, I can't."

I felt his joints. They felt stiff. I grabbed a pair of jeans and a shirt and some sandals from his room, threw them into a shopping bag, ran outside and put them in Jenny's Bug. Then I came back inside. He was slightly bent over, rigid, exactly where I had left him.

"One more time, Charley. Try to walk. We have to go to the hospital one way or the other."

"Dad, I can't move."

I bent down and grabbed him around his legs just above his knees. He was so thin. God, I thought, there was hardly anything to him! But I couldn't worry about that now. Holding his legs, I stood upright and flung him over my shoulder. I locked the door with my free hand and carried him to Jenny's car and folded him into the cramped front seat. He neither helped nor protested. I was amazed at how light he was. Our boy was wasting away and we hadn't been able to do a thing about it.

We drove the mile or so to Santa Monica West in silence. I parked in front of the old, one-story brick building, then got out of the car and opened the passenger-side door. "Come on, Charley," I said when he didn't move, "we have to go in." When he didn't respond I reached in and grabbed him and lifted him out of the car, still in his bathrobe, and got ready to throw him over my shoulder again.

But ah, vanity! The vanity of youth especially—and Charley was as vain as they come. "Wait, Dad," he said. At this moment, dire as his condition was, faced with the prospect of being carried in public, in his bathrobe, over his father's shoulder into a county psych building, he was suddenly, amazingly, able to move. He leaned back into the car to get the bag of clothes. He stood on the sidewalk next to the open car door and put his shirt and pants on, then stepped into his sandals. I looked at him with amazement and admiration as he ran a thin hand—those Chopin fingers!—through his hair to give it a semblance of shape and then ambled, with a bit of panache even, into the building. If he had to go, at least he would go in style.

What happened next threatened to be a repeat of the previous night at the St. John's ER. We were led into the building's admitting area, a spare utilitarian linoleum-floored room with a couple of Depression-era school desks and scarred chairs and walls the color of stale mustard. A minute later a woman about my age came in, Sarah, the admissions person, and began asking Charley what the matter was. He answered dully but coherently, explaining that he had run out of his Cogentin and needed a refill; that was the only problem. Sarah asked what the symptoms were, and Charley answered that he hadn't been able to move because of stiffness caused by the Navane. "Can you move now?" Sarah asked.

"A little." He was at least minimally interactive, roused enough, possibly, to talk his way out of the hospital again. I was determined that this wouldn't happen. I had seen how sick he was. He was more than sick, he was dying. There was no way he was going to get away this time and go home to die. So as Sarah spoke to him, wanting to believe him, to give him the benefit of the doubt, I kept trying to catch her eye. When I did I shook my head.

She went over and took his elbow with one hand and moved his forearm with the other. It swayed easily. She looked at me. "He's not stiff. If it was the side effects of the neuroleptic he wouldn't be able to move at all."

"He couldn't move five minutes ago," I said. I couldn't explain it. Charley had not been pretending at Lin's house and in the car. He obviously had not been able to move. The paralysis may have been psychosomatic, but it wasn't fakery. Was it some kind of subconscious signal?

Sarah turned back to Charley. "Well, we can get you a refill of your prescription. Apart from that, do you want to make an appointment to see our psychiatrist? I can set it up for next Thursday—that's the earliest I can do." Seven days away.

No! I wanted to scream. That's not good enough! He needs help now! I kept looking at her. She saw me looking but didn't get it. To her, at that moment, Charley didn't look so bad.

"I think he needs to be hospitalized," I said carefully.

She looked at me again, uncertain. She seemed like an old hippie, probably antiauthoritarian. Don't trust anybody over thirty. Up the Establishment. She didn't like the idea of grown-ups putting kids away. Was this one of those cases, I imagined her thinking, where the parent was really the crazy one?

I could see that she was getting ready to let Charley go. "Is John here?" I asked. "He's seen Charley before. I wonder if it might be possible to get his opinion." I was being as courteous as possible. The last thing I needed was for this woman to get mad at me or write me off. She looked at me, then at Charley, then nodded. "Yeah, I can do that," she said finally, picking up the phone and dialing an extension. She spoke briefly. A minute later John came into the room.

"Hi, John," I said. "I'm Jonathan Aurthur. I spoke to you a few minutes ago. D'you remember my son Charley?"

"Yes, hi," John said. He was a pleasant-looking man in his forties, with straw blond hair and reddish skin. He could be a camp counselor. A salt-of-the-earth type like Sarah, in the trenches day after day, dealing with the poor and afflicted. He greeted Charley and looked at him with bemusement. "We've met before, haven't we?" Charley half nodded.

"Yeah, we were here a couple of months ago," I said. "You had Charley taken to St. John's."

Now John remembered. "Oh yes." He kept looking at Charley. "You've lost weight, haven't you? You look about fifteen or twenty pounds lighter."

"He has," I said. "We're trying to decide what to do. Sarah is thinking of having him come back here as an outpatient next week, but—I—really—think—he needs—to be—taken—to St. John's. Today."

John turned from me back to Charley, then to Sarah. He had to be diplomatic; they worked together every day. After a brief pause he said to her, "I think he may need more immediate care. He looks like he's lost a lot of weight since I saw him, which was pretty recently."

Things moved quickly after that, and within a half-hour an ambulance had taken him back to St. John's. I went back to work, then home, exhausted, to get some rest. Lin came over around seven-thirty and we walked to the Third Street Promenade—an outdoor mall in downtown Santa Monica—joking about how we were going to get arrested. There had been articles in the papers recently about how local police, at the urging of Promenade businesspeople worried about transients and the homeless loitering outside their shops and scaring away customers, had decided to crack down on people sitting on the curbs and on the sides of fountains. Lin and I were both outraged by what was clearly unconstitutional intimidation. Obviously enforcement would be selective; not everybody sitting on the ledges of fountains or on curbs would be cited, only the homeless and transient-looking. So we decided to stage our own civil disobedience—we would sit someplace illegal and dare the cops to arrest us. It was silly, but it took our minds off other things.

When we arrived at the Promenade we planted ourselves on a fountain ledge and began looking around, glaring, hoping some cops would pass by. Of course there wasn't a cop in sight—there never is when you need one—so we ended up just sitting, physically and emotionally exhausted. At least Charley was safe for a few days, in a hospital that even he didn't hate too much. And we would get a short break.

After a few minutes a young guy came walking by carrying a stack of newspapers, a local tabloid called the *Homeless Advocate*. I flagged him down and he came over. We gave him a dollar and he handed us a paper. Lin looked at the front page. "Do you have anything in here about that new law about people not being allowed to sit down on the streets and fountains?" she asked. "Have you heard about it?"

"Yeah," the paper seller said without enthusiasm. He was thin-faced and had dark bushy hair and crooked teeth. "I heard about it."

"That's why we're here," I said. "We're having a protest because we think it's a fascist law. It's really directed against the homeless, don't you think?"

"Yeah," the paper seller said, still without enthusiasm. He thought for a moment. "But you know," he said suddenly, becoming animated for the first time. "You know what the real problem is—it's the *mentally ill* homeless. The way they look and the way they go around acting. They mess things up for the rest of us. That's why laws like that get passed."

Lin and I glanced at each other. Oh God, I thought, biting my tongue to keep from screaming. Jesus H. *Frigging Christ*—this frigging country! Now the frigging *homeless* movement was being divided, between the good homeless and the bad homeless. There's always somebody worse off than you that you can blame. What's the frigging use?

The guy left after a minute and Lin and I continued our sit-in for a little while more, then left, still shaking our heads at the eye-opening political analysis we had just received. She went back to her place, and I went back to mine and got ready for bed. I hadn't visited Charley at St. John's that evening, mainly out of fatigue and because I didn't think he would want to see me right away. I would bike to the hospital from work tomorrow at lunch.

At 10:15 P.M. the phone rang. I picked it up.

"Hi, Dad."

"Charley . . . ?"

"Yes, it's your son." I could hear the old, slightly mischievous tone in his voice.

"Charley . . . What's going on? You sound completely *normal*."

"Yes, I'm just here chillin'."

I couldn't believe it. Not only did he sound completely normal, but even the humor was back, the lightness in his tone. *This* was my kid, not the scarecrow before.

"What happened, for God's sake? You were a total basket case this afternoon . . . !"

"Yeah, I know. I just needed the Cogentin."

After we hung up, I sat and stared, trying to figure it out. I had never seen him recover so quickly. What did it mean? It couldn't—could it?—have been merely a question of not taking the Cogentin, because Cogentin was only for side effects (the stiffness) of the antipsychotic; it wasn't an antipsychotic itself. And even if he had been off the Navane and then put back on, how could he return to baseline in five hours? It was a little like the first time he had gone to Ryles in Portland, but this time his recovery was even faster and from a lower starting point. Was it being in the hospital, protected from whatever horrific inner presences or impulses he had been experiencing over the past few days?

I never found out exactly what had happened. Later when I asked him he merely said, Yes, he'd been in really bad shape those couple of days, but didn't go into details.

I visited him the next day and he was still much better, back on his regular medicinal regimen, Depakote (the lithium substitute), Navane and Cogentin. He told me he was "damned tired" of the repeated hospitalizations (three or four already this year), and added that I wouldn't be doing this—hospitalizing him and generally overseeing him—for the rest of my life. The whole thing had happened this time because he was "too lazy" to get his prescriptions refilled. He said he didn't belong in the hospital because people there were "the dregs" (I couldn't help thinking back to the paper seller the night before), but added that he didn't want to leave just yet. And, anyway, he couldn't leave; he was on a seventy-two-hour hold, a 5150. He seemed content to stay put.

I had noticed during Charley's hospitalizations that the mood of the various wards affected his mood. If there were a lot of patients who were hyper and jittery, it took him longer to come down off his highs. This time the ward was sparsely populated and calm, and the ill effects of another warehousing seemed to be mitigated. I visited him every day, as always, and he seemed to be in a particularly thoughtful, lucid state, speaking several times about how Lin and I were not going to have to "do this" for the rest of our lives. Of course this could be read two ways: Either he had decided to get better or he had decided, again, to kill himself. He had spoken this way before, and ordinarily we tried to believe that he meant getting well, although we were aware of the other possibility and asked him more than once over the years, when he started talking about how "things were going to change," whether he was thinking about suicide. We made him promise to tell us if he was, and of course he promised, and of course we didn't really believe him.

On August 29, Lin and I picked him up at the hospital and we went out to dinner. She and I had decided not to force him to go to a board-and-care, motel or similar place. Instead we negotiated a simple contract, a retrenched version of our traditional three conditions. We no longer insisted on weekly talk therapy, and we didn't demand that he work or go to school full time. He could stay at Lin's if he saw a psychiatrist regularly (every month at least), stuck to whatever medicinal regimen they agreed on, and either looked for a job or did at least ten hours a week of some kind of work—for example, volunteering at a local social service agency. Charley seemed agreeable. He said that the latest hospital stay had been "a real learning experience." Later that night, which he spent at my apartment, he and I walked up to the coffeehouse where he had worked a year and a half earlier and he commented on the beauty of the night and what a shame it was to have to spend nights like it inside a hospital. He seemed relaxed and stable enough that I decided to go ahead with a three-day vacation to Arizona I had been planning. He would stay at Lin's. On Sunday he wrote in his journal,

> Spending a quiet Sunday at home with Mom. The memories of my last hospital visit still haunt me. I have a grave fear that I'll end up homeless, *wanting* to stay in a psych ward. Thankfully I have parents who care about me. It's really not so bad staying w/Mom.
>
> I'm looking into journalism classes at UCLA extension in an attempt to establish some sort of career. I remember wanting to be a writer at the age of sixteen.

As September wore on, Charley, slipping again into depression, was staying at Lin's but spending a lot of time with me on weekends or after work. On weekdays he would often meet me for lunch near my office. One Saturday, September 21, we went to a movie in the afternoon. I cooked pork chops and after dinner we walked again to the coffeehouse. My journal records that we had a "fairly substantive discussion" about his depression, his future and things related. Although I was always at a loss to understand and talk about his psychotic episodes—his visions, hearing voices, etc.—especially since he spoke so little about them—I felt competent talking about depression, something I had struggled with since I was ten. In addition, when Charley was depressed he often seemed more willing to talk and ask for help than when he was manic, perhaps because he felt more vulnerable, more like the rest of us. During these discussions, which I saw as opportunities, I always tried—and no doubt usually failed—to be helpful without being patronizing, to avoid dispensing Good and Useful Advice and sounding like a Parent. I readily admitted that his "affliction" (his term), whatever name one might give it or however one might characterize it, was far worse than anything I had ever experienced or could even imagine. "Why me?" he would often ask, and I had no answer, and said so. I have never believed, as the current saying goes, that "everything happens for a reason." On the contrary, most things happen for no reason at all. Similarly, I have never pondered the question of why bad things happen to good people. Why shouldn't they? Even the Bible, with the Job story, admits to the fundamental absurdity of the question—the same question that Lin had tackled thirty years before in her Faulkner thesis and answered in the same way: There *is* no reason. So when Charley would ask "why me," I would turn the question around: Why was he handsome, smart and talented? True, he had a terrible affliction but he had so many good things, too, things that often seemed to accompany afflictions like his, and if he just hung in there. . . . Not that giving up in his situation would be cowardly or selfish—I didn't think it was then and don't now—but because— well, *because*. Because of all the obvious, silly things. Where there's life there's hope. If you're dead, there isn't. But I never faulted him for wanting to leave, or for having tried to leave. And later when he left I never faulted him for that either.

The same Saturday as our coffeehouse talk Charley made his next-to-last journal entry, which included a poem with numerous crossed-out lines and rewordings:

My dreams have become completely incomprehensible. Yet it's the only thing I do actively. Just short scene after short scene. Each more surreal than the next. I have a recurring theme in my dreams, that of Uni High. Something is unfinished there. I travel down those empty corridors. I remember the lockers were orange. I remember buying candy at the student store. Could it be I liked the solitude there?

> *Weep not, fair child.*
> *For the dawn is yours.*
> *Each straying star*
> *hands its sparkle to thine eyes.*
>
> *The dewy sunrise*
> *Awakes your eager breath, which*
> *Lost in slumber moments ere*
> *Gains a more fervent course.*
>
> *In this dim light*
> *I will hold you safe.*
> *In this ponderous limbo.*
>
> *Seek again,*
> *That boundless reverie.*
>
> *Under my warm sighs you'll know*
> *the nether world.*
> *In that distant nod*
> *You shall know the secrets.*

What impresses me about Charley's journal entries during these last months is that they show a person who was not nearly as nonfunctional, and certainly not as thought-impoverished, as he often seemed. Arrogant and confused? Yes. "Lacking insight into his condition" (a favorite therapist expression)? That too, often enough, as in the return-to-Reed story where he talks about *other* people's isolation and *their* strangeness and about his inability to understand why the school wouldn't want him on campus. But the image that had flashed through my mind the previous summer when I found the gun pamphlet, the image of the empty-headed loser propositioning supermodels, never materialized. Even when he seemed sullen and withdrawn, or glittery and shallow, the real Charley was still there, thinking and writing, having ideas and feelings. The person in crisis can build a wall between himself and us that is so high and thorny that it seems unscalable. But beyond the wall, out of our sight, life is going on, even as it fades.

His final journal entry comes four days after the "fair child" poem:

I've been somewhat invalid for days now. A weakness has taken possession of me. I'm hesitant to look at the world outside, for it only depresses me more. All seems so crude and graceless. I've taken to thinking about death in a rather thorough way. And it doesn't look so bad. But, alas, I have but one life to endure. Might as well see what it holds for me.

The end came five weeks later.

8

The
Stone Cross

All Saints' Day

From my journal of November 1, 1996: "*11:55 A.M.*—Charley is dead."

An hour earlier I had been at work when my neighbor George called. "There's a man here from the coroner's office," he said, but that's not what I heard.

"Excuse me? A carton?" I thought he said "a man with a carton." I was expecting a UPS package and had asked George, who lived in the apartment next to mine and was home during the day, to accept it if it came while I was at work. I thought that's what he was calling about. The UPS guy needed to talk to me.

"No, not a carton," George said. "There's a man here from the coroner's office."

"Huh?" I must have sounded like a moron. I still wasn't getting it. The final nail. I'd been getting ready for this call for more than five years but when it came I was still totally unprepared.

"He says that Charley"—a pause while George turned away from the receiver and said something I couldn't hear—"jumped onto PCH . . . ? I don't understand. . . ." Speaking away from the receiver again.

"What . . . ?" I wasn't getting the words. George was sounding vague and troubled. I was picking up the tone but not the meaning.

"I really don't understand what this is about," he continued. "Something about Charley jumping. . . ."

Me: "Charley? Charley *Aurthur* . . . ?"

Shock was setting in. Something about Charley and jumping and PCH. Pacific Coast Highway.

"He has a photograph here that he's showing me. . . ." Pause. "Oh God, yes. That's Charley! . . ." George's voice trailed off. He was in shock, too.

Then another voice, a man's, not in shock, came on the line. He told me his name but it didn't register. He said he had come to my apartment, then knocked on George's door when I wasn't home. As he explained, I listened dully, trying to respond appropriately. He offered to wait if I wanted to come home and meet with him in person. I told him I would be coming on my bicycle. Give me twenty minutes.

When I arrived home he was sitting in a deck chair outside my apartment door. We shook hands and he told me his name again, Larry Reiche. He was middle-aged, gray-haired, calmly friendly. What a job to have, I thought. We talked briefly. I asked him to excuse me for a minute, I had to try to get a hold of Charley's mother. I called Lin's office. She wasn't at her desk, although the operator said she thought she was somewhere in the building, but when she paged her, she didn't respond. I went into Lin's voice mail and began telling her what had happened. Almost immediately I sensed that I was making a big mistake—Charley's death on voice mail—but I had started and there was no way to erase what I had said, so I kept going. When I hung up I called her home number praying she was there. She wasn't. This time when I got the voice mail I just told her to call me at home, right away.

When I hung up I was finally able to give my attention to Larry Reiche. He showed me a frontal photo of Charley lying with his eyes closed, ghastly white. The front-on pose reminded me of a mummy; his death mask. I identified him, signed something. I was having a hard time concentrating and apologized when I asked Larry Reiche to repeat a question. "That's all right," he said. "It's entirely likely you won't even remember any of this tomorrow."

I told him about Charley's illness, the previous attempts, the repeated hospitalizations. I said that although Lin and I were always to some extent half-expecting another attempt I was surprised it had come now, since Charley had seemed to be in fairly good spirits recently. And I said what I would say again and again: that although I didn't condemn Charley for it, if I had known he was going to do it then, that day, I would have stuck him back in the hospital. And I would have kept doing it.

Reiche nodded. "Well, when he's in a locked facility you have to keep an eye on him," he said. "Now at least it's over. He's in a hopefully better place." It sounded like he had said this before, which in an odd way was comforting. I excused myself again and again dialed Lin's apartment. No answer. I dialed her office. No answer. Good. It would give me a couple of more minutes. I turned back to Larry Reiche and we finished our business. He was gone in a few more minutes, leaving me the contents of Charley's pockets: his wallet, keys, a few other things. I looked through them dully. I was not in terrible pain. I had no desire to cry. I was simply slightly shaky. The bike ride had helped. I couldn't imagine how I would have been without those twenty minutes alone in the open air, pedaling.

I sat down on the futon—Charley's bed—to wait for Lin's call. Why wasn't she where I could get a hold of her? I started writing in my journal—"*11:55 A.M.*—Charley is dead"—as a way of occupying myself. I talked about meeting with Larry Reiche. Then:

> A feeling—I'm ashamed to say it—of some relief.
> How is one supposed to react to something like this? He finally made it—
> Am I mad at the medical profession? The County of L.A.?—myself? Thank God I didn't get a chance to yell at him this A.M. [I had tried calling him a couple of hours earlier] for walking out of his volunteer job yesterday.
> I'm just scribbling now to keep my mind active—My message to Lin approximately: "Lin: This is Jonathan. The worst has happened. Charley jumped off Lincoln Blvd. Bridge onto Santa Monica Freeway and is dead. I'm sorry I have to tell you like this but I didn't know what else to do. I'm at home with a gentleman from the coroner's office now. Call me here. I'm not going anywhere."
> Somehow appropriate that almost my greatest fear right now is of Lin's reaction—despair—anger at me?
> We talked on phone a couple of hours ago and she said he had taken off on

his bike. Part of me says I should try to track her down—worried about *her*—
but I have to stay put because I have no real idea where she is and I certainly
don't want to drive—

God, how is Jenny going to react?

Jenny was due back the next morning from Asia. After working in Japan for a
few months she had traveled in Malaysia and Thailand, ending up in Indonesia.
She was somewhere between Indonesia and Japan right now, out of phone reach.
She would leave Tokyo in the next few hours and arrive at the L.A. airport the
next morning.

And then dealing with mortuary . . . ?!

Reiche said Ch. went downtown and they'll hold him three days or so,
autopsy (or toxicology test) on Sunday, I think he said. I wonder if he took all
his lithium—falling off bike a couple of times indicates loadedness altho Reiche
said there was no evidence of alcohol.

Am I mad at Charley? No, but . . .

I'm terrified (I'm sitting on futon w/phone beside me) of the call from Lin
altho I desperately want to get it over with. Need to contact Jenny?

Can I imagine meeting her at airport without her knowing . . . ?

Why am I thinking of all these "practicalities"? and subsidiary miseries?

12:15—Heart thumping, but otherwise together except for some shakiness—

Footsteps on landing—thought they were Lin's—weren't—now I'm getting
more afraid . . .

Locked facility—what more could we have done? Obviously a country that
commits mass murder routinely and lets kids die in South-Central has limited
interest even in the relatively privileged.

Poor George—having to be the one to tell me—

Me: "Charley *Aurthur*!?" when he said a man from the coroner's office was
at his apartment. . . .

At least it was fast—He really did it right this time.

The person in Porsche went to hospital for observation/shock, according to
Reiche—

12:23—Part of me is worrying about how I'm going to handle all the sympathy—I don't want to *deal* with it—

When was the last time I talked to him? Yesterday afternoon when I called
to say hi—He was planning to go to the Food Bank [to do volunteer work]—
I said yes, he could stay with me when Jenny came back on Saturday—
tomorrow—Thank *God* I wasn't mean or unsupportive. . . .

12:30—Why no call from Lin?

I'm sitting here in a daze—

Should I have left the message on Lin's machine? As I said to Reiche, phone mail is both a blessing and a curse—

I'm thinking of the other phone call I got—June 22, 1994—from the kid at Ryles while Lin was upstairs at [a friend's]. We have come full cycle. . . .

12:40—"It takes a village. . . ."

Thinking of Lin blaming herself or us—

Trying to image [sic] what he was thinking as he rode the bike. Why did he fall two times?

At least he's out of *his* misery—(Drum roll: *Ours* is just getting going. . . .)

He was so unhappy—so much for the drugs—

Lin's going to talk about how we should've done the nutrition earlier—breast-beating and *mea culpa*ing? Blaming herself for it happening on her watch? Or will she, like me, be relatively calm—as if she'd almost been waiting for it to happen—or crying hysterically?

12:46—I can hear her screaming at me—"How could you tell me like that?! How could you leave a message on my machine!?" . . .

Sitting on futon w/front door closed—chilly . . .

A little anger at him for wimping out? Not going to hospital? Not calling Lin or me? He obviously just finally had it—

Undertone of relief (?)—at least *this* misery is tinged with relief—

The usual clichés (thinking about telling Dr. Gray, Breen)—"We all failed"—the usual bullshit—

To Reiche as he was leaving—"Thank you, sir, for your support"—

12:58—"What could we have done?"—question goes through my mind—in quotes—

Just then the phone rang, Lin. I asked her if she had gotten the voice mail at work. No (thank God!), she hadn't. So I told her what had happened. No tears, no screams, just a kind of anguished acknowledgment. I asked her where she had been. At the airport, she said, picking up her young half-sister Ella—Aunt Ella, Charley's buddy, the artist from San Francisco, who had come down for a couple of days to visit and paint Lin's kitchen and bathroom. The two were at Lin's now. I still had Jenny's car, so I drove over. They were sitting on the couch near the open front door when I came in, arms around each other. They both looked up at me, eyes huge and blurry, their expressions indescribable. I sat down next to Lin. The three of us hugged, then huddled together on the couch and talked. She described fragments of Charley's final night and morning. He had come home upset last night—Halloween—from his volunteer job. He told her that he and Bruce Rankin, the head of the Westside Food Bank, had driven to Westwood in the food bank truck to load some boxes and barrels of food donations from UCLA fraternities. After a couple of hours of lifting and loading he had told Bruce he "just couldn't do it anymore," then walked off abruptly and took the bus home. Lin said he had acted upset with himself. "I'm so ashamed, Mom," he had said. But then this morning he had seemed okay. He had gotten up early, brought her tea, then taken off without saying good-bye while she was in the shower.

After sitting for a while, Lin and I decided to walk to the ocean a half-mile away. The day was chilly and clear-skied, the sun low even at midday in the November sky. We walked to the nearly deserted Venice beach, got some coffee, then walked on the sand toward the water and sat on a little rise above the shoreline. We talked about Charley's recent behavior from the perspective of his previous suicide attempts, trying to see if we had missed anything. He hadn't seemed depressed or particularly manic in recent weeks—a little jittery but not psychotic. Lin had been trying to get him started on a new nutritional regimen of amino acids so that someday he might minimize his other medications or stop them entirely. We talked about how much better he had seemed recently compared to a couple of months earlier, before his final hospitalization, how he probably wouldn't have been able to commit suicide then. He hadn't been alive enough. He had needed to get better in order to kill himself.

We talked about his pattern, more and more noticeable over the past couple of years, of suddenly getting up and walking out of things: walking out of a room, walking away from the dinner table, walking out of movies, walking out on his job the night before. And finally he had walked out of his life.

As we sat and then walked some more along the edge of the calm surf, I mentioned something that had happened a couple of hours earlier when I had arrived home to meet Larry Reiche. It involved the little wooden Oaxacan dragon she had given me for my birthday two years before—the Week of the Long Knives—while Charley was up in Portland getting ready to stab himself. It was a cute, young-looking little dragon, about eighteen inches high, hand-painted black with green spots and multi-colored polka dots. It stood on its hind legs and had wings curved upward like two ends of a smile, big wide eyes, outstretched arms, and a little wooden spit of fire coming out of its grinning mouth. A very friendly little dragon, the kind one could give to a small child. But Charley had never liked it. I was never sure why, and he never said.

A year or so after I got the dragon, somebody else gave Charley or me another figure with wings, a little pink male clay angel made to go in a flower pot, wavy-haired and cherubic. He was about two inches high and sat, legs crossed, head tilted, left cheek leaning against the palm of one hand. His whimsical look immediately reminded me of the Oaxacan dragon, so I sat the little angel down on the dragon's back in the crook of one of the wings, wondering whether he would stay put. He was small compared to the dragon but fit perfectly, and he had perched there comfortably ever since, chin in hand.

Charley hadn't liked the combination of the angel and the dragon either, and he wasn't amused when I put them on a bookshelf in my living room near the phone. He didn't make a big deal about it. He just ignored them.

"Well, when I got to my apartment and went to call you," I said to Lin now as we sat on the beach, "I was so out of it that I hit the dragon with my arm as I was reaching for the phone, and the angel got knocked out of its little nook and fell on the floor, and its head broke off. Can you believe that? Its head broke off. I mean come *on,* the whole thing is like a bad movie. If somebody put that in a script everybody would say, '*No,* we can't do that.'"

But it had happened. And when it did, I said to Lin now—the angel falling and getting broken just hours after Charley had fallen and gotten broken—I had suddenly understood why he hadn't liked the dragon or the angel sitting on its back. He was the angel and the dragon was his illness. What to me was a joke was to him his life.

Later, when I arrived home, I examined the break where the angel's head had come off. It was clean; the head was in one piece and otherwise undamaged. I mixed some A+B epoxy and applied it to the broken area of the neck, then fitted the head back on and secured the two pieces with a rubber band till the glue dried clear and solid, the break barely noticeable. I put the angel back on the dragon, where he sits to this day, in peaceful reverie, on a shelf in my room with other family things.

Obituary

From the Santa Monica *Outlook,* Thursday, November 7, 1996:

Charley Aurthur. Born January 15, 1973, died November 1, 1996. Son of Jonathan and Lin; brother of Jenny; beloved by many. Memorial service will be held at the Unitarian Universalist Community Church, 1260 18th St., Santa Monica 90404, at 3 P.M., Sunday, November 10.

The memorial was attended by several hundred family members, friends and coworkers. Lin and I both prepared something to say. Jenny, who had originally declined to participate, ended up going to the podium as well, carrying a box of Kleenex and speaking extemporaneously. Lin's presentation, written that morning and read by a friend, began as follows:

> The woman sits in her garden under her geraniums and listens to the cars and pickups, the vans and "semis" on Lincoln Boulevard.
> She thinks the sound settles like brown fallout on every leaf and hand.
> In her sleepless mind she sees again her son: He dresses himself and on a Post-It note writes a message to Sting. He swallows sleeping pills, two or three. He gets his bicycle from the laundry room and leaves the house without saying good-bye.
> She thinks: If only I hadn't been in the shower. I would have seen his eyes. I would have known. I would have said, "What's up Babe?" I could have hugged him. I should have known: The Day of the Dead.[1] I could have stopped him then.
> She cries, great heaves from her chest, her face old like her grandmother's.

If only I hadn't . . . I could have . . . I should have . . . The countless self-reproaches of those who have lost a loved one to suicide, particularly parents who have lost a child. Because even the best and most blameless parents have failed in a parent's most fundamental duty, to protect their child from pain and death. Whether that failure was their fault or beyond their control is another question, one of the many that suicide leaves unanswered and unanswerable. The main interlocutor has suddenly upped and unceremoniously left the room and we're left talking to ourselves, and no matter how many of us there are, we're all still one hand clapping. To fill the empty seat, some of us go to psychics to hear from the departed one that he's doing fine, some of us feel or even "see" the departed in familiar places smiling reassuringly, some of us read the departed's letters and journals and pick endlessly over the scraps of his life, tracing and retracing his and our steps and missteps, looking for some sign.

As in Lin's and my return visit to Max Freulich, the suicidologist. Max still had the Ben Shahn–type posters on his office walls and the volumes of Freud in his bookcase when we visited him at his invitation about five weeks after Charley's death. Max greeted us warmly, and we talked about possible explanations, and Max said that for all his study and clinical experience he didn't have any answers. Charley was the toughest case he had had in forty years because—this is what had "scared the hell" out of him—there hadn't seemed to be any psychological reason for the self-destructiveness (this was based on four or five sessions of therapy). He said he thought Charley had been "locked in" to a path toward suicide for a long time and that his illness may have been some kind of pattern of brain seizures, almost like epilepsy, and that he became self-destructive when the seizures occurred, although Max said he knew of no literature on the subject to support any of this. He said he didn't think Charley was a textbook schizophrenic or manic-depressive, that he had never seemed to "surrender himself" to his psychosis—become permanently separated from reality. Apologizing in advance in case Lin and I were religious, Max said that in many cases mentally ill people are like believers who at some point in the development of their psychosis surrender to it, and then, in many cases, live quite contentedly within it. "But Charley wasn't like that."

No, he certainly wasn't. Rather than being peaceful, even if it was the peace of delusion, Charley's life had been full of tension between his illness and his healthy self, punctuated by periodic piercing insight into the "muck" he was making of his present life. A tension that was finally just too much.

More than a year after that meeting with Max, I heard a report on National Public Radio about research being done by John Mann of the New York Psychiatric Institute into the brain chemistry of people who have committed suicide. Researchers are literally dissecting the brains of suicides, studying the prefrontal cortexes and brain stems and comparing them with the brains of people who have died of other causes. The researchers say they are finding physical differences between suicides and nonsuicides—the latter including people who suffer from depression but without suicidality—in the size and structure and number of nerve cells responsible for production and transmission of serotonin, one of the neurotransmitters involved in controlling impulsiveness. Charley had been impulsive from toddlerhood, and he had the scars to prove it. Did a serotonin deficit cause the "seizures" Max theorized about, leading first to Charley's accident-proneness and later to conscious attempts at self-destruction? We would never know. The L.A. County Coroner's office autopsied Charley, but they didn't make cross sections of his brain.

It was an intriguing thought. I wanted to be comforted by Max's seizure theory and the talk about Charley being "locked in" to a suicidal path, because it would let me off the hook. The problem was that it would also let Max off the hook—Max the suicidologist who was supposed to know how to help Charley, but who hadn't. Of course I never blamed him for this. Still, writing in my journal the night Lin and I talked to him I said, " 'Locked in' metaphor. One is always aware in these conversations of the danger of the subconscious desire to justify one's failure to save the person who committed suicide. If we can paint the event as having been inevitable . . ."

But even if it was inevitable, the question remains, Why? Was it some sort of inborn physicochemical inevitability, or an inevitability that was not inborn but somehow came into being through early environmental influences, including parental ones? Despite the current broad acceptance of the brain-disorder theory of mental illness, there is no consensus on what makes people commit suicide. In her book on suicide, *Night Falls Fast* (1999), Kay Redfield Jamison claims that 90 percent of people who kill themselves suffer from serious mental illness, mainly depression, manic-depression, or schizophrenia—which, as we have seen, she considers to be physical disorders of the brain. On the other hand, in another recent book called *The Suicidal Mind* (1996), Edwin Shneidman hardly mentions mental illness at all. Shneidman is not a psychiatric dissident like Peter Breggin or, even more extreme, Thomas Szasz, who rejects the very notion of mental illness as a bad metaphor. Shneidman is a recognized expert on suicide and death, the founder of the American Association of Suicidology and professor emeritus of thanatology at UCLA (and a friend of Max Freulich). But he makes a fundamental distinction between brain condition and behavior. "Obviously, no brain, no mind," he writes.

But slicing Jeffrey Dahmer's brain will no more explain the mysteries of his gross psychological pathology than slicing Einstein's brain will yield $E = mc^2$. On the other hand, severe depression, melancholia, psychoses, and bipolar depressions are related to disorders of brain physiology or even brain structure, but *suicide* is an essentially mental process in the mind. . . .[2]

Most of Shneidman's book is an attempt to explain that process. He writes about a study he did in the early 1970s that tried to identify the common qualities of a group of gifted people who had killed themselves and how they differed from the qualities of people of similar background who hadn't. "In general," Shneidman says, "for the suicidal cases, the relationships with the father turned out to be more critical than relationships with the mother, and these relationships were painful and strained and had a sense of (obvious or subtle) rejection in them."[3] A little later:

> At a somewhat deeper level, and thus more theoretical, in the lives of these suicides there were: elements of childhood or adolescent rejection, disparity between aspiration and accomplishment, early (preadolescent) instability. At a still deeper level (and even more speculative) is the notion that the bright suicidal person is one who believes that he has not had his father's love and seeks it symbolically without success throughout his life, eventually hoping magically to gain it and escape the pain of rejection by a singular act of expiation. Those gifted men who committed suicide did not have that internalized approving parental homunculus that—like a strong heart—seems necessary for a long life. . . .[4]

"Painful and strained" relationships with the father . . . "Believes he has not had his father's love . . ." During Charley's life I never would have believed that any of this applied to him and me. I had always considered us close and was sure he did, too. But something that happened a few days before he killed himself made me begin to doubt—not my love for Charley, but his perception of it.

It was either the Monday or Tuesday evening before his death. He was staying at Lin's and came to my apartment for dinner. I made roast beef and roasted potatoes and green beans, and he ate well. We talked. I had been doing some investigation into the possible nutritional roots of his condition, and I talked about that, reading aloud some literature a coworker had lent me. I had also been looking at books about cognitive therapy and how it might help, and I tried to talk about that.

He listened without any discernible interest. Then: "Dad, do you still love me?"
I was astonished. "Of course I still love you. Why? Do you think I don't?"
"Well, maybe sometimes."

I assured him that I always had loved and always would love him, apologizing for my occasional frustration and harsh tone, pleading human frailty. Later I would ruminate endlessly on this brief exchange and what it meant or didn't mean, especially when I found corroborating evidence in his journals and hospital records that he felt unloved by his parents. Or worse. About six weeks before his death (I believe on September 9; his journal is not absolutely clear) he wrote, "Why it is my father acts like he hates me I cannot grasp. Have I been a disappointment to him?" I have no idea what this refers to; my own journal for September 9 says only, "Tired—didn't sleep enough last night." Had I snapped at him? said something mean? It's entirely possible. It was about ten days after his last hospitalization and we were all very shaky. But on the worst day of my life I never felt, or told Charley, that I was disappointed in him; it would have been unthinkable. Knowing his fragility, I had taken pains to assure him after his crisis began that I could not have asked for a better son, and I meant it. But what about my subtext, my tone and emotional body language, my too-frequent moments of exasperation over the years, when out of weakness or self-pity or exhaustion I lashed out at him? What about my filicidal musings when I found the gun pamphlet? Was some reptilian dragon venom leaking up from the depths of my limbic brain (or serpent heart!), poisoning him and me?

Or was I looking in the wrong places? Was it my pressuring him to take the hated neuroleptics? Or was it, perhaps, my (and Lin's) constant search for causes and cures, like my out-loud musings about cognitive therapy or nutritional disorders that immediately preceded his "Dad, do you still love me?" on that last evening we were together? Was that it? Did my search for solutions make him think I didn't value him as he was? Did he know something about himself that was so much more profound, so much more essential to his being, than vitamin deficiencies and chemical imbalances, that my speaking of these things convinced him that not only did I not know anything about who he really was, but didn't care? ("My dad is very funny and humorous. I think my dad is kinda fun. But in a way I don't want to be around him. He isn't very understanding at all.") Or, another scenario entirely, did he simply "lack insight," as various in-hospital psychologists wrote in his medical records? Was he so narcissistic that anything but total subservience to his boundless needs was evidence of a lack of love? Or, another (related) possibility, was he just being manipulative? Charley was a great kid but he wasn't without flaws. Like any of us, he was capable of skewing things, consciously or not, to get his way or to put himself in a favorable light. I remembered his tearful accusations that I hadn't cared about him enough to send him to River Community, or his statement to the psychologist at San Francisco General that his family had pressured him to play the piano.

But then, even if these last, less flattering (to him) interpretations had merit, how had he become that way? Because *I* hadn't taught him any better! So even here all the problems pointed back to me! One way or the other, whether it was my teasing, my emotional coldness, my bursts of anger, or even my well-meaningness and overinvolvement, the fault was mine. Somehow, some way, I would manage to make myself the center of the drama, even if I had to be the villain. Better to reign in hell than play second harp in heaven.

Of course this is all very overwrought. Not even I am masochistic (or narcissistic) enough to think that Charley committed suicide because I teased him or yelled at him. But might the teasing, or my not-thereness stemming from alcohol, or my occasional impatience or other personality flaws, have been parts of a larger pattern of behavior that played on an inborn vulnerability in a way that it did not play on Jenny, for example, who got basically the same treatment? I mentioned earlier about how around the time of Lin's and my divorce Charley spoke of our failure to appreciate how unhappy he was, the possible subtext being that we cared more about our own selfish needs than we did about his. There may be some truth in this. I talked about it with Lin recently and she, like me, wondered whether if we had had a better understanding of Charley's fragility we would have tried harder to work out our differences and stay together. As it was, we both had a rough-and-ready philosophy toward both kids that reflected our own histories and generational biases: If you love them enough, hug them enough (the defining '70s bumper sticker was "Have You Hugged Your Kid Today?"), everything else will take care of itself. Also, with no family histories or personal experience of major mental illness or suicide, it never occurred to us that Charley might be particularly at risk or in need of some special kind of early intervention.

And in any event, with all the current talk about catching kids at risk early, what does that really mean in practice? Peering and scrutinizing them from the time they're in utero, subjecting them to testing and other "proactive" measures like psychotropic medication before they even manifest any symptoms, in the process inevitably making mistakes, misreading normal patterns, being over-protective, violating young people's privacy and right to be themselves—all cures that may be worse than the disease? It's like the current prostate-cancer debate between those who want to operate at the earliest stages of the cancer, causing impotence, incontinence, etc., and those who want to "watchfully wait," since the cancer develops slowly and the person may die of old age before it becomes a problem. But with young children, even "watchful wait-ing" may take the form of prying and peering and poking. I mean, my God, who wants to live life in a petri dish? If they weren't crazy to begin with . . .

But why even ask these questions about responsibility, especially when I know they are unanswerable? Because they're there, at least for me. And by some perverse dialectic I am free to raise them, particularly the question of my own role—not necessarily guilt, but *role*—in Charley's life and death precisely because nobody else has raised them. Since nobody else blames me, I am free to "blame" myself.

But beyond all questions of guilt and blame and my own perversity, I think there may be something actually useful in this asking, something to do with trying to see and appreciate the subjective experience of the person who is mentally ill or suicidal, to see how *he* sees it, and to begin to redefine, on the basis of that understanding—as I think, for example, the Mark Raginses and the Edward Podvolls and the Edwin Shneidmans try to do—the nature of treatment and recovery. Also something to do with trying to live a more con-scious life.

A little more than three years after Charley died I went to a conference at UCLA called "Suicide Prevention and Survivor Issues" sponsored by the American Foundation of Suicide Prevention. The conference included a work-shop dealing with the loss of a child from a parent's perspective. I decided to attend, hoping to talk about some of these issues. Was I the only parent who had ever tortured him- or herself? I knew I wasn't, but I wanted to get some other views.

I arrived late at the meeting place, a classroom, and sat in back. We all gave our names and said why we were there. Almost all the fifteen or so attendees were parents of suicides, including the couple who led the workshop, Sam and Lois Bloom, activists in the suicide prevention movement; I had met them once or twice before at other events. As we went around the room introducing ourselves, one woman, in tears, described how her son had killed himself just three weeks before. Her loss was new and raw, which was why Sam, when the introductions were completed, announced that he was going to turn the workshop into a support group.

I felt a little cheated. I had come to discuss and debate, not participate in a support group, so when discussion time came I decided to raise some of my points about parental roles anyway, although less assertively than I normally would in deference to the woman who had cried. My questions had the expected result. Sam disagreed and quickly changed the subject, and that was that. I didn't try to prolong the discussion.

One thing he said in his response to me, however, I found fascinating. It was about how, despite what happened or did not happen in our relations with our lost children, we parents of suicide victims need to develop a story, a version of what happened, that will give us comfort.

I found this fascinating because it got to the heart of what I had been trying to do, and not do, since the day of Charley's suicide and especially (although differently) in writing this book. I had been involved in the development of the kind of story Sam was talking about—I called it a narrative—particularly in the first few days after Charley's death, as Lin and I sat around her dining table with friends and relatives and coworkers who came and went (often staying the entire day for days at a time), bringing food, flowers, consolations and talk. Talk. We humans are born storytellers, I began to realize as the days unfolded. That faculty—like denial—is part of our evolutionary equipment, enabling us to organize our sensory perceptions into a coherent picture of the outside world. "You see, but you do not observe," Holmes said to Watson, drawing the distinction between merely taking in sensory information and *understanding* it through verbalizing it, organizing it, metabolizing it, inferring its interconnections, and using what is learned to pick our way along the narrow ledge of existence. Even while Charley was alive I found myself developing a narrative, a story of what he was going through and why. I tried to test this story out on him when he, often such an unwilling interlocutor, would allow it, at the same time as I tried to respect his privacy and his right to have his own story; it was, after all, his life. (*Tried.* My failure to understand and respect the boundaries of his story may, as I mentioned, have been why he asked me whether I still loved him a few days before his death.) Now, after his death, particularly during the first week of endless dining-room-table discussions and rehashings and wonderings and musings and whos and whats and what-ifs, I found myself repeating the story as I understood it at the time—his inborn skittishness, the breakdown that came out of nowhere, our various attempts to help, his passive resistance—and polishing it, refining it, adding to it or subtracting from it, trying it out on new visitors as if the story were new material and they were the audience and I was a monologist or performance artist, until it became burnished and smooth like old wood, comfortable and comforting. By dint of repetition, the narrative—that we were devoted parents and family and friends who loved Charley and who Charley loved and who did everything we could, that Charley may have simply been misplaced, a sprinter who though some cosmic mistake found himself in a marathon—gradually took on a weight, an authority, that gave it the feel of truth.[5]

But lies (or half-truths or incomplete narratives) can also begin to sound true if you repeat them long enough, especially if you (and the people listening to you) want to believe them. The problem with the dining-room-table narrative that I developed about Charley with help from others (group myths being stronger than individual ones) is that I really couldn't know whether it was true, and in my bleaker moments (especially months and years later, after the initial task of self-preservation had been accomplished) I began doubting its truth in direct proportion to the comfort it gave me, especially when other materials and sources began coming to light—Charley's journals, letters and poems I hadn't seen before, or ones I had seen but repressed, like the "Knock on Woody" poem. It was those things that forced me to write *this* narrative, a (one hopes) more complete account of what happened and not just a more elaborate and crafty self-justification. But of course I still don't really know. Charley isn't here to put the check on me himself—"Forget it Dad, you just don't know what I've been through"—so I have to try to be skeptical enough for two, listening for his voice in mine and hoping that for every five or ten "Forget it, Dads" there might be one or two surprised smiles and a grudging,

"Hmm, this really *is* the season for psychoanalysis, isn't it?"

After I got home from the UCLA suicide prevention meeting and Sam and Lois's workshop I wrote them the following letter. I ended up not sending it because, I realized when I finished, it had been written more as self-clarification and self-criticism than as criticism of others. (Months later I sent them a draft of this section of the book, including the letter, but got no answer.)

November 20, 1999

Dear Lois and Sam,

I'm writing this to you while our brief exchange and the rest of your workshop at UCLA today are still fresh in my mind. I'm doing it as much for myself as for you, to try to clarify what I was trying to say. I did feel a little like the bad kid in the back of the room throwing spitballs, and I also felt somewhat constrained by the woman in front who had suffered such a recent loss, so in a way I'm glad you (Sam) moved the discussion away from what I was saying. I certainly wasn't trying to make the woman feel worse than she already did.

On the other hand, this was supposed to be a workshop and not a support group, so I felt entitled at least to raise my point, namely, that parents of child suicides have special issues of guilt and responsibility. Parents *do* have more influence on the lives of their kids than, say, children have on their parents, especially in the early years, both for good and ill. How responsible this makes them for their kids' good or bad outcomes (or suicides) is to me not an easy question that can be answered in some general way. Of course the psychoanalytic theory of mental illness/suicide (and behavior in general) is currently out of fashion and the medical/genetic model is in, but that doesn't mean the pendulum hasn't swung too far in that direction and won't swing back. I've been thinking a lot about this the past three years, since Charley killed himself, and especially the past eighteen months or so that I've been working on my book. I've been reading a lot of stuff on mental illness and the current "brain disease" theory which leads to the idea (expressed particularly by NAMI) that "it's nobody's fault" when somebody is mentally ill or, by extension (since mental illness is now being found in 90 percent of suicides, according to Kay Jamison), commits suicide. But then recently I read Ed Shneidman's latest book, *The Suicidal Mind,* in which he talks about the role of the distant father in many suicides. Shneidman seems to be talking very differently from Jamison et al., and whether I liked it or not when I read his book I was forced to think about what he said in relation to my own relationship with Charley. Should I not do this? Are we saying that we should simply not talk about things like this because they're too painful? Or is Shneidman, whom everybody seems to hold in renown, simply wrong? I don't think we can pretend there's a unified, universally accepted and valid explanation of what makes people kill themselves, much as we would like to think there is, especially if it's an explanation that lets us all off the hook. Something that explains everything explains nothing.

I see a certain whistling-past-the-graveyard aspect to the current "it's nobody's fault" movement. I heard it in what you (Sam) said about the need for the survivor to make up a story that makes him/her feel better. Do we have a responsibility to make the story true? Or is that not a meaningful question? Is "truth" simply in the eye of the beholder? Are we subjective idealists for whom the only truth is what we make ourselves believe? I was thinking as I rode home after the workshop how *American* this idea is. In the case of particularly parent "survivors" it goes something like this: We suicide survivors are good people who would never do anything to hurt our kids. We're kind, we're articulate, we're well meaning. All of which is probably true. We sit around comforting ourselves and each other that of course we did the best we could, that it couldn't have been our fault, which may also be true. But always? It's the same mentality that makes Americans put ourselves in a different category from everyone else and demand special consideration. "We" would never massacre civilians in Vietnam or Korea, "we" would never condone slavery or genocide, "we" would never overthrow democratic governments and support dictators, "we" would never acquiesce in segregation and mistreatment of minorities and the weak. We're Americans. We don't do stuff like that. We're good parents, we'd never abuse our kids.

What am I trying to say? As I try to understand Charley's life and death I'm learning to live with uncertainty, not really knowing how much of his "illness"—he called it his "affliction"—was caused by brain chemistry etc. and how much was caused by his upbringing, environment, parenting, etc. Simply to ignore one side of that contradiction hasn't worked for me. I think that it's somewhere in the struggle of those two opposites—temperament and life circumstances—that the reality lies. I also think that that's what gives life its tragic character, and what gives the works of art that we most value their power. They express and grapple with, rather than try to sweep under the rug, that contradiction between fate and free will, nature and nurture, the individual and the collective, youth and age, parental pride and parental jealousy, Abraham and Isaac, etc., etc.

I'm sure this all sounds very grandiose and holier than thou, like I'm setting myself up as some tragic figure. I really don't mean to do that, only to say that we're all stuck in a world and a culture full of contradiction, of good and bad, of power and powerlessness. I think the current medicalization of mental illness and suicide will ultimately fail as a valid model because it tries to do an end run around the complexity of what is ultimately not merely a physical or medical, but a human and social, problem.

Hope all this isn't too abstract or too awful. As I said, I'm still trying to figure a lot of things out.

Sincerely . . .

Some weeks later, as I read this over while including it here, I suddenly thought, "Oh my God! Lin's paper on Faulkner's tragic vision was right! We *do* spend our lives trying to do the right thing, and even when we come as close as our flawed selves allow, the unthinking universe that doesn't know or care that we exist *still* swats us down like flies! And it's *still* our fault!"

Now, two-plus years after *that,* reading the letter over yet again, I want to add a word more. While the statement about how the reality of mental illness and suicide lies in "the struggle of those two opposites—temperament and life circumstances" is no doubt true as far as it goes, I don't think it goes far enough. This is because in the past few years, as I've noted, even the most fervent apostles of the brain-disorder model have begun talking about how there are other factors besides genetics and biology in these "brain disorders" and about how medication, formerly thought to be a cure-all, is not enough by itself. For example, in *Night Falls Fast* Kay Redfield Jamison writes about how John Mann (and colleagues) of the New York Psychiatric Institute, who as I mentioned earlier have been dissecting the brains of suicide victims to determine the role of serotonin deficits in self-destructiveness, recently (1999) "proposed a 'Stress-Diathesis' model to explain the relationship between the underlying biological predisposition to suicide and the precipitants that trigger it." Aside from "genetic vulnerabilities," the model includes "temperamental variables, such as aggressiveness and impulsivity; chronic alcohol and drug abuse; chronic medical conditions; and certain social factors, such as the early death of a parent, social isolation, or a childhood history of physical or sexual abuse."[6]

Pretty holistic-sounding. Jamison herself, as I have also mentioned, has been for some years now toning down or qualifying the claims of her own brain-disorder camp, criticizing its tendency to oversimplify the role of genes and neurotransmitters in mental illness and underestimate the necessity of psychology and psychotherapy, which were previously thought to be rendered obsolete by lithium and antipsychotic medications.

There is quite a bit of hedging going on these days, in other words. And we are likely to see more hedging as more discoveries are made that contradict conventional scientific wisdom. Examples include recent findings that the brain is not "hard wired" like a building's electrical system, that in fact it develops and changes in response to the environment and even the types of thinking it does—that the term "hard wired," in fact, is rhetorical and misleading. Another example came when the Human Genome Project recently announced that human beings possess only about 30,000 genes rather than the 90,000 to 150,000 previously thought, causing jaws to drop throughout the scientific world. "Albert Einstein only had 1 percent more genes than a mouse and 50 percent more than a roundworm," says a February 18, 2001, *Los Angeles Times* op-ed piece entitled "Stuck with Freedom: Completion of the Human Genome Deals a Blow to Biological Determinism."[7]

This discovery is interesting for a couple of reasons. First, for what it says about the supposedly advanced state of genetic research—research that psychiatry has been using for years to support its claim that mental illness is genetic. It turns out that scientists didn't even know—*really* didn't know—how many human genes there actually are, much less what they do; they were off by a factor of three to five, not even close. And this enormous miscalculation indicates something even more important—namely, the misguidedness of past correlations between genes and behavior. The words of the *Times* article's subtitle—"a Blow to Biological Determinism"— say it: With so few genes (relatively), the previously posited one-to-one correlation between gene and trait or gene and behavior goes out the window, and along with it the idea that there's a shopping gene, an IQ gene, a gay gene, an alcoholism gene, a violence gene, a race gene, a sports gene, a couch-potato gene, a gene for eating Godiva chocolate, or a gene for schizophrenia or manic-depression.

To be fair: Even before the discovery that mice have almost as many genes as humans, the psychiatric research community was moving away from the simple-minded (or is it simple-brained?) idea that there is *one* gene for schizophrenia or manic-depression; it had begun talking about a more complex web of genetic influences.[8] Hedging has also been going on in the discussion of the relative efficacy of psychotropic drugs versus psychotherapy, with talk therapy, previously dismissed as a waste of time (after all, "you can't talk to the disease"), making a comeback.[9]

However, for all the hedging and apparent coming together of the "brain" people and the "mind" people on common ground that I've spoken about before (between Kay Redfield Jamison and Kate Millett, between Edward Podvoll's "groundlessness" and Goodwin and Jamison's postulation that "environmental causality and biological vulnerability need not be viewed as opposing hypotheses"[10])—for all this, there is still a fundamental split between the two camps, similar, say, to the split between Plato and Aristotle or between Ptolemy and Copernicus or between capital and labor. A philosophical difference, one not just of degree but of kind. Which side am I on? After several (post-Yosemite) years of being in the "brain" camp, thinking it was the scientific as opposed to the airy-fairy place to be, I found myself moving, at first tentatively, later with more conviction, into the "mind" camp. Which I no longer think is the airy-fairy place to be, despite the fact that a lot of people with whom I don't agree or identify (some religionists, the people who believe in reincarnation or channeling, the romanticizers of mental illness, the hard-core antimedicationists) are *also* in it. And although I still believe in scientific progress, I have become convinced that "hard" scientific research—biochemistry, molecular biology, brain imaging and so forth—will never be able to explain or effectively treat mental illness, despite the obvious role of brain chemistry in mental disorders and the apparent effectiveness of *some* medications on *some* people for some period of time. (Other people don't get better with any medication; other people get better with therapy or religion; other people recover spontaneously.) To me, believing in "schizophrenia" or "manic-depression" as knowable, physical "brain diseases" is like believing in the abominable snowman. If you believe in the abominable snowman, then you believe that "it's only a matter of time" before advances in heat-detection devices, infrared nighttime sensors and high-tech weapons will allow us to bag it. If you *don't* believe in the abominable snowman, you don't believe we'll *ever* bag it. This doesn't mean that you haven't seen what looks like footprints in the snow, that you haven't heard the screams in the night and haven't found the mutilated bodies of villagers. *Something* is out there. Just not the abominable snowman.[11]

The "Iawaska" Mystery Solved

A couple of years after Charley's death, I accidentally found out what the "iawaska" seeds were that caused the bad drug trip during his freshman year at Reed, the trip Lin and I always thought of as a possible precursor to his breakdown at Yosemite. I had wondered about these "iawaska" seeds for years, but nobody I asked had ever heard of them, and my forays into books on botany and hallucinogenics also proved fruitless. Then, in 1998, while at work on this book, I was half-listening to the news on National Public Radio one evening as I stared at the computer screen, finishing my writing for the day. An anthropologist and ethnobotanist named Wade Davis was being interviewed about a book he had written called *Shadows in the Sun,* dealing with the spiritual experiences of indigenous cultures. Suddenly I felt my ears perking up. Davis was talking about how the Barasana Indians of the Colombian Amazon make extremely powerful hallucinogenic potions from *ayahuasca* plants (pronounced "iawaska" and spelled so by Charley and me), potions that are used in religious ceremonies. Eureka! The misspelling explained why I hadn't found anything in any reference books.

I ran out, bought Davis's book, and read about ayahuasca, which Davis describes as "the most revered and celebrated of Amazonian shamanic preparations . . . the jaguar's nectar, a magical intoxicant that could free the soul."[12] Charley was no doubt aware of the lore surrounding ayahuasca, which I'm sure is why he took it. It was part of his pattern, as Edward Podvoll describes more generally, of looking for a substance to trigger a spiritual transformation.

So why the bad trip in the student union that Brian Marsh had told me about, the breaking of lightbulbs, the intense fear Charley felt of not knowing what was going on around him? As I read Davis's account, some answers began to occur to me. Davis participated in an ayahuasca ceremony while staying among the Barasanas in Colombia. He describes the elaborate structure of that ceremony as well as the Indians' sophistication about the substances they use. The ayahuasca that Davis and his hosts ingested was a "frothy liquid" derived from scraping the fresh bark of two species of forest plant,

> then boiled for several hours until a thick, bitter liquid is produced. The active compounds are the beta-carbolines harmine and harmaline, whose subjective effects are suggested by the fact that, when first isolated, they were known as

telepathine. Taken alone, an infusion of the plant induces subtle visions, blues and purples, undulating waves of color.[13]

One can infer that neither Charley nor other Reedies who consumed ayahuasca performed any of these preparations, or any of the detailed costuming and body-painting and playing of musical instruments that Davis describes as part of the ayahuasca ceremony. And even if they had, such ceremonies would not have had the same meaning for them as they have for the Barasanas. They would have been more like the cultural dilettantism (or cultural imperialism) that causes affluent but dissatisfied Westerners to read Sufi poetry one day, go to lectures on Tibetan Buddhism the next, and then spend the weekend in a Native American sweat lodge. Davis himself touches on this question of authenticity when he speaks about the importance of the context in which drugs are taken, including the expectations of the people taking them. He says that

> the pharmacologically active components do not produce uniform effects. On the contrary, any psychoactive drug has within it a completely ambivalent potential for good or evil, order or chaos. Pharmacologically, it induces a certain condition, but that condition is mere raw material to be worked by particular cultural or psychological forces. . . . [T]he hallucinogenic plants consumed by the Amerindians induce a powerful but neutral stimulation of the imagination. They create a template upon which cultural reliefs may be amplified a thousand times. What individuals see in the visions is dependent not on the drug but on other factors: the physical and mental states of the users; their expectations, based on a rich repository of tribal lore; and, above all the authority, knowledge, and experience of the leader of the ceremony.[14]

"Pharmacologically, it induces a certain condition" . . . *"neutral stimulation of the imagination"* . . . As I read this I wondered, could what is true of psychoactive drugs also be true of the brain neurotransmitters they act on? The case of love, for instance. Don't romantic love and sexual passion, particularly in combination, cause just as much wild brain chemistry and even madness as schizophrenia or mania, at least temporarily? Don't they lead to at least as many suicides? Or dreams. Aren't dreams really just little psychotic episodes? The flights of fantasy in dreams involve the same brain chemicals as one's daytime thoughts, but as long as the dreams stay dreams and do not take over one's waking life

nobody worries about them. What, in other words, does "chemical imbalance" really mean? Is it some absolute state with an objective value, or is it contextual? Even a straight arrow brain-diseaser like Kay Jamison admits that she wouldn't want to give up her manic-depression *as long as its most extreme forms can be controlled;* her "illness," after all, has allowed her to feel, to love, more deeply.

And again, the context is not only personal, but cultural. "Amerindians enter the realm of hallucinogenic visions not out of boredom or to relieve restless anxiety," says Davis, "but rather to fulfill some need of the group. . . . Moreover, the experience is explicitly sought for positive ends. *It is not a means of escaping from an uncertain existence. Rather, it is perceived as a means of contributing to the welfare of all of one's people.*[15] (emphasis added)

The importance of the cultural context of "chemical imbalances" came home to me even more some weeks after I read this, when I had my earlier-described daylong visit with Mark Ragins and the Village to investigate the psychosocial rehab model of treatment. I received a binder with articles, clippings and other material on the organization's philosophy and practice. In one article written by Ragins himself he states, "Schizophrenics in third world countries are regularly reported to have better outcomes than here. Also schizophrenics who explain their conditions spiritually instead of medically apparently fare better."[16] Why? Could it be because, like Lin during Charley's first breakdown, traditional societies see madness in a less rigid and predetermined way than we do, as something that might even have meaning and value, not merely a brain disorder? At the very least a spiritual view of schizophrenia might make a person experiencing it more rather than less hopeful, since the spirit can grow and change, but what can you do about bad genes or a "shrunken brain"?

Ragins's remark about better outcomes in Third World countries also reminded me of what Wade Davis says about the neutral nature of the stimulation caused by hallucinogenic drugs, how their real meaning and effect is determined by culture. Even if a person really does have a chemical "imbalance" for whatever reason (drugs, insomnia, inborn instability), aren't its significance and outcome dependent at least to some extent on how the person him- or herself and the surrounding community see it and deal with it? What happens when the surrounding community's cultural and personal values mainly revolve around the accumulation of twenty-foot-high closets and multiple-stove kitchens in monster mansions? What kind of healing power and healthiness can a society provide that worships such things and the people who possess them? What kind of leadership can it offer to the troubled and confused?

Despite Western civilization's shaky credentials as a model for mental health, however, I do not mean to devalue Western science's contributions to human understanding or to ignore the physical realities of mental illness. There is obviously a physicochemical aspect to psychosis in the sense that *by definition* all activities of the mind involve the chemicals of the brain; we can all agree on that. In fact, it was the Buddhist-oriented Edward Podvoll, firmly in the "mind" camp, who provided me with perhaps the single most interesting bit of brain-chemistry information (aside from Wade Davis's revelations about ayahuasca) that I've found in all my reading. In a section of *The Seduction of Madness* called "Neurotransmitters," Podvoll writes about how the brain's neurotransmitters are chemically almost identical to hallucinogens.

> With only minute changes of atoms on the basic, fixed structure, a neurotransmitter may become a hallucinogen. In this way the essential neurotransmitter serotonin can become the hallucinogen psilocybin ["magic mushrooms"—JA]. Much of the recent manufacture of underground "designer" drugs is based on chemical rearrangements of the neurotransmitter structures. Oddly enough, it seems, our mandatory and precious neurotransmitters, in some variation or other, are also "out there" in the earth in mushrooms, cacti, and vines.[17]

Podvoll adds that just as serotonin is almost identical to psilocybin, so "[d]opamine itself"—the neurotransmitter most often associated with schizophrenia—"is, along with mescaline, one of the alkaloids of the peyote cactus."[18] This link between neurotransmitters and natural and synthetic hallucinogens explains a lot about why peyote, mescaline, LSD and so forth induce psychosis, and about why medications used as antipsychotics are effective (in varying degrees): They act upon these neurotransmitters, blocking, say, the activity of serotonin or dopamine that causes psychosis—or that at least is the immediate "brain" cause of the psychosis.

Now, all this information about the similarities between the brain and mushrooms and cacti is pretty amazing, and interesting, and probably important.

And it's all the result of scientific investigation. Would I ever condemn such investigation and the knowledge that comes from it? Absolutely not. But it's a question of the context in which we view (and what we do with) that knowledge—a little of which, we should always remember, is a dangerous thing. Because no matter how much we know about the brain (or about genes), we still know *very* little.[19] Yes, various medications have been discovered, usually by accident, that reduce psychotic symptoms in some people, at least for a while. The problem (aside from the often debilitating side effects) is that in many cases, even when they do work, the medications become less effective over time because people develop a tolerance for them, the brain and its neurotransmitters realigning themselves to accommodate the foreign substance and eventually returning to something like the status quo. This can cause addiction and further instability. "Typically, and increasingly," says Podvoll, "one hears of the dilemma of psychiatrists who are futilely attempting to regulate the knife-edge dosage of their patient's medications: *'He can't live with it and he can't live without it!'*"[20] (emphasis in the original) This reminded me of Charley's reaction to going back on his antipsychotic and side-effects medication after I rehospitalized him in August 1996—the awful episode where I had to throw him over my shoulder and put him into Jenny's VW Bug because he claimed he couldn't move. Fifteen minutes later he was walking into Santa Monica West on his own, and five hours later he was calling me sounding entirely normal. How much of that was the drug, and how much was feeling safe in the hospital?

With "brain" drugs, more than with other chemicals that affect other organs, such as insulin or heart medication, we confront the ambiguities of physical effects and psychological effects—the psychosomatic nexus—which in turn gets us back to the question of the context in which we see the scientific knowledge we've gained and what we do with it. Clearly, there was a physical aspect to Charley's illness. There was a specifically seasonal component, for one thing, his tendency (as he himself put it) to be affected by the solstice. His manias seemed to originate in the spring and erupt in the summer, although there was never a strict schedule; they could last into fall and winter. Then he would recover. His first insomnia—the "white light" episode—took place in July. The journal entries in which he wrote about that episode and about being a genius took place the following May. The Yosemite breakdown, of course, came in July after weeks of insomnia. And the following year's episode, the "dreams of madness" journal entries in which he speaks of both his fear of psych wards and his longing for god consciousness, also began in May, as did the *M. Butterfly* episode that led to the stabbing. But earlier in his life it was precisely in the spring that his schoolwork tended to improve. Charley often acted dreamy in school, but he often seemed to become more focused toward the end of the school year, sometimes quite suddenly. One of his middle-school teachers mentioned this to me with some wonder one late spring day. She'd always known Charley was smart, but he had a tendency not to pay attention in class or hand in his homework. "But then one day he just suddenly got it together," she said. In late spring. Could that focus have come from the same seemingly sudden infusion of mental energy that when he got older would lead to hypomania and eventually full-fledged mania?

A lot of work has been done on trying to understand the cyclical nature of manic-depression, how it relates to the seasons, to sleep patterns, to the rhythms of the Earth and of the human body, rhythms (both daily and longer) that may get out of sync. But with manic-depression in particular, especially its extreme forms, how much of that cyclicity becomes, over time, if not caused by, at least made worse by, the individual's own worries about (as Kay Redfield Jamison says) "when will it happen again?" As with insomnia, where fear of sleeplessness makes the sleeplessness worse, the fear of a new psychotic break might help bring it on. When I went to Reed at Thanksgiving 1992 after Charley's second breakdown, the dean and the school psychologist talked to me about the "kindling" phenomenon observed in manic-depression or schizoaffective disorder, where over time some people's episodes come closer together and for less apparent reason, "kindled" by progressively less stimulation (or stress). In the brain-research community this tends to be seen as a physical phenomenon, the brain cells becoming further damaged with each episode, less able to cope. But might it instead, or at least also, be caused by anxiety, the "self-fulfilling prophesy" aspect of a life crisis that never entirely goes away? Goodwin and Jamison, in their chapter on the pathophysiology of manic-depression, talk about how "prior episodes may themselves constitute a form of stress that increases the likelihood of subsequent episodes."[21]

So psychology as well as physiology may enter into it, as well as environment. (The same page as the above quote is where Goodwin and Jamison speak of how "environmental causality and biological vulnerability need not be viewed as opposing hypotheses." They also say three paragraphs later, in another bow to the "nurture" side of the nature/nurture debate, "It is likely that stress activation of bipolar illness involves a pathological reaction to the normal stresses associated with adolescence," which certainly would seem applicable to Charley's life, a life that despite family instability and his parents' divorce, fatherly malpractice, and stresses over his sexual identity and his academic future, was certainly not *abnormally* bad and in many ways pretty good.) But again, it's a question of what we do with the knowledge, whether we handle it from the "brain" or "mind" angle. Goodwin and Jamison hope that early intervention in the form of "pharmacological treatment, combined with psychological support," might help steer at-risk children away from, or at least reduce the severity of, subsequent manic-depressive episodes. But then they say, "This prevention strategy depends on the ability to identify vulnerability before the illness has expressed itself, a possibility that awaits the discovery of biological or genetic markers applicable to the general population of manic-depressives."[22] In other words, it's only a matter of time before we bag the abominable snowman with the new night scopes and infrared sensing devices we will soon have. We will "identify" vulnerable children and give them powerful and dangerous medications from the time they're toddlers, and then observe and manipulate them for the rest of their lives. The petri-dish treatment. We'll help these kids if it kills them.

Finally, I must say, talk about "biological or genetic markers" is very strange coming from Kay Redfield Jamison, and as much as I respect her intellect and good intentions I sometimes have to wonder. In her autobiography she tells a story about her time as a researcher on manic-depressive illness at UCLA. One day she went for a physical exam to a new doctor, a man she didn't know. After finding out that she was on lithium, the doctor asked whether she knew that manic-depressive illness was a genetic disease. When she said yes, of course she knew, the man told her calmly, "as though it were God's truth," that she should not have children. Jamison describes her reaction:

> I felt sick, unbelievably and utterly sick. . . . I asked him if his concerns about my having children stemmed from the fact that, because of my illness, he thought I would be an inadequate mother or simply that he thought it was best to avoid bringing another manic-depressive into the world. Ignoring or missing my sarcasm, he replied, "Both." I asked him to leave the room, put on the rest

of my clothes, knocked on his office door, told him to go to hell, and left. I walked across the street to my car, sat down, shaking, and sobbed until I was exhausted.[23]

So much for "genetic markers."[24]

Were there other, *less* "early and aggressive," less intrusive forms of intervention that could have helped Charley? As I read *Shadows in the Sun* and Wade Davis's discussion about ayahuasca, about how variable, contextual and culturally determined brain chemistry can be (or at least the uses to which it is put), I again found myself wondering about Charley's initial breakdown, whether a different kind of intervention, one more attentive to his inner life and better adapted to his extreme fragility in a time of crisis, might have been less "destructive to the psyche." I say this with all due respect to (and appreciation for) Dr. Gray. It was not some power-tripping arrogance that made him advise Lin and me to hospitalize Charley based on a less-than-ten-minute doctor-patient interview the Tuesday after Yosemite. It was the fact that he grasped immediately what Lin and I did not: that the car crash had not been an accident and that Charley was still a danger to himself.

But safety had a price. Over the next five-plus years, in hospital and out, Charley would repeatedly say to me almost these exact words: "Dad, these people don't know what they're doing!" And just as many times I, sounding hollow and guilty even to myself, would say, "Well, we don't know what *we're* doing either. At least they have practical experience. Get what you can. They're not malicious people." And they weren't. Most of them were intelligent and well meaning, and collectively they prolonged his life. But they didn't save it. Whether anyone could have saved it is not clear (Vern the Native American shaman didn't work out either). We'll never know whether Charley was "locked in" (Max Freulich) to his suicidal path, and if he was, when the lock was set—before Yosemite, at Yosemite, or even after Yosemite. But we *do* know that psychiatry's medicalization of Charley's "affliction" did not work. And by the end, I think, it made death look like a better deal. I don't have any direct proof of this; Charley never said it in so many words (although he came close ... *"The memories of my last hospital visit still haunt me. I have a grave fear that I'll end up homeless, wanting to stay in a psych ward"*). But I suspect that the reason he finally killed himself was that his choices had narrowed to two: either successful suicide, in which he was at least an active subject, an actual participant in his existence, or life in a psych ward, in which he would be more and more an object—and not only an object, but an object of contempt—even to himself. Death or dishonor.

Sunday Afternoon in
the Psych Ward with the Kids

Charley was still alive when I had my strongest intuition of how false the rigid category of "mental illness" can be. It came during the best of the good hours I had with him, an October Sunday in 1994 when he was getting ready to leave Harbor-UCLA for the second time. What made the hour so good was that it involved not only Charley but his sister Jenny. I have talked about how hard it had become for the two of them to deal with each other since Charley's crisis began. His arrogance and condescension seemed to grow exponentially whenever he was around Jenny, and her impatience and thin-skinnedness grew right alongside. Family gatherings often degenerated into nasty spats, so I had long made it a policy not to pressure Jenny to "relate" to Charley. But as I talked to her on the phone this Sunday morning and told her I was going to the hospital she said she wanted to come too. It was a beautiful, warm fall day. We drove down after lunch in her old VW Bug, a quick twenty miles on the San Diego Freeway.

When we arrived at 8W Charley was in a good mood. He had long since gotten over the June stabbing psychosis and most of his postpsychotic depression and was looking forward to leaving the hospital in the next few days to go to a halfway house. His mood got even better when he saw Jenny enter the ward with me, cool as he played it. She seemed happy and relaxed, too, and I felt none of the discomfort and resistance I often got from her in these situations. After Charley greeted us we sat in the windowless dining room of the ward for a little while and talked. Then Jenny or I suggested that we ask one of the nurses to open the recreation room down the hall; it had windows and we could bask in the sunshine rather than fluorescent light. Charley didn't think they would do it. It wasn't recreation time yet and the nurses and orderlies tended to withhold doing special favors as a way of demonstrating their control. The excuse would be that one of them would have to stay in the rec room to monitor us (hospital rules), taking them away from their current tasks. But today the staff seemed to be in a good mood, too, so when we asked if they would open the room early, one of the nurses said yes. He let us in and then left, perhaps thinking my presence would be enough adult supervision.

At first we were the only ones in the room, which contained a battered old upright piano with a couple of important keys that didn't work, a pool table, a Ping-Pong table, a stationary bicycle and a bunch of chairs. Jenny sat down near a window while Charley and I played Ping-Pong. The room was quiet and peaceful. I asked Charley if he'd like to play the piano, and he said yes. He sat on the scarred bench in front of the scarred piano with keys the color of old dog teeth and started playing a rippling Chopin prelude. Then he picked up a volume of Scott Joplin I'd brought him some weeks before and started playing "Maple Leaf Rag." I sat next to him watching him in profile. He had his back to Jenny and the rest of the room as he played. The music wafted out the door and down the hall.

Soon other patients began coming in. I had seen them all on earlier visits, some of them just minutes before out in the main ward. All were on medication, and they usually sat in their rooms or in the TV room or shuffled vacant-eyed through the halls. None of them ever seemed to have visitors. Now they came into the room like inanimate objects suddenly enlivened by the music—not only enlivened but made normal. They were walking like regular people, the stiffness of their ordinary medication shuffle and postures smoothed out, made loose and fluid by the mercurial shimmering of the "Maple Leaf." I thought of Disney's cartoon *Pinocchio,* the first movie Charley had ever seen, where the puppets come to life (he was a year old and sat in the theater trans-fixed and unmoving for its entire length). There was an old white-haired man with pale pinkish skin and white stubble; he came in first. Then a middle-aged Asian man who ten minutes before had been wandering the halls in his paja-mas staring straight ahead, talking to no one; now he walked in, smiling faintly, shy eyes engaging us. Then a fortyish Anglo woman who was a little more on the manic-y side. I think she had a crush on Charley; I had seen her hanging around the kitchen trying to make conversation when Lin and I visited him other nights. Then a very large, thirty-something black man.

Charley didn't seem to notice. He just played, his back to the room. I looked over at Jenny. Usually at this point in a visit she would be starting to make eye contact, the "Dad, isn't it time to go?" look. But not today. She was sitting smiling contentedly, as if being here were the one place in the world she wanted to be. A second woman went over to her with a Ping-Pong paddle and asked if she wanted to play. Jenny got up and the two began hitting the ball back and forth in a relaxed way. The woman with the crush on Charley was riding the stationary bike. The Asian man and the white-haired man were playing pool. The large black man was watching the Ping-Pong game, waiting for his turn, and he started rallying with Jenny a few minutes later.

I sat there thinking what an incredible gift Charley had. For years I had had a fantasy of being a barrelhouse or blues pianist like Pine Top Smith or Fats Waller. I would have gladly sold my soul—or traded any talent I had as a writer or painter—for the ability to perform music for an audience, to entertain. What a thing to be able to do—to reach people this directly, especially these "lost souls."

He played for a few minutes more, another Joplin rag. He seemed unaware of what was going on behind him, and I'm not sure he would have cared even if he *had* been aware, although from what Shizuko told me later and from reading his own journals I think he did care. (*"All the composers have left behind traces of themselves. . . . Recognizing their love of humankind as I play their music I am exercising my sense of the commonality of man."*) Whatever the case, the music did what it did, and I was never prouder of him than at that moment. Nor was I ever prouder of Jenny. As I watched her going after the Ping-Pong ball, relaxed, the calm half-smile on her face, I had a sense of her for the first time as a grown woman, and not only grown, but a person of kindness and compassion who could put her own "ego-centricity" away. I have never experienced, nor could I ever imagine, a happier moment.

Epilogue

A View from the Bridge

Several times a week, Lin Aurthur places fresh flowers among the wilted blooms and rain-streaked notes at the rail of the Lincoln Boulevard overpass on the Santa Monica Freeway. "This little altar," she calls it, a shrine to her son, Charley, who jumped to his death there Nov. 1. It is one of the street shrines that are now such a familiar part of the urban landscape, appearing overnight, sometimes disappearing almost as quickly. As on pilgrimages, friends, family and strangers come to lay flowers, light candles, leave poems.

(Los Angeles Times, *about five weeks after Charley's death*)[1]

November 12, 1996

Tuesday. Eleven days after Charley's death. Two days after his memorial. The dining-room discussions over, the immediate work of grieving done. Relatives gone. Me alone, walking on Lincoln Boulevard toward the overpass to visit, for the first time, Charley's shrine at the spot where he had jumped. I was in

an intense, emotional mood, thinking of the events of the past eleven days—
and five years. As I walked I sang to myself the Negro hymn "I Shall Not Be
Moved," a CD version of which (sung by Pop Staples) I had used as exit music
at the memorial. As I approached the overpass and the shrine I was thinking
about all the oppressed and all the damaged souls like Charley, people who
have troubles that we can't always see, who suffer hurts—and express hurt—in
ways that aren't always clear.

I reached the waist-high metal bridge railing where Charley's homemade
shrine had sprung up, a collection of pictures and poems (by him and to him)
and notes (one from a total stranger) taped to the top rail. On the ground
against the railing were little votive candles and vases of flowers that Lin had
brought from the memorial, as well as (how appropriate!) a little empty airline
whiskey bottle. The candles were all out. Except on the calmest days the flames
people lit never lasted long on this windy bridge, and I had no matches with
me now. I stood facing east and looked down at the Santa Monica Freeway, just
as Charley had done. I could see another bridge/overpass a few blocks east—
Eleventh Street—which had a high chain-link fence attached to the railing
across its whole span. That's why Charley had chosen this bridge: It had no
guard fence. As I looked down at the whoosh of cars heading west—a lot of
cars even at eleven in the morning—I felt a touch of vertigo because of the
low railing. It couldn't have been more than four feet high. How little there
was between us, me and the cars. Yet how much. How much it must have taken
for him to throw himself down at those chunks of metal hurtling along that
concrete ribbon.

For the first time the full weight, the sheer physicality, of what he had done
seized hold of me. This was not a very high overpass. It wasn't more than
twenty or twenty-five feet above the roadway. He must have realized that the
jump alone wouldn't kill him. What was his plan? To land in front of a car and
be crushed or knocked flying? To land *on* one, as he had done? But what split-
second timing that would require! How could he know how long the fall
would take? Had he been planning this? Lin had mentioned to me that when
she was tending the shrine an older black man, one of the local transients who
hung out outside a U-Haul rental next to the freeway, had come up to her and
said he had seen Charley a couple of days before he jumped. He had been on
his bike, the man said, and had just sat on it leaning against the overpass railing

watching the freeway for a while, then gone on his way. We weren't sure whether to believe this. They come out of the woodwork, people in these situations do, wanting to be part of the narrative. Had Charley really gone to the bridge before Friday, planning the jump? Maybe he had even tested the distance, dropping a pebble or a penny onto the roadway, timing its fall. He had four or five watches, all with second hands; a couple of them even had stop-watches. He was always preoccupied with time. Had he counted the cars just before the jump? Did he say to himself, I'll do it at the tenth car, or the twentieth, or the hundredth? Is that why he waited for several minutes? *("Witnesses indicated he rode his bicycle to the overcrossing, climbed over the railing, looked down for a few minutes and jumped. . . .")* Or was he waiting for a car like the vintage Porsche, to go out in style?

The cars passed below me, as oblivious to my presence as they had been to Charley's. The Porsche driver had been oblivious, hadn't seen Charley falling. He would tell me this himself a couple of months later when I talked to him on the phone. He was a young guy who even then, months after Charley's fall, sounded a bit shell-shocked. And no wonder. He hadn't seen Charley jump, he told me. He was driving along on his daily commute when he suddenly heard and felt what seemed like an explosion in back of him—Charley landing on the trunk of his car. The driver literally had not known what hit him.

Now, the whoosh of cars below me, rushing toward the ocean. I was thinking "shh" sounds. Porsche. Rush. Whoosh. Ocean. They reminded me of a gesture Charley often made during his episodes, raising a finger to his lips and saying "Shh . . . !" when I asked him a question he didn't want to answer or when I talked too loud. He could be very sensitive to sound, particularly during his manias, when all his senses were operating at an almost painful pitch. "Shh . . . !" he would whisper, and it might be about the voices, too. Sometimes I was interrupting the voices when I spoke, or maybe he didn't want them to hear me, so he would shoosh me. Now he had shooshed everything.

So strong and new was this physical feeling of what Charley had done as I stood there at the railing that I almost imagined he was there with me, that his being had entered mine. I could feel his pull. I could feel the downward pull from the whoosh of the cars below, their forward thrust creating a vacuum in their wakes that tugged at his sleeves resting on the rail, a draw of air that helped lift him over the railing. Here at this ugly intersection of two great roads that make a vast stone cross, Interstate 10 that runs from the Atlantic to the Pacific, from Jacksonville, Florida, to Santa Monica, and Lincoln Boulevard (Route One), part of the Camino Real, the "Royal Road" that runs from Mexico to Canada. Crossing here a mile from the ocean, near the 10's terminus. And Charley's.

After a few minutes of experiencing the power of this spot I left the railing and continued walking, starting to sing "I Shall Not Be Moved" again. But my few moments at the bridge had changed my mood. I felt a sense of liberation now. It is awful to think that I felt liberated coming from the spot of Charley's death, but at that moment I did. His terrible affliction and suffering had imprisoned him but it had also imprisoned me, and now both of us were free. It was not a freedom I had chosen: Standing at the railing minutes before I had also thought about how if I'd been there when he started to go over I would have grabbed him by the scruff of the neck and dragged him back to the hospital. (Was that the reason for his few minutes' hesitation? Was he waiting for someone—me?—to come and make him change his mind, give him a reason to live, pluck him off his death spot?) It was not a freedom I had chosen, but it had come to me anyway. I felt a new sense of authority, that I could look anything or anybody in the world in the eye. Nobody had anything on me. "A totally unexpected feeling of authority and power—almost elation," I wrote in my journal that night. "Charley's death has freed me to do things besides mourn. Almost a warrior feeling. Standing beside the fallen comrade, welcoming the advance of the enemy. Well, come *on*."

This almost theatrical elation was more an end than a beginning, of course, the last gasp of the adrenaline rush I had been feeling since a day or so after Charley's death, and which had allowed me to function. I wasn't really free, and I never would be. But even as my Homeric mood would soon melt away, giving way to the exhaustion I had been expecting, and later to the doubt and confusion (and guilt and shame) I have been describing, a residue would remain and (I think) become a permanent part of who I am. It is the sense that nothing worse can happen to me, and that therefore I have nothing more to fear.

THE END

Acknowledgments

For reasons that are probably obvious by now, this was not an easy book to write—or, I have often feared, to read. To the extent that it is readable I have a number of people to thank, friends and associates who generously volunteered their time to examine and critique the earlier drafts, often in detail. Some of these people knew Charley, some did not. All of them gave me their professional and moral support and constructive criticism. I wish to thank Doris Koenig, Jacquelin Gorman, Russel Lunday, Elizabeth Frank, Janet Lent, Charon D'Aiello and Leslie Laine for having the fortitude (and upper body strength) to heft and then wade through the very long first draft—almost twice as long as the finished book!—and help me figure out how to pare it down to a more manageable size. I also want to thank George Wilson, George Davison, Jan Bramlett, Peter Belsito, Cary Shulman, David Ralicke, Deirdre Sloyan, my sister Kate, Tony Garavente and Renée D'Antoni for reading a later draft and making numerous helpful suggestions. I especially want to thank Danilo Bach and Jeffry Frieden for first reading the manuscript and then giving me substantial personal time to discuss structural matters and other things of substance. Their labor was absolutely crucial in helping me to see certain problems with my presentation and then in suggesting possible solutions.

And I *especially* want to thank my brother, Charley's Uncle Tim, for having the patience to read and critique both drafts and bolster my spirits during the writing.

Also thanks to several in particular of Charley's friends who also became friends of mine after his death and who read and discussed with me various versions of this book and related matters. They—Lisa-Michèle Talamantes, Lysa

Mateu, and Danielle Littell—talked to me at length about Charley and their relationships with him and helped deepen my understanding of him and his connections with other people. Special thanks to Jenny Lewis, a special friend of Charley who, despite everything, remained close to him and his family through it all.

And of all Charley's closest friends, I wish to extend the most profound thanks to Shizuko Imai, who permitted me to quote her letters, provided me with copies of Charley's poems and letters to her, and by doing so enabled me to tell her story as well as his.

I want to thank Lucille Van Ornam, Charley's favorite teacher, who not only read a draft of the book but contributed to it with a letter to me about Charley. She also, on her own initiative, tracked down and gave me a long-lost school journal of Charley's from fifteen years earlier that had lain hidden somewhere in Culver City Middle School.

In the professional community, many thanks to Martha Long, Mark Ragins, David Pilon and Dena Blumgarden of the Village Integrated Service Agency in Long Beach, California, for inviting me to a full-day immersion session to explain the workings of their agency and the theory of psychosocial rehabilitation. David Pilon, in particular, kept in touch with me after the immersion and provided me in a timely fashion with additional information when I requested it.

Thanks to Jeffrey Fortuna, executive director of Windhorse Associates in Northampton, Massachusetts. Jeff, a long-time associate of Dr. Edward Podvoll, granted me a lengthy interview in the spring of 2000 to discuss the Windhorse model of treatment begun by him and Dr. Podvoll. This discussion, and additional materials that Jeff provided me, were enormously helpful as I worked on the book.

Thanks to Dr. Edwin S. Shneidman for responding to my queries about his work on suicide and helping to clarify my thinking on the differences between the "mind" and "brain" camps. And thanks to my friend of more than thirty years, Dr. Bill Schwartzman, for talking to me at length (and depth) about this and other subjects related to healthcare, both physical and mental.

Of the various professional caregivers who dealt with Charley (and me), I want to express my particular deepest and eternal gratitude to Dr. Duane Bietz of Portland, Oregon, whose timely intervention and subsequent surgery on Charley's heart saved his life in 1994.

I want to thank my publisher, Health Communications, Inc., for being willing to take a chance on a difficult book and for treating me with unfailing courtesy and respect. Particular thanks to Christine Belleris, Tom Sand, Kim Weiss, Larissa Hise Henoch (who designed the cover), and my editor, Susan Tobias. I also want to thank Joel Roberts and Bonnie Grey of Joel D. Roberts and Associates for helping me to "hone" my message.

Finally, I want to thank Charley's mother, Lin, and his sister, Jenny, for giving me their permission actually to seek a publisher for this book. Writing it was something I would have done under any circumstances; I simply couldn't avoid it. But I could not and would not have actually tried to get it published without Lin's and Jenny's okay, since the story so intimately involved their lives as well as Charley's and mine.

Appendix A

Selected Poems of Charley's

The following are selected poems of Charley's not included in the body of the text. One of them, "Knock on Wood," is discussed and partially quoted in the text. Some are undated, but I have tried to present them in roughly chronological order.

Crying

(Undated, late 1989)

Crying.
The baby is
     D
     R
     O
     P
     P
     E
     D
       I
         N   *e endless abyss of reality . . .*
             T   h
          O t
       From the dark warm cave of oblivion

He is compelled to see the
Immeasurable light.

Sur le Train
To Brian Marsh—11/14/92

(Written during Charley's autumn 1992 breakdown, about ten days before the Thanksgiving Portland Adventist hospitalization. Charley had visited Lin in Santa Cruz before Halloween and had taken the train back to Reed. See his letter to me on pages 80–81 of the text, where he mentions the parakeets and writing to Brian Marsh.)

In the underworld the people chatter
Like paraqueets in a stolen cave.
In gross cacophony the wheels clatter
With ridiculous anger and moronic rave.

Prometheus' fire and temerity
Are enough to heat the carriage.
Two reckless knights of prosperity
Relax in the comfort of quiet disparage.

Overlooking the sea we eat and drink
Talking to passengers of things of late.
Then to the books, we read and think;
I thank you now, dear goddess Fate.

The new Deal

(Undated, but written around the same time as "Sur le Train," and also before the Thanksgiving hospitalization. The poem's puns and wordplays and non sequiturs are characteristic of people who are experiencing mania. The run-in words and misspellings are as in the original.)

Even if I'm gnarley
You can still call me Charley
Cause the rye is still good
When you're in the rightmood

The New York "Bohemes"
Has still got his rights
On the writings of Engels
And Santa Clause shingls

Dont hope in Despair
Let the Leaf Blower repair
We've all got a job
In saving the mob.

You can call me wise
You can call me a fool.
But you must remember
That charming December.
When the fool and the spool took charge of the ember

Mourning

(Dated 12/31/92, about a month later, after Charley's release from Ryles Center in Portland. I had driven him back to Los Angeles, and he was staying with me in Santa Monica. Seven weeks after the poem was written he would cut his wrists and swallow his lithium.)

To ease the pain;
Halting strife.
To knock the strain of a futile life
To parry the blow
Of a loved one lost
To query the blow and inevitable cost
The price is time; for 'tis ever present
Persevere the mime; it might be pleasant
The night addresses youthful eyes
Interminably worthy of despise.

But yours my friend crystaline
Forget tomorrow, 'tis never thine

Untitled—1993

(Written at St. John's Hospital in late February 1993 when Charley was recovering from the wrist cutting)

The dawn peeks through thick drapes
In the dark somber rooms
A little reminder: life must go on.
Pulse, temperature, blood pressure.
The nurse must collect them.
Informing me I am still alive
Through the halls patients pass
A bland breakfast awaits them.

Outside of the hospitals
Away from the minute corners of despair

The world is happening
Where people are busy
Working, playing, loving.
Outside this torpor and melancholy
Progress and production take place
And folks smile over small accomplishments.

But at the ward idleness resumed
And the burden is carried one more day
The sweet sickly smell pervades
The rooms mixing w/sweat and urine
A stagnant scent, unmistakable.
Withdrawal is so simple
It is healing or merely postponing?
A little of both perhaps.

The doctors pass through briefly
Wearing ties and stethoscopes
And through my mind
Pass the faces and voices of yesterday
Dreams of a pretty girl I used to know
Memories of the world of progress
I shall see it again, I know
A thousand-fold stronger.

"Mourning Malease"

(Undated, probably written in Los Angeles in summer 1993 while Charley was living with me in Santa Monica)

> *As we this week-end old adjourn,*
> *Coming now so nigh the week unborn,*
> *Drink your sleep. First the muddle*
> *And dreamy deep, ere, soft and subtle,*
> *The rising sun does bring the summer Monday Mourn.*
>
> *The land of Nod I could not find*
> *Along the roadways of my mind.*
> *From my room I cannot lumber.*
> *By luck or doom I did not slumber.*
> *Yesterday indeed is passed but still not left behind.*
>
> *My wakeful watch I give to those*
> *Now donning on their working clothes.*
> *I need some rest, a smoke perhaps.*
> *I face the East, while minutes lapse;*
> *And breathe a sign that breaks the muse*
> *Of all the evening's woes.*

Elay

(Undated, from around the same time as "Mourning Malease." Charley was working at Café Athens.)

> *I remember someone once saying*
> *In Elay you're always waiting*
> *For something to happen.*
>
> *The days in Elay pass like*
> *The Elay haze . . .*
> *In overcast gray.*

I have only a bicycle
I am trapped inside
On the West side.
I roam around—timelessly
Looking inside the
Bohemian coffee houses
For life . . . intelligence?

The cars and the wide streets oppress me.
The buildings are new and temporary
Like the people.
The shops come and go making room for more.

The restaurants in which I find work
Are young and expensive, and decorative
Like the Elay women.
The well-to-do stuff themselves
But cannot fill the emptiness.
They're starving.

Something in the air
Defiles the collective conscience
And takes from us our humanity.
It is worse than the smog.

And still I roam the streets
But I cannot escape the emptiness
In my house, on the promenades,
the parks, the freeways.
It's all the same.

Throughout this vast expanse
Of money there is no escape.
Then I visit the beach
That formidable wall which
allows no more expanding.
The people are in awe.
They don't understand it.

And still I'm waiting,
In this confounded desert called Elay.
Where there is little contentment
And little peace.

Knock on Wood

(Also from the summer of 1993, after Charley had recovered from his wrist-cutting episode and before he returned to Reed for his third and final try)

"Knock on wood," said his father with a grin and a chuckle,
And jestingly tapped his son's head with his knuckle.
To Woody's father it was no small revelation
That such fun could be got from the boy's appellation.
He was five at the time and not long thereafter
Would he become the source of indefatigable laughter.

When company parted, driving out in the fog,
They'd first tap on his head like an old maple log.
If Dad had a bet on the week's double header,
He'd knock on poor Woody to make his odds better.

When sister was out late, not home safe in bed,
Before turning in Mother tapped on his head.
And so just like this it became a mere habit
To regard Woody's head as the foot of a rabbit.

And it didn't end there, that banter so cruel.
From home the joke managed to be known at his school.
Out the window from class when clouds dank and grey
Appeared to deter the young students from play,
Each child took a rap to Woody's small pate,
And strangely enough the storm would abate.
The children knew not the ineffable harm
Done to Woody's morale, with his head a luck-charm.
For on one fateful day in the midst of discourse
The teacher, so to give his lecture more force
Knocked on sad Woody's head, the notorious last tap,
For down poor Woody's cheeks streamed not tears but sap!
His eyes lost their lustre. Like wood-knots they seemed.
With incredulous horror all the girls screamed.
An inanimate block did his noggin remain.
All attempts to restore him to life were inane.

So on this regretful note I will end,
With only one word of counsel, dear friend.
Superstition be not a vice on its own
If properly noted that wood *is not* bone.

Sonnet

(Dated "12/30/93," written during winter break from Reed, probably in
Santa Monica)

Every thought, every sigh, each beat of heart I may expend,
Every word spoken, no matter how phrased,
Are of little effect on the women You send,
Who, with smiling lips, and lashes raised,
Seem indifferent. Indifference, the lover will hate the worst.
The carefree female knows not perhaps
How quickly she's sated, how small is her thirst
To the fresh eager spring she so carelessly taps.
Not like the bee, who sucks the rose dry,
Leaving no honey remnant to nurture its grief;
The woman converts love's juice into lye,
Which burns away spirit, and corrodes all belief.
  On the grace of her form, You have ably succeeded,
  But by her cruel flippant ways, it is largely exceeded.

Melancholy

(Undated, probably from 1993 or 1994)

I cannot strike you
  Cancerous thing
I cannot shun you
In all your strength
You're guised by weakness
Deceiving your victim.

So I must embrace you
Hold you tender

Till you tire of me
And release me from
your venomous grasp.

What should we do
In the absence of melancholy?
Awake each morn, perhaps
With glee and fervor?
We might smile at all those
Who look our way
With an earnest twinkle in the eye.

Ode to Guinness Extra Stout

(Dated 3/11/94, toward the end of Charley's final year at Reed. Charley entered the poem in a contest sponsored by the Guinness Company. The winner, as I recall, would acquire a pub in Ireland.)

When I sip your draught that seethes with foam,
To the poet Yeats my thoughts do roam:
He, indeed, with Ire and Love
Who, with guidance from the muse above
Placed his thoughtful plume in ink.
To him I raise my glass to drink—
. . . and taste his bitter tears.

Soap Opera Heroine

(Probably written during Charley's 1993–1994 year at Reed. The person addressed may have been Shizuko. One of her letters to Charley implies that he had called her a "soap opera queen.")

The leading rôle on your daytime drama
Invokes the sensitive but sustaining heart.
An actress who thrives on the throes of trauma
Will bring her best to the thankless part.

Could your day progress without this strife
And histrionics of which you seem so fond?
Could love be rather for the sake of life,
Than the means to secure a weary bond?

Appendix B

Short Story

The following short story, dated February 13, 1990, was written during Charley's senior year of high school while he was living with his grandparents in San Francisco. It is followed by a brief commentary by me.

The Pool Lesson

Somewhere off in the land of Missouri or Kansas, one of those lower midwestern states lies a tiny, lost town by the name of Shingledale. It's a borough not distinct or memorable by any means, but a place where folks with modest incomes reside peacefully; oblivious to the rapidly changing world beyond.

One of Shingledale's prominent businesses and most popular "hotspots" is Arnie's Bar-Pool Hall situated in the center of town adjacent to Harry's Meat Market. Arnie, an amiable man in his sixties, gets the bulk of his patronage from travelers off route 52, who stay the night at the nearby inn. But there is also Shingledale's indolent, dissipated crowd, mostly men of their senior years, who have little to do but loiter about, tipple in front of their TV's, and play pool at Arnie's. Most of them are friends of the owner from high school.

At one time the most regular frequenter was Carl Jenkins, a kind-hearted geezer who told jokes and drank a great deal with the other regulars. For the most part Carl was good natured and virtuous. At this particular time, his wife,

Margaret, had been dead for eight years, leaving him alone, with no offspring. After her death he began drinking more than he ever had before, and started to grow cynical and rather indifferent to life. He did have one passion though—playing pool. Loneliness and the monotony of his existence drove him to be the greatest player at Arnie's, which meant he was the best in Shingledale.

On an average night when Carl was at Arnie's consuming scotch at his usual rapid pace he eyed two young men, not older than twenty-five, walking through the door. These youths had definitely come from some distance. Their reserved gait and body language suggested New England breeding. Something, however, about their jocular way of talking and looking around this unfamiliar bar said they were a little bold, and rebellious toward their conservative backgrounds. When they each took up a pool cue and began playing at one of Arnie's six tables Carl looked at them, envious yet derisive of their youthful charm and ignorance.

Michael Kelly (Micky to his friends), a lad of six feet and short, curly brown hair, started the game. As he set his fingers' bridge for the break he said, "I hope you'll learn something from this pool lesson, Jimmy."

And when the cue ball scattered the other fifteen but sank into a side pocket, his friend James Lewis remarked, "It looks like you've got the white ones."

Thus they played. Micky proved to be a much more adept player and not a bit reluctant to press the point. Every shot he made was followed by a sharp smirk. Whenever James made a shot, which wasn't nearly as often, his friend would effect fear and give an exaggerated, "Uh-oh." James, who was a little shorter than Micky and more refined, had never been competitive by nature. He was rather amused by his friend's cockiness. After five games, though, he no longer had the energy to be a good sport nor the patience to see another victorious smile of Micky's. The score of wins was four to one if you count Micky's eight ball scratch where James still had five of his balls on the table. Of course, Micky couldn't honor James's win but clapped him on his back and said, "You really kicked my ass that time. Won't you give me a chance to win back my title?" So they played a fifth game and Micky gained his title back in two turns.

Alone, James walked to the bar where old Carl was putting away spirits in impressive quantities. James sat next to him and sighed. He was not vexed, as so many young people would be, when Arnie asked for his identification to prove his right to liquor. Carl leaned close to the boy and with a breath tainted with Jack Daniels and non-filtered cigarettes, said "Your friend over there," looking at Micky slamming balls violently one by one into the holes, "he plays pretty good but he's a smarty pants."

"Oh, he doesn't mean any harm. Just likes to win. I suppose I'm used to his attitude, though."

"Well, I figure when a man's on a losing streak he don't need his face rubbed in it. A man's pride is like his woman. A part of him that makes him complete that everybody else should respect. But I guess you yankee boys don't think much of propriety."

"No, that's not it at all. My friend likes to think he's good for something so he flaunts it when he wins. It's just a game anyway. He's not a bad guy. Only a little crazy. Last week he was kicked out of the college we go to. We need to get away from Connecticut. We're going to California."

Carl persisted in lecturing James about old fashioned morality. The latter perceived him to be quite tipsy. And since he wasn't in opposition with anything the old man said, he nodded every few moments to pacify his bitterness, not wanting to provoke him. He was glad to see his friend join them at the bar. But before Micky could order a drink Carl spoke to him. "How about a couple games. I could use a few pointers from a young shark like yourself." Micky accepted eagerly.

"Let's say five dollars a game. I'm too old to play for nothing."

Micky couldn't see why a modest player would propose to wager. He figured something sneaky about the guy and wanted to find out what it was. Micky was not a young man of any especial intelligence but being somewhat of a prankster himself he could intuit when a man was not one hundred percent. "Who cares," he said to himself. "I'll beat'm whether he thinks he's good or not."

So they went to work. When all of the old-time regulars gathered around to watch their friend Carl play, they were surprised to see this young stranger beat him five games straight. Micky was so high on winning so easily he felt himself invincible, and didn't think twice when Carl suggested putting fifty up for the sixth game. Here was where Micky lost his high and [got] flustered.

Carl put away every striped ball on the table in one turn, leaving himself a perfect shot on the eight. This he pushed in every so smoothly. The color began to drain from Micky's cheeks at the same time it returned to the smiling faces of Carl's friends. Micky started the next game with vengeance in his eyes. He was actually able to sink all of the solid balls but could not make the complicated bank shot he left himself on the eight ball. Here again Carl performed what he did in the prior game, but when it came to knocking in the winning ball which was on the edge of a pocket, he paused. The bet was only twenty-five dollars, enough for Micky to break even. He then tightened his grip on the stick and shot at the white ball. The cue scraped the ball awkwardly, moving it to the right about three inches, giving Micky a perfect angle on the winning shot. Solemnly he uttered, "Damn." James, standing in the corner, was struck by this decisive occurrence.

With a shaky stroke, Micky made that shot, then collected his twenty-five, and left with James in a confused state of mind.

★ ★ ★

This story, which could be called "A Connecticut Yankee in King Arnie's Pool Parlor," is very, very Charley, the Charley who existed before the onset of his illness and intermittently afterward. At the time he wrote it he was living with Grandpa Bob, and the two of them often played pool in the family basement, so the story comes out of his experience spending time with a much older man, one in many ways as eccentric as he and whom he respected and emulated. On the surface, the story is about a cocky, grandiose youth who gets a (somewhat confusing) life lesson. Micky is "high" on winning, feeling "invincible," his self-image tied up with his skill. An older man lets him win, but in such a way as to throw him into confusion about why, upsetting his apple cart.

The character of the not-very-bright Micky is Charley's ironic self-portrait. (In real life, his best friend in middle school in Culver City was named Jimmy.) It is the rational, balanced Charley's view of the grandiose, somewhat crazy Charley. But there's more to it than that. The old man, Carl, is also a self-portrait (denoted, for example, by the similarity in the character's and author's names). Carl "tipples," as Charley did in real life, carrying around a little hip flask. Carl is lonely and childless. He has lost his wife and is thus incomplete—since a woman, like pride, is necessary to make a man whole, *as Charley had written in his journal at the beginning of his love affair with Stephanie. ("The Pool Lesson" was written a few months after their traumatic breakup.) Carl understands from his own experience that a man "on a losing streak doesn't need his face rubbed in it." He himself has been on a losing streak, gently dissipating after his wife's death. (He is still the best pool player in town, though, so he is not a complete loser.) Micky, by contrast, has no self-knowledge. He is unaware of how others see him and is thus isolated by his own arrogance; only people who make allowances for him, like Jimmy, can stand being around him. On an immediate level, then, Carl's letting Micky win is a way of saving Micky's pride even though Micky doesn't deserve it. It is the act of grace of a damaged god, but one designed to make Micky think. On a deeper level, it is not only Carl's gift to Micky but to himself, because he sees Micky as his younger self, one still salvageable if he is able to become self-aware.* Whether Micky actually learns anything is left in doubt at the end. But there is no question that the author, presenting himself in two halves, is on some level aware of his own rivenness.*

---

*A rewritten version of the final paragraph, changed by Charley in response to class-room criticism, makes this identification explicit—in fact overexplicit. I have left the original, more interesting version in place.

Appendix C

Apples, Big Apples and Tangerines

Internal Contradictions in the
Brain-Disorder Model of Mental Illness

In the days when psychoanalysis ruled, when hours were fifty minutes long and lives were measured out not in coffee spoons but in the lengths of analyst couches, parents, particularly mothers, received most of the credit or blame—usually blame—for their children's outcomes. This was the post–World War II era of Refrigerator Mom, Schizophrenigenic Mom, and Jewish Mother Mom. If Mom was not affectionate enough she caused autism; if she was too affectionate she caused narcissism and homosexuality. Poor old Mom was damned if she did, damned if she didn't. Is it any wonder that many a mother took refuge in Valium and gin? Blaming Mom became so prevalent that Leo Kammer, who had coined the term *autism* in 1943 and been responsible for much of the "bad parenting" view, felt compelled to write a book called *In Defense of Mothers: How to Bring Up Children in Spite of the More Zealous Psychologists*.

How things have changed. With the fragmentation and decline of the Freudian school, the development of antipsychotic drugs (starting with Thorazine in the 1950s) and advances in brain research, the pendulum has swung away from psychological explanations of mental illness and toward the physical—or, more accurately, has swung back. Because from the time of the father of Western medicine, Hippocrates (fifth century B.C.), to the rise of Freud, Western doctors and philosophers considered mental illnesses to be physical ailments caused by an imbalance in the bodily "humours" or a diseased brain. It was treated by physical means: bloodletting, blistering, spinning on a rotating chair, mineral baths or lobotomy. The Freudian psychological theory that replaced the physical theory lasted less than a hundred years. The current idea that mental illness is a brain disease is thus not new. In the words of two historians of psychiatry, it is a return to the "traditional and prevalent approach."[1]

Whether it is a return based on a new and better understanding remains to be seen. What does not remain to be seen is that the physical theory of mental illness has become conventional wisdom. Mental illness is a medical condition, scientists and laymen alike instruct us, that exists independent of parental and other environmental causes. In my book I noted, among many other examples, Kay Redfield Jamison's unshakable view that manic-depression is a medical disorder and that not using medication to treat it is almost always malpractice.[2]

The medicalization of mental illness brings with it a number of supposed benefits, including specificity of treatment (e.g., just as diabetes is treated with insulin, schizophrenia is treated with antipsychotics) and destigmatization. If mental illness is neither a personality defect nor a result of bad parenting (or of bad medicine or social imbalances), nobody should have to feel guilty about it. On the National Alliance for the Mentally Ill's suggested reading list, for example, we find the title *It's Nobody's Fault: New Hope and Help for Difficult Children and Their Parents,* by Harold Koplewicz. "This work," the NAMI blurb says, "emphasizes that while parents are responsible for the treatment of their child's disorder, they are not to blame for the existence of the disorder."

The supposedly destigmatizing effect of the brain-disorder theory is no doubt one of the reasons it has done so well so quickly in supplanting the guilt- and angst-ridden Freudian view and become the new orthodoxy. Take, for example, a *New York Times* review of the book *Welcome to My Country* (1997) by psychologist Lauren Slater, which is an account of Slater's work as a talk therapist with the severely mentally ill in Boston. The reviewer, Michael Winerip (himself a writer about mental illness), while finding much to praise in Slater's book, faults her for seeming "to give serious weight to the theory that schizophrenia can be caused by bad parenting. Most experts agree that it is an organic brain dysfunction that has little or nothing to do with an individual's environment." Similarly with manic-depressive illness, a disease with "indisputable biological roots."[3]

Physical Problem, Physical Solution

The brain-disorder theory does more than take away blame and stigma, we are told. Defining mental illness as physical seems to pull it out of the clouds of psychology and "mind" and settle it in the earthly world of bodily ailments like diabetes, heart disease, hypertension and tuberculosis, which, fearsome as they may be, are at least physically knowable and thus physically treatable. Such apparent demystification has enormous appeal because it seems to allow us to grasp, and therefore control, something that previously was smoky and elusive. It fits particularly well with the American national character, our positive, can-do spirit and belief in scientific progress. With its new-world, no-nonsense Yankee optimism, the biochemical model seems to stand in shining contrast to the gloomier Europeanism of Freud, who, far from promising that his insights would facilitate "life, liberty, and the pursuit of happiness," seemed to think that the best one could hope for in this life was to crawl out of the depths of abject misery and, through long and arduous introspection, eventually arrive at the summit of "ordinary unhappiness."

Long and arduous and *expensive* introspection. Beyond its alleged power to destigmatize and demystify, the brain-disorder model promises economy of treatment. Medication, the current standard of care for mental disorders major and minor, is cheaper than long years of psychotherapy and apparently more effective. Lithium does, after all, control wild mood swings in most cases, and antipsychotics do tend to tamp down delusions and hallucinations. Even in fuzzy cases like Charley's, more and more the notion is that *some* medication or medications will eventually work. It's a question of making the right "differential diagnosis" for a given patient based on observation of symptoms as listed in the *Diagnostic and Statistical Manual of Mental Disorders,* then finding the right medication or medications, then adjusting the medication and, if necessary, the diagnosis.

Given the appeal of the biological model—no blame, no stigma, no big therapists' bills—who could possibly object to it? The common view is that no one in his right mind would. The few dissidents in the psychiatric community like Thomas Szasz or Peter Breggin or Edward Podvoll are written off as flat-earthers, cranks and curmudgeons—or worse, malpracticers—because they don't like medication. Refractory "psychiatric survivors" like Kate Millett or refractory nonsurvivors like Charley are shrugged off as just not knowing what's good for them. The small percentage of persons diagnosed as mentally ill who are violent—like the Unabomber Ted Kaczynski—are pointed to as reasons for increasing government power to hospitalize and medicate people against their will. Since everybody knows that mental illness is a physical, treatable brain disorder, seeing it any other way is frivolous or even dangerous. Not to use drugs or (increasingly) electroconvulsive therapy is malpractice.

"Most Experts Agree . . ."

> The public should take scientific discoveries with a grain of salt—the bigger the claim, the more salt. . . . "It would not hurt the public to pick up on the feeling that when experts say something it isn't necessarily true," [NASA astronomer Stephen P.] Maran said. "It's just what the experts are saying."[4]

Frederick K. Goodwin and Kay Redfield Jamison's 1990 book, *Manic-Depressive Illness,* is an enormous work, not only physically (938 pages) but in scholarship and scope; the bibliography alone runs more than 120 pages. And yet, toward the end of its section on the biology (or "pathophysiology") of manic-depression, itself more than two hundred pages long, the authors indicate how little is still known about the most basic things. For example: "There is some suggestion of a rough similarity in some anatomical measures between manic-depressive illness and schizophrenia."[5] The tentativeness of the phrasing, like that of the National Institute of Mental Health's discussion of schizophrenia cited in the text of this book (see pages 93–94), illustrates how unsettled so much of the research is. For example, are the disruptions of brain neurotransmitters the cause of manic-depression or its effects? Goodwin and Jamison talk about "the relatively unsophisticated way that the concept of causality has been applied. All too often, pathophysiology is taken as etiology, at least implicitly."[6]

In plain English: the chemical malfunctioning (the pathophysiology) that characterizes manic-depression is assumed to be the cause or origin (etiology) of the illness, an assumption that Goodwin and Jamison term a "reductionist fallacy." Other fallacies "include reasoning backward from the effects of drugs to pathophysiology and the (usually implicit) assumption that understanding the components is tantamount to understanding the whole."[7]

That was 1990. Five years later, in her memoir *An Unquiet Mind* (1995), Jamison doesn't have that much to add. Toward the end she writes about attending a conference on the latest findings on "structural abnormalities" in the brains of bipolar patients found through magnetic resonance imaging (MRI) and positron emission tomography (PET), which view the living brain. She talks about the "intuitive appeal" of the images derived. PET, for example, shows a depressed brain as a chilly blue, a hypomanic brain as bright red and orange. Yet she admits that such images in themselves do not tell us whether the "hyperintensities" (nicknamed "unidentified bright objects" or UBOs) are the cause or the effect of the illness.[8] After talking about how the conference pushed her to do further reading on "structural brain abnormalities" and "subcortical abnormalities" detected using MRI, Jamison concludes that

> it was unclear what any of these findings really meant: they could be due to problems in measurement, they could be explained by dietary or treatment history [e.g., the effects of medication—JA], they could be due to something totally unrelated to manic-depressive illness; there could be any number of other explanations. The odds were very strong, however, that the UBOs meant *something*.[9] (emphasis in the original)

We are still not sure, in other words, whether brain abnormalities are the cause or the effect of manic-depressive illness, although we're pretty sure they mean "something." Four years later, in her book on suicide, *Night Falls Fast,* Jamison says in a parenthetical sentence during a discussion of schizophrenia, "Not surprisingly, brain-imaging studies reveal pronounced differences in structure and functioning between individuals who have schizophrenia and those who do not."[10] What *is* surprising is that Jamison, in a book that has ninety-five pages of notes, does not provide a single reference to back up the assertions made in this sentence, which goes far beyond what NIMH says about the same questions of brain structure, functioning, etc. (again, see pages 93–94 of my book).

Taking Away the Stigma?

And what about stigma? Does the brain-disease model really destigmatize mental illness?

In *An Unquiet Mind*, as I have noted (see page 344), Kay Redfield Jamison talks about the moral and ethical issues that will arise when and if manic-depression is proven to be genetic and its specific gene or genes are located.[11] Will pregnant women with family histories of manic-depression have prenatal genetic testing done on their fetuses? Will they be encouraged to have abortions if the tests prove that the child is likely to be manic-depressive? As I have also noted, Jamison talks of being reduced to tears by a physician's telling her she shouldn't have children because she is manic-depressive.[12] What will happen when women with far less knowledge or self-assurance or fewer resources are confronted with similar godlike pronouncements?

Despite the supposedly enlightened nature of current scientific thinking, the asylum model of treating mental illness—that is, the practice of quarantining people in conceptual categories if not always in actual psych wards—is still alive and well. It is only the locus of the stigma that has changed, from personality (or parents) to genes, which in a way is even more devastating because you can work on your personality or escape (or forgive) your parents, but how can you change your genes? (Gene therapy so far has, to say the least, not given grounds for much encouragement.) Kay Jamison is told not to have children. Schizophrenics are told that people with their disease seldom get better and that the best they can do is manage their condition, which means not expecting too much out of life since they must avoid "stress." Too much stress—the wear and tear of what most people call living—will counteract their medication and bring back their psychoses. Better to stay home or at a board-and-care or halfway house and at most work at a low-stress (translation: dull and repetitive) job.

This supposed destigmatization is leading in other unintended directions as well. Traditionally, particularly in the United States, manic-depressive illness has been underdiagnosed and confused with schizophrenia. As I discuss in this book, I saw this firsthand in the confusion at Ryles Center, where a bipolar staff person told me that Charley was bipolar, while Gayle, the director, told me he was probably schizophrenic. Except for Dr. Gray, who never made a definitive diagnosis, the first thumbnail diagnosis that Charley's other psychiatrists and psychologists made was schizophrenia or something related to it (such as "schizophreniform" or "schizotypal" or schizoaffective disorder.)

Recently, though, a countertrend has been developing in the form of a sort of definitional enlargement of the mood disorder "box" (or pigeon hole) and a shrinking of the schizophrenia box. Artists in particular, as well as "leaders" of various stripes, from Lincoln to Churchill, are being placed in the mood-disorder (manic-depression or depression) box. Van Gogh, for example, who was once assumed to be schizophrenic, has been recategorized as manic-depressive. (Not by everybody. Some people believe he had a physical disease called porphyria.) In fact Kay Jamison wrote an entire other book, *Touched with Fire,* about the connection between creativity and mood disorder. She claims that manic-depressive illness is skewed not only toward artists (particularly poets and musicians) but toward the (ostensibly more energetic and creative) upper classes, and may even be part of the reason for their success. She theorizes that the positive features of manic-depressive illness have had evolutionary advantages that counteract its negative qualities and perhaps explain the illness's continued genetic survival in the species.

We might think that seeing more mood disorder and less schizophrenia is good news, since mood disorder is supposedly easier to treat. But for every winner there's a loser. Since all the creative people and high achievers are now out of the schizophrenia box and in the mood disorder box, only the uncreative dregs are left in the schizophrenia box. The new categorization system is, again, taking on a class bias, with mood disorders becoming the upper-class disease and schizophrenia the lower-class. In a recent book from Australia, a neuropsychologist named Richard Gates writes,

> There is considerable evidence that although schizophrenia affects people from all levels of society, it tends to occur more frequently among the lower socioeconomic groups. Some studies suggest that the ratio may be as high as eight to one. One interpretation of this disproportionate representation is that sufferers of the disease are more likely to slide downwards because they are unable to maintain themselves at higher economic and social levels. . . . It seems probable that the illness pushes individuals into a lower socioeconomic status, rather than their coming from such status to begin with.[13]

I remember falling into this way of thinking with Charley. If you have to be crazy, it's better to be manic-depressive than schizophrenic, not only because manic-depression is supposedly more treatable but because it's more socially acceptable. This is fine unless you happen to be diagnosed as schizophrenic. Or what if you were told before that you're manic-depressive and then a new psychiatrist tells you, no, you're schizophrenic or schizoaffective (which also happened to Charley)? Such a "demotion" could have a very demoralizing effect.

The constantly shifting diagnostic boundaries, changing with every new addition of the *Diagnostic and Statistical Manual,* attest to the extreme subjectivity and arbitrariness of the current methodology of categorizing mental illnesses.[14]

Apple or Tangerine?

Frederick Goodwin and Kay Redfield Jamison, both in their joint work and in Jamison's solo efforts, grapple with the uncertainties and confusion that continue to plague the efforts of researchers to define and fix the conceptual categories of mental illnesses, particularly mood disorders. But instead of seeing these uncertainties and confusions as reflecting the uncertainties and confusions of real life, Goodwin and Jamison believe that they are temporary, solvable problems that will be swept away by the march of science; the more precise our understanding of brain chemistry and genetics becomes, the more precise the categories of mental disease will become. But is this really true? In order to suggest an answer, let us talk for a moment about apples and tangerines. This discussion, if it is as fruitful as its subjects, will help us further understand the belief system or mindset that underlies the brain-disease school of mental illness, a belief system that (in my opinion) only seems to stem from the science but in fact precedes and in the end undermines it.

In her books on mood disorders, Jamison, like other researchers, wrestles with the question of whether different mental illnesses are discrete "disease entities" with hard borders between them or whether they exist on a continuum or spectrum, shading into each other. In *Manic-Depressive Illness,* she and Goodwin use the analogy of the citrus fruit versus the apple. Does mental illness have separate segments, like a tangerine—one segment being manic depression, another segment being schizophrenia, another segment being schizoaffective disorder, another segment being "personality disorders," and so on—or is it like an apple, which must be artificially sliced up with a conceptual knife? In that book, written in 1990, Goodwin and Jamison do not answer this question, although they seem at times to "shade" toward the "apple" model. In her later solo works, Jamison seems to move closer toward the apple model and even beyond it to what might be called the "big apple" model—the idea that, at least in the case of affective (mood) disorders, these disorders exist not only on a spectrum but on the *same* spectrum as "normal" moods. There is one big continuum compromising all moods, in other words, both disordered and normal, healthy and diseased.

In *Touched with Fire,* Jamison's book on manic-depression and the artistic temperament, her views almost seem to evolve in the course of her analysis. On page 81, she talks about how "[t]he affective continuum that ranges from normal states through hypomania and then mania is very important, but poorly understood. It remains unclear whether the overlap in cognitive and mood changes represents etiologically related syndromes or phenomenologically similar but causally unrelated patterns of expression."[15] This is science-speak for saying we don't know whether different mood states are, or just seem to be, related. Fifty pages later, however, Jamison appears to be inclined toward taking a bite out of what I'm calling the "big apple" (they *are* all related) model, although she doesn't exactly say it herself. She cites studies by other researchers comparing the "infradian" rhythms[16] of bipolar and "healthy" control subjects, quoting them as saying:

> The principal difference between patients and control subjects is the amplitude of cycles, and hence, affective symptoms may be considered *a variant of normal hedonic states. . . . Affective symptoms seem to be universal,* with a periodic component that differs *in degree rather than kind;* the pattern of cycles for ill persons is defined by amplitude. This makes affective disorder akin to hypertension and diabetes, wherein a physiological variable *shades into* a pathological variant.[17] (emphasis added by me—JA)

Mood disorders like manic-depression, in other words, are merely extreme forms of normal behavior.

Thirty pages later in a chapter on Lord Byron, whose brief, tumultuous

life in many ways reminded me of Charley's, Jamison returns to the diabetes/
hypertension analogy:

> Byron's fiery and melancholic temperament at times crossed over *the fine line*
> that separates illness from health. (This is analogous to many other medical con-
> ditions—for example, diabetes, thyroid disease, and hypertension—in which the
> underlying predisposition flares up, from time to time, into acute disease. Such
> exacerbations of ongoing metabolic and other states may be temporary and ulti-
> mately self-correcting, representing only short-term discomfort and possible
> danger, or they may be progressive and life threatening. But they can also be
> both, and manic-depressive illness tends to fit this latter description.) In Byron's
> case aspects of his underlying temperament often worsened into periods of
> painful melancholia and disruptive, perturbed mental states; by the end of his life
> these periods of emotional distress began to outweigh periods of health. His tem-
> perament also, however, made him exquisitely responsive to virtually everything
> in his physical and psychological world; it gave to him much of his great capac-
> ity for passion and understanding, as well as for suffering.[18] (emphasis added)

All of these passages point toward a continuum or "big apple" model of
manic-depression. Now compare them with the epilogue—the final summation—of *Manic-Depressive Illness*. Here Goodwin and Jamison also speak of the
importance of correctly differentiating between pathological and normal, but
then seem to draw a different conclusion, one based on the tangerine model:

> Diagnostic issues remain an important part of the clinical practice and sci-
> entific understanding of manic-depressive illness. The very fact that an illness
> can be expressed in various ways—as temperament, seasonal swings of mood,
> morbid melancholia, mixtures of mania and depression, or unmanageable psy-
> chosis—speaks to the complexity of the manic-depressive spectrum. The ten-
> dency of clinicians to underdiagnose bipolar disorder in favor of schizophrenia
> or borderline personality disorders is now being replaced by an opposite ten-
> dency to diffuse *the core concept* of manic-depressive illness by including mild sea-
> sonal affective disorders and often unclearly defined bipolar-II conditions.
> Clearly, underinclusiveness results in an unacceptably large number of patients
> being denied effective treatment. Overinclusion, on the other hand, risks trivi-
> alization of a serious disease, inappropriate treatment, *blurring of meaningful*
> *diagnostic and genetic borders,* and the labeling as pathological that which is in
> many people *simply a variant of normal temperament.* These diagnostic subtleties
> *will, no doubt, be clarified* by increasingly sophisticated diagnostic criteria using
> combined measures of biological markers, family history, subtypings on the basis

of natural course and treatment response, and, eventually, neuropsychiatric profiles, brain-imaging patterns, laboratory techniques, and chromosome specification.[19] (emphasis added)

Here, particularly in that last sentence—the "will, no doubt"—we come to the gist of the matter, the underlying (and unproven) belief system of the "brain disorder" school. We'll get to that in a moment. But first: If I'm reading this epilogue correctly, it's saying something different from the previous passages, where we find statements like "affective symptoms may be considered *a variant of normal hedonic states,*" that is, different from good health in quantity ("amplitude"), not quality.[20] The epilogue, by contrast, insists that there is a *qualitative* difference not only between manic-depression and health but between manic-depression and such things as "mild seasonal affective disorders and often unclearly defined bipolar-II conditions," which in many people, Goodwin and Jamison say, are "simply a variant of normal temperament." Lumping them together with manic-depression diffuses the core concept of the illness, they insist, leading to "overinclusion" and the "blurring of meaningful diagnostic and genetic borders."

But does an "unblurred" distinction in fact exist, or is the blurring—which Goodwin and Jamison themselves engage in elsewhere—being done for good reason, namely that *reality itself is blurry,* the boundaries within it at most "shadings" and "fine lines" and "variants"?

In this epilogue to *Manic-Depressive Illness,* Goodwin and Jamison seem to sense the corner they have painted themselves into: They have tried for eight hundred pages to isolate a "serious disease" but even now can't really say what it is. Is it a slice of an apple (whether a small one or a big one), or a section of a tangerine? Is it a variation of normal mood states, or something unique? Was Kraepelin right in making a firm distinction between manic-depression and schizophrenia, or do hybrids like "schizoaffective disorder" and other ambiguous conditions throw the whole analytical scheme into disarray?

Goodwin and Jamison cannot answer any of these questions. But instead of dealing with the possibility that they find themselves painted into a corner because of a basic problem with their painting technique (they started from the wrong end of the room), they perform a little rhetorical leap out of their corner, attributing the conceptual blurriness ("diagnostic subtleties") not to the fact that reality itself is blurry but to the inadequacy of current knowledge. "No doubt" such subtleties will be clarified some time down the road. In other words, they assume as a given the very thing that needs to be proved. A verbal wave of the hand—"no doubt"—substitutes for argument. It's "no doubt" just a matter of time before we bag the abominable snowman.

I'm not trying to play word games, and I'm not accusing Goodwin and Jamison of consciously trying to deceive. Their problem is something different, so basic that they're probably not even aware of it. It's that the direction of research—*toward* blurriness, *toward* the "big apple" model of affective (and cognitive) states—is tending to contradict their theoretical belief system, a system that says that mental illnesses are objective, physical brain disorders that exist in traditional, discrete categories. When reality and mindset collide, mainstream psychiatry assures us that the pileup is just temporary. The now-blurry reality will "no doubt" become clearer and better defined as the diagnostic tools—biological markers, family history, brain imaging, etc.—become sharper.

But what if this is not true? What if it is precisely the increasing *sharpness* of the tools (mapping the genome, for example) that is leading *to* the greater *blurring* of distinctions, not away from them? Eighty years ago, with Kraepelin, the distinction between schizophrenia and manic-depressive illness was clear—or seemed to be. It has become steadily more confused ever since then, not because scientists know *less* but because they know *more*. It is like looking at a photograph in a newspaper. It looks coherent from a distance, but the closer we get, particularly as we look through a magnifying glass and then a microscope, the more the recognizable image dissolves into a chaos of dots. Why should we expect this trend suddenly to reverse?

I apologize for what may seem like "angels on the head of a pin" nitpicking. I have argued in this way for two reasons. The first is to try to show the internal inconsistencies of even the most advanced mainstream psychiatry, the worm of doubt that is gnawing within the belly of the beast itself—whether that "beast" is an apple, a tangerine or the abominable snowman. Second, and related to this, my experience with Charley convinced me of the critical importance of framing the question of what mental illness is in the right way, neither underestimating its seriousness nor (so to speak) absolutizing it, attributing to it more independent reality than it has. Mainstream psychiatry has done the latter. Rather than illuminating the individual's psychological landscape as a whole, the brain-disorder model has distorted that landscape even more by casting an extremely strong but narrow light on one small patch of mental territory, throwing the rest, by contrast, into even deeper shadow.

Finally, a note on angels: For a long time I wondered how medieval theologians could waste their time on questions like how many angels can dance on the head of a pin. But then one day I found out that I had misunderstood what the argument was really about. It was not about whether, say, four as opposed to seven angels can dance on the head of a pin, but whether *any* can— that is, whether angels have mass. If they do have mass, then not even one angel can dance on a pin. If they are pure spirit, any number can. The debate, in other words, was about the *nature* of angels, not their size. Similarly, the current debate about mental illness is about the nature, not the size, of dragons.

Appendix D

Charley's Smoking List

Reasons to not smoke
1. Costs money ($2.30–2.60/pack)
2. Smells up breath
3. Smells up clothing
4. Stains teeth
5. Can be antisocial
6. Smells up rooms
7. Causes cancer, emphysema, etc.
8. Inhibits exercise
9. Causes lethargy
10. Dulls nose and taste buds
11. Causes a certain lifestyle paralysis
12. Becomes obsessive
13. Can be enslaving
14. Bothers my mom
15. Smoking is considered a weakness
16. Irritates throat and lungs and can cause asthma
17. I wake up feeling languid
18. Inhibits creativity
19. Addiction can cause inconvenience
20. Just generally *vile*

Reasons to smoke

1. Helps me sleep
2. I enjoy it
3. Helps me relax
4. Fills a certain emptiness inside
5. I'm addicted
6. Creates a social ambiance
7. Stimulates me
8. Goes well after sex
9. Goes well after meals
10. Goes great with coffee
11. Gives hands an occupation
12. Fulfills infantile craving to have something in mouth
13. My folks don't smoke
14. Goes well with a drink
15. Keeps me company in solitude, i.e. allows private time
16. Helps me focus sometimes
17. Goes great after getting stoned

Appendix E

Contact Information for
Alternative Recovery Facilities

Below is contact information for the two recovery facilities/models whose theories and practices I talk about in the book and with which I have had personal contact. Windhorse, based on the work of Dr. Edward Podvoll, has two facilities in the United States, and I am providing available information for both of them. (When this book went to press, the Colorado facility was in the process of being set up and did not yet have a phone number.) Both the Village and Windhorse have Web sites where further information is available.

The Village Integrated Service Agency
456 Elm Avenue
Long Beach, California 90802
Phone: (562) 437-6717
Web site: *www.village-isa.org*

Windhorse Associates
31 Trumbull Road, Suite 2
Northampton, Massachusetts 01060
Phone: (413) 586-0207
Web site: *www.WindhorseAssociates.org*

Windhorse Community Services
3050 15th Street
Boulder, Colorado 80304
Web site: *www.WindhorseCommunityServices.com*

Notes

Chapter 1: Prologue

[1] Sidebar, *Santa Monica Outlook,* 2 November 1996, sec. B, 1.

Chapter 2: Wrong Turn at Yosemite

[1] *www.mentalhealth.com,* 1999.

[2] Ibid.

[3] This turned out to be not strictly correct according to current usage. In recent years the time frame for brief reactive psychosis has been extended to thirty days. Such changes from edition to edition of the *DSM* are common.

[4] Charley's journals indicate that it was probably Brian Marsh.

Chapter 3: "The Brightest Little Boy in the Whole Park"

[1] See Appendix A for the entire poem.

[2] See Appendix B for a short story Charley wrote around this time that demonstrates his own awareness of his two-sidedness.

Chapter 4: "One More Bloody Year of Reed"

[1] I am inferring this from a journal entry of about five weeks later (June 19) where Charley talks about "learning the proletarian lifestyle" (as Lin and I had done years before) by working at Café Athens. He's having problems saving money, which he attributes to his relations with his parents. "My parents have a problem with money, with being comfortable with it. Both Mom and Dad have a sort of money complex (perhaps owing to their former political ideology, their familial backgrounds—something or other—I really don't know) but my plan is to break away from these detrimental

patterns and live a healthy financial existence. . . ."

2   In a journal entry about five weeks later Charley expresses this himself in
a very interesting way:

> It's 1:20 A.M. Sunday morning, time to make another entry. I'm sitting at
> the kitchen table of my father's apartment, with lots of stuff on my mind. I've
> just taken a shower, having washed myself of the restaurant business. That's
> another subject I'm tired of thinking about, but while I'm on it I may as well
> mention the dream I had last night. I had just matriculated into the San
> Francisco Conservatory of Music and I was arranging my accommodations
> (the school does not provide this in reality) and was incorporating myself
> into the place when I noticed two busboys from my restaurant came in plan-
> ning to attend. All else I can remember is that I felt threatened by this, quite
> deeply. My interpretation of this is simple. My feeling threatened by the bus-
> boys represents the desire I have to live a lifestyle above the working class,
> not among them. It's a wish to be separated by [sic] that "cruel" world and
> have values which they cannot appreciate. This subconscious phenomenon is
> incongruous with reality because I fraternize openly with my coworkers and
> do not take a haughty attitude with them in the least. Perhaps this dream is
> impertinent [doesn't pertain] to the busboys per se and is mostly demonstra-
> tive of my true desire to live outside the mainstream.

In other words, the busboys in the dream invading SFCM weren't the
Central American and Mexican refugees "who work like mules for rich
men," as Charley had written earlier, people he worked with and respected.
They were the part of him—the ordinary, proletarian part—that he was
trying to escape but that kept dogging him, both in his dreams and in his
actual life. He also, as I mentioned, associated this part of himself with his
parents, with our history, which he could not really understand, of giving
up our educational and other advantages to go to work in factories and
other less-remunerative jobs.

3   Years later, after Charley's death, I found a sheet of paper in his desk entitled
"The Warren W. Wilcox Hallucinogenic State," which outlines eight steps
to achieving that state. After presenting steps for relaxing (correct body
position, deep breathing, concentration), it culminates with steps six and
seven:

6. **Hypnagogic Imagery.** If you have been able to relax fully, and not become distracted, an image may suddenly appear in your mind. Often the image is a clear picture, like on a postcard. These images come from deep in your mind and may or may not be familiar to you. Again, during this stage, it is important not to consciously think about anything, or try to *make* something appear. Let your mind create for you and just watch. Later we will work on controlling your images.

7. **Goal Imagery.** As you gain skill in relaxation technique, it will become possible for you to control your imagery. Pick a habit or fault, or a project for self-improvement, and imagine yourself as free and happy as you would really like to be. Then go through the Scale and create a hypnagogic image that helps you toward this goal. For instance, a worried, nervous person could picture himself as smiling and relaxed. A person trying to quit smoking could see herself as relaxed and free from the habit, able to smell again, etc. You will find that *being able to see yourself* as you really want to be helps you to *be* that way.

⁴ Years later I learned about a town in Belgium near Antwerp called Geel (also spelled "Gheel"), which for hundreds of years has functioned as a kind of therapeutic village, taking in the mentally ill, who are adopted by families and treated as family members. A recent account includes the following:

> **Geel, Belgium Uses The Legend Of St. Dimpna As A Model Of Treatment.** The system of care in Geel for the mentally ill and retarded is based on a religious tradition stemming from the legend of St. Dimpna. According to legend, supplemented by bits of historical fact, an Irish king made incestuous demands of Dimpna, his daughter, after the death of his wife. Dimpna fled the country accompanied by her confessor and tutor, Gerebernus, in a boat across the North Sea and landed in Belgium. The two traveled overland and hid in the region of Geel. The king pursued and beheaded them both with a sword in approximately 600 A.D. At the moment of Dimpna's beheading it is said the king's sanity was restored.
>
> Many of the boarders in Geelian families are severely mentally ill and retarded individuals who are not considered to be suitable candidates for the majority of community care programs in the United States. Taking into account the type of patient Geel attracts, mainly chronic patients with no viable family or community ties, these individuals would otherwise spend their lives on the back wards of state hospitals. To the dismay of professionals, Geelians just do not see the boarders as psychiatric patients. Boarders are

included in the work and recreational activities of their families and are also free to participate on their own in the community sphere. Boarders are quite visible in the churches, cafes, local fairs, the movie house and at sports events. Cafes, of which there are 143 in the town, are places of social interaction for all Geelians. Boarders socialize with others in cafes, some spend their time actively hallucinating at a corner table, others cannot be distinguished from the "normal" customers. . . . The police, too, tend to be protective of the boarders. According to the chief of police, Geel has a lower crime rate than the surrounding communities. ("Geel, Belgium: A Radical Model for the Integration of Deviancy," in Ellen Baxter, *The Community Imperative,* reproduced on Mental Health Consumer Network, Consumer Network News, Cincinnati, *www.mentalhealthconsumers.org/connet/cnn/9711/november.htm.*)

It is possible that Dr. Gray, who said that he had read about the French therapeutic village many years earlier, was actually referring to Belgium's Geel.

[5] *www.mentalhealth.com,* 1999.

[6] Some researchers make a distinction between the terms "manic-depressive disorder" and "bipolar disorder," saying that the former category includes unipolar depression. This is part of the trend toward reducing the three major mental illnesses to two (mood disorder and thought disorder). In keeping with general usage, however, I will use the terms as meaning the same thing.

[7] In a recent book about suicide, *Night Falls Fast,* Kay Redfield Jamison (of whom I will speak more later) states that although she believes firmly in the organic or brain-disease hypothesis of mental illness, there is still a lot that isn't known about neurotransmitters, whose imbalances are thought to cause much of mental illness. "No one knows how many transmitters there are, nor does anyone fully understand the actions of the more than one hundred identified to date. . . . For scientists to focus on one or two substances [such as serotonin or dopamine—JA] at the expense of others known or yet to be discovered, or to minimize the complexity of the chemical interactions within the brain or the synapses, would be a damning mistake, a late-twentieth-century equivalent of earlier, primitive views that deranged minds were caused by satanic spells or an excess of phosphorous and vapors" (Kay Redfield Jamison, *Night Falls Fast* [New York: Knopf, 1999], 183–84).

[8]   *www.nimh.nih.gov/publicat/schizoph.*

[9]   Ibid.

[10]   The brain-diseasers don't rule out *all* psychotherapy, as I will talk about later, but they narrow it down, sometimes insistently (as I will also talk about later), to basically helping the person cope with having a brain disease and having to take often unpleasant and "stigmatizing" medications. Psychotherapy, in other words, is at best a subsidiary treatment, and thus the first to go when something has to be cut back.

[11]   Frederick K. Goodwin, M.D., and Kay Redfield Jamison, Ph.D., *Manic-Depressive Illness* (New York and Oxford: Oxford University Press, 1990), 17–8.

[12]   Ibid., 24.

[13]   W. Mayer-Gross, E. Slater, and M. Roth, *Clinical Psychiatry* (second edition) (London: Cassell & Co., 1960, 213–14), quoted in ibid., 24–5.

[14]   Emil Kraepelin, *Manic-Depressive Insanity and Paranoia* (translated by R. M. Barclay, edited by G. M. Robertson) (Edinburgh: E & S Livingstone, 1921), 70–1, quoted in ibid., 25.

[15]   Ibid., 27.

[16]   D. L. Murphy and A. Beigel, "Depression, Elation, and Lithium Carbonate Responses in Manic Patient Subgroups," *Archives of General Psychiatry,* 31 (1974): 647, quoted in ibid., 30–1.

[17]   Jamison talks in various places (e.g., Jamison 1999, 179; and Jamison 1993 [see note 1, chapter 5 on the following page], 87) about how mood disorders may actually have evolutionary benefits, and how especially manic-depression seems to correlate with upper-class status. The energy associated with mania or hypomania, in other words, can lead to evolutionary and social success. Schizophrenia, by contrast, in a kind of polarization and ghettoization process that has gone on in mental health research and writing, has become associated with social failure and lower-class status. As a result, in a self-fulfilling-prophesy kind of way, the rich (and/or the artistic) tend to be diagnosed with manic–depression, the poor with schizophrenia. See Appendix C for a fuller discussion of this and other aspects of the hidden presuppositions and biases in current psychiatric research.

[18]   Carlos Tejada and Patrick Barta, *The Wall Street Journal,* 7 January 2000, sec. A, 1.

19 Ibid.

20 Ibid., sec. A, 6.

21 Ibid.

22 Ibid.

23 Kate Millett, *The Loony-Bin Trip,* (New York: Touchstone [Simon & Schuster], 1990), 11.

24 Ibid., 31.

25 Ibid., 94–5.

26 Ibid., 72.

27 Ibid., 309.

28 Kay Redfield Jamison, *An Unquiet Mind* (New York: Knopf, 1995), 93–5.

29 Ibid., 161–62.

30 Ibid., 112.

31 Ibid., 166.

32 Ibid., 102.

33 Ibid., 204. *Cyclothymia* means "mood swings."

34 Ibid., 217–18.

35 Ibid., 92.

36 Ibid., 98.

37 Ibid., 102.

Chapter 5: M. Butterfly and Mr. Lithy

1 Kay Redfield Jamison, *Touched with Fire: Manic-Depressive Illness and the Artistic Temperament* (New York: The Free Press [div. of Macmillan], 1993), 15.

2 *www.mentalhealth.com*, 1999.

3 The number 22 is important in numerology, which Charley had taken up. I think numerology, which *Webster's Dictionary* defines as "the study of the occult significance of numbers," appealed to Charley for a couple of reasons. First, it appealed to his need for structure in a world in which he had never been fully at home and which tended to appear increasingly fragmented and pointless as his illness evolved. (He also expressed an interest in other secret "orders" like Freemasonry or, as we have seen, TM with its ascending stages of consciousness.) Also, I think numerology especially appealed to Charley's hypomanic or manic side. When one is in especially the early, god-like stage of mania, the mind can be incredibly supple and

quick, delighting in puns and wordplay and the seeming fluidity and inter-connectedness of all things, their ability to change form, to transmogrify into each other at enormous speed. Charley used to love to rattle off, say, a string of associations between the numbers involved in the letters that spelled his name, or his birthday, or other dates, or other things related to him or me. It seemed like a way of controlling the world and his place in it by turning the fragmented and ordinary into a magical unity.

4 But even the piano was not without problems. Some time in late winter/spring—unfortunately I can't pinpoint the date—Charley got stage fright at a Friday afternoon recital he had been preparing for, and he was unable to perform. The experience, in the Reed chapel in front of an audi-ence, was mortifying. I wonder now, although I have no direct evidence, whether the months of piano playing rather than studying might have rep-resented the continuation of Charley's vision of switching from Reed—that is, path C, the somewhat boring life of the mind—to music school and becoming a concert pianist—path B, the great artist. If this is true, the humiliation of the stage fright could have loomed larger in what came after than anyone suspected at the time.

5 The Englishman John Custance, who wrote a book called *Wisdom, Madness, and Folly,* published in 1952.

6 This is true of psychoses other than mania—even of paranoid schizophre-nia, where "everybody is out to get" the paranoid individual. This seems log-ically impossible. How can paranoid thinking be solipsistic? That is, if nobody else exists, how can "everybody" be out to get the one being who *does* exist? Because they exist *only* to get him, and so have no *independent* existence. Similarly with depression, where the person has an excessively low rather than high sense of self-worth. AA people have an expression for such negative self-aggrandizement: "I'm the worthless piece of shit the entire uni-verse revolves around."

7 *www.mentalhealth.com,* 1999.

8 Ibid.

9 The main problem I have with *Toxic Psychiatry* is that Breggin makes the ques-tion of medication vs. no medication *the* question, and thus becomes a kind of (weirdly symbiotic) "intimate enemy" or flip side of mainstream psychiatry, which does the same thing from the opposite side. It is not enough for Breggin

to point out the health dangers of psychiatric drugs. He must also condemn their use *in principle* as being a crutch, a moral failure like street drugs or alcohol. "We must ask ourselves," says Breggin,

> whether drugs actually help people understand and take better control over their inner mental lives and their conduct, and we must ask ourselves whether the potential *moral downside* isn't too great. Taking psychoactive drugs on a regular basis readily becomes a symbolic gesture that interferes with personal growth and even fosters personal failure.... I don't believe that the desire to handle life through a psychiatric drug is essentially different from the desire to do it with alcohol, and I don't believe that physicians should look upon it more favorably. (Peter R. Breggin, M.D., *Toxic Psychiatry* [New York: St. Martin's Press], 1991, 182, emphasis added)

Well, maybe. But a lot of people I love and admire have handled their lives through alcohol (and drugs), and some of them have done great things. Who am I to say they were moral or personal failures? And who is "we"? To me it sounds too much like the "royal" we. I value Breggin as a crusader who is fundamentally on the right side, struggling against the brain-disease theory of mental illness, the false claims by drug companies, the foisting of heavy drugs on children, etc. But self-righteousness, the occupational hazard of crusaders, is all too often effectively used by their enemies to paint them as cranks and kooks—which I don't believe Breggin is. But Breggin has no more right to finger-shakingly "forbid" people to take medication than psychopharmacological psychiatrists have a right to force medication on them. Some medications work for some people. The answer, it seems to me, has to be an attitude of extreme skepticism about any claims made on behalf of any medications, full disclosure of their nature and side effects and long-term dangers, fully informed consent by people taking them, and a constant search for alternatives.

Chapter 6: Weaving the Shroud

[1] Robert Lowell, *Day by Day* (New York: Farrar, Straus and Giroux, 1977), 113, quoted in Goodwin and Jamison, 732.

[2] Edward M. Podvoll, M.D., *The Seduction of Madness* (New York: HarperCollins, 1990), 122.

3   Ibid.

4   InteliHealth, Johns Hopkins Drug Resource Center Web site, 1999.

5   Actually, the River Community bridge was not entirely burned. In my efforts to get my refund, I negotiated and (despite my threatening letters) developed cordial relations with River Community's head, an old activist about my age who was also an avid cyclist. As our negotiations concluded he told me that Charley, whom he had met at one of our negotiating sessions, had a standing invitation to come back to River Community any time he wanted for as long as he wanted, and I wouldn't have to pay. They would accept his SSI check for the first month as well as every one afterward. I told Charley this, but he didn't seem interested.

6   Goodwin and Jamison, 588.

7   Ibid., 594, emphasis added.

8   Ibid.

9   Aside from journal entries I have cited, see Appendix D regarding Charley's attitude toward smoking. In *Night Falls Fast* Kay Redfield Jamison says, "Smoking cigarettes . . . is far more common in those who commit suicide than those who do not—and also more common in patients with schizophrenia, alcoholism, depression, and antisocial personality disorder . . ." (Jamison 1999, 192. Also see reference, 372). She talks about links that have been found between smoking and low serotonin levels, although the causality—whether low serotonin causes people to smoke or is caused by smoking—is not clear.

Chapter 7: The Final Year

1   Years later I heard a radio account of an experience a suicidal woman— who was also a physician—had had with the mental health system. In her case the payer was her private HMO, not Medi-Cal, but the issues were the same. She felt herself sliding into a suicidal depression and went to her local ER to put herself in the hospital, but the staff refused to admit her because she wasn't sick enough to meet her insurance company's criteria for reimbursement. In desperation she went home and swallowed a bottle of sleeping pills, then went back to the ER and told them what she had done, saying "*Now* will you take me?!" This time they did; she met the criteria. In the end, her insurance company had to pay not only for the psych ward

but for getting her stomach pumped and all the intensive care costs as well.

2   A note on these "anti–side effect" drugs (such as Artane and Cogentin, both of which Charley took at one time or another): During Charley's lifetime I didn't think much about them, assuming they had been developed specifically to counter the side effects of neuroleptic drugs like Navane and thus had no side effects of their own; no one ever mentioned any. This turned out not to be correct. Cogentin was developed to counteract parkinsonism, a chronic nervous disorder that causes rigidity similar to that caused by antipsychotics; it was not developed to be used in the context of mental illness. In fact, one medical source says, "When benztropine mesylate [the chemical name of Cogentin] is used to treat extrapyramidal symptoms due to CNS [central nervous system] drugs such as phenothiazine derivatives and reserpine in patients with a psychiatric illness, *occasionally there may be intensification of psychiatric illnesses.* Although benztropine mesylate need not be discontinued when this occurs, the psychotogenic potential of antiparkinsonian drugs should be considered when planning the management of patients with psychiatric illnesses" (*www.mentalhealth.com,* 1999, emphasis added). Other side effects of Cogentin can include "nervousness, impaired memory, numbness of fingers, listlessness, depression. Mental confusion, excitement and visual hallucinations with high doses" (Ibid.). My point is that even the secondary medications Charley was taking— Cogentin for neuroleptic side effects, Xanax or Klonopin for sleep—are by any definition extremely powerful substances with all kinds of potential unintended consequences, and even Charley's most straightforward and experienced therapists never really dealt straightforwardly with the negative possibilities of these drugs and their various combinations—most likely, I can't help thinking, because they didn't want to think about such possibilities themselves.

3   Breggin 1991, 34.

4   Ibid. Charley, while often critical, never expressed hatred for Lin or me, so I didn't think Breggin's remarks about abusive parents were relevant to us. And in fact Breggin himself qualifies his anti-NAMI remarks later in the same book. "[N]ot all NAMI parents have caused their children's problems," he says, "but the NAMI *leadership* has aggressively sought to suppress those with whom it disagrees" (Ibid., 363n., emphasis Breggin's).

5   *www.nami.org*, 1998.

6   George L. Engel, "A Unified Concept of Health and Disease," *Perspectives in Biology and Medicine* 3 (1960): 459–85, quoted in Larry Davidson and John S. Strauss, "Beyond the Biopsychosocial Model: Integrating Disorder, Health, and Recovery," *Psychiatry* 58 (1990): 44.

7   "Quiet Tragedies: A Roundtable Discussion of Mental Illness," *Los Angeles Weekly*, 23–29 October 1998, 38.

8   Ibid.

9   Joyce Thompson and Karen Strand, "Psychiatric Nursing in a Psychosocial Setting," *Journal of Psychosocial Nursing* 32, 2 (1994): 27.

10   Podvoll, 279; referring to Manfred Bleuler, "Some Results of Research in Schizophrenia," *Behavioral Science* 15 (1970).

11   In *The Seduction of Madness,* Podvoll wrestles with the question of medication vs. no medication. Although he's much closer to the antimedicationists both philosophically and practically (he understands the physical and psychological dangers of the drugs), he ends up with a position not entirely in one camp or the other. Podvoll feels that at times the medications may be useful if they are used not to control behavior (the chemical straitjacket idea) but more temporarily, to "lower the 'amplitude' of outrageous sensory phenomena . . . or the excitement and panic caused when the senses are in disarray." As I have mentioned, antipsychotics are major tranquilizers. Used as such, sparingly and "with great care" *("given in as small a dose as possible, and incrementally . . . withdrawn as soon as their therapeutic effect is achieved"),* medication "may give a patient an opportunity to live with some relatively quiet moments, when the sensory phenomena are not so imperious, and when one can turn away from the hallucinatory demands to 'live in two places at once'" (Ibid., 228, emphasis in the original).

12   Courtenay M. Harding et al., quoted in *Village Immersion* binder, 19 March 1999.

13   For its core population of 276 members, the Village's case rates—the money allocated to each member's care—are based on a two-tier structure corresponding to the severity of a member's diagnosis. The more severely ill (high-cost) members are funded at $18,500 per year, the less severely ill (moderate-cost) are funded at $6,500 per year (thus the average amount spent per member is $12,500). The total pool of money is fungible; that is,

if less money is spent on a particular member during the year than was allocated to his or her care, what is not spent is available for someone whose care cost more than what was budgeted. (The additional 200-plus members added by the state in 1999 are funded under a different structure, at about $12,000 per person per year. Much of that money is for housing.)

Chapter 8: The Stone Cross

1   In Mexico, All Saints' Day (November 1) is known as *El Día de los Muertos.*
2   Edwin S. Shneidman, *The Suicidal Mind* (New York/Oxford: Oxford University Press, 1996), 18.
3   Ibid., 87.
4   Ibid., 90.
5   An expansion and variation of this early narrative—what I call the cancer version—came later, as I worked on the first draft of this book. It went like this:

> What is certain is that his breakdown at Yosemite was only the first major outburst of an extremely cruel, virulent, terminal illness. The illness was particularly cruel because its episodes invariably began as beautiful and seductive highs, full of feelings of power and elation and transcendent love, only later crashing into self-hatred and despair. From what I've been able to learn about Charley's "affliction" (his term), much of it from him, it was a sort of cancer of the mind. Like cancer, it involved the malfunctioning of normal cells and bodily functions rather than the introduction of a foreign substance (like a bacteria or poison) into the body, and thus, like cancer, seemed to erupt from within, viciously and insidiously and without warning, attacking the very fiber of his being. Like cancer, it had no single cure but merely different forms of treatment that could have side effects that often seemed as bad as the disease. Like some cancers, it periodically went into remission, seeming to disappear entirely or almost entirely, giving the sufferer the idea that he was cured and didn't have to be treated anymore. Like cancer, its flare-ups tended to get worse over time as the disease metastasized, taking over greater and greater parts of his life. And like cancer, it tended to drain the sufferer of all hope, so that by the end death seemed the lesser of two evils.

Beware of any metaphor involving cancer. As much truth as may lie hidden in the description, the very word tends to overpower the reader's (and the writer's!) critical faculties.
6   Jamison 1999, 199.

7   Gary Stix, "Stuck with Freedom: Completion of the Human Genome Deals a Blow to Biological Determinism," *Los Angeles Times*, 18 February 2001, sec. M, 1.

8   The main reason for this is that past experiments (twin studies, for example) that claimed to find a direct genetic cause of mental illness have never been replicated, and many have been called into question for their methodology, suppositions, etc.

9   In her NAMI-approved book *When Madness Comes Home*, Victoria Secunda writes, "After a long period of disfavor in parts of the scientific community, talking therapies have recently enjoyed a comeback. . . . [R]ecent studies suggest that these therapies can be as effective as drugs in treating even the more severe forms of depressive illness, for example, and *in some cases may be preferable to drugs*" (Victoria Secunda, *When Madness Comes Home: Help and Hope for the Families of the Mentally Ill* [New York: Hyperion, 1997], 36) (emphasis added).

10 See chapter 6, Weaving the Shroud, note 6, page 208.

11 See the last section of Appendix C, entitled "Apples, Big Apples and Tangerines," for more discussion of this.

12 Wade Davis, *Shadows in the Sun* (Washington, DC/Covelo, Calif.: Island Press, 1998), 155.

13 Ibid., 163.

14 Ibid., 167. Davis gives another example of the importance of expectation and preparedness. When people mistakenly consume certain species of hallucinogenic mushrooms found in Oregon rain forests, thinking they are ordinary ones, they often end up in the poison units of hospitals. People who eat the same hallucinogenic mushrooms deliberately, however, "experience a pleasant intoxication."

15 Ibid., 166–68.

16 Mark Ragins, M.D., "Recovery with Severe Mental Illness: Changing from a Medical Model to a Psychosocial Rehabilitation Model" (1996); Village Immersion, 1999.

17 Podvoll, 17–9.

18 Ibid.

19 "[T]he role of dopamine," says Podvoll, "with its various molecular actions and reactions at the junction of nerve cells, has turned out to be far more

complicated than originally suspected. Also, dopamine is only one of a dozen other neurotransmitters that can be shown to have tremendous power in effecting neural transmission, the wiring of the brain. The best estimates indicate that there are as many as two hundred such substances residing in the brain and elsewhere in the body. We are swimming in neurotransmitters" (Podvoll, 179). Kay Jamison speaks similarly, as I've mentioned (see chapter 4, "One More Bloody Year of Reed," note 7, page 330).

[20] Podvoll, 183.

[21] Goodwin and Jamison, 588.

[22] Ibid.

[23] Jamison 1995, 191.

[24] Again, to be fair: Subsequent to Jamison's collaboration with Frederick Goodwin on *Manic-Depressive Illness,* she herself began expressing misgivings about the desirability of genetic screening, etc. In her autobiography, for example, two pages after the just-quoted doctor visit story, Jamison, despite her "strong commitment to the scientific efforts that are being made to track down the genes for manic-depressive illness," expresses "concerns about what finding the genes might actually mean" (Jamison 1995, 193). Prenatal diagnostic testing, for instance, might lead prospective parents to abort fetuses that carry the genes for manic-depression "even though it is a treatable disease" (Ibid.)—and not only treatable, but a condition that can "confer advantages on both the individual and society" (Ibid., 194). Whether her position has actually evolved since 1990, when she and Goodwin were stressing "the clinical importance of early and aggressive treatment" (Goodwin and Jamison, 782), or whether she's merely hedging her biological-psychopharmacological bets, is not clear. So far, the latter seems to be the case. *Night Falls Fast,* Jamison's book on suicide (published in 1999, four years after the autobiography), still places her firmly in the "brain" camp, even though her understanding—based on an extreme ambivalence about her own manic-depression—is certainly more nuanced than that of many "brain-diseasers" such as NAMI.

Chapter 9: Epilogue

[1] Beverly Beyette, "Public Devotions," *Los Angeles Times,* 6 December 1996, sec. E, 1.

Appendix C: Apples, Big Apples and Tangerines

[1] Franz G. Alexander and Sheldon T. Selesnick, *The History of Psychiatry: An Evaluation of Psychiatric Thought and Practice from Prehistoric Times to the Present* (New York: Harper and Row, 1966), 293.

[2] Jamison 1995, 102.

[3] Goodwin and Jamison, 245.

[4] K. C. Cole and Robert Lee Hotz, "Science, Hype, and Profit: A Perilous Mix," *Los Angeles Times,* 24 January 1999, sec. A, 24.

[5] Goodwin and Jamison, 584.

[6] Ibid., 577.

[7] Ibid.

[8] Jamison 1995, 197.

[9] Ibid., 198.

[10] Jamison 1999, 120.

[11] Ibid., 191 et seq.

[12] Ibid.

[13] Richard Gates, Afterword to Ross David Burke, *When the Music's Over* (New York: BasicBooks/HarperCollins, 1995), 231.

[14] This methodology is increasingly coming under criticism from people besides Thomas Szasz, Peter Breggin, Edward Podvoll and other psychiatric dissidents, and there is reason to believe that the pendulum is swinging again, this time from a mechanistic, purely medical model of mental illness back toward a view that gives more weight to individual psychology and environment. Other recent and well-publicized critiques of this mechanistic view—critiques that have been taken seriously and not simply dismissed as flat-earthism—are embodied in T. M. Luhrmann's book *Of Two Minds: The Growing Disorder in American Psychiatry* (Knopf, 2000), and John Horgan's *The Undiscovered Mind: How the Human Brain Defies Replication, Medication, and Explanation* (Free Press, 1999).

[15] Jamison 1993, 81.

[16] *Infradian* rhythms are rhythms that last for more than one day, i.e., seasonal rhythms. *Circadian* rhythms are more or less daily rhythms.

[17] M. R. Eastwood et al., "Infradian Rhythms: A Comparison of Affective Disorders and Normal Persons," *Archives of General Psychiatry* 42 (1985):

295–99, quoted in Jamison 1993, 135. The same passage is also quoted in Goodwin and Jamison, 565.

[18] Jamison 1993, 165.

[19] Goodwin and Jamison, 781–82.

[20] Admittedly, the quoted language is that of other researchers (Eastwood et al.; see note 17 above), but the passage is cited with seeming approval in *both* Jamison's own book *(Touched with Fire)* and in her collaboration with Goodwin.

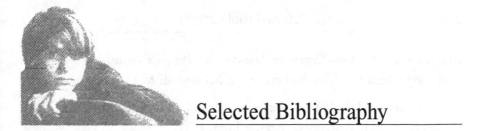

Selected Bibliography

Alexander, Franz G., and Sheldon T. Selesnick. *The History of Psychiatry: An Evaluation of Psychiatric Thought and Practice from Prehistoric Times to the Present.* New York: Harper and Row, 1966.

Alvarez, A. *The Savage God: A Study of Suicide.* New York: Bantam Books (div. of Random House), 1972.

Breggin, Peter R., M.D., *Toxic Psychiatry.* New York: St. Martin's Press, 1991.

Cole, K. C., and Robert Lee Hotz. "Science, Hype, and Profit: A Perilous Mix." *Los Angeles Times,* 24 January 1999, sec. A, 24.

Davis, Wade. *Shadows in the Sun.* Washington, DC/Covelo, Calif.: Island Press, 1998.

Engel, George L. "A Unified Concept of Health and Disease." *Perspectives in Biology and Medicine 3* (1960): 459–85.

Gates, Richard. Afterword to Ross David Burke. *When the Music's Over.* New York: BasicBooks/HarperCollins, 1995.

Goodwin, Frederick K., M.D., and Kay Redfield Jamison, Ph.D. *Manic-Depressive Illness.* New York and Oxford: Oxford University Press, 1990.

Horgan, John. *The Undiscovered Mind: How the Human Brain Defies Replication, Medication, and Explanation.* New York: The Free Press (div. of Simon & Schuster), 1999.

Jamison, Kay Redfield. *An Unquiet Mind.* New York: Knopf, 1995.

———. *Night Falls Fast.* New York, Knopf, 1999.

———. *Touched with Fire: Manic-Depressive Illness and the Artistic Temperament.* New York: The Free Press (div. of Macmillan), 1993.

Kraepelin, Emil. *Manic-Depressive Insanity and Paranoia* (translated by R. M. Barclay, edited by G. M. Robertson). Edinburgh: E & S Livingstone, 1921.

Kushner, Howard J. *Self-Destruction in the Promised Land: A Psychocultural History.* Piscataway, N.J.: Rutgers University Press, 1991.

Lindner, Robert. *The Fifty-Minute Hour.* New York: Bantam Books, 1955.

Luhrmann, T. M. *Of Two Minds: The Growing Disorder in American Psychiatry.* New York: Knopf, 2000.

Mayer-Gross, W., E. Slater, and M. Roth. *Clinical Psychiatry* (second edition). London: Cassell & Co., 1960.

Millett, Kate. *The Loony-Bin Trip.* New York: Touchstone (div. of Simon & Schuster), 1990.

Podvoll, Edward M., M.D. *The Seduction of Madness.* New York: HarperCollins, 1990.

"Quiet Tragedies: A Roundtable Discussion of Mental Illness." *Los Angeles Weekly,* 23–29 October 1998.

Ragins, Mark, M.D. "Recovery with Severe Mental Illness: Changing from a Medical Model to a Psychosocial Rehabilitation Model," 1996. Published in Village Integrated Services Agency, Village Immersion, March 19, 1999.

Secunda, Victoria. *When Madness Comes Home: Help and Hope for the Families of the Mentally Ill.* New York: Hyperion, 1997.

Shneidman, Edwin S. *The Suicidal Mind.* New York/Oxford: Oxford University Press, 1996.

Slater, Lauren. *Welcome to My Country: A Therapist's Memoir of Madness.* New York: Random House, 1996.

Stix, Gary. "Stuck with Freedom: Completion of the Human Genome Deals a Blow to Biological Determinism." *Los Angeles Times,* 18 February 2001, sec. M.

Szasz, Thomas S., M.D. *The Myth of Mental Illness: Foundations of a Theory of Personal Conduct.* New York: HarperCollins, 1974.

Thompson, Joyce, and Karen Strand. "Psychiatric Nursing in a Psychosocial Setting." *Journal of Psychosocial Nursing* 32, 2 (1994): 27.

www.mentalhealth.com

www.nami.org, National Alliance for the Mentally Ill Web site.

www.nimh.nih.gov/publicat/schizoph, National Institute of Mental Health Web site.

Index

Numbers in *italics* indicate photographs.

About the Author

Jonathan Aurthur was born in New York City in 1948 and attended St. John's College in Annapolis, Maryland, and the University of California, Los Angeles, where he majored in motion pictures. In the late 1960s through the early 1980s, he worked as a community organizer and documentary filmmaker. He was also the editor of a journal of political theory called *Appeal to Reason* and the author of a book on political economy called *Socialism in the Soviet Union*. He currently lives in Santa Monica, California. Aside from his late son, Charley, he has a surviving daughter, Jenny.